Give & Take
The Ins and Outs of Western Visual Fine Art

Second Custom Edition for Indiana Wesleyan University

Taken from:
Prebles' Artforms: An Introduction to the Visual Arts, Tenth Edition
by Patrick Frank

A World of Art, Sixth Edition
by Henry M. Sayre

The Art of Seeing, Eighth Edition
by Paul Zelanski and Mary Pat Fisher

Cover Art: Courtesy of Darby Bannard.

Taken from:

Prebles' Artforms: An Introduction to the Visual Arts, Tenth Edition
by Patrick Frank
Copyright © 2011, 2009, 2006, 2004, 2002 by Pearson Education, Inc.
Published by Prentice Hall
Upper Saddle River, New Jersey 07458

A World of Art, Sixth Edition
by Henry M. Sayre
Copyright © 2010 by Pearson Education, Inc.
Published by Prentice Hall

The Art of Seeing, Eighth Edition
by Paul Zelanski and Mary Pat Fisher
Copyright © 2011, 2007, 2005, 2002, 1999, 1994, 1991, 1988 by Pearson Education, Inc.
Published by Prentice Hall

Pearson Learning Solutions, 501 Boylston Street, Suite 900, Boston, MA 02116
A Pearson Education Company
www.pearsoned.com

Printed in the United States of America

1 2 3 4 5 6 7 8 9 10 V011 17 16 15 14 13 12

000200010271684484

MM/LP

ISBN 10: 1-256-84009-2
ISBN 13: 978-1-256-84009-1

CONTENTS

STUDENT TOOLKIT

This short section is designed to introduce the overarching themes and aims of *Give and Take* as well as provide you with a guide to the basic elements of art that you can easily access whenever you interact with works of art—in these pages, in museums, and anywhere else you encounter them. The topics covered here are developed much more fully in later chapters, but this overview brings all this material together in a convenient, quick-reference format.

WHY STUDY ART?

We study art because it is among the highest expressions of culture, embodying its ideals and aspirations, challenging its assumptions and beliefs, and creating new visions and possibilities for it to pursue. That said, "culture" is itself a complex phenomenon, constantly changing and vastly diverse. The "world of art" is composed of objects from many, many cultures—as many cultures as there are and have been. In fact, from culture to culture, and from cultural era to cultural era, the very idea of what "art" even has changed. It was not until the Renaissance, for instance, that the concept of fine art, as we think of it today, arose in Europe. Until then, the Italian word *arte* meant "guild"—any one of the associations of craftspeople that dominated medieval commerce—and *artista* referred to any student of the liberal arts, particularly grammarians.

But, since the Renaissance, we have tended to see the world of art through the lens of "fine art." We differentiate those one-of-a-kind expressions of individual creativity that we normally associate with fine art—painting, sculpture, and architecture—from craft, works of the applied or practical arts like textiles, glass, ceramics, furniture, metalwork, and jewelry. When we refer to "African art," or "Aboriginal art," we are speaking of objects that, in the cultures in which they were produced, were almost always thought of as applied or practical. They served, that is, ritual or religious purposes that far outweighed whatever purely artistic skill they might evidence. Only in most recent times, as these cultures have responded to the West's ever-more-expansive appetite for the exotic and original, have individual artists in these cultures begun to produce works intended for sale in the Western "fine arts" market.

To whatever degree a given object is more or less "fine art" or "craft," we study it in order to understand more about the culture that produced it. The object gives us insight into what the culture values—religious ritual, aesthetic pleasure, or functional utility, to name just a few possibilities.

THE CRITICAL PROCESS

Studying these objects engages us in a critical process that is analogous, in many ways, to the creative process that artists engage in. One of the major features of this text is a series of spreads called Works in Progress.

One of the greatest benefits of studying art is that it teaches you to think critically. Art objects are generally "mute." They cannot explain themselves to you, but that does not mean that their meaning is "hidden" or elusive. They contain information—all kinds of information—that can help you explain and understand them if you approach them through the critical thinking process outlined on page vii.

Student Toolkit and Seven Steps to Thinkinig Critically About Art were taken from *A World of Art,* Sixth Edition by Henry M. Sayre.

Seven Steps to Thinking Critically about Art

1. **Identify the artist's decisions and choices.**
   Begin by recognizing that, in making works of art, artists inevitably make certain decisions and choices—What color should I make this area? Should my line be wide or narrow? Straight or curved? Will I look up at my subject or down on it? Will I depict it realistically or not? What medium should I use to make this object? And so on. Identify these choices. Then ask yourself why these choices were made. Remember, though most artists work somewhat intuitively, every artist has the opportunity to revise or redo each work, each gesture. You can be sure that what you are seeing in a work of art is an intentional effect.

2. **Ask questions. Be curious.**
   Asking yourself why the artist's choices were made is just the first set of questions to pose. You need to consider the work's title: What does it tell you about the piece? Is there any written material accompanying the work? Is the work informed by the context in which you encounter it—by other works around it, or, in the case of sculpture, for instance, by its location? Is there anything you learn about the artist that is helpful?

3. **Describe the object.**
   By carefully describing the object—both its subject matter and how its subject matter is formally realized—you can discover much about the artist's intentions. Pay careful attention to how one part of the work relates to the others.

4. **Question your assumptions.**
   Question, particularly, any initial dislike you might have for a given work of art. Remember that if you are seeing the work in a book, museum, or gallery, then someone likes it. Ask yourself why. Often you'll talk yourself into liking it too. But also examine the work itself to see if it contains any biases or prejudices. It matters, for instance, in Renaissance church architecture, whether the church is designed for Protestants or Catholics.

5. **Avoid an emotional response.**
   Art objects are supposed to stir up your feelings, but your emotions can sometimes get in the way of clear thinking. Analyze your own emotions. Determine what about the work set them off, and ask yourself if this wasn't the artist's very intention.

6. **Don't oversimplify or misrepresent the art object.**
   Art objects are complex by their nature. To think critically about an art object is to look beyond the obvious. Thinking critically about the work of art always involves walking the line between the work's susceptibility to interpretation and its integrity, or its resistance to arbitrary and capricious readings. Be sure your reading of a work of art is complete enough (that it recognizes the full range of possible meanings the work might possess), and, at the same time, that it doesn't violate or misrepresent the work.

7. **Tolerate uncertainty.**
   Remember that the critical process is an exercise in discovery, that it is designed to uncover possibilities, not necessarily certain truths. Critical thinking is a process of questioning; asking good questions is sometimes more important than arriving at "right" answers. There may, in fact, be no "right" answers.

   Critical thinking is really a matter of putting yourself in a *questioning* frame of mind. Our culture is increasingly dominated by images, and all students today must learn to see and interpret the visual world around them. As you question what you see, as you actively engage the world of art—and not just passively "receive" its images, like some television set—you will find that you are at once critical and self-critical. You will see better and understand more—about both the work of art and yourself.

A WORLD OF ART

On February 12, 2005, across the 843-acre expanse of New York City's Central Park, 7,503 saffron-colored fabric panels were dropped from the top of 7,503 saffron-painted steel gates, each 16 feet tall, to billow in the wind about 7 feet above the ground. The gates were positioned 12 feet apart (except where low-hanging tree branches extended above the walkways) and were of various widths, depending on the widths of the walkways they covered (there are 25 different widths of walkways in the park's 23 miles of paths). Seen from the skyscrapers that surround the park, the gates looked like golden-orange rivers meandering through the bare branches of the park's trees (**Fig. 1.1**). In the

1.1 Christo and Jeanne-Claude.
The Gates, New York City, Central Park, aerial view, 1979–2005.
Courtesy of Wolfgang Volz/Laif/Redux.

Chapter 1: A World of Art was taken from *A World of Art,* Sixth Edition by Henry M. Sayre.

bright sun of New York's chilly February days, they glowed with an autumnal warmth.

The Gates, New York City, Central Park was the creation of Christo and Jeanne-Claude, the husband-and-wife team that for the last 40 years has wrapped buildings around the world. Like their other projects, *The Gates* was a temporary work, up for a few weeks and then dismantled, leaving no trace of their presence behind. The total cost of the project was $21 million, financed entirely by the artists, as is true of all their projects, through the sale of preparatory studies, drawings, collages, scale models, and other works (**Fig. 1.2**). All of the materials used in the project were recycled—the fabric went to a firm in Pennsylvania, where it was shredded and respun; the vinyl framing was ground into half a million pounds of orange chips used to make fencing; and the steel, including the screws, went to a scrap yard in New Jersey, where it was melted down and sold worldwide. Christo and Jeanne-Claude donated

merchandising rights to a not-for-profit environmental organization dedicated to preserving nature in New York City's urban setting, which in turn shared its profits from the project with the Central Park Conservancy.

New Yorkers generally received *The Gates* with enthusiasm. For many, the work represented the rejuvenation of the city after the tragedy of 9/11, a festive celebration of life. The gates' presence certainly revitalized the city's economy, as more than four million people visited the park in just over two weeks, contributing an estimated $1/4$ billion dollars to city businesses. Those who complained generally found the steel, vinyl, and fabric constructions an intrusive violation of the natural landscape. But, Christo was quick to point out, the geometric grid pattern of the hundreds of city blocks surrounding Central Park—to say nothing of the rectangular design of the park as a whole—was reflected in the rectangular structure of the gates themselves. Furthermore, the park itself

1.2 Christo.
The Gates, Project for Central Park, New York City, 2003.
Drawing in two parts, pencil, charcoal, pastel, wax crayon, technical data, fabric sample, aerial photograph, and tape on paper, 15 3 96 in. and 42 3 96 in.
Courtesy of Wolfgang Volz/Laif/Redux.

was a man-made construction. More than 150 years ago, the original architects, Frederick Law Olmsted and Calvert Vaux, were commissioned by the city to create a park out of a rocky, swampy, and almost treeless landscape to the north of what was then the city proper. So barren was the area that the soil was inadequate to sustain the trees and shrubs that were purchased for the site. Olmsted and Vaux had 500,000 cubic feet of topsoil carted in from New Jersey. They created lakes, blasted out boulders, and sculpted hillsides. If today the park looks natural, it was originally as artificial—as constructed—as Christo and Jeanne-Claude's work of art.

If, as critic Michael Kimmelman wrote in the *New York Times*, "*The Gates* is a work of pure joy, a vast populist spectacle of goodwill and simple eloquence, the first great public art event of the 21st century," viewers from Japan saw it in a different light. For them, it echoed the famous Fushimi Inari Shrine in Kyoto (**Fig. 1.3**), dedicated to the Shinto god of rice, where more than 10,000 orange

1.3 *Torii* gates, Fushimi Inari Shrine,
Kyoto, Japan, eighth century.

and black *torii* gates line 4 kilometers of mountain trails. The similarity between the two structures suggested an important environmental message to Japanese audiences. They saw *The Gates*, especially in its commitment to recycling and its support of the environmental organization, as a commentary on the refusal of the United States to ratify the 1997 Kyoto Protocol, an international agreement designed to lower the overall emissions of six greenhouse gases that are believed to be a factor in global warming.

If the experience of *The Gates* project was undoubtedly different for its Japanese and American viewers, both groups nevertheless asked themselves the same questions. What is the purpose of this work of art (and what is the purpose of art in general)? What does it mean? What is my reaction to the work and why do I feel this way? How do the formal qualities of the work   such as its color, its organization, its size and scale—affect my reaction? What do I value in works of art? These are some of the questions that this book is designed to help you address. Appreciating art is never just a question of accepting visual stimuli, but of intelligently contemplating why and how works of art come to be made and have meaning. By helping you understand the artist's creative process, we hope that your own critical ability, the process by which you create your own ideas, will be engaged as well.

THE WORLD AS ARTISTS SEE IT

The Gates project demonstrates how two different cultures might understand and value the same work of art in different ways. Similarly, different artists, responding to their world in different times and places, might see the world in apparently divergent terms. They do, however, share the fundamental desire to *create*. All people are creative, but not all people possess the energy, ingenuity, and courage of conviction that are required to make art. In order to produce a work of art, the artist must be able to respond to the unexpected, the chance occurrences or results that are part of the creative process. In other words, the artist must be something of an explorer and inventor. The artist must always be open to new ways of seeing. The landscape painter

John Constable spoke of this openness as "the art of seeing nature." This art of seeing leads to imagining, which leads in turn to making. Creativity is the sum of this process, from seeing to imagining to making. In the process of making a work of art, the artist also engages in a self-critical process—questioning assumptions, revising and rethinking choices and decisions, exploring new directions and possibilities. In other words, the artist is also a *critical thinker*, and the creative process is, at least in part, an exercise in critical thinking.

Exploring the creative process is the focus of this book. We hope you take from this book the knowledge that the kind of creative and critical thinking engaged in by artists is fundamental to every discipline. This same path leads to discovery in science, breakthroughs in engineering, and new research in the social sciences. We can all learn from studying the creative process itself.

Roles of the Artist

Most artists think of themselves as assuming one of four fundamental roles—or some combination of the four—as they approach their work: 1) they help us to see the world in new and innovative ways; 2) they create a visual record of their time and place; 3) they make functional objects and structures more pleasurable by imbuing them with beauty and meaning; and 4) they give form to the immaterial ideas and feelings.

1.4 Yayoi Kusama.
You Who Are Getting Obliterated in the Dancing Swarm of Fireflies, 2005.
Mixed media.
The Phoenix Museum of Art. Museum purchase with funds provided by Jan and Howard Hendler (2005.146). © Yayoi Kusama.

1) Artists help us to see the world in new or innovative ways.

This is one of the primary roles that Christo and Jeanne-Claude assumed in creating *The Gates*. In fact, almost all of their work is designed to transform our experience of the world, jar us out of our complacency, and create new ways for us to see and think about the world around us. As visitor after visitor to *The Gates* commented, Christo and Jeanne-Claude's art transformed their experience of Central Park forever, altering their sense of its space, deepening their understanding of its history, and heightening their appreciation for its beauty.

The work of Japanese artist Yayoi Kusama has much the same effect. Kusama is widely known for her fascination with polka-dots. In the late 1950s, she began to produce paintings that she called "Infinity Nets," huge canvases painted all over in tiny circles. The paintings were a means of coming to grips with an obsessive hallucinatory vision that she first experienced as a child:

One day I was looking at the red flower patterns of the tablecloth on a table, and when I looked up I saw the same pattern covering the ceiling, the windows and the walls, and finally all over the room, my body and the universe. I felt as if I had begun to self-obliterate, to revolve in the infinity of endless time and the absoluteness of space, and be reduced to nothingness.

Over a career that has spanned the last 50 years, she has covered people, rooms, buildings, and landscapes with her polka-dot patterns, and she has created installations—room-sized environments—that quite literally reflect her sense of "the infinity of endless time." *You Who Are Getting Obliterated in the Dancing Swarm of Fireflies* (**Fig. 1.4**) is an example. Created for the new 2005 addition to the Phoenix Museum of Art—where it has quickly become the most popular work of art in the collection—it consists of a room, the ceiling, floor, and walls of which are covered with mirrors that reflect the flickering glow of tiny dots of LED lights suspended in the space on small strings. Passing through, the viewer feels literally awash in a space so vast that all sense of self—or at least

self-importance—is obliterated. Kusama makes us aware of just how small we are in the grand scheme of things.

2) Artists make a visual record of the people, places, and events of their time and place.

Sometimes artists are not so much interested in seeing things anew as they are in simply recording, accurately, what it is that they see. The sculpture of *Pat* (**Fig. 1.5**) almost looks as if it is alive, and certainly anyone meeting the real "Pat" would recognize her from this sculpture. In fact, *Pat* is one of many plaster casts made from life by John Ahearn and Rigoberto Torres, residents of the South Bronx in New York City. In 1980, Ahearn moved to the South Bronx and began to work in collaboration with local resident Torres. Torres had learned the art of plaster casting from his uncle, who had cast

1.5 John Ahearn and Rigoberto Torres.
Pat, 1982.
Painted cast plaster, 28½ 3 16½ 3 11 in.
Courtesy Alexander and Bonin, New York. Collection Norma and William Roth, Winter Haven, Florida. Photo courtesy of Sotheby's.

1.6 Attributed to Manohar.
Jahangir in Darbar, Mughal period, India, about 1620.
Opaque watercolor and gold on paper, 13³/₄ 3 7⁷/₈ in.
Museum of Fine Arts, Boston. Francis Bartlett Donation of 1912 and Picture
Fund 14.654.

plaster statues for churches and cemeteries. Together Ahearn and Torres set out to capture the spirit of a community that was financially impoverished but that possessed real, if unrecognized, dignity. "The key to my work is life—lifecasting," says Ahearn. "The people I cast know that they are as responsible for my work as I am, even more so. The people make my sculptures."

Portraiture is, in fact, one of the longest standing traditions in art. Until the invention of photography, the portrait—whether drawn, painted, or sculpted—was the only way to preserve the physical likeness of a human being. And artists have always understood that in the myriad expressions and attitudes visible in the faces of the people who make up their world, something like the spirit of their age might be discovered.

In the sixteenth century, portraiture became especially valued by the Muslim Mughal leaders of India. When the Mughal ruler Akbar took the throne in 1556 at the age of just 14 years, he established a school of painting in India, open to both Hindu and Islamic artists, taught by masters brought from Tabriz, Persia. He also urged his artists to study the Western paintings and prints that Portuguese traders began to bring into the country in the 1570s. By the end of Akbar's reign, a state studio of more than 1,000 artists had created a library of over 24,000 illuminated manuscripts.

Akbar ruled over a court of thousands of bureaucrats, courtiers, servants, wives, and concubines. Fully aware that the population was by and large Hindu, Akbar practiced an official policy of religious toleration. He believed that a synthesis of the world's faiths would surpass the teachings of any one of them. Thus he invited Christians,

Jews, Hindus, Buddhists, and others to his court to debate with Muslim scholars. Despite taxing the peasantry heavily to support the luxurious lifestyle that he enjoyed, he also instituted a number of reforms, particularly banning the practice of immolating surviving wives on the funeral pyres of their husbands.

Under the rule of Akbar's son, Jahangir, portraiture found even greater favor in India. The painting *Jahangir in Darbar* is exemplary (**Fig. 1.6**). It shows Jahangir, whose name means "World Seizer," seated between the two pillars at the top of the painting, holding an audience, or *darbar*, at court. His son, the future emperor Shah Jahan, stands just behind him. The figures in the street are a medley of portraits, composed in all likelihood from albums of portraits kept by court artists. Among them is a Jesuit priest from Europe dressed in his black robes. The stiff formality of the figures, depicted in profile facing left and right toward a central axis, makes a sharp contrast to the variety of faces with different racial and ethnic features that fills the scene. But the painting does, nevertheless, fully document the variety and tolerance of the Mughal court.

No one would mistake Claude Monet's representation of the Gare Saint-Lazare (**Fig. 1.7**) for a portrait. And yet his depiction of the Paris train station that by 1868 was handling over 13 million commuter passengers a year captures, as fully as *Jahangir in Darbar*, the spirit of its age. Beginning in 1852, Paris had undergone a complete transformation. Long, straight, wide boulevards had been extended across the city. Working-class citizens, who had previously lived in the labyrinth of ancient streets that the boulevards replaced, were removed to the suburbs, along with the industry they supported. Shops, cafés, and the world's first department stores lined the broad sidewalks of the new prome-nades. New parks, squares, and gardens were built, and the avenues were lined with over 100,000 newly planted trees. In order to allow traffic to flow seamlessly around the train station, a massive new bridge, the Pont de l'Europe, was built over the tracks. By the time Monet painted the Gare Saint-Lazare in 1877, these changes had been effected. His painting captures the transformation of not only Paris, but modernity itself. Here is a portrait of the new modern world, for better or worse—both the promise of the railroad, of modern speed and industry, and the atmosphere of steam and smoke created in its wake. All around this scene—and Monet painted it seven times in 1877—are the new open avenues of airy light, but here, Monet seems to suggest, just below ground level, lies the heart of the new modern city. In describing the world, the artist is free to celebrate and praise it, or critique and ridicule it, or, as is the case here, acknowledge its ambiguities.

1.7 Claude Monet.
Le Pont de l'Europe, Gare Saint-Lazare, 1877.
Oil on canvas, 25^{1}/$_{4}$ 3 31^{7}/$_{8}$ in.
Courtesy of Bridgeman-Giraudon/Art Resource, NY.

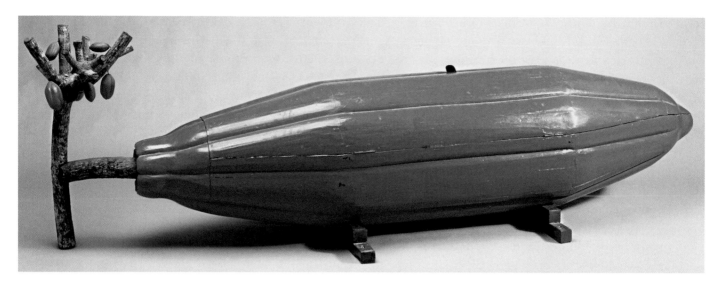

1.8   Kane Kwei (Teshi tribe, Ghana, Africa).
Coffin Orange, in the Shape of a Cocoa Pod, c. 1970.
Polychrome wood, 34 3 105½ 3 24 in.
The Fine Arts Museums of San Francisco. Gift of Vivian Burns, Inc., 74.8.

3) Artists make functional objects and structures (buildings) more pleasurable and elevate them or imbue them with meaning.

It is, perhaps, somewhat surprising to recognize that the sculpture of a cocoa pod by African artist Kane Kwei (**Fig. 1.8**) is actually a coffin. Trained as a carpenter, Kwei first made a decorative coffin for a dying uncle, who asked him to produce one in the shape of a boat. In Ghana, coffins possess a ritual significance, celebrating a successful life, and Kwei's coffins delighted the community. Soon he was making fish and whale coffins for fishermen, hens with chicks for women with large families, Mercedes Benz coffins for the wealthy, and cash crops for farmers, such as the 8½-foot cocoa bean coffin illustrated here. In 1974, an enterprising San Francisco art dealer brought examples of Kwei's work to the United States, and today the artist's large workshop makes coffins for both funerals and the art market.

Perhaps the object upon which cultures lavish their attention most is clothing. Clothing serves many more purposes than just protecting us from the elements: It announces the wearer's taste, self-image, and, perhaps above all, social status. The

Karaori kimono illustrated here (**Fig. 1.9**) was worn by a male performer who played the part of a woman in Japanese Noh theater. In its sheer beauty, it announced the dignity and status of the actor's character. Made of silk, brocaded with silver and gold, each panel in the robe depicts autumn grasses, flowers, and leaves. Thus, the kimono is more an aesthetic object than a functional one—that is, it is conceived to stimulate a sense of beauty in the viewer.

Almost all of us apply, or would like to apply, this aesthetic sense to the places in which we live. We decorate our walls with pictures, choose apartments for their visual appeal, ask architects to design our homes, plant flowers in our gardens, and seek out well-maintained and pleasant neighborhoods. We want city planners and government officials to work with us to make our living spaces more appealing.

Public space is particularly susceptible to aesthetic treatments. One of the newest standards of aesthetic beauty in public space has become its compatibility with the environment. A building's beauty is measured, in the minds of many, by its self-sufficiency (that is, its lack of reliance on nonsustainable energy sources such as coal), its use of

1.9 Karaori kimono, Middle Edo Period, Japan, c. 1700.
Brocaded silk, length 60 in.
Tokyo National Museum.

sustainable building materials (the elimination of steel, for instance, since it is a product of iron ore, a nonrenewable resource), and its suitability to the climate and culture in which it is built (a glass tower, however attractive in its own right, would seem out of place rising out of a tropical rainforest). These are the principles of what has come to be known as "green architecture."

The Jean-Marie Tjibaou Cultural Center in Nouméa, New Caledonia, an island in the South Pacific, illustrates these principles (**Fig. 1.10**). The architect is Renzo Piano, an Italian, but the principles guiding his design are anything but Western. The Center is named after a leader of the island's indigenous people, the Kanak, and it is dedicated to preserving and transmitting Kanak culture. Piano studied Kanak culture thoroughly, and his design blends Kanak tradition with green archi-

tectural principles. The buildings are constructed of wood and bamboo, easily renewable resources of the region. Each of the Center's ten pavilions represents a typical Kanak dwelling (in a finished dwelling the vertical staves would rise to meet at the top, and the horizontal elements would weave in and out between the staves, as in basketry). Piano left the dwelling forms unfinished, as if under construction, but to a purpose—they serve as wind scoops, catching breezes off the nearby ocean and directing them down to cool the inner rooms, the roofs of which face south at an angle that allows them to be lit largely by direct daylight. As in a Kanak village, the pavilions are linked with a covered walkway. Piano describes the project as "an expression of the harmonious relationship with the environment that is typical of the local culture. They are curved structures resembling huts, built

1.10 Renzo Piano.
Jean-Marie Tjibaou Cultural Center, Nouméa, New Caledonia, 1991–1998.
© Hans Schlupp / architekturphoto.

out of wooden joists and ribs; they are containers of an archaic appearance, whose interiors are equipped with all the possibilities offered by modern technology."

For many people, the main purpose of art is to satisfy our aesthetic sense, our desire to see and experience the beautiful. Many of Pablo Picasso's representations of women in the late 1920s and early 1930s are almost demonic in character. Most biographers believe images such as his *Seated Bather by the Sea* (**Fig. 1.11**) to be portraits of his wife, the Russian ballerina Olga Koklova, whom he married in 1918. By the late 1920s, their marriage was in shambles, and Picasso portrays her here as a skeletal horror, her back and buttocks almost crustacean in appearance, her horizontal mouth looking like some archaic mandible. Her pose is ironic, inspired by classical representations of the nude, and the sea behind her is as empty as the Mediterranean sky is gray. Picasso means nothing in this painting to be pleasing, except our recognition of his extraordinary ability to invent expressive images of tension. His entire career, since his portrayal of a brothel in his 1907 *Les Demoiselles d'Avignon* (see *Works in Progress*, pp. 12–13), he represented his relation to women as a sort of battlefield between attraction and repulsion. There can be no doubt which side has won the battle in this painting.

From a certain point of view, the experience of such dynamic tension is itself pleasing, and it is the ability of works of art to create and sustain such moments that many people value most about them. That is, many people find such moments *aesthetically* pleasing. The work of art may not itself be beautiful, but it triggers a higher level of thought and awareness in the viewer, and the viewer experiences this intellectual and imaginative stimulus— this higher order of thought—as a form of beauty in its own right.

4) Artists give form to the immaterial—hidden or universal truths, spiritual forces, personal feelings.

Picasso's treatment of women in both *Seated Bather* and *Les Demoiselles d'Avignon* gives form to his own, often tormented, feelings about the opposite sex. In *Les Demoiselles d'Avignon*, the power of these feelings was heightened by his incorporation of African masks into the composition.

When Westerners first encountered African masks in the ethnographic museums of Europe

1.11 Pablo Picasso.
Seated Bather (La Baigneuse), 1930.
Oil on canvas, 64¼ 3 51 in.
© 2011 Estate of Pablo Picasso/Artists Rights Society (ARS), New York.
Digital Image © The Museum of Modern Art/Licensed by SCALA/Art Resource, NY.

The Creative Process and Pablo Picasso's
Les Demoiselles d'avignon

NO ONE COULD LOOK at Picasso's large painting of 1906–07, *Les Demoiselles d'Avignon* (**Fig. 1.14**), and call it aesthetically beautiful, but it is, for many people, one of his most aesthetically interesting works. Nearly 8 feet square, it would come to be considered one of the first major paintings of the modern era—and one of the least beautiful. The title, chosen not by Picasso but by a close friend, literally means "the young ladies of Avignon," but its somewhat tongue-in-cheek reference is specifically to the prostitutes of Avignon Street, the red-light district of Barcelona, Spain, Picasso's hometown. We know a great deal about Picasso's process as he worked on the canvas from late 1906 into the early summer months of 1907, not only because many of his working sketches survive but also because the canvas itself has been submitted to extensive examination, including X-ray analysis. This reveals early versions of certain passages, particularly the figure at the left and the two figures on the right, which lie under the final layers of paint.

An early sketch (**Fig. 1.12**) reveals that the painting was originally conceived to include seven figures— five prostitutes, a sailor seated in their midst, and, entering from the left, a medical student carrying a book. Picasso probably had in mind some anecdotal or narrative idea contrasting the dangers and joys of both work and pleasure, but he soon abandoned the male figures. By doing so, he involved the viewer much more fully in the scene. No longer does the curtain open up at the left to allow the medical student to enter. Now the curtain is opened by one of the prostitutes as if she were admitting us, the audience, into the bordello. We are implicated in the scene.

And an extraordinary scene it is. Picasso seems to have willingly abdicated any traditional aesthetic sense of beauty. There is nothing enticing or alluring here. Of all the nudes, the two central ones are the most traditional, but their bodies are composed of a series of long lozenge shapes, hard angles, and only a few traditional curves. It is unclear whether the second nude from the left is standing or sitting, or possibly even lying down. (In the early drawing, she is clearly seated.) Picasso seems to have made her position in space intentionally ambiguous.

We know, through X-rays, that all five nudes originally looked like the central two. We also know that sometime after he began painting *Les Demoiselles*, Picasso visited the Trocadero, now the Museum of Man, in Paris, and saw its collection of African sculpture, particularly African masks. He was strongly affected by the experience. The masks seemed to him imbued

1.12 Pablo Picasso.
Medical Student, Sailor, and Five Nudes in a Bordello (study for *Les Demoiselles d'Avignon*), Paris, early 1907.
Charcoal and pastel, 18$\frac{1}{2}$ 3 25 in.
Oeffentliche Kunstsammlung, Kupferstichkabinett Basel. Photo: Oeffentliche Kunstsammlung, Martin Buhler. © 2007 Estate of Pablo Picasso / Artists Rights Society (ARS), New York.

with power that allowed him, for the first time, to see art, he said, as "a form of magic designed to be a mediator between the strange, hostile world and us, a way of seizing power by giving form to our terrors as well as our desires." As a result, he quickly transformed the faces of three of the five prostitutes in his painting into African masks. The masks freed him from representing exactly what his subjects looked like and allowed him to represent his idea of them instead.

That idea is clearly ambivalent. Picasso probably saw in these masks something both frightening and liberating. They freed him from a slavish

concern for accurate representation, and they allowed him to create a much more emotionally charged scene than he would have otherwise been able to accomplish. Rather than offering us a single point of view, he offers us many, both literally and figuratively. The painting is about the ambiguity of experience.

Nowhere is this clearer than in the squatting figure in the lower-right-hand corner of the painting. She seems twisted around on herself in the final version, her back to us, but her head is impossibly turned to face us, her chin resting on her grotesque, clawlike hand. We see her, in other words, from

both front and back. (Notice, incidentally, that even the nudes in the sketch possess something of this "double" point of view: Their noses are in profile though they face the viewer.) But this crouching figure is even more complex. An early drawing (**Fig. 1.13**) reveals that her face was originally conceived as a headless torso. What would become her hand was originally her arm. What would become her eyes were her breasts. And her mouth would begin as her bellybutton. Here we are witness to the extraordinary freedom of invention that defines all of Picasso's art, as well as to a remarkable demonstration of the creative process itself.

1.13 Pablo Picasso.
Study for Les Demoiselles d'Avignon.
Head of the Squatting Demoiselle,
1907. Inv.: MP 539. Gouache
and Indian ink on paper, 24³/₄ 3
18⁷/₈ in.
Musée Picasso, Paris. Reunion des Musées
Nationaux / Art Resource, NY. © 2007 Estate
of Pablo Picasso / Artists Rights Society (ARS),
New York.

1.14 Pablo Picasso.
Les Demoiselles d'Avignon, 1907.
Oil on canvas. 8 ft. 3 7 ft. 8 in.
© 2011 Estate of Pablo Picasso / Artists Rights Society (ARS), New York.

in the late nineteenth and early twentieth centuries, they saw them in a context far removed from their original settings and purposes. In the West, we are used to approaching everyday objects made in African, Oceanic, Native American, or Asian cultures in museums as "works of art." But in their cultures of origin, such objects might serve to define family and community relationships, establishing social order and structure. Or they might document momentous events in the history of a people. They might serve a simple utilitarian function, such as a pot to carry water or a spoon to eat with. Or they might be sacred instruments that provide insight into hidden or spiritual forces believed to guide the universe.

A fascinating example of the latter is a type of magical figure that arose in the Kongo in the late nineteenth century (**Fig. 1.15**). Known as a *minkisi* ("sacred medicine"), for the Kongo tribes such figures embodied their own resistance to the imposition of foreign ideas as European states colonized the continent. Throughout Central Africa, all significant human powers are believed to result from communication with the dead. Certain individuals can communicate with the spirits in their roles as healers, diviners, and defenders of the living. They are believed to harness the powers of the spirit world through *minkisi* (singular *nkisi*). Among the most formidable of *minkisi* is the type known as *minkonde* (singular *nkonde*), which are said to pursue witches, thieves, adulterers, and wrongdoers by night. The communicator activates a *nkonde* by driving nails, blades, and other pieces of iron into it so that it will deliver similar injuries to those worthy of punishment.

Minkonde figures usually stand upright, as if ready to spring forward. One arm is raised and holds a knife or spear (often missing, as here), suggesting that it is ready to attack. A hole in the figure's stomach contained magical "medicines," often kaolin, a white clay believed to be closely linked to the world of the dead, and red ocher, linked symbolically to blood. Such horrific figures—designed to evoke awe in the spectator—were seen by European missionaries as direct evidence of African idolatry and

witchcraft, and the missionaries destroyed many of them. More accurately, the *minkonde* represented a form of **animism**, a foundation to many religions referring to the belief in the existence of souls and the conviction that nonhuman things can also be endowed with a soul. However, European military commanders saw them as evidence of an aggressive native opposition to colonial control. Despite their

1.15 Magical figure, *nkisi nkonde*, Kongo (Muserongo), Zaire, late nineteenth century.
Wood, iron nails, glass, resin, height 20 in.
The University of Iowa Museum of Art, Iowa City, IA. The Stanley Collection, X1986.573.

suppression during the colonial era, such figures are still made today and continue to be used by the peoples of the Kongo.

In the West, the desire to give form to spiritual belief is especially apparent in the traditions of Christian religious art. For example, the idea of daring to represent the Christian God has, throughout the history of the Western world, aroused controversy. In seventeenth-century Holland, images of God were banned from Protestant churches. As one contemporary Protestant theologian put it, "The image of God is His Word"—that is, the Bible—and "statues in human form, being an earthen image of visible, earthborn man [are] far away from the truth." In fact, one of the reasons that Jesus, for Christians the son of God, is so often represented in Western art is that representing the son, a real person, is far easier than representing the father, a spiritual unknown who can only be imagined.

Nevertheless, one of the most successful depictions of the Christian God in Western culture was painted by Jan van Eyck nearly 600 years ago as part of an altarpiece for the city of Ghent in Flanders (**Figs. 1.16 and 1.17**). Van Eyck's God is almost frail, surprisingly young, apparently merciful and kind, and certainly richly adorned. Indeed, in the richness of his vestments, van Eyck's God apparently values worldly things. Van Eyck's painting seems to celebrate a materialism that is the proper right of benevolent kings. Behind God's head, across the top of the throne, are Latin words that, translated into English, read: "This is God, all powerful in his divine majesty; of all the best, by the gentleness of his goodness; the most liberal giver, because of his infinite generosity." God's mercy and love are indicated by the pelicans embroidered on the tapestry behind him, which in Christian tradition symbolize self-sacrificing love, for pelicans were believed to wound themselves in order to feed their young with their own blood if other food was unavailable. In the context of the entire altarpiece, where God is flanked by Mary and John the Baptist, choirs of angels, and, at the outer edges, Adam and Eve, God rules over an earthly assembly of worshippers, his divine beneficence is protecting all.

1.16 Jan van Eyck.
God. Panel from *The Ghent Altarpiece*, c. 1432.
Church of St. Bavo, Ghent, Belgium.
Scala / Art Resource, New York.

1.17 Jan van Eyck.
The Ghent Altarpiece, c. 1432.
11 ft. 5 in. 3 15 ft. 1 in. Church of St. Bavo, Ghent, Belgium.
Scala / Art Resource, New York.

In a group of works known as the *Siluetas* (**Fig. 1.18**), done in the 1970s, Cuban-born Ana Mendieta attempted to come to grips with her own complicated heritage by transferring the silhouette of her own body into the landscape. In 1961, following the Communist Revolution of Fidel Castro, Mendieta's parents arranged to have her flown out of Cuba along with thousands of other children in what was known as Operation Peter Pan. For several years after, she lived in a Catholic orphanage in Iowa. "The making of my *silueta*," she explained, "makes the transition between my homeland and my new home. It is a way of reclaiming my roots and becoming one with nature. Although the culture in which I live is part of me, my roots and cultural identity are a result of my Cuban heritage." That heritage, on her mother's side, extends back to the sixteenth-century Spanish conquest of the Americas. When she created the *Silueta* pictured here, in Mexico, she stained it with red paint to evoke the oppression, even genocide, endured by the native peoples of the Americas after the conquest. Here the silhouette of the body seems transformed into the imprint of a large, bloody sword on the earth, the head and arms its hilt, the body its blade. The imprint of the live body evokes the

1.18 Ana Mendieta.
Silueta Works in Mexico, 1973–1977.
Color photograph, $19^{3}/_{8}$ 3 $26^{9}/_{16}$ in.
The Museum of Contemporary Art, Los Angeles. Purchased with grant
provided by the Judith Rothschild Foundation.

grave of her forebears and gives form to the tragedy of her ancestral past.

THE WORLD AS WE PERCEIVE IT

Many of us assume, almost without question, that we can trust our eyes to give us accurate information about the world. Seeing, as we say, is believing. Our word "idea" derives, in fact, from the Greek word *idein*, meaning "to see," and it is no accident that when we say "I see" we really mean "I understand."

The Process of Seeing

But the act of seeing is not a simple matter of our vision making a direct recording of the reality. Seeing is both a physical and psychological proc-

ess. Physically, visual processing can be divided into three steps:

reception   extraction   inference

In the first step, *reception*, external stimuli enter the nervous system through our eyes—"we see the light." Next, the retina, which is a collection of nerve cells at the back of the eye, *extracts* the basic information it needs and sends this information to the visual cortex, the part of the brain that processes visual stimuli. There are approximately 100 million sensors in the retina, but only 5 million channels to the visual cortex. In other words, the retina does a lot of "editing," and so does the visual cortex. There, special mechanisms capable of extracting specific information about such features as color, motion, orientation, and size "create" what is finally seen. What you see is the *inference* your visual cortex extracts from the information your retina sends it.

Seeing, in other words, is an inherently creative process. The visual system makes conclusions about the world. It represents the world for you by selecting out information, deciding what is important and what is not. Consider, for example, what sort of visual information you have stored about the American flag. You know its colors—red, white, and blue—and that it has 50 stars and 13 stripes. You know, roughly, its shape—rectangular. But do you know its proportions? Do you even know, without looking, what color stripe is at the flag's top, or what color is at the bottom? How many short stripes are there, and how many long ones? How many horizontal rows of stars are there? How many long rows? How many short ones? The point is that not only do we each perceive the same things differently, remembering different details, but also we do not usually see things as thoroughly or accurately as we might suppose. As the philosopher Nelson Goodman explains, "The eye functions not as an instrument self-powered and alone, but as a dutiful member of a complex and capricious organism. Not only how but what it sees is regulated by need and prejudice. It selects, rejects, organizes, discriminates, associates, classifies, analyzes, constructs. It does not so much mirror as take and make." In other words, the eye mirrors each individual's complex perceptions of the world.

Active Seeing

Everything you see is filtered through a long history of fears, prejudices, desires, emotions, customs, and beliefs. Through art, we can begin to understand those filters and learn to look more closely at the visual world. Jasper Johns's *Three Flags* (**Fig. 1.19**) presents an opportunity to look closely at a familiar image. According to Johns, when he created this work, the flag was something "seen but not looked at, not examined." *Three Flags* was painted at a time when the nation was obsessed with patriotism, spawned by Senator Joseph McCarthy's anti-communist hearings in 1954, by President Eisenhower's affirmation of all things American, and by the Soviet Union's challenge of American supremacy through the space race. Many of the

painting's first audiences saw the fact that the flag becomes less grand and physically smaller the closer it gets to the viewer as a challenge to their idea of America. While contemporary viewers may not have experienced that Cold War era, the work still asks us to consider what the flag represents.

Faith Ringgold's *God Bless America* (**Fig. 1.20**) has as its historical context the Civil Rights movement. In it, the American flag has been turned into a prison cell. Painted during a time when white prejudice against African Americans was enforced by the legal system, the star of the flag becomes a sheriff's badge, and its red and white stripes are transformed into the black bars of the jail. The white woman portrayed in the painting is the very image of contradiction, at once a patriot, pledging allegiance to the flag, and a racist, denying blacks the right to vote. She is a prisoner to her own bigotry.

Flags inevitably raise questions of national pride and identity. In a series of museum instal-

1.19 Jasper Johns.
Three Flags, 1958.
Encaustic on canvas, 30⁷/₈ 3 45¹/₂ 3 5 in.
50th Anniversary Gift of the Gilman Foundation, Inc., the Lauder Foundation, A. Alfred Taubman, an anonymous donor, and purchase 80.32. Collection of Whitney Museum of American Art, New York. Photo: Geoffrey Clements. Art © Jasper Johns / Licensed by VAGA, New York.

1.20 Faith Ringgold.
God Bless America, 1964.
Oil on canvas, 31 3 19 in.
© Faith Ringgold, Inc. 1964.

lations, Yukinori Yanagi has used ant farms as a means to make witty assaults on nationalism. For a museum installation entitled *America* (**Fig. 1.21**), Yanagi created a grid of plastic boxes, each filled with colored sand in the pattern of a national flag—representing the 36 countries of the Americas. Each box was connected to adjacent boxes by plastic tubing. Yanagi then introduced ants into the system, which immediately began carrying colored sand between flags, transforming and corrupting the flags' original designs. As each flag's integrity was degraded by these "border crossings," a new "cross-cultural" network of multinational symbols and identities began to establish itself.

Yanagi's work directly addresses the permeable boundaries that exist between countries sharing a single land mass; his other work makes a similar statement about border crossings on a global scale. Audiences have interpreted the work as an image of the destruction of local cultures or as the creation of a new multiculturalism. While the meaning of the work is open for interpretation, there is no question of its power to draw us into a closer examination of our perceptions of the world.

1.21 Yukinori Yanagi.
America, 1994.
Ants, colored sand, plastic boxes, and plastic tubes, 36 boxes, each 8 3 12 in.
Installation view at Museum of Contemporary Art, San Diego, 1994.
Collection of the artist.

Thinking about Making and Seeing

IN THIS CHAPTER, we have discovered that the world of art is as vast and various as it is not only because different artists in different cultures see and respond to the world in different ways, but also because each of us sees and responds to a given work of art in a different way. Artists are engaged in a *creative process*. We respond to their work through a process of *critical thinking*. At the end of each chapter of *A World of Art* is a section like this one titled *The Critical Process* in which, through a series of questions, you are invited to think for yourself about the issues raised in the chapter. In each case, additional insights are provided at the end of the text, in the section titled *The Critical Process: Thinking Some More about the Chapter Questions*. After you have thought about the questions raised, turn to the back and see if you are headed in the right direction.

Here, Andy Warhol's *Race Riot* (**Fig. 1.22**) depicts events of May 1963 in Birmingham, Alabama, when police commissioner Bull Connor employed attack dogs and fire hoses to disperse civil rights demonstrators led by Reverend Martin Luther King, Jr. The traditional roles of the artist—to help us see the world in new or innovative ways; to make a visual record of the people, places, and events of their time and place; to make functional objects and structures more pleasurable and elevate them or imbue them with meaning; and to give form to the immaterial, hidden or universal truths, spiritual forces, or personal feelings—are all part of a more general creative impulse

that leads, ultimately, to the work of art. Which of these is, in your opinion, the most important for Warhol in creating this work? Did any of the other traditional roles play a part in the process? What do you think Warhol feels about the events (note that the print followed soon after the events themselves)? How does his use of color contribute to his composition? Can you think why there

are two red panels, and only one white and one blue? Emotionally, what is the impact of the red panels? In other words, what is the work's psychological impact? What reactions other than your own can you imagine the work generating? These are just a few of the questions raised by Warhol's work, questions to help you initiate the critical process for yourself.

1.22 Andy Warhol.
Race Riot, 1963.
Acrylic and silkscreen on canvas, four panels, each 20 3 33 in.
© 2007 Andy Warhol Foundation for the Visual Arts / Artists Rights Society (ARS), New York.

ART CRITICISM

What makes a work of art worthwhile? Is it visually interesting? Does it move our feelings? Is it skillfully done? Which criteria are even relevant to judging art? Who is qualified to make such judgments? As we consider answers to these questions, we will find that there are many ways of judging the quality of art. Further, we will see that our assessments of quality are usually connected to other values that we also hold about the function of art in society; hence, our preferences about art generally embody other deeply held beliefs.

ART CRITICISM

The term **art criticism** refers to making discriminating judgments, both favorable and unfavorable. We all do art criticism, but professionals tend to follow one or more of three basic theories:

- Formal theories, which focus attention on the composition of the work and how it may have been influenced by earlier works
- Contextual theories, which consider art as a product and of a culture and value system
- Expressive theories, which pay attention to the artist's expression of a personality or worldview.

These theories emphasize the work, the culture, and the artist, respectively. Let us consider each in turn, as they might be used to analyze three paintings that are pictured in this chapter.

Formal Theories

Critics who use formal theories look carefully at how a work is made: how the parts of the composition come together to create a visual experience that may interest us, or not. They generally believe that the most important influence on a work is other works that the artist has seen or studied. Because the formal organization of the work is the most important factor in evaluating it, the theories are called **formal**. The subject or theme of the work is less important than how the artist presented it. Formalist critics value innovation in style above all; thus, they always want to know when a work was done, so that they can compare it (at least mentally) with its predecessors and contemporaries. They value such stylistic novelty because they believe that art can be an important source of visual refreshment, unconnected to our complicated and strife-torn world.

From a formal perspective, Titian's *Pietà* is very innovative in its brushwork. His immediate predecessors in Italian art were the Renaissance masters Raphael, Michelangelo, and Leonardo, among others. Titian understood the painting methods that they used, but he went beyond them by making his brushwork much bolder and

Chapter 2: Art Criticism was taken from *Prebles' Artforms: An Introduction to the Visual Arts,* Tenth Edition by Patrick Frank.

2.1 Titian.
Pietà. 1576.
Oil on canvas. 149″ 3 136″.
SCALA\Art Resource, N.Y.

looser, adding a new element of expressiveness to painting that influenced artists for generations to come. The work also uses an innovative composition: the center is an empty niche surrounded by a diagonal row of heads that is balanced by the two figures at the upper right. This emptiness at the center is a bold compositional device for that time.

Sonia Delaunay-Terk was similarly innovative when she painted *Simultaneous Contrasts* in 1913. The work was influenced by Cubism (see Chapter 11), but Delaunay-Terk did not overlap the planes as earlier Cubists did; the elements of this work fit together like a jigsaw puzzle. Yet she used shading to model each zone, as if the zones were curved surfaces. The work is innovative for how it sug-

2.2 Sonia Delaunay-Terk.
Simultaneous Contrasts. 1913.
Oil on canvas. 46 3 55 cm.
Museo Thyssen-Bornemisza, Madrid. 518 (1976.81). L & M Services
B. V. Amsterdam.

gests and denies a third dimension at the same time. This painting is also more innovative in its color than most early Cubist works. This painting explores how one bright color can have an impact on our perception of a neighboring one.

Horn Players by Jean-Michel Basquiat is also innovative from a formal standpoint: It uses techniques that the artist learned from making graffiti, something that few artists had done at that time. The parallel arrangement of three vertical panels is also interesting, suggesting a Japanese screen. The composition as a whole barely hangs together, but it does cohere. Note the repeated heads, boxes, and white paint strokes in each panel.

2.3 Jean-Michel Basquiat.
Horn Players. 1983.
Acrylic and oil paintstick on three canvas panels.
Overall 8′ 3 6′5″ (2.44 3 1.91 m).
Broad Art Foundation, Santa Monica, California. © 2010 The Estate of
Jean-Michel Basquiat/ADAGP, Paris/ARS, New York.

Thus, we can conclude that each of these three paintings is formally interesting, but for different reasons.

Contextual Theories

Critics who use these theories tend to look first at the environmental influences on a work of art: the economic system, the cultural values, and even the politics of the time; because the context matters a great deal, they are termed **contextual theories**. Just as formalist critics will want to know the date of a work, contextual critics are likely to ask, "What else was going on in the culture at that time?" Contextual critics tend to favor works that either cogently embody important cultural values, or memorably express resistance to them. Let us see how they might judge our three paintings.

Titian's *Pietà* is an altarpiece, destined for public viewing in a chapel at a church in Venice; altarpieces generally took up important Christian themes, and this one is no exception. However, Titian painted it during an epidemic of the plague, and its theme of mortality and grief takes on added meaning in that context. The vacant niche probably symbolizes death, and Titian's eloquent depiction of the dead Christ must have given comfort to the many Venetians who lost relatives in the epidemic. The work expresses grief over current events, but Titian has successfully taken it out of its time, so that even today we can still appreciate its mournful aspect.

Simultaneous Contrasts by Sonia Delaunay is less interesting from a contextual perspective, because its subject seems to be a simple sunlit landscape. The work tells us very little about its time (the early twentieth century). The title of the work refers to an optical theory that many artists studied in those days, which dealt with the interaction of colors. Delaunay also did fabric designs, and she used her discoveries in painting to give her ideas for her fashion work. This painting fueled her innovative clothing designs, which she called "Simultaneous Dresses".

In contrast, *Horn Players* is filled with contextual information. Basquiat admired the leaders of the bebop movement in jazz, and this work is an homage to them. Saxophonist Charlie Parker is at the upper left, red musical notes pouring out of his instrument. The ear that seems about to be cut off may refer to Vincent van Gogh, an artist of similar innovative power who indeed cut off his ear. (Both Parker and van Gogh died young, "cut off" in their prime.) We can make out the name of trumpeter Dizzy Gillespie at the top center and see him pictured at the right. The word "ornithology" refers to one of Parker's musical compositions that the two of them recorded in a famous track. Together they must have created the "alchemy" (magically transformative mixture) that the artist scrawled at the lower right.

Expressive Theories

All artworks are made by people. The skill level, personal intent, emotional state, mind-set, and gender of the creator must play a role in the creative process. Artist-centered theories are thus termed **expressive theories**. If formalists want to know dates, and contextualists want to know about the background culture, an expressive critic will want to know "Who made it? And who is she or he?" Critics who favor this approach tend to look for powerful personal meanings, deep psychological insight, or profound human concern. Expressive approaches have value because we all wish to be known, and finding artists similar to us in the museum is reassuring. Moreover, art is a means of communication between artist and viewer, and this communication can be done well or poorly. Each of our three paintings is quite expressive.

Titian painted the *Pietà* in the last year of his life; hence, its somber reflection on death expresses the artist's own mortality. Indeed, the figure at the lower right in the red shawl is Titian himself. Anyone who has ever mourned can probably identify with Mary's mournful attitude in this painting. The brushwork here is loose and expressive: Many critics believe that this represents an "old age style" in which the artist cast off the restraint of his younger days.

Sonia Delaunay's ebullient personality comes across in *Simultaneous Contrasts*. No clouds darken its sunlit skies. Her bright and exuberant color palette comes from her memories of brightly colored folk costumes in her native Ukraine, especially wedding costumes that were festooned with ribbons.

Critics of an expressive bent tend to like Jean-Michel Basquiat because his works are full of personal meaning. Most interesting is his use of line: it seems both intent and intense. That intensity contrasts nicely with the seemingly casual arrangement of the figures and script. The painting seems to have

come together like a three-verse song. This work also explores the artist's personal history as an African American by upholding examples from the music world. In *Horn Players*, he shares with us some people who are important to him, which is a good way to get a conversation going in almost any context.

WHAT MAKES IT GREAT?

The most obvious answer to this question is, "It's great if you think it is!" And everyone has their own personal list of great artworks. However, with our three theories in hand, we can now say how a work of art comes to be regarded as a "masterpiece," and commands the place of honor in a museum (or appears in a book like this): Some degree of innovation, important cultural meanings, and a recognizable personal statement are key ingredients. Not all three are necessary, but at least one must be strongly present.

Most works hanging in museums have been selected by the specialists on the staff because they embody at least one of the three theories. Your judgments may not agree with theirs, and that is OK.

But to go deeper is rewarding. The three theories of art criticism presented here give us three standards of quality, and three ways of judging artworks. Often we apply one or more of these without thinking, and we say something like, "I like art that I can relate to." Well, why do you relate to it? What are you looking for? A little self-examination should help you to uncover what values are motivating your choices, and can help open an interesting discussion about art with other viewers.

For the non-specialist, formal innovation is the hardest quality to recognize in a work of art. Many artworks hanging in museums are quite innovative (especially modern works), but unless we are visually literate, the innovation will likely be lost on us.

DEVELOPING VISUAL LITERACY

Visual art can be powerfully persuasive, and one of the purposes of this book is to help you to recognize how this is so. Yet it is important for you to understand from the outset that you can neither recognize nor understand—let alone communicate—how visual art affects you without using language. In other words, one of the primary purposes of any art appreciation text is to provide you with a descriptive vocabulary, a set of terms, phrases, concepts, and approaches that will allow you to think critically about visual images. It is not sufficient to say, "I like this or that painting." You need to be able to recognize why you like it, how it communicates to you. This ability is given the name *visual literacy*.

The fact is, most of us take the visual world for granted. We assume that we understand what we see. Those of us born and raised in the television era are often accused of being nonverbal, passive receivers, like TV monitors themselves. If television, the Internet, movies, and magazines have made us virtually dependent upon visual information, we have not necessarily become visually literate in the process. This chapter will introduce you to some essential concepts in visual literacy—the relationships among words, images, and objects in the real world; the idea of representation; and the distinctions among form and content in art, conventions in art, and iconography.

WORDS AND IMAGES

The Belgian artist René Magritte offered a lesson in visual literacy in his painting *The Treason of Images* (**Fig. 3.1**). Magritte reproduced an image of a pipe similar to that found in tobacco store signs and ads

3.1 René Magritte.
The Treason of Images, 1929.
Oil on canvas, 21¹/₂ 3 28¹/₂ in.
Los Angeles County Museum. ©
Bridgeman–Giraudon / Art Resource,
New York.
© 2007 C. Herscovici, Brussels / Artists
Rights Society (ARS), New York.

Chapter 3: Developing Visual Literacy was taken from *A World of Art,* Sixth Edition by Henry M. Sayre.

of his time. The caption under the pipe translates into English as "This is not a pipe," which at first seems contradictory. We tend to look at the image of a pipe as if it were really a pipe, but of course it isn't. It is the representation of a pipe. Both images and words can refer to things that we see, but they are not the things themselves. Magritte's painting invites us to think critically about the representations that bombard us in daily life.

The work of photographer Lorna Simpson consistently challenges the relations between words and images. Consider her photographs of a black female sitting in a chair, entitled *She* (**Fig. 3.2**). She is dressed in a brown suit, as if at an interview. Without the title and the italic script label at the top—"female"—the sitter's gender would be in doubt. If the work were called, say, *Interviewee*, the sitter's head cut off at the chin, there would be no way to know the gender of the sitter. In fact, Simpson has said that black women in the United States are treated by society as if they are faceless— without identity, personality, or individuality. Here, *She* challenges gender stereotypes, seemingly usurping man's place. It is as if, in the old phrase, *She* is wearing the pants in the family. And even if the words do somewhat diminish the ambiguity of

the piece, it remains as open to interpretation as the sitter's hand gestures, which are expressive even if we don't know what precisely they express. The **subject matter** of the work—what the image literally depicts—barely hints at the complexity of its content—what the image means.

In a series of photographs focused on the role of women in her native Iran and entitled *Women of Allah*, Shirin Neshat combines words and images in startling ways. In *Rebellious Silence* (**Fig. 3.3**), Neshat portrays herself as a Muslim woman, dressed in a black *chador*, the traditional covering that extends from head to toe revealing only hands and face. A rifle divides her face, upon which Neshat has inscribed in ink a Farsi poem by the devout Iranian woman poet Tahereh Saffarzadeh. Saffarzadeh's verses express the deep belief of many Iranian women in Islam. Only within the context of Islam, they believe, are women truly equal to men, and they claim that the *chador*, by concealing a woman's sexuality, prevents her from becoming a sexual object. The *chador*, in this sense, is liberating. It also expresses women's solidarity with men in the rejection of Western culture, symbolized by Western dress. But to a Western audience, the values embodied in the poem are indecipherable, a

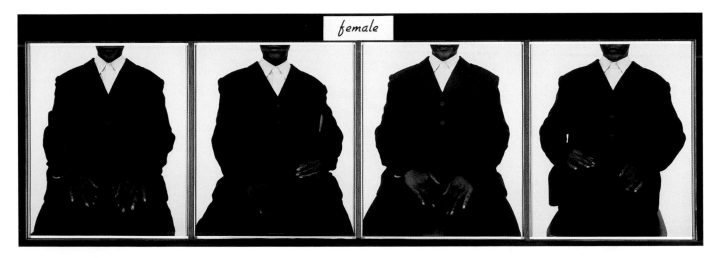

3.2 Lorna Simpson.
She, 1992.
Photographs, four dye-diffusion transfers (Polaroids) and plaque, 29 3 85¼ in.
Reproduced with permission. Ellen Kelleran Gardner Fund, 1992.204a-e. Museum of Fine Arts, Boston.
Photo © 2006 Museum of Fine Arts, Boston.

3.3 Shirin Neshat.
Rebellious Silence, from the series
Women of Allah, 1994.
Gelatin silver print and ink,
11 3 14 in.
Photo: Cynthia Preston. © Shirin Neshat,
courtesy Gladstone Gallery, NY.

fact that Neshat fully understands. Thus, because we cannot understand the image, it is open to stereotyping, misreading, misunderstanding—the very conditions of the division between Islam and the West, imaged in the division of Neshat's body and face by the gun.

In Islamic culture, in fact, words take precedence over images, and calligraphy—that is, the fine art of handwriting—is the chief form of Islamic art. The Muslim calligrapher does not so much express himself as act as a medium through which Allah (God) can express himself in the most

3.4 *Triumphal Entry* (page from a manuscript of the *Shahnamah of Firdawsi*), Persian, Safavid culture, 1562–1583. Opaque watercolor, ink, and gold on paper, 18^{11}/16 3 13 in.

beautiful manner possible. Thus, all properly pious writing, especially poetry, is sacred. This is the case with the page from the poet Firdawsi's *Shahnamah* (**Fig. 3.4**).

Sacred texts are almost always decorated with designs that aim to be visually compelling but not representational. Until recent times, in the Muslim world, every book, indeed almost every sustained statement, began with the phrase "In the name of Allah, the Beneficent, Ever-Merciful"—the *bismillah*, as it is called—the same phrase that opens the Qur'an. On this folio page from the *Shahnamah*, the *bismillah* is in the top right-hand corner (Arabic texts read from right to left). To write the *bismillah* in as beautiful a form as possible is believed to bring the scribe forgiveness for his sins.

The Islamic emphasis on calligraphic art derives, to a large degree, from the fact that at the heart of Islamic culture lies the word, in the form of the recitations that make up the Qur'an, the messages the faithful believe that God delivered to the prophet Muhammed through the agency of the angel Gabriel. The word could be trusted in a way that images could not. In the *hadith*, the collections of sayings and anecdotes about Muhammed's life, Muhammed is quoted as having warned, "An angel will not enter a house where there is a dog or a painting." Thus, images are notably absent in almost all Islamic religious architecture. And because Muhammed also claimed that "those who make pictures will be punished on the Day of Judgment by being told: make alive what you have created," the representation of "living things," human beings especially, is frowned upon. Such thinking would lead the Muslim owner of a Persian miniature representing a prince feasting in the countryside to erase the heads of all those depicted (**Fig. 3.5**). No one could mistake these headless figures for "living things."

The distrust of images is not unique to Islam; at various periods in history Christians have also debated whether it was sinful to depict God and his creatures in paintings and sculpture. In the summer of 1566, for instance, Protestant **iconoclasts** (literally "image breakers," those who wished to destroy images in religious settings) threatened to destroy van Eyck's *Ghent Altarpiece* (see Figs. 1.16 and 1.17), but just three days before all Ghent's churches were sacked, the altarpiece was dismantled and hidden in the tower by local authorities. In Nuremberg, Germany, a large sculpture of Mary and Gabriel hanging over the high altar of the Church of San Lorenz was spared destruction, but only after the town council voted to cover it with a cloth that was not permanently removed until the nineteenth century. The rationale for this wave of destruction, which swept across northern Europe, was a strict reading of the Ten Commandments: "Thou shalt not make any graven image, or any likeness of any thing that is in heaven above, or that is in the earth beneath, or that is in the water

3.5 Page from a copy of Nezami's *Khamseh* (the "Quintet") illustrating a princely country feast, Persian, Safavid culture, 1574–75. Illuminated manuscript, 9 3/4 3 6 in.
India Office, London.

under the earth: Thou shalt not bow down thyself to them nor serve them" (Exodus 20:4–5). But whatever the religious justification, it should be equally clear that the distrust of visual imagery is, at least in part, a result of the visual's power. If the worship of "graven images," that is, idols, is forbidden in the Bible, the assumption is that such images are powerfully attractive, even dangerously seductive.

Race and Gender Criticism

AT PRESENT, ART is undergoing intense scrutiny on the basis of criteria that are new to art criticism. At issue is the extent to which women artists and artists of color have been marginalized by the white, male-dominated Western art establishment and their humanity trivialized or oppressed through art.

One problem has been racial and gender stereotyping, rather than recognition of the full humanity of those without political power. Women have often been depicted as seductive sex objects rather than as complete and independent individuals. From the 1970s onward, some women artists have themselves begun creating art about the female body, not as an object but as a subject. To redefine their own sexuality, they have explored the female body in images, celebrated its links with nature and natural processes, and documented its abuses.

Another issue is the low value placed on the work of women and people of color in the West. In the art market centered in New York, it has been difficult for many such artists to be accepted or taken seriously. Women have rarely been acknowledged as fine artists—as painters or sculptors or printmakers, for instance. And traditional crafts which they have mastered, such as quiltmaking, have not been recognized as valuable art until recent years. In 1997, a prominent show of contemporary artists at the Museum of Modern Art in New York included only three white women, one woman of color, and no men of color, out of a total of seventy-one artists. If the work of women or people of color is shown, it may be specifically as "feminist" or "black" art, rather than simply as art, or it may be shown only in alternative

Art Issues: Race and Gender Criticism was taken from *The Art of Seeing*, Eighth Edition by Paul Zelanski and Mary Pat Fisher.

3.6 Imna Arroyo.
Ancestors of the Passage: A Healing Journey Through the Middle Passage, 2005.
Mixed-media installation, heads with hands 19 3 8 3 9½ ins (48.3 3 20.3 3 24.1 cm), background collagraph prints on paper 49 3 90 ins (124.5 3 228.6 cm), overall dimensions variable. Exhibited at Widener Gallery, Trinity College, Hartford, Connecticut, January–March 2005.

spaces, such as cooperative galleries. Daryl Chin asserts:

"The art world, so tied to an ideology of a market economy, reflects the sociopolitical consciousness of that ideology. And that ideology maintains a hierarchy of stratification, with minority artists lacking a definable place within the structure …. If the majority fails to recognize the exclusionary tactics now being practiced, then the realm of aesthetics is no longer imaginary; it is downright pathological."[1]

One could argue that the art of disempowered peoples should be judged by the same aesthetic standards as the art of the powerful. But it can also be argued that the criticism of art is based on aesthetic principles developed in the mainstream of Western culture. How then to judge quality in works that are not part of that tradition?

One solution is to try to evaluate work in terms of its own intentions. Consider the work of Imna Arroyo. She is a Puerto Rican artist whose work self-consciously reflects her African-Caribbean heritage and also her indigenous Taino ancestry. Although much of her work investigates the role of women in those cultures, *Ancestors of the Passage: A Healing Journey Through the Middle Passage* (**Fig. 3.6**) has different intentions. She explains:

"My imagery reflects both my physical and spiritual world. I use both two- and three-dimensional forms to resurrect the ancestors from their watery graves and give voice to the millions of people who

died as a result of greed, disease, and inhuman treatment during the Atlantic slave trade. *Ancestors of the Passage* is an affirmation of the memory of this loss. Only half of the slave ship cargo of 40 million to 90 million people, kidnapped from their homeland, survived. The *Ancestors of the Passage* is an important artwork for me because it has informed me of my richer African heritage and allows me to bear witness and to acknowledge the great loss. At the same time, I want the viewer to become aware of the great gifts brought forth by the ancestors who survived and to honor their legacy. As human beings we continue to witness atrocities and yet forget them all too quickly."[2]

If this work is to be judged on its own terms, we should not ask, "Is it well-designed or skillfully made?" but rather, "Does it touch us, reach out to us, educate us, remind us of a horrible page in human history?"

The serious consideration of multicultural and women's art is challenging and broadening critical tastes in art in the West. Some non-Western societies already value variety in their own art. India, for instance, which is home to sixteen different official languages, takes pride in displaying historic, folk, and contemporary works from the many artistic traditions woven into the cultural fabric of the country.

Notes

1. Daryl Chin, "Some Remarks on Racism in the American Arts," M/E/A/N/I/N/G, #3, May 1988, pp. 22, 25.
2. Imna Arroyo, personal communication to co-author, 30 October, 2005.

DESCRIBING THE WORLD

In the last section, we explored the topic of visual literacy by considering the relationship between words and images. Words and images are two different systems of describing the world. Words refer to the world in the abstract. Images represent the world, or reproduce its appearance. Traditionally, one of the primary goals of the visual arts has been to capture and portray the way the natural world looks. But, as we all know, some works of art look more like the natural world than others, and some artists are less interested than others in representing the world as it actually appears. As a result, a vocabulary has developed that describes how closely, or not, the image resembles visual reality itself. This basic set of terms is where we need to begin in order to talk or write intelligently about works of art.

Representational, Abstract, and Nonrepresentational Art

Generally, we refer to works of art as either **representational**, **abstract**, or **nonrepresentational** (or **nonobjective**). A **representational** work of art portrays natural objects in recognizable form. The more the representation resembles what the eye sees, the more it is said to be an example of **realism**. The less a work resembles real things in the real world, the more it is said to be an example of **abstraction**. When a work does not refer to the natural or objective world at all, it is said to be **nonrepresentational** or **nonobjective**.

Nonobjective or nonrepresentational works of art do not refer to the natural or objective world at all. Kasimir Malevich's *Suprematist Painting* (**Fig. 3.7**) is concerned primarily with questions of form. When we speak of a work's form, we mean everything from the materials used to make it, to the way it employs the various formal elements (discussed in Part 2), to the ways in which those elements are organized into a **composition**. **Form** is the overall structure of a work of art. Somewhat misleadingly, it is generally opposed to **content**, which is what the work of art expresses or means.

Obviously, the content of nonobjective art *is* its form. Malevich's painting is really *about* the relation between the black rectangle, the blue triangle, and the white ground behind them. Though it is a uniform blue, notice that the blue triangle's color seems to be lighter where it is backed by the black rectangle, and darker when seen against the white ground. This phenomenon results from the fact that our perception of the relative lightness or darkness of a color depends upon the context in which we see it, even though the color never actually changes. If you stare for a moment at the line where the triangle crosses from white to black, you will begin to see a vibration. The two parts of the triangle will seem, in fact, to be at different visual depths. Malevich's painting demonstrates how purely formal relationships can transform otherwise static forms into a visually dynamic composition.

Form and Content

One way to understand how art communicates experience is to compare works that have the same subject but differ greatly in form and content. *The Kiss* by Auguste Rodin and *The Kiss* by Constantin Brancusi show how two sculptors interpret an embrace. In Rodin's work, the life-size human figures represent Western ideals of the masculine and feminine: Rodin captured the sensual delight of that highly charged moment when lovers embrace. Our emotions are engaged as we overlook the hardness of the marble from which he carved it. The natural softness of flesh is heightened by the rough texture of the unfinished marble supporting the figures.

In contrast to Rodin's sensuous approach, Brancusi used the solid quality of a block of stone to express lasting love. Through minimal cutting of the block, Brancusi symbolized—rather than illustrated—the concept of two becoming one. He chose geometric abstraction rather than representational naturalism to express love. We might say that Rodin's work expresses the feelings of love while Brancusi's expresses the idea of love.

Form and Content section was taken from *Prebles' Artforms: An Introduction to the Visual Arts*, Tenth Edition by Patrick Frank.

3.7 Kasimir Malevich. *Suprematist Painting, Black Rectangle, Blue Triangle,* 1915. Oil on canvas, 26⅛ 3 22½ in. Stedelijk Museum, Amsterdam. Erich Lessing / Art Resource, New York.

Meaning and Culture

Consider another set of examples: an ancient sculpture of the Greek god Apollo and a carved mask from the Sang tribe of Gabon in West Africa (**Figs. 3.10 and 3.11**). In the late 1960s, art historian Kenneth Clark compared the two images through an ethnocentric lens and concluded that the image of the messenger god Apollo demonstrated the superiority of classical Greek civilization. Clark understood the conventions of Greek sculpture and recognized the meaning of the idealized sculptural form: "To the Hellenistic imagina-tion it is a world of light and confidence, in which the gods are like ourselves, only more beautiful, and descend to earth in order to teach men reason and the laws of harmony." His interpretation of the African mask, however, reveals his ignorance of the conventions of the West African tribe that created it: "To the Negro imagination it is a world of fear and darkness, ready to inflict horrible pun-ishment for the smallest infringement of a taboo." However, the features of the African mask are exaggerated at least in part to separate it from the "real." Clark's ethnocentric reading of it neglects

3.8   Auguste Rodin.
The Kiss. 1886.
Marble. Height 5′11¼″.
Musée Rodin, Paris, France. Photograph: Bruno Jarret.
© 2010 Artists Rights Society (ARS), New York/ADAGP, Paris.

3.9   Constantin Brancusi.
The Kiss. c. 1916.
Limestone.
23″ 3 13″ 3 10″.
Photo by Graydon Wood, 1994. 1950–135–4.
Art Resource/Philadelphia Museum of Art.
© 2010 Artists Rights Society (ARS),
New York/ADAGP, Paris.

its ritual, celebratory social function in African society. Worn in ceremonies, masks are seen as vehicles through which the spirit world is made available to humankind.

Iconography

Cultural conventions are often carried forward from one generation to the next by means of **iconography**, a system of visual images the meaning of which is widely understood by a given culture or cultural group. These visual images are **symbols**—

that is, they represent something more than their literal meaning. The subject matter of iconographic images is not obvious to any viewer unfamiliar with the symbolic system in use. Furthermore, every culture has its specific iconographic practices, its own system of images that are understood by the culture at large to mean specific things. Christian audiences, for instance, can easily read incidents from the story of Christ, such as those represented in the lower nine panels of the center window in the west front of Chartres Cathedral in France (**Fig. 3.12**). This

3.10　*Apollo Belvedere* (detail), Roman copy after a fourth-century BCE Greek original.
Height of entire sculpture 7 ft. 4 in.
Vatican Museums, Rome. © Alinari / Art Resource, NY.

3.11　African mask, Sang tribe, Gabon, West Africa.
Courtauld Gallery, Courtauld Institute, London.

3.12　Lower nine panels of the center lancet window in the west front of Chartres Cathedral, showing the Nativity, Annunciation of the Shepherds, and the Adoration of the Magi, c. 1150. Chartres Cathedral, France.
Courtesy of Bridgeman-Giraudon/Art Resource, NY.

window was made about 1150 and is one of the oldest and finest surviving stained-glass windows in the world. The story can be read like a cartoon strip, beginning at the bottom left and moving right and up, from the Annunciation (the angel Gabriel announcing to Mary that she will bear the Christ Child) through the Nativity, the Annunciation to the Shepherds, and the Adoration of the Magi. The window is usually considered the work of the same artist who was commissioned by the Abbot Suger to make the windows of the relic chapels at Saint-Denis, which portray many of the same incidents.

"The pictures in the windows are there," the Abbot explains in his writings, "for the sole purpose of showing simple people, who cannot read the Holy Scriptures, what they must believe." But he understood as well the expressive power of this beautiful glass. It transforms, he said, "that which is material into that which is immaterial." Suger understood that whatever story the pictures in the window tell, whatever iconographic significance they contain, and whatever words they generate, it is, above all, their art that lends them power.

3.13   Jan van Eyck.
Giovanni Arnolfini and His Wife Giovanna Cenami, c.1434.
Oil on wood, 32¼ 3 23½ in.
© National Gallery, London.

When Jan van Eyck painted his portrait of *Giovanni Arnolfini and His Wife Giovanna Cenami* in 1434 (**Fig. 3.13**), its repertoire of visual images was well-understood, but today, much of its meaning is lost to the average viewer. For example, the bride's green dress, a traditional color for weddings, was meant to suggest her natural fertility. She is not pregnant—her swelling stomach was a convention of female beauty at the time, and her dress is structured in a way to accentuate it. The groom's removal of his shoes is a reference to God's commandment to Moses to take off his shoes when standing on holy ground. A single candle burns in the chandelier above the couple, symbolizing the presence of Christ at the scene. And the dog, as most of us recognize even today, is associated with faithfulness and, in this context, particularly, with marital fidelity.

But what would Islamic culture make of the dog in the van Eyck painting, as in the Muslim world dogs are traditionally viewed as filthy and degraded? From the Muslim point of view, the painting verges on nonsense. Even to us, viewing van Eyck's work more than 500 years after it was painted, certain elements remain confusing. An argument has recently been made, for instance, that van Eyck is not representing a marriage so much as a betrothal, or engagement. It was also widely understood in van Eyck's time that a touching of the hands, the woman laying her hand in the palm of man, was the sign, especially in front of witnesses, of a mutual agreement to wed.

The painter himself stands in witness to the event. On the back wall, above the mirror, are the words *Jan de Eyck fuit hic, 1434*—"Jan van Eyck was here, 1434" (**Fig. 3.14**). We see the backs of Arnolfini and his wife reflected in the mirror, and beyond them, standing more or less in the same place as we do as viewers, two other figures, one a man in a red turban who is probably the artist himself.

3.14 Jan van Eyck.
The Marriage of Giovanni Arnolfini and Giovanna Cenami (detail), 1434.
Oil on oak panel.
National Gallery, London, UK. Bridgeman Art Library.

Thinking about Visual Conventions

VERY RARELY CAN WE FIND the same event documented from the point of view of two different cultures, but two images, one by John Taylor, a journalist hired by *Leslie's Illustrated Gazette* (**Fig. 3.15**), and the other by the Native American artist Howling Wolf (**Fig. 3.16**), son of the Cheyenne chief Eagle Head, both depict the October 1867 signing of a peace treaty between the Cheyenne, Arapaho, Kiowa, and Comanche peoples, and the United States government, at Medicine Lodge Creek, a tributary of the Arkansas River, in Kansas. Taylor's illustration is based on sketches done at the scene, and it appeared soon after the events. Howling Wolf's work, actually one of several depicting the events, was done nearly a decade later, after he was taken east and imprisoned at Fort Marion in St. Augustine, Florida, together with his father and 70 other "ringleaders" of the continuing Native American insurrection in the Southern Plains. While in prison, Howling Wolf made many drawings such as this one, called "ledger" drawings because they were executed on blank accountants' ledgers.

Even before he was imprisoned, Howling Wolf had actively pursued ledger drawing. As Native Americans were introduced to crayons, ink, and pencils, the ledger drawings supplanted traditional buffalo hide art,

3.15 John Taylor.
Treaty Signing at Medicine Creek Lodge, 1867.
Drawing for *Leslie's Illustrated Gazette*, September–December 1867, as seen in Douglas C. Jones, *The Treaty of Medicine Lodge*, page xx, Oklahoma University Press, 1966.

but in both the hide paintings and the later ledger drawings, artists depicted the brave accomplishments of their owners. The conventions used by these Native American artists differ greatly from those employed by their Anglo-American counterparts. Which, in your opinion, is the more representational? Which is the more abstract?

Both works possess the same overt content—that is, the peace treaty signing—but how do they differ in form? Both Taylor and Howling Wolf depict the landscape, but how do they differ? Can you determine why Howling Wolf might want to depict the confluence of Medicine Creek and the Arkansas in his drawing? It is as if Howling Wolf portrays the events from above, so that simultaneously we can see tipis, warriors, and women in for-

mal attire, and the grove in which the United States soldiers meet with the Indians. Taylor's view is limited to the grove itself. Does this difference in the way the two artists depict space suggest any greater cultural differences? Taylor's work directs our eyes to the center of the image, while Howling Wolf's does not. Does this suggest anything to you?

Perhaps the greatest difference between the two depictions of the event is the way in which the Native Americans are themselves portrayed. In Howling Wolf's drawing, each figure is identifiable—that is, the tribal affiliations and even the specific identity of each individual are revealed through the iconography of the decorations of his or her dress and tipi. How, in comparison, are the Native Americans por-

trayed in Taylor's work? In what ways is Taylor's work ethnocentric?

One of the most interesting details in Howling Wolf's version of the events is the inclusion of a large number of women. Almost all of the figures in Howling Wolf's drawing are, in fact, women. They sit with their backs to the viewer, their attention focused on the signing ceremony before them. Their braided hair is decorated with customary red paint in the part. This convention is of special interest. When the Plains warrior committed himself to a woman, he ceremonially painted her hair to convey his affection for and commitment to her. Notice the absence of any women in Taylor's depiction, as opposed to their prominence in Howling Wolf's. What does this suggest to you about the role of women in the two societies?

3.16 Howling Wolf
Treaty Signing at Medicine Creek Lodge, 1875–1878. Ledger drawing, pencil, crayon, and ink on paper, 8 3 11 in.
New York State Library, Albany, NY.

SEEING THE VALUE IN ART

4

Henry Geldzahler, then Cultural Commissioner for New York City, saw Jean-Michel Basquiat's paintings at P. S. 1 and "just flipped out." Alauna Heiss, founder of P. S. 1, recalls "standing in front of Jean-Michel's work with a director of Philip Morris. We were paralyzed. It was so obvious that he was enormously talented."

By 1982, Basquiat was earning an average of about $4,000 a week by painting. Two years later, at age 24, he became the first black artist to grace the cover of *The New York Times Magazine*. At the time of his death, four months before his 28th birthday, the victim, according to the medical examiner's report, of "acute mixed drug intoxication (opiates–cocaine)," his paintings were selling for about $30,000 each (normally a dealer keeps 50 to 60 percent of the sale price). Soon after his death, the auction house Christie's sold a 1981 canvas for $110,000. Now, 20 years since his death, the current auction record for a Basquiat is $14.6 million for *Untitled*, a painting featuring a figure with large hands. It sold at Sotheby's in 2007. As an obituary ironically entitled "Banking on Basquiat," put it, "There's no artist like a dead artist, some dealers are fond of saying."

If these numbers seem staggering, it is worth remembering that the monetary value of works of art is closely tied to the business of art, and, from a business point of view, art works are commodities to be bought and sold like any others, ideally for profit. Sylvie Fleury's *Serie ELA 75/K*

(Plumpity . . . Plump) (**Fig. 4.1**) is a wry commentary on this fact. Here the art work is literally a shopping cart, placed on a revolving pedestal and plated in 24K gold. Art, Fleury's work implies, is literally shopping.

And very high-end shopping, at that. The art market depends on the participation of

4.1 Sylvie Fleury.
Serie ELA 75/K (Plumpity . . . Plump), 2000.
Gold-plated shopping cart, plexiglas handle with vinyl text, rotating pedestal (mirror, aluminum, motor).
$32^{3}/4 \times 37^{3}/4 \times 21^{5}/8$ in. Pedestal $12^{1}/4 \times 39^{3}/8$ in.
Courtesy of the artist and Galerie Eva Presenhuber, Zürich, Switzerland.

Chapter 4: Seeing the Value in Art was taken from *A World of Art*, Sixth Edition by Henry M. Sayre.

wealthy clients through their investment, ownership, and patronage. It is no accident, then, that the major financial centers of the world also support the most prestigious art galleries, auction houses, and museums of modern and contemporary art. Art galleries bring artists and collectors together. They usually sign exclusive contracts with artists whose works they believe they can sell. Collectors may purchase work as an investment but, because the value of a given work depends largely upon the artist's reputation, and artists' reputations are finicky at best, the practice is very risky. As a result, what motivates most collectors is the pleasure of owning art and the prestige it confers upon them (the latter is especially important to corporate collectors).

It is at auction that the monetary value of works of art is most clearly established. But auction houses are, after all, publicly owned corporations legally obligated to maximize their profits, and prices at auction are often inflated. The business of art informs the practices of museums as well, which market their exhibitions as "events" in every way comparable to a rock concert or major motion picture. In fact, in order to finance their work, museums have increasingly relied on corporate sponsorship. Consider, for instance, the Guggenheim Museum's 2000–01 exhibition dedicated to the fashion design of Giorgio Armani (**Fig. 4.2**), whose company, not coincidentally, had entered into a $15 million sponsorship agreement with the museum. It is no accident, either, that the exhibition took place over the Christmas shopping season.

4.2 Installation view of Giorgio Armani exhibition at the Solomon R. Guggenheim Museum, New York, October, 20, 2000–January, 17, 2001.
Photo: Ellen Labenski © SRGF, NY.

Art as Investment

WHEN JAPANESE BUSINESSMAN Ryoei Saito bought Van Gogh's *Portrait of Dr. Gachet* for $82.5 million in 1990, he called the price "very reasonable."[1] Prices of artworks up for auction had reached extraordinary heights at that time, driven by international wealth and an increasing trend on the art scene. Instead of being purchased by people who primarily love and live with art, works by artists who are in vogue are more than ever before being bought as investments, for later auction at a higher price.

In 2004, a new world record was set at Sotheby's auction house in New York for an auctioned painting—$104 million for *Boy with a Pipe*, an early painting by Picasso that had been purchased in 1950 by private collectors for $30,000 (**Fig. 4.3**). Then, in 2006, that record was broken by the sale of a Gustav Klimt painting, *Adele Bloch-Bauer I* (**Fig. 4.4**) for a reported $135 million. The Klimt sale is of particular historical as well as artistic interest because it capped a long effort by the family of Adele Bloch-Bauer to recover the painting, which had been stolen from them by the Nazis in 1938, along with four other paintings by Klimt. They had ended up in an Austrian museum, but a law passed in Austria in 1998 required its museums to return art that Nazis had seized. The aged niece of Adele Bloch-Bauer, Maria Altmann, was there when the paintings were taken away from her family. She fought the case for seven years, and now that the family has won, they have sold the painting to a small New York museum so that it can be viewed by the public in memory of Jews in the Holocaust.

Art has become a sought-after commodity because the prices that people are willing to pay for art have rapidly escalated. Not surprisingly, this situation raises many new issues, both for artists and for those who buy art.

For buyers of art offered for resale at auctions, there are the risks of buying on speculation—being sure that one is buying an original rather than a copy, assessing its quality, preserving its condition, insuring it, and then at a later date arranging to sell it for much more than was paid for it. In 1990, prices had become so inflated that the market for artworks crashed. However,

4.3 Pablo Picasso.
Boy with a Pipe, 1905.
Oil on canvas 39⅓ × 32 ins
(100 × 81 cm).
Collection of Mr and Mrs John Hay Whitney, New York, USA. *Picasso painted this image of a young Parisian boy when he was only twenty-four years old, during his "Rose period."* Courtesy of Réunion des Musées Nationaux/Art Resource, NY.

Art Issues: Art as Investment was taken from *The Art of Seeing*, Eighth Edition by Paul Zelanski and Mary Pat Fisher.

4.4 Gustav Klimt.
Adele Bloch-Bauer I, 1907.
Oil and gold on canvas, 54⅓ × 54⅓ ins (138 × 138 cm). *This gold-flecked portrait by Gustav Klimt (1862–1918) will now hang in the Neue Galerie, a New York museum owned by cosmetics magnate Ronald S. Lauder devoted to German and Austrian art.*
Neue Galerie New York/Art Resource.

the art market heated up again, with especially high prices being paid for Impressionist paintings. As the supply of Impressionist art dwindled, people were paying huge sums for mediocre or little-known works by famous artists. In 1996, Christie's in New York sold a Van Gogh painting of empty tables at a restaurant, with a few people in the background, for $10.3 million. The auction house explained that this might be the last Van Gogh interior ever to come up for auction.

In sales of both pre-owned art through auctions and new art through galleries, prices are determined by a star system. It is ruled by what one artist characterizes as "a headless entity consisting of auctions, rumors, the media, newspapers, art magazines, interviews and so on. If you're out, you're out—you simply don't count. There is no opposition, no different opinion. [In this system] a painting which consists of a

few square inches of paper can cost more than a building. The building is much larger and, when it rains, people can go inside. But nobody asks what this is all about."[2]

For living artists, the lure of big money may lead people to concentrate on making art that sells rather than art that comes from the urge to create. And should they receive a percentage of profits that buyers make on reselling their work? Are they only economic pawns in a high-risk game?

Where do museums stand in this game? With prices so high, small museums cannot compete with the larger ones. There are only a limited number of true masterpieces, but museums may nevertheless try to have something from every period and many famous artists in their collections. Some observers therefore think that museums have become repositories of second-rate art. Furthermore, some pieces in museum

collections are antiquities taken out of other countries without permission. And some works may not have been executed by the famous artists whose names they bear. In the workshop system, which is not uncommon even today, the master artist creates the visual idea but employs helpers and apprentices for jobs such as—in the case of paintings—preparing the supports, grounds, and paints, painting the underlayers, painting certain details such as clouds and horses, and perhaps executing the whole painting under the master's supervision. Rubens had a large studio since his work was so popular, and even when he traveled abroad, the production of paintings continued in his absence. In the output of Rembrandt's workshop, we do not now know which pieces were created solely by the hand of the master or what the "Rembrandt" signature meant at the time. The Rembrandt Research Project suggests that of the 711 existing works that were thought in 1920 to be created by Rembrandt, perhaps fewer than 300 were actually done by Rembrandt himself. In recent years, contemporary Chinese and Indian artworks have rapidly escalated in market value, as new international attention to contemporary Asian art has also fueled domestic interest among nouveau-riche Asians. But the global financial meltdown in the fall of 2008 put the brakes on everescalating prices for art everywhere. After the preceding "feeding frenzy" in which all sorts of works were being quickly snatched up at greatly inflated prices, a Danish gallery owner commented, "It's nice that it's going back to normal and that it's time to talk about art again, instead of investment."[3]

Notes

1. Ryoei Saito, quoted in Charles Danziger, "Where the Buyers Are," *Art in America*, July 1990, p. 55.
2. Sandro Chia, quoted in "Making Art, Making Money," *Art in America*, July 1990, p. 138.
3. Claus Andersen, in Jill Lawless, "Meltdown hits world of art, prices plunge," *Asian Age*, October 21, 2008

ART AND ITS RECEPTION

The artist's relation to the public, it should be clear, depends on the public's understanding of what the artist is trying to say. But the history of the public's reception of art abounds with instances of the public's misunderstanding. In 1863, for example, Edouard Manet submitted his painting *Luncheon on the Grass,* more commonly known by its French name, *Déjeuner sur l'herbe* (**Fig. 4.5**), to the conservative jury that picked paintings for the annual Salon exhibition in Paris. It was rejected along with many other paintings considered "modern," and the resulting outcry forced Napoleon III to create a Salon des Refusés, an exhibition of works refused by the Salon proper, to let the public judge for itself the individual merits of the rejected works. Even at the Salon des Refusés, however, Manet's painting created a scandal. Some years later, in his novel *The Masterpiece,* Manet's friend Emile Zola

4.5 Edouard Manet.
Luncheon on the Grass (Le Déjeuner sur l'herbe), 1863.
Oil on canvas, 7 ft. × 8 ft. 10 in. (2.13 × 2.6 m).
Courtesy of Réunion des Musées Nationaux/Art Resource, NY.

wrote a barely fictionalized account of the painting's reception:

It was one long-drawn-out explosion of laughter, rising in intensity to hysteria. . . . A group of young men on the opposite side of the room were writhing as if their ribs were being tickled. One woman had collapsed on to a bench, her knees pressed tightly together, gasping, struggling to regain her breath. . . . The ones who did not laugh lost their tempers. . . . It was an outrage and should be stopped, according to elderly gentlemen who brandished their walking sticks in indignation. One very serious individual, as he stalked away in anger, was heard announcing to his wife that he had no use for bad jokes. . . . It was beginning to look like a riot . . . and as the heat grew more intense faces grew more and more purple.

Though it was not widely recognized at the time, Manet had, in this painting, by no means abandoned tradition completely to depict everyday life in all its sordid detail. *Déjeuner sur l'herbe* was based on a composition by Raphael that Manet knew through an engraving, *The Judgment of Paris*, copied from the original by one of Raphael's students, Marcantonio Raimondi (**Fig. 4.6**). The pose of the three main figures in Manet's painting directly copies the pose of the three figures in the lower right corner of the engraving. However, if Manet's sources were classical, his treatment was anything but. In fact, what

4.6 Marcantonio Raimondi.
 The Judgment of Paris (detail), c. 1488–1530.
 Engraving, after Raphael. Clipped impression, Plate line 11⅝ × 17¼ in.
 Photograph © The Metropolitan Musueum of Art/Art Resource.

4.7 Marcel Duchamp.
Nude Descending a Staircase, No. 2, 1912.
Oil on canvas, 58 × 35 in.

most irritated both critics and the public was the apparently "slipshod" nature of Manet's painting technique. He painted in broad visible strokes. The body of the seated nude in *Déjeuner* was flat. The painting's sense of space was distorted, and the bather in the background and the stream she stands in both seemed about to spill forward into the picnic.

Manet's rejection of traditional painting techniques was intentional. He was drawing attention to his very modernity, to the fact that he was breaking with the past. His manipulation of his traditional sources supported the same intentions. In the words of his contemporary, Karl Marx, Manet was looking "with open eyes upon his conditions of life and true social relations." Raphael had depicted the classical judgment of Paris, the mythological contest in which Paris chose Venus as the most beautiful of the goddesses, a choice that led to the

4.8   Etienne-Jules Marey.
Man Walking in Black Suit with White Stripe Down Sides, 1883.
Collection Musée Marey, Beaune, France. Photo: Jean-Claude Couval.

Trojan War. In his depiction of a decadent picnic in the Bois de Bologne, Manet passed judgment upon a different Paris, the modern city in which he lived. His world had changed. It was less heroic, its ideals less grand.

The public tends to receive innovative artwork with reservation because it usually has little context, historical or otherwise, in which to view it. It is not easy to appreciate, let alone value, what is not understood. When Marcel Duchamp exhibited his *Nude Descending a Staircase* (**Fig. 4.7**) at the Armory Show in New York City in 1913, it was a scandalous success, parodied and ridiculed in the newspapers. Former President Teddy Roosevelt told the papers, to their delight, that the painting reminded him of a Navajo blanket. Others called it "an explosion in a shingle factory," or "a staircase descending a nude." The American Art News held a contest to find the "nude" in the painting. The winning entry declared, "It isn't a lady but only a man."

The Armory Show was most Americans' first exposure to modern art, and more than 70,000 people saw it during its New York run. By the time it closed, after also traveling to Boston and Chicago, nearly 300,000 people had seen it. If not many understood the *Nude* then, today it is easier for us to see what Duchamp was representing. He had read, we know, a book called *Movement,*

published in Paris in 1894, a treatise on human and animal locomotion written by Etienne-Jules Marey, a French physiologist who had long been fascinated with the possibility of breaking down the flow of movement into isolated data that could be analyzed. Marey began to photograph models dressed in black suits with white points and stripes, which allowed him to study, in images created out of a rapid succession of photographs, the flow of their motion. These images, called "chronophotographs," literally "photographs of time" (**Fig. 4.8**), are startlingly like Duchamp's painting. "In one of Marey's books," Duchamp later explained, "I saw an illustration of how he indicated [movement] . . . with a system of dots delimiting the different movements. . . . That's what gave me the idea for the execution of [the] *Nude.*"

Marey and Duchamp had embarked, we can now see, on the same path, a path that led to the invention of the motion picture. On December 28, 1895, at the Grand Café on the Boulevard des Capucines in Paris, the Lumière brothers, who knew Marey and his work well, projected motion pictures of a baby being fed its dinner, a gardener being doused by a hose, and a train racing directly at the viewers, causing them to jump from their seats. Duchamp's vision had already been confirmed, but the public had not yet learned to see it.

Censorship of Offensive Art

DOES THE PURSUIT of art require complete freedom of expression for all artists? Should limits be drawn as to what is acceptable in publicly displayed art or publicly funded art?

These questions came to the fore in 1990 in the United States when funding by the National Endowment for the Arts for a traveling exhibition of sexually explicit photographs by Robert Mapplethorpe became the subject of intense debate and even an obscenity court case. It was filed against the director of the Contemporary Art Center in Cincinnati. Jurors were shown only the seven most controversial photographs from the exhibit. They were asked to determine whether they met all three criteria of obscenity, as defined in a 1973 US Supreme Court ruling. The Supreme Court had ruled that a work is obscene if it depicts sexuality "in a patently offensive way," if "the average person, applying contemporary community standards," finds that it appeals to "prurient interest," and if it "lacks serious literary, artistic, political, or scientific value."[1]

None of the jurors had any background in art appreciation and they did not like the pictures. Nevertheless, they acquitted the director after ten days of expert testimonies designed to prove that Mapplethorpe's work did indeed have serious artistic value and therefore should not be judged legally obscene. The director of the Cleveland Museum of Art argued that the photographs were metaphoric "images of rejection, aggression, anxiety." The director of the Walker Art Center in Minneapolis told the jury:

"I recognize that they are difficult. I recognize that they are confrontational. I recognize that they tell us things maybe we would rather not hear. But they do shine lights in some rather dark corners of the human psyche. And they symbolize, in disturbing, eloquent fashion, an attitude. And they do reflect an attitude that is not necessarily limited to the artist."[2]

One of the jurors later said, "We learned that art doesn't have to be pretty."[3] Nevertheless, the potential for funding for art on the edge to be withdrawn continues to hang over the heads of artists and museums.

In 1999, the mayor of New York threatened to withdraw the city's financial support of the Brooklyn Museum of Art, evict it from its premises, and replace its governing board because of its exhibition of the work of ninety-two young British artists, entitled "Sensation." The works included slices of animals in formaldehyde-filled cases, a portrait of a child abuser and murderer made of small children's hand-prints, and statues of children with genitalia where their faces should be. The mayor termed it "sick stuff," and pointed to a work by Chris Ofili, *The Holy Virgin Mary*, as being particularly offensive to people of Roman Catholic faith. Ofili's black Madonna is ornamented with cutouts of buttocks and lumps of elephant dung. The resulting controversies involving use of public funds, vested interests, religion, race, moral sensitivities, animal rights, freedom of expression, and mixing of aesthetics and politics notwithstanding, the exhibition was held, and record crowds queued up to see it.

Art that is intentionally provocative or sensational arouses strong passions around the globe. In 2005, Buenos Aires was rocked by controversy over a retrospective of the antireligious, explicitly sexual, and politically satirical works of Leon Ferrari. The archbishop of the city declared the exhibition blasphemous, and the cultural center, staff, and artist received threats of violence. After the exhibit was closed by a judge to avoid hurting people's religious sentiments, the cultural center and city hall won their appeal to reopen it, on the basis of the artist's right to free expression. The cultural secretary of Buenos Aires observed, "The exhibition may be provocative, but nobody was obliged to see it."[4]

Moscow witnessed violent protests over an exhibition of the work of forty Russian artists exploring religion in Russian life. Held at the Sakharov Museum and Public Center in 2003, the exhibit was entitled "Caution! Religion." The exhibition was vandalized by Orthodox fundamentalists and the organizers were brought to trial in 2005 on charges of provoking religious hatred. Mobs of fundamentalists built altars for prayer vigils in the courthouse corridors and shouted anti-Semitic epithets at the defendants. The court demanded that the artists submit statements explaining why they had created their works; one artist had to defend her depiction of Adam and Eve as naked. Psychologists and art historians called by the prosecution said that they detested contemporary art and felt that it should not be shown in public museums. Despite outcries by the international intellectual community, the organizers were found guilty and fined.

Controversy erupted again in 2007 in Moscow over an exhibition of political art at the prestigious State Tretyakov Gallery. Among the pieces found most offensive by critics such as the Minister of Culture were photographs of the Blue Noses collective in which members wearing masks of

---

Art Issues: Censorship of Offensive Art was taken from *The Art of Seeing,* Eighth Edition by Paul Zelanski and Mary Pat Fisher.

famous people including Lenin and Stalin were depicted in sexual escapades with each other. Although the show went on in Moscow, many pieces were pulled from the exhibit before it was sent to Paris.

Censorship of art has long been an issue. Michelangelo's monumental painting on the end wall of the Sistine Chapel, *The Last Judgment* (detail in **Fig. 4.9**), was violently attacked in the sixteenth century shortly after it was painted. In the Council of Trent, Roman Catholic Church officials had ruled that sacred images must adhere closely to scriptural descriptions, lest any viewer be misled. Critics felt that Michelangelo had taken too much artistic license. His angels did not have wings, for instance, and the angels blowing trumpets announcing the apocalypse were all grouped together, rather than at the four corners of the earth in accordance with scripture. The most controversial aspect of the work was the voluptuous nudity of the figures, which prompted one critic to refer to Michelangelo as "that inventor of filthiness."[5] People tried physically to attack *The Last Judgment*. So as to save the masterpiece, two successive popes ordered that the naked figures should be overpainted with loincloths to cover their genitals and breasts; the bits of clothing now seen did not exist in Michelangelo's original work (Fig. 4.9).

More recently, in 1937 Nazi Germany confiscated over 16,000 pieces of modern German art of all sorts, burned much of it in a huge fire, and exhibited some of the rest with the label "Degenerate Art." At the opening of the exhibit, the president of the Reich Chamber of Visual Arts explained:

"We now stand in an exhibition that contains only a fraction of what was bought with the hard-earned savings of the German people and exhibited as art by a large number of museums all over Germany. All around us you see the monstrous offspring of insanity, impudence, ineptitude, and sheer degeneracy. What this exhibition offers inspires horror and disgust in us all."[6]

Among the works confiscated from German museums were fifty-seven paintings by Wassily Kandinsky.

Questions arise: What are the ramifications of institutional censorship of artistic creation? Can art be dangerous for social health? Can censorship of art be dangerous for social health? If there should be limits, who should define them? Should the depiction of violence, sexism, racism, or sacrilege be censored, or only overt depictions of sexuality?

4.9 Michelangelo Buonarroti. *The Last Judgment* (detail), end wall of the Sistine Chapel, old print of the original.

Notes

1. *Miller vs. California*, US Supreme Court ruling 1973.
2. As quoted in Robin Cembalest, "The Obscenity Trial," *ARTnews*, December 1990, p. 138.
3. Ibid., p. 137.
4. Gustavo Lopez, in Peter Hudson, "The Show That Had All Buenos Aires Talking," *ARTnews*, April 2005, p. 62.
5. Gaye, *Carteggio Inedito*, vol. ii, p. 500, as quoted in Anthony Blunt, *Artistic Theory in Italy 1450–1600*, The Clarendon Press, Oxford, 1940, p. 119.
6. Quoted in "Decadent, Un-German, Morally Offensive," *ARTnews*, May 1991, p. 123.

Cleaning and Restoring Paintings

OVER THE CENTURIES, great paintings are vulnerable to damage by aging processes, dampness, and filth. They may be further damaged by the methods used by restorers to attempt to clean and repair their surfaces. And attempts to repaint areas that are damaged are inevitably controversial, for restorers, no matter how skillful, do not have the rare talent and aesthetic judgment of the original masters.

Attempts to clean and restore great paintings are now undertaken with considerable caution. Restorer Pinin Brambilla Barcilon worked on a miniature scale for over twelve years trying to bring Leonardo da Vinci's *The Last Supper* (Fig. 9.8) back to life as the master had originally painted it. Such restorations are now matters of high technology, including infrared and ultraviolet photographic analyses of what lies beneath the surface, and microscopic examination of paint chips to determine their layers. Even so, the restorer's task is quite daunting and, in some cases, nearly impossible.

The Last Supper is a restorer's nightmare. It is painted on a wall in the convent of Santa Maria delle Grazie, but it is not a fresco. Leonardo had apparently treated the wall as if it were a wood panel and painted it in tempera on a pitch and mastic ground. Art historians speculate that this approach allowed Leonardo to work at his own pace and make corrections to the painting, whereas fresco cannot be handled in this way. But soon after its completion in 1497, the paint surface began to decay and crumble off the refectory wall, due to dampness from a spring 20 feet (6 m) below the wall. To try to save the masterpiece, it was repainted twice in the eighteenth century and three more times in the nineteenth century. It is thought that what

then remained to be seen was only 20 percent Leonardo's work; the rest was painted by restorers.

How can anyone, even working with the most sophisticated of means, now be sure what the original looked like? The surface of the mural has disintegrated into myriad delicate flakes, each no bigger than a grain of rice. No single pattern can be discerned in the layers of the flakes after the painting has been reworked with different painting approaches and additions of glues, waxes, and lacquers. "There is an incredible variety of materials in the painting, meaning that a cleaning technique that might have worked in one section could be totally ineffective or even harmful a few centimeters away,"[1] says Brambilla.

Despite the treacherous difficulties, Brambilla claims that repainters' work is easily distinguished from Leonardo's original painting when each flake is examined under a microscope, cleaned, and then reattached to the wall. It has thus been determined that the roof beams as shown in Fig. 9.8 are the work of a repainter; Leonardo's beams are actually in a different place, beneath the ceiling that was apparently added to the painting in the eighteenth century. The restored painting of the figures is also different, more three-dimensional than earlier repaintings. Are we now seeing the true hand of Leonardo revealed afresh or the hand of the latest restorer at work?

The question of authenticity has brought great controversy into some restoration projects. Most notably, controversy raged throughout the major twentieth-century restoration of the Sistine Chapel ceiling in Rome. Opponents of the project particularly object to the newly brilliant but rather flat and simple colors, convinced that

they are not those originally used by the artist. Critics also assert that the new cleaning has removed delicate *a secco* overpaintings by which Michelangelo had finished the modeling of his figures and added details. Supporters of the restoration claim that Michelangelo worked only in the best *buon fresco* tradition, with very little *a secco* overpainting, so that nothing significant has been lost during the restoration, and that the newly cleaned fresco reveals Michelangelo's extraordinary use of color.

Even routine removal of aged varnish to clean the surface of paintings may engender controversy. Artists have traditionally used varnish on their paintings to protect the surface and keep the underlying image clean. The idea was that the varnish would be removed from time to time, again revealing the clean surface, which would then be revarnished. The varnish itself would get dirty and change color as it aged, usually turning yellow. Grays and greens then tend to look brown, and blues turn green. Other materials have accumulated on top of the yellowing varnish. In addition to being darkened by the soot from the candles of the devout, church paintings in Italy and elsewhere were often rubbed with bacon rind before major holidays. To remove these coatings without harming the glazes of the painting itself is very difficult. Even water brushed lightly over the surface may dissolve glazes as well as varnish.

Leonardo's *Mona Lisa* is extremely dirty, as you can see in Fig. 9.7, but it is otherwise in good condition and is only dusted lightly each year. Cleaning has been eschewed to avoid outraging a public who are accustomed to the painting as it is, with thick yellowed varnishes. A clue to its original colors is revealed when *Mona Lisa*'s

Art Issues: Cleaning and Restoring Paintings was taken from *The Art of Seeing*, Eighth Edition by Paul Zelanski and Mary Pat Fisher.

frame is annually removed for dusting: a clear blue color can be seen on the untrimmed and unvarnished edges of Leonardo's painting of the sky. Elsewhere the built-up layers of varnish are reportedly a quarter of an inch (0.63 cm) thick. The Louvre's chief curator of paintings, Pierre Rosenberg, explains that the painting has not been cleaned because it was treated with reverence from the beginning and thus escaped harmful restorations. Now, he says, "We are not afraid of the job— it's a simple procedure—but of reactions nationally and internationally."[2] When other oil paintings by Leonardo have been restored, it has been discovered that he worked with extraordinarily fine strokes, some as minute as 0.0013 of an inch (0.03 mm), and sometimes he blended areas with his fingers for a soft-focus *sfumato* effect.

Public reactions and technical difficulties in rejuvenating a masterwork are not the only problems in restoration. Aesthetics may be lost in the process. Art historian Professor James Beck of Columbia University argues that, especially in the case of the restoration of Michelangelo's huge *Last Judgment* fresco on the end wall of the Sistine Chapel, restorers have worked piece by piece among scaffolds and thus have lost the aesthetic harmony of the whole. Beck explains:

"The fundamental problem was that no viewing distance was possible. Seen at arm's length, the oversized details, segments, and fragments were overwhelming but fundamentally misleading."[3]

After four years of section-by-section work, the scaffolds were removed and the restoration unveiled. According to Beck, it was a "garish and disharmonious" mistake. No

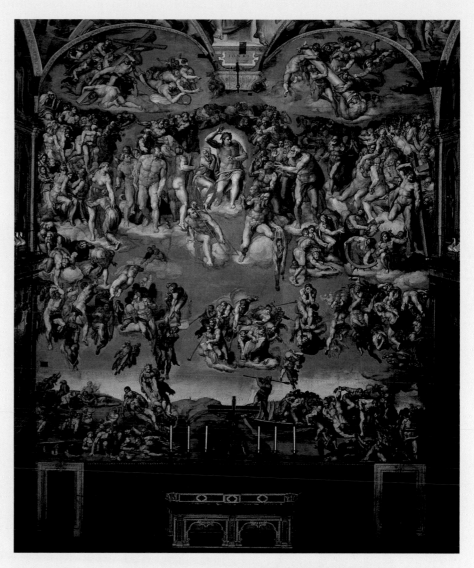

4.10   Michelangelo's *Last Judgment,* end wall of the Sistine Chapel, after latest restoration (completed c. 1994). Vatican City, Rome.

consistent light source remained, and the figures appear flat, with loss of the modeling effects of careful differences in value. Another loss, claims Beck, is Michelangelo's shifting use of outlines sometimes as borders and sometimes as shadows. **Figure 4.10** shows the entire *Last Judgment* after its recent restoration.

Notes

1. Pinin Brambilla Barcilon, quoted in Ken Shulman, "Like Seeing Leonardo for the First Time," *ARTnews,* November 1991, p. 53.
2. Pierre Rosenberg, quoted in Ginger Danto, "What Becomes a Legend Most," *ARTnews,* Summer 1989, p. 153.
3. James Beck with Michael Daly, *Art Restoration: The Culture, the Business, and the Scandal,* W. W. Norton and Company, New York, 1996, p. 194.

ART, POLITICS, AND PUBLIC SPACE

A certain segment of the public has always sought out art in galleries and museums. But as a general rule (except for statues of local heroes mounted on horseback in the public square—of interest mainly to pigeons), the public could ignore art if it wished. In 1967, when Congress first funded the National Endowment for the Arts (NEA), that changed. An Arts in Public Places Program was initiated, quickly followed by state and local programs nationwide that usually required 1 percent of the cost of new public buildings to be dedicated to purchasing art to enhance their public spaces. Where artists had

before assumed an interested, self-selected audience, now everyone was potentially their audience. And, like it or not, artists were thrust into activist roles—their job, as the NEA defined it, to educate the general public about the value of art.

The Endowment's plan was to expose the nation's communities to "advanced" art, and the Arts in Public Places Program was conceived as a mass-audience art appreciation course. Time and again, throughout its history, it commissioned pieces that the public initially resisted but learned to love. Alexander Calder's *La Grande vitesse* (**Fig. 4.11**) in Grand Rapids, Michigan, was the first

4.11   Alexander Calder
La Grande vitesse, 1969.
Sheet metal, bolts, and paint. 43 × 55 × 25 ft. Calder Plaza, Vandenberg Center, Grand Rapids, Michigan.
© 2011 Calder Foundation, New York / Artists Rights Society (ARS), New York.

piece commissioned by the Program. The selection committee was a group of four well-known outsiders, including New York painter Adolph Gottlieb and Gordon Smith, director of the Albright-Knox Art Gallery in Buffalo, New York, and three local representatives, giving the edge to the outside experts, who were, it was assumed, more knowledgeable about art matters than their local counterparts. In the case of *La Grande vitesse*, the public initially reacted negatively to the long organic curves of Calder's praying mantis–like forms but soon adopted the sculpture as a civic symbol and a source of civic pride. The NEA and its artists were succeeding in teaching the public to value art for art's sake.

Public Sculpture

To value art for art's sake is to value it as an aesthetic object, to value the beauty of its forms rather than its functional practicality or its impact on social life. The NEA assumed, however, that teaching people to appreciate art would enhance the social life of the nation. Public art, the Endowment believed, would make everyone's lives better by making the places in which we live more beautiful, or at least more interesting. The public sculpture considered in this section tests this hypothesis.

Richard Serra's controversial *Tilted Arc* (**Fig. 4.12**) received an entirely different reception. When it was originally installed in 1981 in Federal Plaza in Lower Manhattan, there was only a minor flurry of negative reaction. However, beginning in March 1985, William Diamond, newly appointed Regional Administrator of the General Services Administration, which had originally commissioned the piece, began an active campaign to have it removed. At the time, nearly everyone believed that the vast majority of people working in the Federal Plaza complex despised the work. In fact, of the approximately 12,000 employees in the complex, only 3,791 signed the petition to have it removed, while nearly as many—3,763—signed a petition to save it. Yet the public perception was that the piece was "a scar on the plaza" and "an arrogant, nose-thumbing gesture," in the words of one observer. During the night of March 15,

4.12   Richard Serra.
Tilted Arc, 1981.
Cor-Ten steel, 12 ft. × 120 ft. × 2½ in. Installed, Federal Plaza, New York City. Destroyed by the U.S. Government March 15, 1989.
© 2007 Richard Serra / Artists Rights Society (ARS), New York.

1989, against the artist's vehement protests and after he had filed a lawsuit to block its removal, the sculpture was dismantled and its parts stored in a Brooklyn warehouse. It has subsequently been destroyed.

From Serra's point of view, *Tilted Arc* was destroyed when it was removed from Federal Plaza. He had created it specifically for the site, and once removed, it lost its reason for being. In Serra's words: "Site-specific works primarily engender a dialogue with their surroundings. . . . It is necessary to work in opposition to the constraints of the context, so that the work cannot be read as an affirmation of questionable ideologies and political power."

Serra *intended* his work to be confrontational. It was political. That is, he felt that Americans were divided from their government, and the arc divided the plaza in the same way. Its tilt was ominous—it seemed ready to topple over at any instant. Serra

4.13   Michelangelo.
David, 1501–1504.
Copy of the original as it stands in the Piazza della Signoria, Florence. Original in the Galleria dell'Accademia, Florence. Marble, height 13 ft. 5 in.

succeeded in questioning political power probably more dramatically than he ever intended, but he lost the resulting battle. He made his intentions known and understood, and the work was judged as fulfilling those intentions. But those in power judged his intentions negatively, which is hardly surprising, considering that Serra was challenging their very position and authority.

One of the reasons that the public has had difficulty, at least initially, accepting so many of the public art projects that have been funded by both the NEA and percent-for-art programs is that they have not found them to be aesthetically pleasing. The negative reactions to Serra's arc are typical. If art must be beautiful, then Serra's work was evidently not a work of art, at least not in the eyes of the likes of William Diamond. And yet, as the public learned what the piece meant, many came to value the work, not for its beauty but for its insight, for what it revealed about the place they were in. Serra's work teaches us a further lesson about the value of art. Once public art becomes activist, promoting a specific political or social agenda, there are bound to be segments of the public that disagree with its point of view.

A classic example is Michelangelo's *David* (**Fig. 4.13**). Today, it is one of the world's most famous sculptures, considered a masterpiece of Renaissance art. But it did not meet with universal approval when it was first displayed in Florence, Italy, in 1504. The sculpture was commissioned three years earlier, when Michelangelo was 26 years old, by the Opera del Duomo ("Works of the Cathedral"), a group founded in the thirteenth century to look after the Florence cathedral and to maintain works of art. It was to be a public piece, designed for outdoor display in the Piazza della Signoria, the plaza where public political meetings took place on a raised platform called the *arringhiera* (from which the English word "harangue" derives). Its political context, in other words, was clear. It represented David's triumph over the tyrant Goliath and was meant to symbolize Republican Florence—the city's freedom from foreign and papal domination, and from the rule of the Medici family as well.

Michelangelo Buonarroti on Marble-Quarrying

MICHELANGELO BUONARROTI (1475–1564) was a true "Renaissance man"—sculptor, painter, architect, and poet. As a sculptor, he is best known for some of his earliest work, especially the colossal *David* (**Fig. 4.14**) and the tender *Pietà* (Fig. 6.21), both of which were executed when he was in his twenties. Whereas *David* was carved from a huge block of marble that had been unsuccessfully begun by another sculptor, Michelangelo took personal responsibility for supervising the quarrying of other blocks of marble he was to use, as well as having them transported. In some cases he hired *scarpellini* (stonemasons) to do the initial rough carving of the forms. The following excerpts from his letters suggest some of the difficulties he faced in these processes:

March, 1518: "As the marbles [in the mountains of Seravezza] have turned out to be excellent for me and as those that are suitable for the work at St. Peter's are easy to quarry and nearer the coast than the others, that is, at a place called Corvara; and from this place no expense for a road is involved, except over the small stretch of marsh land near the coast. But for a choice of the marble for figures, which I need myself, the existing road will have to be widened for about two miles from Corvara to Seravezza and for about a mile of it or less an entirely new road will have to be made, that is, it must be cut into the mountains with pickaxes to where the said marbles have to be loaded."

April 2, 1518: "Commend me to His Magnificence and beg him to commend me to his agents in Pisa, so that they may do me the favor of finding barges to transport the marbles from Carrara. I went to Genoa and got four barges sent to the quayside to load them. The Carrarese bribed the masters of the said barges and are bent on balking me, so that I achieved nothing."

April 18, 1518: "These scarpellini whom I brought from Florence know nothing on earth about quarrying or about marble. They have already cost me more than a hundred and thirty ducats and haven't yet quarried me a chip of marble that's any use … . In trying to tame these mountains and to introduce the industry into these parts, I've undertaken to raise the dead."

December, 1523: "When I was in Rome with [Pope Julius], and when he had given me a commission for his Tomb, into which a thousand ducats' worth of marbles were to go, he had the money paid to me and sent me to Carrara to get them. I remained there eight months to have the marbles blocked out and I transported nearly all of them to the Piazza of St. Peter, but some of them remained at Ripa. Then, after I had completed the payment for the freight of the said marbles, I had no money left from what I had received for the said work, but I furnished the house I had in the Piazza of St. Peter with beds and household goods out of my own money, in anticipation of the Tomb, and I brought assistants from Florence, some of whom are still living, to work on it, and I paid them in advance out of my own money. At this point Pope Julius changed his mind and no longer wanted to go on with it."[1]

4.14 Michelangelo Buonarroti
David, 1501–4.
Marble, height approx. 18 ft (5.5 m).
Galleria dell'Accademia, Florence.

Note

1. Excerpted from *The Letters of Michelangelo*, trans. E. H. Ramsden, vol. 1, Stanford University Press, Stanford, California, 1963, pp. 108, 110, 112, 148. [Reprinted by kind permission of the publisher.]

Artists on Art: Michelangelo Buonarroti on Marble-Quarrying was taken from *The Art of Seeing*, Eighth Edition by Paul Zelanski and Mary Pat Fisher.

The *David* was, as everyone in the city knew, a sculptural triumph in its own right. It was carved from a giant 16-foot-high block of marble that had been quarried 40 years earlier. Not only was the block riddled with cracks, forcing Michelangelo to bring all his skills to bear, but earlier sculptors, including Leonardo da Vinci, had been offered the problem stone and refused.

When the *David* was finished, in 1504, it was moved out of the Opera del Duomo at eight in the evening. It took 40 men four days to move it the 600 yards to the Piazza della Signoria. It required another 20 days to raise it onto the *arringhiera*. The entire time, its politics hounded it. Each night, stones were hurled at it by supporters of the Medici, and guards had to be hired to keep watch over it. Inevitably, a second group of citizens objected to its nudity, and before its installation a skirt of copper leaves was prepared to spare the general public any possible offense. Today, the skirt is long gone. By the time the Medici returned to power in 1512, the *David* was a revered public shrine, and it remained in place until 1873, when it was replaced by a copy (as reproduced here in order to give the reader a sense of its original context) and moved for protection from a far greater enemy than the Medici—the natural elements themselves. Michelangelo's *David* suggests another lesson about the value of art. Today, we no longer value the sculpture for its politics but rather for its sheer aesthetic beauty and accomplishment. It teaches us how important aesthetic issues remain, even in the public arena.

The "Other" Public Art

Public art has been associated particularly with sculptural works. Whatever social issues or civic pride they may symbolize, there are kinds of public art that are designed to have direct impact on our lives. For example, in their 1994 piece *The Cruci-fiction Project* (**Fig. 4.15**), performance artists Guillermo Gómez-Peña and Roberto Sifuentes crucified themselves for three hours on 16-foot-high crosses at Rodeo Beach, in front of San Francisco's Golden Gate Bridge. "The piece was designed for the media," Gómez-Peña explains, "as a symbolic pro-

4.15   Guillermo Gómez-Peña and Roberto Sifuentes. *The Cruci-fiction Project,* 1994. Site-specific performance, Marin headlands, California.
Photo: Victor Zaballa. Courtesy Headlands Center for the Arts.

test against the xenophobic immigration politics of California's governor Pete Wilson." The artists identified themselves as modern-day versions of Dimas and Gestas, the two small-time thieves who were crucified along with Jesus Christ, and they dressed as Mexican stereotypes: "I was an 'undocumented bandido,' crucified by the INS [Immigration and Naturalization Service]," Gómez-Peña recalls, "and Roberto was a generic 'gang member,' crucified by the LAPD [Los Angeles Police Department]." Gómez-Peña describes what happened at the performance:

Our audience of over 300 people each received a handout, asking them to "free us from our martyrdom as a gesture of political commitment." However, we had miscalculated their response. Paralyzed by the melancholia of the image, it took them over three hours to figure out how to get us down. By then, my right shoulder had become dislocated and Roberto had passed out. We were carried to a nearby bonfire and nurtured back to reality, while some people in the crowd rebuked those who were trying to help us, saying, "Let them die!"

Photographs of the event were quickly picked up by the media, and the piece became international news. The image appeared in, among other publications, Der Spiegel (Germany), Cambio 16 (Spain), Reforma and La Jornada (Mexico), and various U.S. newspapers. The photos have since reappeared in major news media and art publications as the debates on immigration and arts funding continue to be the focus of the political right.

The Cruci-fiction Project was designed to draw public attention to immigration issues in California. Similarly, when Thai artist Sakarin Krue-On was invited to participate in an exhibition of contemporary Thai art at Tang Contemporary Art in Beijing, China, he took the opportunity to draw the attention of the Chinese public to the fact that the city of Xuchang in Henan province had become one of the largest centers of human hair distribution in the world. Across China, common people trade hair that has often taken years to grow for whatever money they can get in return (in some cases, just enough to buy a pair of pants). In Xuchang today, there are 112 hair-product manufacturing companies. The irony is that it was in Henan province, in 1958, that the then-Communist government of Mao Zedong established its first commune, designed to abolish private ownership and maximize the effectiveness of the rice harvest—hence the title of Krue-On's work, *Since 1958*, spelled out on the gallery wall and composed of 10,000 locks of human hair, which Krue-On purchased from a Bangkok wholesaler who had in turn ordered it from China (**Fig. 4.16**). "From rice harvest to human-hair harvest," Krue-On says.

A final example of this activist direction in art is artist Krzysztof Wodiczko's *Homeless Vehicle* (**Figs. 4.17 and 4.18**), a shopping cart representing the very opposite of Sylvie Fleury's (see Fig. 4.1), which opened this chapter. Wodiczko, who had fled Poland in 1984 and had lived in the United

4.16   Sakarin Krue-On.
Since 1958, 2007.
10,000 locks of human hair on gallery wall,
4 ft. 1 in. × 30 ft. 6 in. Installation view and inset detail. Tang Contemporary Art, Beijing, China, 2007.
Artwork © Sakarin Krue-On.

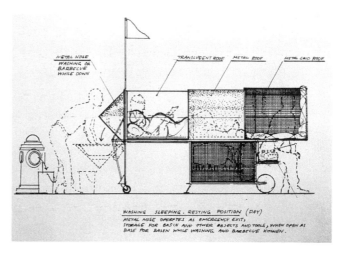

4.17   Krzysztof Wodiczko.
Homeless Vehicle, 1988.
Preliminary drawing showing vehicle in washing, sleeping, and resting position (day).
Courtesy of the artist and Gallery Lelong, New York.

4.18   Krzysztof Wodiczko.
Homeless Vehicle in New York City, 1988–1989.
Color photograph.
Courtesy of the artist and Gallery Lelong, New York.

States for only four years, was appalled during the winter of 1987–88 that an estimated 70,000 people were homeless in New York City alone. While he felt that "the fact that people are compelled to live on the streets is unacceptable," he also proposed to do something about it. Given the failure of the city's shelter system, he asked himself, "What can we do for individuals struggling for self-sufficiency on the streets today?" His solution was a vehicle for the homeless. As ingenious as the vehicle itself is, providing a level of safety and some creature comforts on the streets, Wodiczko's project is also motivated by more traditional issues. He draws attention to what the viewer has failed, or refused, to see, and thus attempts "to create a bridge of empathy between homeless individuals and observers."

Early Encounters with the Artists Within

I'd like to study the drawings of kids. That's where the truth is, without a doubt.

André Derain[1]

THE ARTS COME from inborn human needs to create and to communicate. They come from the desire to explore, confirm, and share special observations and insights—a fact readily apparent in nine-year-old Kojyu's *Searching for Bugs in the Park.* The arts are one of the most constructive ways to say "I did it. I made it. This is what I see and feel. I count. My art is me." Unfortunately, the great value of this discover-and-share, art-making process is only rarely affirmed in today's busy homes and schools.

We include art by children as the best way—other than actual hands-on art-making processes—to help you reexamine your relationship to your own creative powers and perhaps even to guide you as you prepare to become a parent, a teacher, or a caregiver for children.

Children use a universal visual language. All over the world, drawings by children ages two to six show similar stages of mental growth, from exploring with mark making to inventing shapes to symbolizing things seen and imagined. Until they are about six years old, children usually depict the world in symbolic rather than realistic ways. Their images are more mental constructions than records of visual observations.

During the second year of life, children enjoy making marks, leaving traces of their movements. Sensitive exploration is visible in *First Lines,* by a one-and-a-half-year-old child. After marking and scribbling, making circles and other shapes fascinates young children. The *House* shape is by a two-year-old. *Hand with Line and Spots* is by a three-year-old, as is the smiling portrait of *Grandma* in which self-assured lines

Kojyu, age 9.
Searching for Bugs in the Park.

Anonymous Child, age 18 months.
First Lines.

Jeff, age 3.
Hand with Line and Spots.

Alana, age 3.
Grandma.
Photographs: Duane Preble.

Alana, age 2.
House.

Art in the World: Early Encounters with the Artists Within was taken from *Prebles' Artforms: An Introduction to the Visual Arts,* Tenth Edition by Patrick Frank.

symbolize a happy face, shoulders, arms, body, belly button, and legs.

Being the son of a salt-water fish collector, and watching an octopus, gave almost four-year-old Jason the idea for his drawing of a smiling *Mother Octopus with Babies*. The excitement of joyful play with friends on unicycles inspired eight-year-old Yuki's *I Can*

Jason, almost 4.
Mother Octopus with Babies.

Yuki, age 8.
I Can Ride, I Can Ride My Unicycle.
Photographs: Duane Preble.

Ride, I Can Ride My Unicycle. Notice how she emphasized her own image by greatly exaggerating her size relative to others and how she included important information, such as her right leg seen through the spokes of the wheel.

Young children often demonstrate an intuitive sense of composition. Unfortunately, we lose much of this intuitive sense of balanced design as we begin to look at the world from a conceptual, self-conscious point of view. Most children who have been given coloring books, workbooks, and predrawn printed single sheets become overly dependent on such impersonal, stereotyped props. In this way, children often lose the urge to invent unique images based on their own experiences. A child's two drawings of *Birds* show this process: The child first interprets the bird in a personal, fresh way, but later adopts the trite forms of a conventional workbook. Without ongoing opportunities for personal expression, children lose self-confidence in their original creative impulses.

Children begin life as eager learners. If they are loved and cared for, they soon express enthusiasm for perceiving and exploring the world around them. Research shows that parents' ability to show interest in and empathy for their child's discoveries and feelings is crucial to the child's brain development. Before the age of one, and well before they talk, babies point tiny fingers at wonderful things they see. Bodies move in rhythm to music. Ask a group of four-year-olds "Can you dance?" "Can you sing?" "Can you draw?" and they all say, "Yes! Yes!" Ask twelve-year-olds the same questions, and they will too often say "No, we can't." Such an unnecessary loss has ominous implications for the spiritual, economic, social, and political health of society.

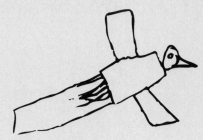

Anonymous Child.
Birds.
a. This picture shows one child's drawing of a bird before exposure to coloring books.

b. Then the child colored a workbook illustration.

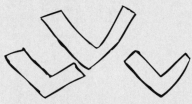

c. After coloring the workbook birds, the child lost creative sensitivity and self-reliance.
(a,b, and c) From Creative Mental Growth by Lowenfeld, ©1975, p. 23.
Reproduced by permission of Pearson Education Inc, Upper Saddle River, NJ.

Most abilities observed in creative people are also characteristic of children during interactions with the world around them. What becomes of this extraordinary capacity? According to John Holt, author of *How Children Fail,*

We destroy this capacity above all by making them afraid—afraid of not doing what other people want, of not pleasing, or of making mistakes, of failing, of being wrong. Thus we make them afraid to gamble, afraid to experiment, afraid to try the difficult and unknown.[2]

Notes

1. André Derain, *ArtNews* (April 1995): 118.
2. John Holt, *How Children Fail* (New York: Pitman, 1964), 167.

THE VISUAL ELEMENTS

5

The language of vision determines, perhaps even more subtly and thoroughly than verbal language, the structure of our consciousness.

S. I. HAYAKAWA[1]

The most direct path to the mind is through the eyes. As philosopher and educator S. I. Hayakawa pointed out, our visual experience of the world is so profoundly influential that it constitutes a nonverbal language all its own. This is the language that artists use to communicate. In this chapter we will first discuss the art of looking and then consider various visual tools that artists use.

LOOKING AND SEEING

The verbs "look" and "see" indicate varying degrees of awareness. Looking implies taking in what is before us in a purely mechanical way; seeing is a more active extension of looking. If we care only about function, we simply need to look quickly at a doorknob in order to grasp and turn it. But when we get excited about the shape and finish of a doorknob, or the bright, clear quality of a winter day, we go beyond simple functional looking to a higher level of perception called "seeing."

The twentieth-century French artist Henri Matisse wrote about the effort it takes to move beyond stereotypes and to see intently:

To see is itself a creative operation, requiring an effort. Everything that we see in our daily life is more or less distorted by acquired habits, and this is perhaps more evident in an age like ours when cinema, posters, and magazines present us every day with a flood of ready-made images which are to the eye what prejudices are to the mind. The effort needed to see things without distortion takes something very like courage.[2]

But, since words and visual images are two different "languages," talking about visual arts with words is always an act of translation one step removed from actually experiencing art. In fact, our eyes have their own connections to our minds and emotions. By cultivating these connections, we can take better advantage of what art has to offer.

Chapter 5: The Visual Elements was taken from *Prebles' Artforms: An Introduction to the Visual Arts,* Tenth Edition by Patrick Frank.

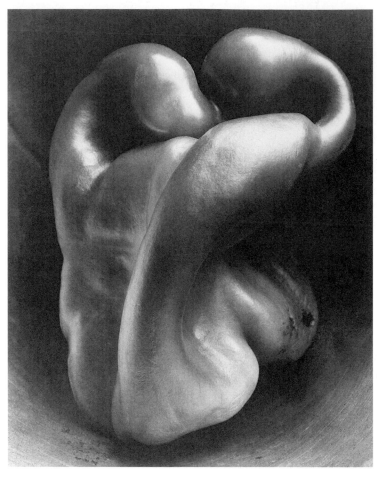

5.1 Edward Weston.
Pepper #30. 1930.
Photograph.
Photograph by Edward Weston.
Collection Center for Creative Photography, The University of Arizona.
©1981 Arizona Board of Regents.

Ordinary things become extraordinary when we see them deeply. Is Edward Weston's photograph of a pepper meaningful to us because we like peppers so much? Probably not. To help us truly see, Weston created a memorable image on a flat surface with the help of a common pepper. A time exposure of over two hours gave *Pepper #30* quality of glowing light—a living presence that resembles an embrace. Through his sensitivity to form, Weston revealed how this pepper appeared to him. Notes from his *Daybook* communicate his enthusiasm about this photograph:

I could wait no longer to print them—my new peppers, so I put aside several orders, and yesterday afternoon had an exciting time with seven new negatives.

First I printed my favorite, the one made last Saturday, August 2, just as the light was failing—quickly made, but with a week's previous effort back of my immediate, unhesitating decision. A week?—Yes, on this certain pepper,—but twenty-eight years of effort, starting with a youth on a farm in Michigan, armed with a No. 2 Bull's Eye [Kodak] 3½ 3 3½, have gone into the making of this pepper, which I consider a peak of achievement.

It is a classic, completely satisfying—a pepper—but more than a pepper: abstract, in that it is completely outside subject matter . . . this new pepper takes one beyond the world we know in the conscious mind.[3]

Weston's photograph of a seemingly common object is a good example of the creative process at work. The artist was uniquely aware of something in his surroundings. He worked for a long time (perhaps 28 years!) to achieve the image he wanted. The photograph that resulted not only represents the object but also communicates a deep sense of wonder about the natural world.

THE VISUAL TOOLBOX

Remember that a picture—before being a war horse, a nude woman, or some anecdote—is essentially a plane surface covered with colors assembled in a certain order.
MAURICE DENIS[4]

Painter Maurice Denis might have gone on to say that the surface can also be covered with lines, shapes, colors, and other aspects of visual form. Sculpture consists of these same elements organized and presented in three-dimensional space. Because of their overlapping qualities, it is impossible to draw rigid boundaries between the elements of visual form.

A glance at Swiss artist Paul Klee's *Landscape with Yellow Birds* shows his fluent use of several visual tools. Fluid, curving **lines** define abstract **shapes**. Klee simplified and flattened the solid **masses** of natural plant

Edward Weston on Photography as a Way of Seeing

EDWARD WESTON (1886–1958), one of the great figures in American photography, initially created out-of-focus, dreamy portraits. But in the 1920s he began a movement he called "straight photography," in which objects were shot in sharp focus, with attention to their details. One of the most influential members of the f/64 group, he particularly loved the "sculptural" forms of vegetables, rocks, trees, the human figure. For him photography was an intense way of seeing, as well as the technical expertise to capture what he saw. The following are excerpts from his daybooks:

"B. sat next to me again. As she sat with legs bent under [**Fig 5.3**], I saw the repeated curve of thigh and calf—the shin bone, knee and thigh lines forming shapes not unlike great sea shells,—the calf curved across the upper leg, the shell's opening ....

These simplified forms I search for in the nude body are not easy to find, nor record when I do find them. There is that element of chance in the body assuming an important movement: then there is the difficulty in focussing close up with a sixteen-inch lens: and finally the possibility of movement in an exposure of from 20sec. to 2min.,— even the breathing will spoil a line .... My after exhaustion is partly due to eye-strain and nerve strain. I do not weary so when doing still-life and can take my own sweet time."

"I hold to a *definite attitude of approach,* but the camera can only record what is before it, so I must await and be able to grasp the right moment when it is presented on my ground glass. To a certain point I can, when doing still-life, feel my conception before I begin work, but in portraiture,

5.2 Edward Weston
Knees, 1927.
Gelatin-silver print, 6¼ 3 9³/₁₆ ins (15.9 3 23.4 cm).
San Francisco Museum of Modern Art, California. Albert M. Bender Collection. Albert M. Bender Bequest Fund Purchase.
© 1981 Center for Creative Photography, Arizona Board of Regents

figures, clouds,— trying to record ever-changing movement and expression, everything depends upon my clear vision, my intuition at the important instant, which if lost can never be repeated. This is a great limitation and at the same time a fascinating problem in photography.

"Imagine if you had to create in, at the most, a few seconds of time, without the possibility of pre-visioning, a complete work, supposed to have lasting value. Of course my technique is rapid, and serves me if coordinated at the time with my perception."

"I am the adventurer on a voyage of discovery, ready to receive fresh impressions, eager for fresh horizons, not in the spirit of a militant conqueror to impose myself or my ideas, but to identify myself in, and unify with, whatever I am able

to recognize as significantly part of me: the 'me' of universal rhythms. Nature must not be recorded with a viewpoint colored by psychological headaches or heartaches .... [I want] an honest, direct, and reverent approach when granted the flash of revealment."

"I have been training my camera on a cantaloup—a sculptural thing. I know I shall make some good negatives for I feel its form deeply. Then last eve green peppers in the market stopped me: they were amazing in every sense of the word,—the three purchased. But a *tragedy* took place. Brett ate two of them!"[1]

Note

1. Excerpted from Nancy Newhall, ed., *The Daybooks of Edward Weston,* vol. 2, Horizon Press, New York, in collaboration with the George Eastman House, Rochester, 1966, pp. 10, 18, 37, 206.

Artists on Art: Edward Weston on Photography as a Way of Seeing was taken from *The Art of Seeing,* Eighth Edition by Paul Zelanski and Mary Pat Fisher.

5.3 Paul Klee.
Landscape with Yellow Birds. 1923.
Watercolor, newspaper, black base. 14"317⅞".
Photograph: Hans Hinz/Artothek.
© 2010 Artists Rights Society (ARS), New York/VG Bild-Kunst, Bonn.

basic means for recording and symbolizing ideas, observations, and feelings; it is a primary means of visual communication.

A line is an extension of a point. Our habit of making all kinds of lines obscures the fact that pure geometric line—line with only one dimension, length—is a mental concept. Such geometric lines, with no height or depth, do not exist in the three-dimensional physical world. Lines are actually linear forms in which length dominates over width. Wherever we see an edge, we can perceive the edge as a line—the place where one object or plane appears to end and another object or space begins. In a sense, we often "draw" with our eyes, converting edges to lines.

In art and in nature, we can consider lines as paths of action—records of the energy left by moving points. Many intersecting and contrasting linear paths form the composition in Lee Friedlander's photograph *Bismarck, North Dakota.* Wires, poles, railings, building edges, and the shadows they cast all present themselves as lines in this work.

and bird forms so that they read as flat shapes against a dark background **space**. Such **abstraction** emphasizes the fantastic, dreamlike quality of the subject. The whimsical positioning of the upside-down bird suggests a moment in **time** without **motion**. **Light** illuminates and enhances the yellow **color** of the birds and the unusual colors of the leaves.

This chapter introduces the visual tools identified in *Landscape with Yellow Birds:* line, shape, mass, space, time, motion, light, and color, and abstraction. Not all these elements are important, or even present, in every work of art; many works emphasize only a few elements. To understand their expressive possibilities, it is useful for us to examine, one at a time, some of the expressive qualities of each of these aspects of visual form.

LINE

We write, draw, plan, and play with lines. Our individualities and feelings are expressed as we write our one-of-a-kind signatures or make other unmechanical lines. Line is our

5.4 Lee Friedlander.
Bismarck, North Dakota. 2002.
Photograph.
© Lee Friedlander, courtesy Fraenkel Gallery, San Francisco.

5.5 *Line Variations.*

a. Actual line

b. Implied line

c. Actual straight lines and implied curved line

d. Line created by an edge

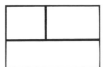

e. Vertical line (attitude of alert attention); horizontal line (attitude of rest).

f. Diagonal lines (slow action, fast action).

g. Sharp, jagged line.

h. Dance of curving lines.

i. Hard line, soft line.

j. Ragged, irregular line.

Characteristics of Line

Lines can be active or static, aggressive or passive, sensual or mechanical. Lines can indicate directions, define boundaries of shapes and spaces, imply volumes or solid masses, and suggest motion or emotion. Lines can also be grouped to depict light and shadow and to form patterns and textures. Note the line qualities in these *Line Variations.*

Consider the range of uses artists found for lines in the works pictured on these two pages. In Anselm Reyle's *Untitled* neon work, colored lights describe lines in three-dimensional space. But artists have put lines to many other uses.

Bridget Riley created a powerful energy field of parallel, wavy lines in her painting *Current.* We cannot focus steadily on one spot in this work, and as our eyes move, the work seems to vibrate even though nothing in it moves. Jackson Pollock made his *Drawing* by pouring and dripping ink from a stick without touching the paper. The swirling

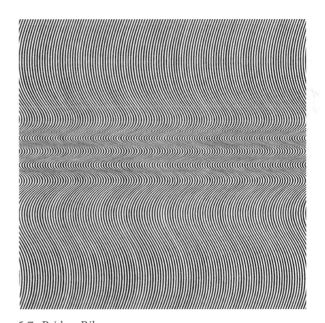

5.7 Bridget Riley.
Current. 1964.
Synthetic polymer paint on composition board.
58⅜"358⅞" (148.1 3 149.3 cm).

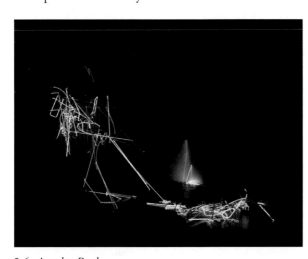

5.6 Anselm Reyle.
Untitled. 2006.
119 neon tubes, chains, cable, and 13 transformers.
16′4″ 3 32′8″ 3 26′4″.

5.8 Jackson Pollock.
Drawing. 1950. Duco on paper. 28.2 3 152.2 cm.
Staatsgalerie Stuttgart/Graphische Sammlung. © 2010 The Pollock-Krasner Foundation/Artists Rights Society (ARS), New York.

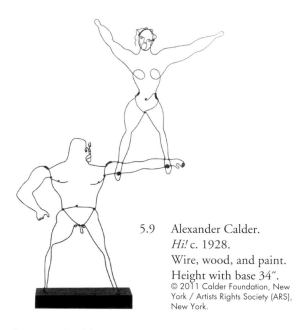

5.9   Alexander Calder.
Hi! c. 1928.
Wire, wood, and paint.
Height with base 34″.
© 2011 Calder Foundation, New York / Artists Rights Society (ARS), New York.

5.10   Attributed to Torii Kiyonobu I (1664–1729).
Woman Dancer with Fan and Wand (or possibly *Tsugawa Handayu*). c. 1708.
Woodblock print. 21¾″311½″.
The Metropolitan Museum of Art, Harris Brisbane Dick Fund and Rogers Fund, 1949 (JP 3098). Photograph © 1979 The Metropolitan Museum of Art. Art Resource, NY.

5.11   Torii Kiyotada (Japanese, worked c. 1710–1740).
An Actor of the Ichikawa Clan in a Dance Movement of Violent Motion. c. 1715.
Hand-colored woodcut. 11¼″36″.
The Metropolitan Museum of Art, Harris Brisbane Dick Fund and Rogers Fund, 1949. (JP 3075). Photograph © 1979 The Metropolitan Museum of Art. Art Resource, NY.

lines tracked his expressive hand motions, varying the thickness with the speed of his wrist. The two acrobats in *Hi!* by Alexander Calder are drawn in space using wire that the artist flexed into shape with pliers; his dynamic lines captured their exuberant maneuvers. Many Japanese prints take as subject matter popular entertainers such as dancers and actors. The two prints pictured here use black contour lines in contrasting ways: *Woman Dancer* is curvy and sensuous, suggesting rhythmic motion, whereas Torii Kiyotada's *Actor* uses angular lines to express violent and swift action.

Many types of prints are made up almost entirely of lines, with little shading or color. Kiki Smith etched lines in a metal plate to create *Ginzer*, a depiction of her cat. She painstakingly drew one line for each of *Ginzer*'s hairs, it seems. The eyes and foot pads are slightly shaded, but all else was done with line. She successfully captured the cat's flexible limbs and back as *Ginzer* reclined, but she also showed a hint of the cat's wild side in the mouth and alert eyes.

5.12   Kiki Smith.
Ginzer. 2000.
Etching, aquatint, and drypoint on mold-made paper.
22½″331″.
© Kiki Smith, Published by Harlan & Weaver, New York.

Implied Line

Implied lines suggest visual connections. Implied lines that form geometric shapes can serve as an underlying organizational structure. In *I and the Village*, Marc Chagall used implied lines to create a large circle at the lower center that brings together scenes of Russian Jewish village life. Notice that he also drew in the implied sightline between man and animal with a fine line.

SHAPE

The words *shape*, *mass*, and *form* are sometimes used interchangeably, but they mean different things in the visual arts. Here *shape* is used to refer to the expanse within the outline of a two-dimensional area or within the outer boundaries of a three-dimensional object. When we see a three-dimensional object in natural light, we see that it has mass, or volume. If the same object is silhouetted against a sunset, we may see it only as a flat shape. Enclosing lines or changing color sets a shape apart from its surroundings so that we recognize it.

We can group the infinite variety of shapes into two general categories: geometric and organic. **Geometric shapes**—such as circles, triangles, and squares—tend to be precise and regular. **Organic shapes** are irregular, often curving or rounded, and seem relaxed and more informal than geometric shapes. The most common shapes in the human-made world are geometric. Although some geometric shapes exist in nature—in such forms as crystals, honeycombs, and snowflakes—most shapes in nature are organic. A related term with a similar meaning is **biomorphic**, which also suggests shapes based on natural forms.

In *I and the Village,* Chagall used a geometric structure of circles and triangles to organize the organic shapes of people, animals, and plants. He softened the severity of geometric shapes to achieve a natural flow between the various parts of the painting. Conversely, he abstracted natural subjects toward geometric simplicity in order to strengthen visual impact and symbolic content.

When a shape appears on a **picture plane** (the flat picture surface), it simultaneously cre-ates a second shape out of the background area. The dominant shapes are referred to as **figures** or **positive shapes**; background areas are **ground** or **negative shapes**. The figure–ground relationship is a fundamental aspect of perception; it allows us to sort out and interpret what we see. Because we are conditioned to see only objects, and not the spaces between and around them, it takes a shift in awareness to see the white negative shapes in *A Shape of Space*. Most artists consider both positive and negative shapes simultaneously and treat them as equally important to the total effectiveness of a composition.

5.13 Marc Chagall.
I and the Village. 1911.
Oil on canvas. 6′3⅜″ 3 59⅝″ (192.1 3 151.4 cm).
The Museum of Modern Art/Licensed by Scala-Art Resource, NY.
Mrs. Simon Guggenheim Fund.
Photograph © 2002 The Museum of Modern Art, New York.
© 2010 Artists Rights Society (ARS), New York/ADAGP, Paris.

5.14 *A Shape of Space.*
Implied shape.

Interactions between figure shapes and ground shapes are heightened in some images. *Night Life* can be seen as white shapes against black or as black shapes against white. Or, to say it another way, the figure–ground relationship can shift back and forth. In both this and M. C. Escher's woodcut *Sky and Water*, shifting of figure and ground contributes to a similar content: the interrelatedness of all things.

In the upper half of Escher's print, we see dark geese on a white ground. As our eyes move down the page, the light upper background becomes fish against a black background. In the middle, however, fish and geese interlock so perfectly that we are not sure what is figure and what is ground. As our awareness shifts, fish shapes and bird shapes trade places, a phenomenon called **figure–ground reversal**.

MASS

A two-dimensional area is called a shape, but a three-dimensional area is called a mass—the physical bulk of a solid body of material. When mass encloses space, the space is called **volume**.

5.16 M. C. Escher.
Sky and Water I. 1938.
Woodcut. 17⅛″317¼″.

Mass in Three Dimensions

Mass is often a major element in sculpture and architecture. For example, immense or bulky mass was an important characteristic of ancient Egyptian architecture and sculpture. Egyptians sought this quality and perfected it because it expressed their desire to make art for eternity.

Sennefer, Steward of the Palace was carved from hard black granite and retains the cubic, block-like appearance of the quarried stone. None of the limbs project outward into the surrounding space. The figure sits with knees drawn up and arms folded, the neck obscured by a ceremonial headdress. The body is abstracted and implied with minimal suggestion. This piece is a good example of **closed form**—form that does not openly interact with the space around it. Here, compact mass symbolizes permanence. Egyptian portrait sculpture acted as a symbolic container for the soul of an important person to ensure eternal afterlife.

5.17   *Sennefer, Steward of the Palace.*
c. 1450 B.C.E.
Black granite. Height 2'9".
The British Museum, Department of Egyptian Antiquities.
© The British Museum/Art Resource, NY.

In contrast to the compact mass of the Egyptian portrait, modern sculptor Alberto Giacometti's *Man Pointing* conveys a sense of fleeting presence rather than permanence. The tall, thin figure appears eroded by time and barely existing. Because Giacometti used little solid material to construct the figure, we are more aware of a linear form in space than of mass. The

5.18   Alberto Giacometti (1901–1966).
Man Pointing. 1947.
Bronze. 70½"×40¾"×16⅜", at base, 12"×13¼".
Gift of Mrs. John D. Rockefeller 3rd. (678.1954) The Museum of Modern Art, New York, NY, U.S.A. Digital Image The Museum of Modern Art/Licensed by SCALA/Art Resource, NY. © 2010 Succession Giacometti/Artists Rights Society (ARS), New York/ADAGP, Paris.

figure reaches out; its **open form** interacts with the surrounding space, which seems to overwhelm it, suggesting the fragile, impermanent nature of human existence.

5.19 Elizabeth Catlett.
Bread. 1962.
Linocut on paper. 15⅝" 3 11⅝".
Courtesy of the Library of Congress.
© Elizabeth Catlett/Licensed by VAGA, New York, NY.

5.20 Cesar Pelli and Associates.
Ronald Reagan Washington National Airport. 1997.
Courtesy of Andre Jenny/Alamy.

Giacometti's art reveals an obsession with mortality that began when he was twenty, following the death of an older companion. Later, expressing the fleeting essence of human life became a major concern of his work. For Giacometti, both life and art making were continuous evolutions. He never felt that he succeeded in capturing the changing nature of what he saw, and therefore he considered all of his works unfinished.

Mass in Two Dimensions

With two-dimensional media such as painting and drawing, mass must be implied. In *Bread*, Elizabeth Catlett drew lines that seem to wrap around and define a girl in space, implying a solid mass. The work gives the appearance of mass because the lines both follow the curvature of the head and build up dark areas to suggest mass revealed by light. Her use of lines convinces us that we are seeing a fully rounded person.

SPACE

Space is the indefinable, general receptacle of all things—the seemingly empty space around us. How artists organize space in the works they create is one of their most important creative considerations.

Space in Three Dimensions

Of all the visual elements, space is the most difficult to convey in words and pictures. To experience three-dimensional space, we must be in it. We experience space beginning with our own positions in relation to other people, objects, surfaces, and voids at various distances from ourselves. Each of us has a sense of personal space—the area surrounding our bodies—that we like to protect, and the extent of this invisible boundary varies from person to person and from culture to culture.

Architects are especially concerned with the qualities of space. Imagine how you would feel in a small room with a very low ceiling. What if you raised the ceiling to fifteen feet? What if you added skylights? What if you replaced the walls with glass? In each case you would have changed the character of the space and, by doing so, would have radically changed your experience.

We experience the outside of a building as mass, but we experience the inside as volume, and as a sequence of enclosed spaces. Cesar Pelli's design for the *North Terminal* at Ronald Reagan Washington National Airport takes the passenger's experience of space into account. Large windows offer views of the runways and also of the Potomac River and the nearby Washington Monument. The architect divided the huge interior space into smaller modules to give the concourse a more domestic feel: "The module has an important psychological value in that each one is like a very large living room in size," the architect said.[5] "It's a space that we experience in our daily life. . . . The domes make spaces designed on the scale of people, not on the scale of big machines."

Space in Two Dimensions

With three-dimensional objects and spaces, such as sculpture and architecture, we must move around to get the full experience. With two-dimensional works, such as drawing and painting, we see the space of the surface all at once. In drawings, prints, photographs, and paintings, the actual space of each picture's surface (picture plane) is defined by its edges—usually the two dimensions of height and width. Yet within these boundaries, a great variety of possible pictorial spaces can be implied or suggested, creating depth in the picture plane.

Paintings from ancient Egypt, for example, show little or no depth. Early Egyptian painters made their images clear by portraying objects from their most easily identifiable angles and by avoiding the visual confusion caused by overlap and the appearance of diminishing size. *Pool in the Garden* demonstrates this technique. The pool is shown from above while the trees, fish, and birds are all pictured from the side.

Implied Depth

Almost any mark on a picture plane begins to give the illusion of a third dimension: depth. Clues to seeing spatial depth are learned in early childhood. A few of the major ways of indicating space on a picture plane are shown in the diagrams of *Clues to Spatial Depth*.

When shapes overlap, we immediately assume from experience that one is in front of the other (diagram a). Overlapping is the most basic way to achieve the effect of depth on a flat surface. (Note that *Pool in the Garden* uses very little overlapping.) The effect of overlap is strengthened by diminishing size, which gives a sense of increasing distance between each of the shapes (diagram b). Our perception of distance depends on the observation that distant objects appear smaller than near objects. A third method of achieving the illusion of depth is vertical placement: objects placed low on the picture plane (diagram c) appear to be closer to the viewer

5.21 *Pool in the Garden.*
Wall painting from the tomb of Nebamun.
Egypt. c. 1400 B.C.E.
Paint on dry plaster.
© The Trustees of the British Museum, London.

5.22 *Clues to Spatial Depth.*

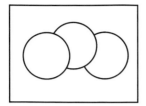
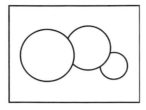
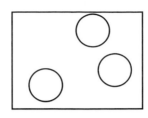
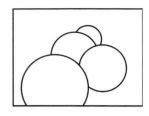

a. Overlap.

b. Overlap and diminishing size.

c. Vertical placement.

d. Overlap, vertical placement, and diminishing size.

5.23 Mu Qi (Japanese, d. after 1279).
Six Persimmons (Six Kakis). c. 1269.
Pen and ink on paper, width 36.2 cm.
Daitoku–ji Monastery, Kyoto, Japan.
The Bridgeman Art Library International Ltd.

painters have paid careful attention to the relationship between the reality of the flat picture plane as well as the illusion of depth they wish to imply. Mu Qi's ink painting *Six Persimmons* has only a subtle suggestion of depth in the overlap of two of the persimmons. By placing the smallest persimmon lowest on the picture plane, Mu Qi further minimized the illusion of depth; because we interpret the lower part of the picture as being closer to us, we might expect the persimmon there to be larger.

The persimmons appear against a pale background that works as both flat surface and infinite space. The shapes of the fruit punctuate the open space of the ground. Imagine what would happen to this painting if some of the space at the top were cut off. Space is far more than just leftovers; it is an integral part of the total visual design.

Linear Perspective. In general usage, the word perspective refers to point of view. In the visual arts, perspective refers to any means of representing three-dimensional objects in space on a two-dimensional surface. In this sense it is correct to speak of the perspective of Persian miniatures, Japanese prints, Chinese Song Dynasty paintings, or Egyptian murals—although none of these styles are similar to the **linear perspective** system, which was developed during the Italian Renaissance. Different traditions, rather than mere skill, give us various ways of depicting depth.

In the West, we have become accustomed to linear perspective (also called simply, perspective) to depict the way objects in space appear to the eye. This system was developed by Italian architects and painters in the fifteenth century, at the beginning of the Renaissance.

than objects placed high on the plane. This is the way we see most things in actual space. Creating illusions of depth on a flat surface usually involves one or more such devices (diagram d).

When we look at a picture, we may be conscious of both its actual flat surface and the illusion of depth that the picture contains. Artists can emphasize either the reality or the illusion, or strike a balance between these extremes. For centuries, Asian

Linear perspective is based on the way we see. We have already noted that objects appear smaller when seen at a distance than when viewed close up. Because the spaces between objects also appear smaller when seen at a distance, parallel lines appear to converge as they recede into the distance, as shown in the first of the *Linear Perspective* diagrams below. Intellectually, we know that the edge lines of the road must be parallel, yet they seem to converge, meeting at last at what is called a **vanishing**

5.24 *Linear Perspective.*

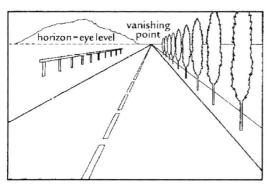

a. One-point linear perspective.

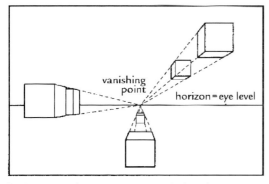

b. One-point linear perspective. Cubes above eye level, at eye level, and below eye level.

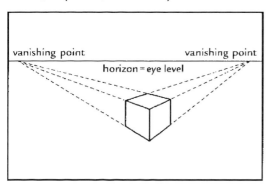

c. Two-point linear perspective.

point on the horizon—the place where land and sky appear to meet. On a picture surface, the horizon (or **horizon line**) also represents your eye level as you look at a scene.

Eye level is an imaginary plane, the height of the artist's eyes, parallel with the ground plane and extending to the horizon, where the eye level and ground plane appear to converge. In a finished picture, the artist's eye level becomes the eye level of anyone looking at the picture. Although the horizon is frequently blocked from view, it is necessary for an artist to establish a combined eye-level/horizon line to construct images using linear perspective.

With the linear perspective system, an entire picture can be constructed from a single, fixed position called a **vantage point**, or viewpoint. Diagram a shows **one-point perspective**, in which the parallel sides of the road appear to converge and trees in a row appear smaller as their distances from the vantage point increase. A single vanishing point is used for all shapes.

Diagram b shows cubes drawn in one-point linear perspective. The cubes at the left are at eye level; we can see neither their top nor their bottom surfaces. We might imagine them as buildings.

The cubes in the center are below eye level: we can look down on their tops. These cubes are drawn from a high vantage point: a viewing position above the subject. The horizon line is above these cubes, and their perspective lines go up to it. We may imagine these as boxes on the floor.

The cubes at the right are above our eye level; we can look up at their bottom sides. These cubes are drawn from a low vantage point. The horizon line is below these cubes, and their perspective lines go down to it. Imagine that these boxes are sitting on a glass shelf high above our heads.

In one-point perspective, all the major receding "lines" of the subject are actually parallel, yet visually they appear to converge at a single vanishing point on the horizon line. In two-point perspective, two sets of parallel lines appear to converge at two points on the horizon line, as in diagram c.

When a cube or any other rectilinear object is positioned so that a corner, instead of a side, is

5.25a Raphael.
The School of Athens. 1508. Fresco. Approximately 18′3 26′. Stanza della Segnatura, Vatican Palace, Vatican State.
Copyright Erich Lessing/Art Resource, NY.

Perspective lines showing eye level, main vanishing point, and left vanishing point for
the stone block in the foreground.

5.25b Raphael.
The School of Athens. 1508.
Stanza della Segnatura, Vatican Palace, Vatican State.
Copyright Erich Lessing/Art Resource, NY.

5.25c *Study of The School of Athens*
Stanza della Segnatura, Vatican Palace, Vatican State.
Copyright Erich Lessing/Art Resource, NY.

closest to us, we need two vanishing points to draw it. The parallel lines of the right side converge to the right; the parallel lines of the left side converge to the left. There can be as many vanishing points as there are sets and directions of parallel lines. Horizontal parallel lines moving away from the viewer above eye level appear to go down to the horizon line; those below eye level appear to go up to the horizon line.

In *The School of Athens*, Raphael invented a grand architectural setting in the Renaissance style to provide an appropriate space for his depiction of the Greek philosophers Plato and Aristotle and other important thinkers. The size of each figure is drawn to scale according to its distance from the viewer; thus, the entire group seems natural. Lines superimposed over the painting reveal the basic one-point perspective system Raphael used. However, the cube in the foreground is not parallel to the picture plane or to the painted architecture and is in two-point perspective.

Raphael used perspective for emphasis. We infer that Plato and Aristotle are the most important figures in this painting because of their placement at the center of receding archways in the zone of greatest implied depth.

If the figures are removed, as shown in the *Study of the School of Athens*, our attention is pulled right through the painted setting into implied infinite space. Conversely, without their architectural background defined by perspective, Plato and Aristotle lose importance; picking them out from the crowd becomes difficult.

Atmospheric Perspective. **Atmospheric** or **aerial perspective** is a nonlinear means for giving an illusion of depth. In atmospheric perspective, the illusion of depth is created by changing color, value, and detail. In visual experience of the real world, as the distance increases between the viewer and faraway objects such as mountains, the increased quantity of air, moisture, and dust causes the distant objects to appear increasingly bluer and less distinct. Color intensity is diminished, and contrast between light and dark is reduced.

Asher Brown Durand used atmospheric perspective in his painting *Kindred Spirits* to provide

a sense of the vast distances in the North American wilderness. The illusion of infinite space is balanced by dramatically illuminated foreground details, by the figures of the men, and by Durand's lively portrayal of trees, rocks, and waterfalls. We identify with the figures of painter Thomas Cole and poet William Cullen Bryant as they enjoy the spectacular landscape. As in *The School of Athens*, the implied deep space appears as an extension of the space we occupy.

Traditional Chinese landscape painters have another way of creating atmospheric perspective. In Shen Zhou's painting *Poet on a Mountain Top*, near and distant mountains are suggested by washes of ink and color on white paper. The light gray of the

5.26 Asher Brown Durand.
Kindred Spirits. 1849.
Oil on canvas. 44" 3 36".
Courtesy Crystal Bridges Museum of American Art, Bentonville, Arkansas.

5.27 Shen Zhou (Chinese, 1427–1509).
Poet on a Mountain Top. Ming Dynasty (1368–1644). From series: *Landscape Album: Five Leaves*
Album leaf mounted as a handscroll. Ink and watercolor on paper. Silk mount.15¼" 3 23¾"
(38.73 3 60.32 cm) overall.
The Nelson-Atkins Museum of Art, Kansas City, Missouri.
(Purchase: Nelson Trust) 46-51/2. Photo credit: Robert Newcombe

farthest mountain at the upper right implies space and atmosphere. Traditional Chinese landscape paintings present poetic symbols of landforms rather than realistic representations. Whereas *Kindred Spirits* draws the viewer's eye into and through the suggested deep space, *Poet on a Mountain Top* leads the eye across (rather than into) space.

TIME AND MOTION

Time is the non-spatial continuum, the fourth dimension, in which events occur in succession. Because we live in an environment combining space and time, our experience of time often depends on our movement in space and vice versa. Although time itself is invisible, it can be made perceptible in art. Time and motion become major elements in visual media such as film and video.

5.28 *Aztec Calendar Stone.* 1479.
Courtesy of Mark Wiener/Alamy.

Many traditional non-Western cultures teach that time is cyclic. The Aztecs of ancient Mexico, for example, held that the Earth was subject to periodic cycles of destruction and recreation, and their calendar stone embodies this idea. At the center of the *Aztec Calendar Stone* is a face of the sun god representing the present world, surrounded by four rectangular compartments that each represent one previous incarnation of the world. The whole stone is round, symbolizing the circular nature of time.

The Judeo-Christian tradition of Western culture teaches that time is linear—continually moving forward. The early Renaissance painter Sassetta implied the passage of linear time in his painted narration of *The Meeting of St. Anthony and St. Paul*. The painting depicts key moments during Saint Anthony's progression through time and space, including the start of his journey in the city, which is barely visible behind the trees at the top center. He first comes into view as he approaches the wilderness in the upper left; we next see him encountering the centaur at upper right; finally, he emerges into the clearing in the foreground, where he meets Saint Paul. The road on which he travels implies continuous forward movement in time.

Comics also generally express a linear conception of time, as we read the frames from left to

5.29 Sassetta and Workshop of Sassetta.
The Meeting of Saint Anthony and Saint Paul. c. 1440.
Tempera on panel, .475 3 .345 cm (18¾″ 3 13⅝″) framed: .616 3 1.254 3 .076 cm (24¼″ 3 49⅜″ 3 3″).
Samuel H. Kress Collection. Photograph © 2001 Board of Trustees, National Gallery of Art, Washington. 1939.1.293.(404)/PA

5.30 Doug Aitken (b. 1968).
Doug Aitken: Sleepwalkers. 2007.
Installation view of the exhibition.
January 16, 2007 through February 12, 2007.
(IN1991.25) Location: The Museum of Modern
Art, New York, NY, U.S.A. Courtesy 303
Gallery, New York.

right and top to bottom. Gary Panter's six-panel comic *Back to Nature* shows the progression of his thoughts as he comes to grips with the attacks of September 11, 2001. Although he thinks of the past and hopes for the future, the sequence of frames implies succession in time.

Manipulated Time

Most movies compress time to varying degrees. Doug Aitken's 2007 video work *Sleepwalkers* manipulated time by presenting five parallel narratives of actors awakening at sunset and going about urban rounds in the city at night. The five actors played various roles, from bike messenger to corporate executive. Their stories were edited down to 13 minutes each and projected in random sequence onto eight exterior walls of the Museum of Modern Art in New York. The piece interacted with viewers' urban errands as well, since the work was on view from 5 to 10 P.M. each night for a month. The artist said of the work, "I wanted to create something that transformed architecture into a moving, flowing space." As viewers moved about the city block that the museum occupies, they saw five workers in parallel narratives also moving about the city.

Implied Motion

To give lifelike feeling, artists often search for ways to create a sense of movement. Sometimes movement

5.31 *Dancing Krishna.*
Tanjor, Tamil Nadu. South
India. Chola dynasty. c. 1300.
Bronze, 23⅜".
Honolulu Academy of Arts. Partial gift of
Mr. and Mrs. Christian H. Aall; partial purchase, The Jhamandas Watumull Family Fund,
1997. (8640.1) Photo by Shuzo Uemoto.

Auguste Rodin on Implied Movement

THE SCULPTOR AUGUSTE RODIN (1840–1917) worked intently with naturally moving living models, creating vigorously realistic sculpture that flew in the face of prevailing French academic traditions. His marvelous *Monument to Balzac* (**Fig. 5.32**), though commissioned by the Society of Men of Letters, was rejected by the Society because it did not coincide with their ideas of what a portrait should look like. Yet his genius in coaxing apparent life into cast metal and sculpted marble is now highly celebrated. The following are excerpts from conversations with his friend Paul Gsell, on the illusion of movement in sculpture:

"I have always sought to give some indication of movement. I have very rarely represented complete repose. I have always endeavored to express the inner feelings by the mobility of the muscles.

"Art cannot exist without life. If a sculptor wishes to interpret joy, sorrow, any passion whatsoever, he will not be able to move us unless he first knows how to make the beings live which he evokes. For how could the joy or the sorrow of an inert object— of a block of stone—affect us? Now, the illusion of life is obtained in our art by good modeling and by movement. These two qualities are like the blood and the breath of all good work."

"Note, first, that *movement is the transition from one attitude to another* .... You remember how in Dante's Inferno a serpent, coiling itself about the body of one of the damned, changes into man as the man becomes reptile. The great poet describes this scene so ingeniously that in each of these two beings one follows the struggle between two natures which progressively invade and supplant each other.

"It is, in short, a metamorphosis of this kind that the painter or the sculptor effects in giving movement to his personages. He represents the transition from one pose to another— he indicates how insensibly the first glides into the second. In his work we still see a part of what was and we discover a part of what is to be.

"The sculptor compels, so to speak, the spectator to follow the development of an act in an individual .... Have you ever attentively examined instantaneous photographs of walking figures? What did you notice? If, in instantaneous photographs, the figures, though taken while moving, seem suddenly fixed in mid-air, it is because, all parts of the body being reproduced exactly at the same twentieth or fortieth of a second, there is no progressive development of movement as there is in art.

"It is the artist who is truthful and it is photography which lies, for in reality time does not stop, and if the artist succeeds in producing the impression of a movement which takes several moments for accomplishment, his work is certainly much less conventional than the scientific image, where time is abruptly suspended."

"Note besides that painters and sculptors, when they unite different phases of an action in the same figure, do not act from reason or from artifice. They are naively expressing what they feel. Their minds and their hands are as if drawn in the direction of the movement, and they translate the development by instinct. Here, as everywhere in the domain of art, sincerity is the only rule."

5.32 Auguste Rodin
Monument to Balzac, 1897.
Bronze, 8 ft 10¼ ins 3 3 ft 11½ ins
4 ft 2½ ins (2.7 3 1.2 3 1.3 m).
Musée Rodin, Paris.

Artists on Art: Auguste Rodin on Implied Movement was taken from *The Art of Seeing*, Eighth Edition by Paul Zelanski and Mary Pat Fisher.

5.33 Gino Severini
(1883–1966).
*Suburban Train
Arriving in Paris.*
1915.
Oil on canvas.
35″ 3 45½″.
Tate Gallery, London,
Great Britain © 2011
Artists Rights Society (ARS),
New York/ADAGP, Paris.
Photo Credit: Tate, London/
Art Resource, NY.

itself is the subject or a central quality of the subject. An appealing depiction of movement, *Dancing
Krishna* portrays the Indian Hindu god as a playful
child who just stole his mother's butter supply and
now dances with glee. The cast bronze medium provides the necessary strength to hold the dynamic pose
as the energy-radiating figure stands on one foot,
counterbalancing arms, legs, and torso.

Artists of the Futurist movement in the early
twentieth century found innovative ways to depict
motion and speed, which they regarded as the most
important new subjects for art. Gino Severini lived
near railroad tracks outside Paris and he made
the churning, chugging trains a subject of several
works. *Suburban Train Arriving in Paris* needs very
little explanation, as the train shatters the landscape
into jagged, slanting forms. The overlapping planes
and diagonal lines suggest powerful left-to-right
motion. The inscription at the top (Kneipp) refers
to a billboard advertisement for a drink.

Contemporary artist Jenny Holzer made a
clever use of implied motion in an *Untitled* work, in
which she installed light boards on the inner edge
of the spiral ramp in the Guggenheim Museum in

5.34 Jenny Holzer.
Untitled.
(Selections from Truisms, Inflammatory Essays, The Living Series,
The Survival Series, Under a Rock, Laments, and Child Text),
1989. Extended helical tricolor L.E.D. electronic display signboard.
Site-specific dimensions: 41.9 cm 3 49 m 3 37.8 cm 3 15.2 cm
(16½″ 3 162′ 3 6″).

Solomon R. Guggenheim Museum, New York. Partial gift of the artist, 1989, 89.3626.
Photograph by David Heald © The Solomon R. Guggenheim Foundation, New York. © 2010
Jenny Holzer, member Artists Rights Society (ARS), New York.

New York. These boards are commonly used for advertising, but she populated this extended helix with sayings of her own invention. The sayings seem to progress down the ramp in a continuous flow, but in reality the lights go on and off only at carefully programmed intervals. In this welter of constantly shifting slogans, she hoped to show how the mass media bombard us with input.

Actual Motion

Before the advent of electric motors, artists created moving sculpture by harnessing the forces of wind and water. Fountains, kites, banners, and flags have been popular since ancient times.

Alexander Calder's mobiles, such as his *Untitled* work in the National Gallery, rely on air movement to perform their subtle dances. As viewers enter and leave the galleries of the East Building, the sculpture slowly moves in space. Calder, a leading inventor of **kinetic art**, was one of the first twentieth-century artists who made actual motion a major feature of their art.

5.35 Alexander Calder.
Untitled. 1976.
Aluminum and steel. 9.103 3 23.155 cm (358½" 3 912").
© 2011 Calder Foundation, New York / Artists Rights Society (ARS), New York.

LIGHT

Our eyes are light-sensing instruments. Everything we see is made visible by the radiant energy we call light. Sunlight, or natural light, although perceived as white, actually contains all the colors of light that make up the visible part of the electromagnetic spectrum. Light can be directed, reflected, refracted, diffracted, or diffused. The source, color, intensity, and direction of light greatly affect the way things appear; as light changes, surfaces illuminated by it also appear to change.

Seeing Light

A simple shift in the direction of light dramatically changes the way we perceive the sculpture of *Abraham Lincoln* by Daniel Chester French. When the monumental figure was first installed in the Lincoln Memorial in Washington, D.C., the sculptor was disturbed by the lighting: Sunlight reflected off the floor seemed to radically change Lincoln's character, making it seem that the president had seen a ghost! The problem was corrected by placing spotlights in the ceiling above the statue. This made Lincoln resemble the inspiring leader that the sculptor intended to portray. Because the spotlights are stronger than the natural light reflected from the white marble floor, they illuminate the figure with overhead light that creates an entirely different expression.

Most of us know this from trying to take pictures outdoors: Light coming from a source directly in front of or behind objects seems to flatten three-dimensional form and emphasize shape. Light from above or from the side, and slightly in front, most clearly reveals the form of objects in space.

5.36 Daniel Chester French (1850–1931).
Abraham Lincoln (1911–1922). Detail, seated statue, Lincoln Memorial.
a. As originally lit by daylight.
b. With the addition of artificial light.
Historical professional composite photograph (1922) of full-sized plaster model of head (1917–1918). 50½" tall.
Chapin Library, Williams College; gift of the National Trust for Historic Preservation Chesterwood Archive.
Photographer: De Witt Ward.

In the terminology of art, **value** (sometimes called *tone*) refers to the relative lightness and darkness of surfaces. Value ranges from white through various grays to black. Value can be considered a property of color or an element independent of color. Subtle relationships between light and dark areas determine how things look. To suggest the way light reveals form, artists use changes in value. A gradual shift from lighter to darker tones can give the illusion of a curving surface, while an abrupt value change usually indicates an abrupt change in surface direction.

5.37 *Dark/Light Relationships.*
Value scale compared to uniform middle gray.

5.38 Annibale Carracci
(1560–1609).
Head of a Youth.
Charcoal and white chalk
on green/gray paper.
27.1 3 24 cm.
Hermitage, St. Petersburg, Russia.
The Bridgeman Art Library
International Ltd.

Light in Art

The diagram *Dark/Light Relationships* shows that we perceive relationships rather than isolated forms: the gray bar has the same gray value over its entire length, yet it appears to change from one end to the other as the value of the background changes.

Using charcoal and white chalk on middle-value paper, Annibale Carracci used **chiaroscuro** (shading from light to dark) to create the illusion of roundness in his drawing *Head of a Youth*. The face on its brighter side is close to the shade of the paper. At times the distinction between subject and background is difficult to see, as in the clothing. On the areas where light strikes the subject most directly, the artist used white chalk, as on the forehead and nose, making these areas brighter than the background.

Areas around the mouth and chin are delicately shaded, showing that the artist is sensitive to the subtlest curves of the face. The shadowy areas stand in contrast both to the white highlights and to the color of the paper; the darkest area, at the left, forms a silhouette against the background.

The choice of colored paper is in some ways advantageous because we tend to perceive white areas as flooded with light. Middle-value paper tends to heighten the contrasts of light and dark within the subject itself.

The preoccupation with mass or solid form as revealed by light is a Western tradition that began in the Renaissance. When the Japanese first saw Western portraits, they wanted to know why one side of the face was dirty!

Color, direction, quantity, and intensity of light strongly affect our moods, mental abilities, and general well-being. California architect Vincent Palmer has experimented with the color and intensity of interior light, and he has found that he can modify the behavior of his guests by changing the color of the light around them. Light quality affects people's emotions and physical comfort, thereby changing the volume and intensity of their conversations and even the lengths of their visits.

COLOR

Color, a component of light, affects us directly by modifying our thoughts, moods, actions, and even our health. Psychologists, as well as designers of schools, offices, hospitals, and prisons, understand that colors can affect work habits and mental conditions. People surrounded by expanses of solid orange or red for long periods often experience nervousness and raised blood pressure. In contrast, some blues have a calming effect, causing blood pressure, pulse, and activity rates to drop to below normal levels.

Dressing according to our color preferences is one way we express ourselves. Designers of everything from clothing and cars to housewares and interiors recognize the importance of individual color preferences, and they spend considerable time and expense determining the colors of their products.

Most cultures use color symbolically, according to established customs. Leonardo da Vinci was influenced by earlier European traditions when he wrote, "We shall set down for white the representative of light, without which no color can be seen; yellow for earth; green for water; blue for air; red for fire; and black for total darkness."[6] In traditional painting in North India, flat areas of color are used to suggest certain moods, such as red for anger and blue for sexual passion. A modern artist may paint the sky or the ground with a bright shade that relates not to the appearance of the area, but to the feeling appropriate to the work. In Austrian slang, yellow describes a state of envy or jealousy, while blue means intoxicated.

Between the fifteenth and nineteenth centuries, color was used in limited, traditional ways in Western art. In the 1860s and 1870s, influenced by the new discoveries in optics, the French Impressionist painters revolutionized the way artists used color.

The Physics of Color

What we call "color" is the effect on our eyes of light waves of differing wavelengths or frequencies. When combined, these light waves make white light, the visible part of the spectrum. Individual colors are components of white light.

The phenomenon of color is a paradox: color exists only in light, but light itself seems colorless to the human eye. Objects that appear to have color are merely reflecting the colors that are present in the light that illuminates them. In 1666, British scientist Isaac Newton discovered that white light is composed of all the colors of the spectrum. He found that when the white light of the sun passes through a glass prism, it is separated into the bands of color that make up the visible spectrum, as shown in the diagram *White Light Refracted by a Prism.*

Because each color has a different wavelength, each travels through the glass of the prism at a different speed. Red, which has the longest wavelength, travels more rapidly through the glass than blue, which has a shorter wavelength. A rainbow results when sunlight is refracted and dispersed by the spherical forms of raindrops, producing a combined effect like that of the glass prism. In both cases, the sequence of spectral colors is: red, orange, yellow, green, blue, and violet.

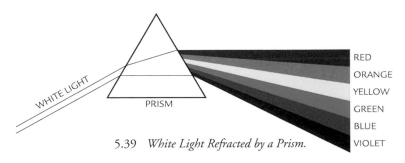

5.39 *White Light Refracted by a Prism.*

Pigments and Light

Our common experience with color is provided by light reflected from pigmented surfaces. Therefore, the emphasis in the following discussion is on pigment color rather than on color coming from light alone.

When light illuminates an object, some of the light is absorbed by the surface of the object and some is reflected. The color that appears to our eyes as that of the object (called **local color**) is determined by the wavelengths of light being reflected. Thus, a red surface illuminated by white light (full-spectrum light) appears red because it reflects mostly red light and absorbs the rest of the spectrum. A green surface absorbs most of the spectrum except green, which it reflects, and so on with all the hues.

When all the wavelengths of light are absorbed by a surface, the object appears black; when all the wavelengths are reflected, the surface appears white. Black and white are not true colors: white, black, and their combination, gray, are **achromatic** (without the property of hue) and are often referred to as **neutrals**.

Each of the millions of colors human beings can distinguish is identifiable in terms of just three variables: hue, value, and intensity.

- **Hue** refers to a particular wavelength of spectral color to which we give a name. Colors of the spectrum—such as yellow and green—are called hues.

- Value refers to relative lightness or darkness from white through grays to black. Pure hues vary in value. On the color chart shown in *The Three Dimensions of Color*, hues in their purest state are at their usual values. Pure yellow is the lightest of hues; violet is the darkest. Red and green are middle-value hues. Black and white pigments can be important ingredients in changing color values. Adding black to a hue produces a **shade** of that hue. For example, when black is added to orange, the result is a brown; when black is mixed with red, the result is maroon. White added to a hue produces a **tint**. Lavender is a tint of violet; pink is a tint of red.

5.40 *The Three Dimensions of Color.*

a. Hue—the color wheel.

b. Value—from light to dark. Value scale from white to black.

+ WHITE   PURE HUE   + BLACK

c. Value variation in red.

PURE HUE   DULLED   PURE HUE

d. Intensity—from bright to dull.

- **Intensity**, also called **saturation**, refers to the purity of a hue or color. A pure hue is the most intense form of a given color; it is the hue at its highest saturation, in its brightest form. With pigment, if white, black, gray, or another hue is added to a pure hue, its intensity diminishes and the color is thereby dulled.

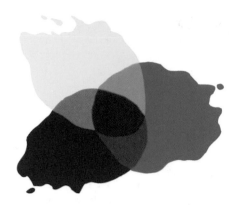

5.41 *Pigment Primaries: Subtractive Color Mixture.*

Most people are familiar with the three *Pigment Primaries*: red, yellow, and blue. Mixtures of these are what we usually experience as local color when we look at a leaf, a wall, or a painting. When the pigments of different hues are mixed together, the mixture appears duller and darker because pigments absorb more and more light as their absorptive qualities combine. For this reason, pigment mixtures are called **subtractive color mixtures**. Mixing red, blue, and yellow will produce a dark gray, almost black, depending on the proportions and the type of pigment used.

A lesser-known triad is the three *Light Primaries*: red-orange, green, and blue-violet. These are actual electric light colors that produce white light when combined; they are the colors that our televisions and computer screens use. Such mixtures are called *additive color mixtures*. Combinations of the light primaries produce lighter colors: red and green light, when mixed, produce yellow light.

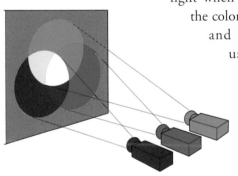

5.42 *Light Primaries: Additive Color Mixture.*

Color Wheel

The color wheel is a twentieth-century version of a concept first developed in the seventeenth century by Isaac Newton. After Newton discovered the spectrum, he found that both ends could be combined into the hue red-violet, making the color wheel concept possible. Numerous color systems have followed since that time, each with its own basic hues. The color wheel shown here is based on twelve pure hues and can be divided into the following groups:

- **Primary hues** (see 1 on the color wheel): red, yellow, and blue. These pigment hues cannot be produced by an intermixing of other hues. They are also referred to as primary colors.

- **Secondary hues** (see 2 on the color wheel): orange, green, and violet. The mixture of two primaries produces a secondary hue. Secondaries are placed on the color wheel between the two primaries of which they are composed.

- **Intermediate hues** (see 3 on the color wheel): red-orange, yellow-orange, yellow-green, blue-green, blue-violet, and red-violet. Each intermediate is located between the primary and the secondary of which it is composed.

The blue-green side of the wheel seems **cool** in psychological temperature, and the red-orange side is **warm**. Yellow-green and red-violet are the poles dividing the color wheel into warm and cool hues. The difference between warm and cool colors may come chiefly from association. Relative warm and cool differences can be seen in any combination of hues. Color affects our feelings about size and distance as well as temperature. Cool colors appear to contract and recede; warm colors appear to expand and advance, as in the *Warm/Cool Colors* diagram.

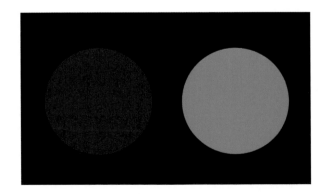

5.43 *Warm/Cool Colors.*

The most vibrant color sensations come not from blending colors, but from placing tiny dots of purer hues next to each other so that they blend in the eye and the mind. This is what happens in modern four-color printing, in which tiny dots of ink in the printer's three primary colors—magenta, yellow, and cyan—are printed together in various amounts with black ink on white paper to achieve the effect of full color. See the *Color Printing* separations and the enlarged detail of the reproduction of Botticelli's *Birth of Venus*; the eye perceives subtle blends as it optically mixes tiny dots of intense color.

5.44 *Color Printing.*

a. Yellow.

b. Magenta.

c. Yellow and magenta.

d. Cyan.

e. Yellow, magenta, and cyan.

f. Black.

g. Yellow, magenta, cyan, and black.

h. Color printing detail of Sandro Botticelli's *Birth of Venus*, 1486. Detail. Tempera on canvas, 69″ 3 52¾″. Erich Lessing/Pearson Education/PH College.

Color Schemes

Color groupings that provide distinct color harmonies are called color schemes.

Monochromatic color schemes are based on variations in the value and intensity of a single hue. In a monochromatic scheme, a pure hue is used alone with black and/or white, or mixed with black and/or white. Artists may choose a monochromatic color scheme because they feel that a certain color represents a mood. Pablo Picasso, for example, made many blue paintings in the early years of the twentieth century, at a time in his life when he was poor.

Other artists adopt the monochromatic color scheme as a kind of personal discipline, in order to experiment with the various shades and gradations of a relatively narrow band of the spectrum. James Abbott McNeill Whistler did just that in the 1870s when he embarked on a series of works called *Nocturnes*. The series began when he noticed that after sunset the world becomes in effect more monochromatic as the brightest hues disappear. We see his exploration in *Nocturne: Blue and Gold—Old Battersea Bridge*, where he created a visually rich surface with limited tonal means. The gold flecks are the only counterfoil to the monochromatic blue-green scheme.

Analogous color schemes are based on colors adjacent to one another on the color wheel, each containing the same pure hue, such as a color scheme of yellow-green, green, and blue-green. Tints and shades of each analogous hue may be used to add variations to such color schemes.

Jennifer Bartlett's three-dimensional installation *Volvo Commission* uses the analogous colors yellow-orange, yellow, and yellow-green, which are adjacent to one another in the spectrum and on the

5.45 James Abbott McNeill Whistler.
Nocturne: Blue and Gold—Old Battersea Bridge.
1872–1875.
Tate Gallery, London, Great Britain. Copyright Erich Lessing/
Art Resource, NY.

5.46 Jennifer Bartlett.
Volvo Commission. 1984.
Relaxation room, detail: table, painted wood,
29″ 3 35″ 3 35″; chair, painted wood,
35″ 3 18″ 3 18″; portfolio of twenty-four drawings, pen, brush, and ink on paper, 20″ 3 16″;
house cigarette box, painted wood, 5″ 3 5″; boat ashtray, silver, 5″ 3 2″; screen, enamel on six wood panels, 6″ 3 10′3″.
Volvo Corporate Headquarters, Sweden. Courtesy of the artist.

color wheel. The analogous color scheme supports the mood of quiet relaxation appropriate to the pleasant rural subject.

Complementary color schemes emphasize two hues directly opposite each other on the color wheel, such as red and green. When actually mixed together as pigments in almost equal amounts, complementary hues form neutral grays, but when placed side by side as pure hues, they contrast strongly and intensify each other. Complementary hues red-orange and blue-green tend to "vibrate" more when placed next to each other than do other complements because they are close in value and produce a strong warm/cool contrast. The complements yellow and violet provide the strongest value contrast possible with pure hues. The complement of a primary is the opposite secondary, which is obtained by mixing the other two primaries. For example, the complement of yellow is violet.

Keith Haring's *Untitled* shows the effect of complementary colors. The bright red and green are near-opposites on the color wheel. When seen together they vibrate. This "loud" color scheme supports the simple execution and brash subject matter of the painting in providing an almost comically crude effect. The artist used Dayglo paints, which are known for their gaudy brightness.

These examples provide only a basic foundation in color theory. In fact, most artists work intuitively with color harmonies more complex than the schemes described above.

Notes

1. Gyorgy Kepes, *The Language of Vision* (Chicago: Paul Theobald, 1944), 9.
2. Henri Matisse, "The Nature of Creative Activity," *Education and Art,* edited by Edwin Ziegfeld (New York: UNESCO, 1953), 21.
3. Edward Weston, *The Daybooks of Edward Weston,* edited by Nancy Newhall (Millerton, NY: Aperture, 1973), vol. 2, 181.
4. Maurice Denis, *Theories 1870–1910* (Paris: Hermann, 1964), 13.
5. Quoted in "National Airport: A New Terminal Takes Flight," *Washington Post* (July 16, 1997). http://www .washingtonpost.com/wp-srv/local/longterm/library/ airport/architect.htm (accessed May 14, 2000).

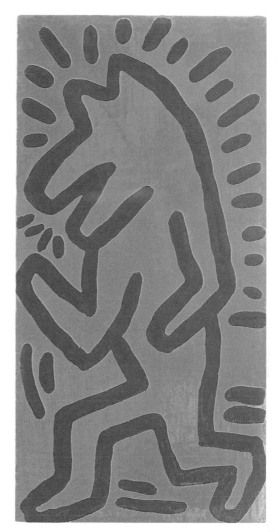

5.46 Keith Haring.
Untitled. 1982.
Dayglo paint on wood. 8½" 3 4½".
© The Keith Haring Foundation

A Quick Reference Guide to the Elements of Art

BASIC TERMS

Three basic principles define all works of art, whether two-dimensional (painting, drawing, printmaking, and photography) or three-dimensional (sculpture and architecture):

- **Form**—the overall structure of the work;
- **Subject Matter**—what is literally depicted;
- **Content**—what it means.

If the subject matter is recognizable, the work is said to be representational. Representational works that attempt to depict objects as they are in actual, visible reality are called realistic. The less a work resembles real things in the real world, the more abstract it is. Abstract art does not try to duplicate the world, but instead reduces the world to its essential qualities. If the subject matter of the work is not recognizable, the work is said to be nonrepresentational, or nonobjective.

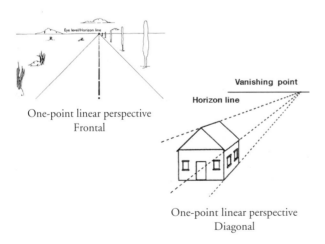

One-point linear perspective
Frontal

Vanishing point

Horizon line

One-point linear perspective
Diagonal

THE FORMAL ELEMENTS

The term form refers to the purely visual aspects of art and architecture. Line, space, levels of light and dark, color, and texture are among the elements that contribute to a work's form.

Line is the most fundamental formal element. It delineates shape (a flat two-dimensional area) and mass (a solid form that occupies a three-dimensional volume) by means of outline (in which the edge of a form or shape is indicated directly with a more or less continuous mark) or contour (which is the perceived edge of a volume as it curves away from the viewer). Lines can be implied—as in your line of sight. Line also possesses certain emotional, expressive, or intellectual qualities. Some lines are loose and free, gestural and quick. Other lines are precise, controlled, and mathematically and rationally organized.

Loose, gestural line   Precise, controlled line

Line is also fundamental to the creation of a sense of deep, three-dimensional space on a two-dimensional surface, the system known as linear perspective. In one-point linear perspective, lines are drawn on the picture plane in such a way as to represent parallel lines receding to a single point on the viewer's horizon, called the vanishing point. When the vanishing point is directly across from the viewer's vantage point, the recession is frontal. When the vanishing point is to one side or the other, the recession is diagonal.

In two-point linear perspective, more than one vanishing point occurs, as, for instance, when you look at the corner of a building

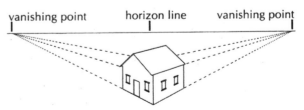

vanishing point   horizon line   vanishing point

Two-point linear perspective

A Quick Reference Guide to the Elements of Art was taken from *A World of Art,* Sixth Edition by Henry M. Sayre.

Light and Dark are also employed by artists to create the illusion of deep space on a two-dimensional surface. In atmospheric perspective—also called aerial perspective—objects further away from the viewer appear less distinct as the contrast between light and dark is reduced by the effects of atmosphere. Artists depict the gradual transition from light to dark around a curved surface by means of modeling. Value is the relative degree of lightness or darkness in the range from white to black created by the amount of light reflected from an object's surface (see the gray scale).

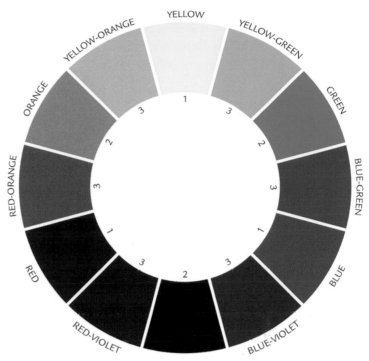

a. Hue—the color wheel.

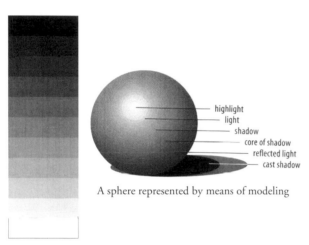

A sphere represented by means of modeling

Gray scale

b. Value—from light to dark. Value scale from white to black.

+ WHITE   PURE HUE   + BLACK

c. Value variation in red.

PURE HUE   DULLED   PURE HUE

d. Intensity—from bright to dull.

Color has three components: hue, value and saturation. What we call hues are your biological interpretation of different wavelengths of light. Value is the lightness or darkness of a color. Adding white to a color raises its value, creating a tint. Adding black to a color lowers its value, creating a shade. Saturation refers to a color's purity. Adding anything besides the initial hue to a color lowers the colors saturation. The visible spectrum—that you see, for instance, in a rainbow—runs from red to orange to yellow (the so-called warm hues) to green, blue, and violet (the so-called cool hues). The spectrum can be rearranged in a conventional color wheel. The three primary colors—red, yellow, and blue (designated by the number 1 on the color wheel)—are those that cannot be made by any mixture of the other colors. Each of the secondary colors—orange, green, and violet (designated by the number 2)—is a mixture of the two primaries it lies between. The intermediate colors (designated by the number 3) are mixtures of a primary and a neighboring secondary. Analogous color schemes are those composed of hues that neighbor each other on the color wheel. Complementary color schemes are composed of hues that lie opposite each other on the color wheel. When the entire range of hues is used, the color scheme is said to be polychromatic.

Texture is the tactile quality of a surface. It takes two forms: the actual surface quality—as marble is smooth, for instance—and a visual quality that is a representational illusion—as a marble nude sculpture is not soft like skin.

THE PRINCIPLES OF DESIGN

In 1928, American artist Charles Demuth set out to make a portrait of his friend, the poet William Carlos Williams. Demuth visualized a line from a poem that Williams wrote when he saw a fire engine racing through the streets on a rainy night: "I saw the figure 5 in gold." To Demuth, that vivid line of poetry seemed to symbolize the poet, and it provided a compelling subject for an artwork. He named the painting after the line: *The Figure 5 in Gold*.

Artists design their works in order to communicate a message or a vision. The process of creation involves choosing between and among methods of arrangement in order to arrive at a final design that will best say what the artist had in mind.

In creating *The Figure 5 in Gold*, Demuth used the large numeral 5 to **unify** the composition. Though the work is not symmetrical, it seems **balanced**. The other inscriptions on the work, such as "Bill" at the top for William Carlos Williams, are **subordinated** to the central figure 5. The diagonals in the work suggest slanting raindrops, establishing a strong **directional force**. The red color (presumably of the fire engine) **contrasts** with the gray background of the rainy city night. The numeral is **repeated** in a way that suggests the approach and passing of the truck. We see the numeral in various **scales** of size.

6.1 Charles Demuth (1883–1935).
   The Figure 5 in Gold. 1928.
   Oil on cardboard. 35½" 3 30" (90.2 3 76.2 cm).
   Alfred Stieglitz Collection, 1949 (49.59.1). The Metropolitan Museum of Art, New York, NY, U.S.A. Image copyright © The Metropolitan Museum of Art/Art Resource, NY.

Chapter 6: The Principles of Design was taken from *Prebles' Artforms: An Introduction to the Visual Arts*, Tenth Edition by Patrick Frank.

In the preceding chapter, we considered the basic elements of the visual vocabulary that artists use; now we need to examine how they use those building blocks to create artworks. In two-dimensional arts, such as painting and photography, this organization is usually called **composition**, but a broader term that applies to the entire range of visual arts is **design**. The word "design" indicates both the process of organizing visual elements and the product of that process.

As he created *The Figure 5 in Gold,* Demuth used seven key principles of design that we will consider in this chapter:

unity and variety
balance
emphasis and subordination
directional forces
contrast
repetition and rhythm
scale and proportion

These terms provide an understanding not only of how artists work, but also of how design affects us. The process at its best is a lively give-and-take between the creator and the viewer. The organization of the work is perhaps the most important task for an artist; it can be done well or poorly, effectively or ineffectively. The Pop artist Roy Lichtenstein recognized this when he said, "Organized perception is what art is all about."[1]

UNITY AND VARIETY

Unity and **variety** are complementary concerns. Unity is the appearance or condition of oneness. In design, unity describes the feeling that all the elements in a work belong together and make up a coherent and harmonious whole. When a work of art has unity, we feel that any change would diminish its quality.

Yet very few artworks are absolutely unified into one homogeneous thing; most such works were created as experiments. For example, the French artist Yves Klein made several paintings in the 1960s that were solid blue in color, with no variation. An example from sculpture is *Die* by Tony Smith. This block is a six-foot cube, resembling one of a huge pair of unmarked black dice. The title may also refer to the finality of death. Few works have ever been as unified as this.

6.2 Tony Smith (1912–1980).
Die. 1962.
Steel. Overall: 72⅜″ 3 72⅜″ 3 72⅜″.
Whitney Museum of American Art, New York; Purchase, with funds from the Louis and Bessie Adler Foundation, Inc., James Block, The Sondra and Charles Gilman, Jr. Foundation Inc., Penny and Mike Winton, and the Painting and Sculpture Committee 89.6 © Estate of Tony Smith/Artists Rights Society (ARS), New York.

6.3   Jacob Lawrence.
Going Home. 1946.
Gouache.
21½″ 3 29½″.
Private collection, courtesy of DC Moore Gallery, New York. ©2010 The
Jacob and Gwendolyn Lawrence Foundation, Seattle/Artists Rights Society
(ARS), New York.

Variety, on the other hand, provides diversity. Variety acts to counter unity. The sameness of too much unity can be boring, and the diversity of uncontrolled variety may be chaotic; most artists strive for a balance between unity and variety that can yield interesting compositions.

In his painting *Going Home*, Jacob Lawrence balanced unity and variety. He established visual themes with the lines, shapes, and colors of the train seats, figures, and luggage, and then he repeated and varied those themes. Notice the varied repetition in the green chair seats and window shades. As a unifying element, the same red is used in a variety of shapes. The many figures and objects in the complex composition form a unified design through the artist's skillful use of abstraction, theme, and variation.

Lawrence was known for the lively harmony of his distinctive compositions. Although he worked in a manner that may seem unsophisticated, he was always resolving his designs through adjustments of unity and diversity. Lawrence studied other artists' work, and he was influenced by painters who were design problem solvers. He said, "I like to study the design to see how the artist solves his problems and brings his subjects to the public."[2]

The flat quality of *Going Home* contrasts with the illusion of depth in *Interior of a Dutch House* by Pieter de Hooch. Each artist depicted daily life in a style relevant to his times. In both, the painter's depiction of space provides the unity in the composition. De Hooch used the unity of the room to unify pictorial space and provide a cohesive setting for the interaction of figures.

Pattern refers to a repetitive ordering of design elements. In de Hooch's painting, the patterns of floor tiles and windows play off against the larger rectangles of map, painting, fireplace, and ceiling.

These rectangular shapes provide a unifying structure. The nearly square picture plane itself forms the largest rectangle. He then created a whole family of related rectangles, as indicated in the accompanying diagram. In addition, the shapes and colors in the figures around the table relate to the shapes and colors of the figures in the painting above the fireplace—another use of theme and variation.

Just as few works strive for perfect unity, even fewer display absolute chaos. Robert Rauschenberg sought to duplicate the randomness of modern life in his works, such as *Gift for Apollo*. He began with a sawed-off door, turned it upside down, and casually applied paint strokes in various colors. He then attached a green necktie, some old postcards, a cloth pocket from a shirt, and part of a sign. He then placed the whole assemblage on small, spoked wheels, and "finished" the work by chaining a bucket to it. Yet even this level of disorder still has some sense of harmony: As in *Interior of a Dutch House*, we see repeated rectangles; the chain

6.4 Pieter de Hooch.
Interior of a Dutch House. 1658.
Oil on canvas. 29" 3 35".
© National Gallery, London/Art Resource, NY.

extends at a right angle to the axles and seems to anchor the work. Glue and gravity still hold it all in place. Rauschenberg made this work over 50 years ago, so the passage of time probably makes it seem less random than it was at first. Complete disorder in art is very difficult to achieve, though some works such as this one attempt it.

Alberto Giacometti's sculpture *Chariot* also combines diverse elements—a standing female figure and two wheels. Unity is achieved through the thin lines and rough texture in the figure, wheels, and axle, as well as through the use of bronze for the entire piece. The unity of handling leads us to see the sculpture as a single mysterious entity. Our interest is held by the varied components and by the precariousness of the figure poised

atop a two-legged table on two wheels. And these bring us to the principle called balance.

BALANCE

For sculptors such as Giacometti, balance is both a visual issue and a structural necessity. The interplay between the opposing forces of unity and variety is a common condition of life. The dynamic process of seeking balance is equally basic in art, though many artists seek lack of balance in their work for one expressive reason or another.

Balance is the achievement of equilibrium, in which acting influences are held in check by opposing forces. We strive for balance in life and in art, and we may lack peace of mind in its absence. In art, our instinct for physical balance finds its

6.5 Robert Rauschenberg.
Gift for Apollo. 1959.
Combine: oil, paint fragments, necktie, wood, fabric, newspaper, printed reproductions on wood with metal bucket, metal chain, door knob, L brackets, metal washer, nail and rubber wheels with metal spokes. 43¾" 3 29½" 3 41" (111.1 3 74.9 3 104.1 cm).
The Museum of Contemporary Art, Los Angeles. The Panza Collection.
Art © Estate of Robert Rauschenberg/Licensed by VAGA, New York, NY.

6.6 Alberto Giacometti.
Chariot. 1950.
Bronze. 57" 3 26" 3 26⅛"
(114.8 3 65.8 3 66.2 cm).
The Museum of Modern Art/Licensed by Scala-Art Resource, NY. Purchase. Photograph © 2002 The Museum of Modern Art, New York. © 2010 Succession Giacometti/Artists Rights Society (ARS), New York/ADAGP, Paris.

parallel in a desire for visual balance. The two general types of balance are symmetrical (formal) and asymmetrical (informal).

Symmetrical Balance

Symmetrical balance is the near or exact matching of left and right sides of a three-dimensional form or a two-dimensional composition. Such works have **symmetry**.

Architects often employ symmetrical balance to give unity and formal grandeur to a building's facade or front side. For example, in 1792 James Hoban won a competition for his *Design for the President's House*, a drawing of a symmetrical, Georgian-style mansion. Today, two centuries and several additions later, we know it as the *White House*.

Symmetrical design is useful in architecture because it is easier to comprehend than asymmetry. Symmetry imposes a balanced unity, making large complex buildings comprehensible in a glance. Symmetry connotes permanence and poise. We generally want our symbolically important

buildings to seem motionless and stable. All the qualities that make symmetry desirable in architecture make it generally less desirable in sculpture and two-dimensional art. Too much symmetry can be boring. Although artists admire symmetry for its formal qualities, they rarely use it rigidly. Artists usually do not want their work to seem static.

Few works of art are perfectly symmetrical, but *Posterity—The Holy Place* by Damien Hirst is

6.7 James Hoban.
   A Design for the President's House. 1792.
   a. Elevation.
   Maryland Historical Society, Baltimore.
   b. *White House.*
   Front view. 1997.
   Photograph: Antonio M. Rosario/Getty Images Inc. – Image Bank.

6.8 Damien Hirst.
   Posterity—The Holy Place. 2006.
   Butterflies and household gloss on canvas, 89⅝″ 3 48″.
   © Damien Hirst. Courtesy of Gagosian Gallery.
   Photograph: Purcence Cuming Associates, Inc. © 2010 Hirst Holdings Limited and Damien Hirst. All rights reserved, ARS, New York/DACS, London.

one. The artist formed it entirely out of butterflies, and it is symmetrical at every level: each butterfly, each unit of the composition, and the work as a whole. It resembles a stained-glass window, but is even more symmetrical than most of those. The stability of symmetry is a useful tool for religious art, which suggests the divine. But the sheer luminosity of *Posterity—The Holy Place* exceeds even that of a stained-glass window because butterfly wings do not depend on direct sunlight to show brilliance. (The artist bought the butterflies from a dealer who raises them.) Because the work is made up of so many small parts, the levels of symmetry help to structure the composition. We can prove this by merely imagining a work of similarly large size without a symmetrical arrangement.

Asymmetrical Balance

With **asymmetrical balance**, the left and right sides are not the same. Instead, various elements are balanced, according to their size and meaning, around a felt or implied center of gravity. For example, in *Noli Me Tangere* by Lavinia Fontana, the composition as a whole seems balanced, but only because dramatic imbalances are held in check. The painting illustrates a New Testament story in which Mary Magdalene went to the empty tomb of Jesus and saw the risen Christ, whom she at first took for the gardener. The story thus requires two people in the foreground, one of them prostrate.

This presents a difficult balancing problem, but Fontana solved it with a few ingenious steps. First, she gave the center of the composition strong weight, with Mary's large figure dressed in warm colors; above Mary is a glow in the sky. These anchor the composition. Christ occupies the right foreground, but he does not disrupt the equilibrium of the whole, because he is balanced by the higher and more massive tomb on the left. The small figure in red just outside the tomb also helps balance the strong figure of Christ.

What exactly are the visual weights of colors and forms, and how does an artist go about balancing them? As with design itself, there are no rules, only principles. Here are a few about visual balance:

- A large form is heavier, more attractive, or more attention-getting than a small form. Thus, two or more small forms can balance one large form.
- A form gathers visual weight as it nears the edge of a picture. In this way, a small form near an edge can balance a larger form near the center.
- A complex form is heavier than a simple form. Thus, a small complex form can balance a large simple form.

The introduction of color complicates these principles. Here are three color principles that counteract the three principles of form just given:

- Warm colors tend to be heavier than cool colors. A single small yellow form can sometimes balance a large dark blue form.

6.9 Lavinia Fontana.
Noli Me Tangere. 1581.
Oil on canvas. 47⅜″ 36⅝″.

6.10   Nicolas Poussin (French, 1594–1665).
      The Holy Family on the Steps. 1648.
      Oil on canvas. 72.4   111.7 cm.
      © The Cleveland Museum of Art, 2001, Leonard C. Hanna, Jr., Fund, 1981.18.

- Related to the point above, warm colors tend to advance toward the viewer, while cool colors tend to recede. This means that when considering two similar forms of opposing temperature, the warmer will be visually heavier because it seems closer to the viewer.

- Intense colors are heavier than weak or pale colors (tints and shades). Hence, a single small bright blue form near the center can balance a large pale blue form near an edge.

- The intensity, and therefore the weight, of any color increases as the background color approaches its complementary hue. Thus, on a green background, a small simple red form can balance a large complex blue form.

Although guidelines such as these are interesting to study and can be valuable to an artist if she or he gets "stuck," they are really "laboratory" examples. The truth is that most artists rely on a highly developed sensitivity to what "looks right" to arrive at a dynamic balance. Simply put, a work of art is balanced when it feels balanced.

A classic example of balance in Western art is Nicolas Poussin's *Holy Family on the Steps*, where he combined both asymmetrical and symmetrical elements in a complex composition. He grouped the figures in a stable, symmetrical pyramidal shape. The most important figure, the infant Jesus, is at the center of the picture, the strongest position. In case we don't notice that immediately, Poussin guided our attention by making the traditional red and blue of Mary's robes both light and bright, and by placing Jesus' head within a halo-like architectural space.

But then Poussin offset the potential inertness of this symmetry with an ingenious asymmetrical color balance. He placed Joseph, the figure at the right, in deep shadow, undermining the clarity of the stable pyramid. He created a major center of interest at the far left of the picture by giving St. Elizabeth a bright yellow robe. The interest created by the blue sky and clouds at the upper right counterbalances the figures of St. Elizabeth and the infant John the Baptist. But the final master stroke that brings complete balance is Joseph's

foot, which Poussin bathed in light. The brightness of this small, isolated shape with the diagonal staff above it is enough to catch our eye and balance the color weights of the left half of the painting.

An extreme case of dynamic balancing is *Jockeys Before the Race* by Edgar Degas. The artist boldly located the center of gravity on the right. To reinforce it, he drew it in as a pole. At first glance, all our attention is drawn to our extreme right, to the nearest and largest horse. But the solitary circle of the sun in the upper left exerts a strong fascination. The red cap, the pale pink jacket of the distant jockey, the subtle warm/cool color intersection at the horizon, and the decreasing sizes of the horses all help to move our eyes over to the left

6.11 Edgar Degas (1834–1917).
Jockeys Before the Race. c. 1878–1879.
Oil essence, gouache, and pastel.
42½" 3 29".
The Barber Institute of Fine Arts, University of Birmingham.
Bridgeman Art Library.

6.12 Mark di Suvero.
Declaration. 1999–2001.
Steel beams. Height 60′.
Copyright Mark di Suvero. Courtesy L.A. Louver, Venice, CA.

lack of balance affects the picture. Cover the jockey's red cap in the Degas, and you'll see a spark of life go out of the painting.

Besides whatever visual balance the creator may seek, works of sculpture and architecture need structural balance or they will not stand up. Mark di Suvero's *Declaration* was erected in 2001 on a spot near the beach in Venice, California. As a work of public art, *Declaration* required a building permit and official structural checks to ensure its safety in earthquakes and tsunamis. The artist used his engineering ability to balance the long V-shaped wings that seem to leap out from the three-legged base. The artist described the work as "a painting in three dimensions with the crane as my paintbrush." Originally intended for a four-month viewing period, the dynamic geometries of *Declaration* have remained on the site ever since.

EMPHASIS AND SUBORDINATION

Artists use **emphasis** to draw our attention to an area. If that area is a specific spot or figure, it is called a **focal point**. Position, contrast, color intensity, and size can all be used to create emphasis.

Through **subordination**, an artist creates neutral areas of lesser interest that keep us from being distracted from the areas of emphasis. We have seen them at work in the two paintings we have just examined.

In *Holy Family on the Steps* (page 102), Poussin placed the most important figure in the center, the strongest location in any visual field. In *Jockeys Before the Race*, Degas took a different approach, using size, shape, placement, and color to create areas of emphasis *away* from the center. The sun is a separate focal point created through contrast (it is lighter than the surrounding sky area and the only circle in the painting) and through placement (it is the only shape in that part of the painting). Sky and grass areas, however, are muted in color with almost no detail so that they are subordinate to, and thus support, the areas of emphasis. Generally, using emphasis and subordination, the artist shows us where to look in a work.

portion of the picture, where a barely discernible but very important vertical line directs our attention upward.

In this work, a trail of visual cues moves our attention from right to left. If we are sensitive to them, we will perform the act of balancing the painting. If we are not, the painting will seem forever unbalanced. Degas, who was known for his adventurous compositions, relied on the fact that seeing is an active, creative process and not a passive one.

A good way to explore a picture's balance is to imagine it painted differently. Block out Joseph's light-bathed foot in the Poussin, then see how the

DIRECTIONAL FORCES

Like emphasis and subordination, artists use **directional forces** to influence the way we look at a work of art. Directional forces are "paths" for the eye to follow, provided by actual or implied lines. Implied directional lines may be suggested by a form's axis, by the imagined connection between similar or adjacent forms, or by the implied continuation of actual lines. Studying directional lines and forces often reveals a work of art's underlying energy and basic visual structure.

Looking at *Jockeys Before the Race*, we find that our attention is pulled to a series of focal points: the horse and jockey at the extreme right, the vertical pole, the red cap, the pink jacket, and the blue-green at the horizon. The dominant directional forces in this work are diagonal. The focal points mentioned above create an implied directional line. The face of the first jockey is included in this line.

The implied diagonal line created by the bodies of the three receding horses acts as a related directional force. As our eyes follow the recession, encouraged by the attraction of the focal points, we perform the act of balancing the composition by correcting our original attraction to the extreme right.

Just as our physical and visual feelings for balance correspond, so do our physical and visual feelings about directional lines and forces. The direction of lines produces sensations similar to standing still (|), being at rest (—), or being in motion (/). Therefore, a combination of vertical and horizontal lines provides stability. For example, columns and walls and horizontal steps provide a stable visual foundation for *Holy Family on the Steps*. The vertical pole and horizon provide stability in *Jockeys Before the Race*.

Francisco Goya's print *Bullfight* provides a fascinating example of effective design based on a dramatic use of directional forces. To emphasize the drama of man and bull, Goya isolated them in the foreground as large, dark shapes against a light background. He created suspense by crowding the spectators into the upper left corner.

Goya evoked a sense of motion by placing the bullfighter exactly on the diagonal axis that runs from lower left to upper right (diagram a). He reinforced the feeling by placing the bull's hind legs along the same line.

Goya further emphasized two main features of the drama by placing the man's hands at the intersection of the image's most important horizontal and vertical lines. He also directed powerful diagonals from the bull's head and front legs to the pole's balancing point on the ground (a). The resulting sense of motion to the right is so powerful that everything in the rest of the etching is needed to balance it.

By placing the light source to the left, Goya extended the bull's shadow to the right, to create a relatively stable horizontal line. The man looks down at the shadow, creating a directional force

a.

b.

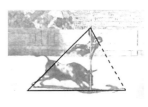

c.

6.13 Francisco Goya.
Bullfight: The Agility and Daring of Juanito Apinani.
Plate 20. Etching with aquatint. 9½" 3 14".
Ashmolean Museum, Oxford, England, UK.

that causes us also to look. When we do, we realize that the implied lines reveal the underlying structure to be a stable triangle (diagram b). Formally, the triangle serves as a balancing force; psychologically, its missing side serves to heighten the tension of the situation.

The dynamism of the man's diagonal axis is so strong that the composition needed additional balancing elements; thus, Goya used light to create two more diagonals in the opposite direction (diagram c). The area of shadow in the background completes the balance by adding visual weight and stability to the left.

It has taken many words and several diagrams to describe the visual dynamics that make the design of Goya's etching so effective. However, our eyes take it in instantly. Good design is efficient; it communicates its power immediately.

CONTRAST

Contrast is the juxtaposition of strongly dissimilar elements. Dramatic effects can be produced when dark is set against light, large against small, bright colors against dull. Without contrast, visual experience would be monotonous.

Contrast can be seen in the thick and thin areas of a single brush stroke. It can also be seen in the juxtaposition of regular geometric and irregular organic shapes, or in hard (sharp) and soft (blurred) edges. Contrast can provide visual interest, emphasize a point, and express content.

In the *Luster-Painted Bowl*, for example, the gold luster contrasts strongly with the blue accents. There is also a great deal of contrast among the eight petal-shaped segments that radiate from the central starburst. These segments are divided and decorated quite differently, creating a richly varied surface. Four of the petals have a blue tree shape, which evokes the idea of paradise described in the Koran, the Muslim holy book. They provide the major **rhythm** of the composition, while the other four petals alternate between a simple zigzag and a doubled

tree separated by a band. After a moment's look, we realize that the vivid and rich contrasts of this piece are subjected to a rigorous balancing scheme based on the repetition of radiating shapes. This discovery soon gives way to admiration for the designer's ability to harmonize such disparate elements.

REPETITION AND RHYTHM

The repetition of visual elements gives a composition unity, continuity, flow, and emphasis. As we saw earlier, *Interior of a Dutch House* (page 98) is organized around the repetition of rectangular shapes.

In Liubov Popova's *The Pianist*, the white shape at the center (the pianist's shirt front) is related visually to the pages of music, which form a strong rhythm leading the eye rightward and toward the keyboard. Likewise, the gray area of his face is repeated in organic shapes to the right

6.14 *Luster-Painted Bowl.*
Hispano-Moresque, Manises. Spain. c. 1400.
Tin-glazed earthenware painted in cobalt blue and luster. Height 5½″, diameter 17⅞″. (E643)
Courtesy of The Hispanic Society of America, New York.

and upward. (Both of these rhythmic sequences lead the eye in the same left-to-right direction that Westerners normally use in reading either music or books.) The angled shapes of the fingers suggest rhythmic motion across the keyboard just above. Indeed, the fragmentary shapes that dominate this painting suggest the rapidly ticking rhythm of the composition that *The Pianist* seems to play.

In the visual arts, rhythm is created through the regular recurrence of elements with related variations. Rhythm refers to any kind of movement or structure of dominant and subordinate elements in sequence. We generally associate rhythm with temporal arts such as music, dance, and poetry. Visual artists also use rhythm, as an organizational and expressive device.

6.15   Liubov Popova.
The Pianist. 1915.
Oil on canvas. 106.5 3 88.7 cm.
National Gallery of Canada, Ottawa.
Photo: © NGC.

6.16 Ogata Korin (1658–1716).
Cranes. c. 1700. Japanese, Edo period (1615–1868).
Ink, color, gold, and silver on paper. 166 H 3 371 cm (65⅜″ 3 146⅛″).
Freer Gallery of Art, Smithsonian Institution, Washington, DC: Purchase, F1956.20.

6.17 José Clemente Orozco.
Zapatistas. 1931.
Oil on canvas. 45″ 3 55″ (114.3 3 139.7 cm).
The Museum of Modern Art, New York, NY, U.S.A © 2011 Artists Rights Society (ARS), New York/SOMAAP, Mexico City. Digital Image © The Museum of Modern Art/Licensed by SCALA/Art Resource, NY.

Japanese artist Ogata Korin used repetition and rhythm to charming effect in *Cranes*, one of a pair of folding screens. The landscape is a flat yet opulent background of gold leaf, interrupted only by a suggestion of a curving stream at the right. The birds are severely simplified, their bodies and legs forming a pattern that is repeated with variations. The heads and beaks of the cranes create a strong directional force toward our left, leading the eye to an ironically empty rectangle. The heads are held high, and their location near the top of the composition enhances this loftiness, making the birds seem just a bit pretentious. Their procession in marching steps in a seemingly straight line supports this note of humor.

Strong rhythm dominates José Clemente Orozco's *Zapatistas.* The line of similar, diagonally placed figures grouped in a rhythmic sequence expresses the determination of oppressed people in revolt. The rhythmic diagonals of their hat brims, bayonets, and swords all contribute to a feeling of action. In fact, diagonal lines dominate the entire composition.

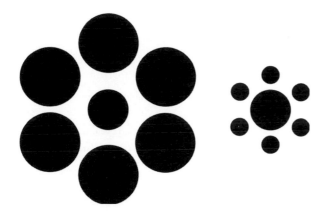

6.18 *Scale Relationships.*

6.19 Claes Oldenburg and Coosje van Bruggen.
Shuttlecocks. 1994. One of four.
Aluminum, fiberglass-reinforced plastic, and
paint. 215¾" 3 209" 3 191¾".
North façade of The Nelson-Atkins Museum of Art, Kansas City, Missouri
including one of four "Shuttlecocks," 1994, by Claes Oldenburg and
Coosje van Bruggen. Purchase; acquired through the generosity of the
Sosland Family. © Claes Oldenburg and Coosje van Bruggen. F94-1/1
Photograph by Jamison Miller.

6.20 Rembrandt van Rijn.
*Self-Portrait in a Cap, Open-Mouthed
and Staring.* 1630.
Etching. 2" 3 1⅞".
© The Trustees of The British Museum.

SCALE AND PROPORTION

Scale is the size relation of one thing to another.
Proportion is the size relationship of parts to a
whole.

Scale is one of the first decisions an artist
makes when planning a work of art. How big will it
be? We experience scale in relation to our own size,
and this experience constitutes an important part
of our response to works of art.

We see many relationships in terms of scale.
You have probably noticed that when a short
person stands next to a tall person, the short one
seems shorter and the tall one taller. Their relationship exaggerates the relative difference in their
heights. In the diagram *Scale Relationships*, the
inner circles at the center in both groups are the
same size, but the center circle at the right seems
much larger.

Many artists since the twentieth century have
distorted scale for visual effect. Claes Oldenburg and
Coosje van Bruggen's *Shuttlecocks* used distortion
in a humorous way. The artists arrayed four huge
metal shuttlecocks on the lawns outside the north
and south façades of the Nelson-Atkins Museum of
Art in Kansas City, Missouri. Each *Shuttlecock* is an
outlandish seventeen feet high and weighs over five
thousand pounds. Because badminton is played on
grass, it appears that the shuttlecocks fell during a
game between giants who used the museum as a net.
Shuttlecocks thus uses distortion of scale to poke gentle fun at the museum, mocking its rather prim look
with a playfully irreverent attitude.

When the size of any work is modified for
reproduction in a book, its character changes.
This is true of every picture in this book, with
this exception: Rembrandt's *Self-Portrait in a Cap*.
This tiny etching, which the artist created when

he was twenty-four years old, is reproduced here at the actual size of the original. It captures a fleeting expression of intense surprise. At this scale, it reads as an intimate notation of human emotion. On the other hand, many large-sized works have been reduced in this book to tiny fractions of their actual sizes, thereby altering their impact. Because works of art are distorted in a variety of ways when they are reproduced, it is important to experience original art whenever possible.

The term **format** refers to the size and shape—and thus to the scale and proportion—of a two-dimensional picture plane, such as a piece of paper, a canvas, a book page, or a video screen. For example, the format of this book is a vertical 8½ by 11–inch rectangle, the same format used for computer

6.21 Michelangelo Buonarroti.
Pietà, 1501.
Marble. Height 6′8½″.
Canali Photobank.

paper and most notebooks. Rembrandt's etching uses a tiny format; some modern artists have used huge ones.

The format an artist chooses strongly influences the total composition of a particular work. Henri Matisse made this clear in his *Notes of a Painter*:

Composition, the aim of which should be expression, is modified according to the surface to be covered. If I take a sheet of paper of a given size, my drawing will have a necessary relationship to its format. I would not repeat this drawing on another sheet of different proportions, for example, rectangular instead of square.[3]

Change in proportion can make a major difference in how we experience a given subject. This becomes apparent when we compare two *pietàs* (*pietà*, Italian for "pity," refers to a depiction of Mary holding and mourning over the body of Jesus).

Creating a composition with an infant on its mother's lap is much easier than showing a fully grown man in such a position. In his most famous *Pietà*, Michelangelo solved the problem by dramatically altering the human proportions of Mary's figure. Michelangelo made the heads of the two figures the same size but greatly enlarged Mary's body in relation to that of Christ, disguising her immensity with deep folds of drapery. Her seated figure spreads out to support the almost horizontal curve of Christ's limp body. Imagine how the figure of Mary would appear if she were standing. Michelangelo made Mary's body into that of a giant; if she were a living human being rather than a work of art, she would stand at least eight feet tall!

Because the proportions of the figure of Christ are anatomically correct and there are abundant naturalistic details, we overlook the proportions of Mary's figure, yet the distortion is essential to the way we experience the content of the work.

Compare Michelangelo's work with the *Roettgen Pietà*, created about two centuries earlier. Unlike the Renaissance work, the German sculptor carved both figures of similar height. Making Christ bony and emaciated helped to alleviate the

problem of how Mary can support a person of similar size; Christ's gaunt body also expresses the truth of his suffering in a way that Michelangelo avoided. The anonymous creator of *Roettgen Pietà* also carved both heads larger, out of proportion to the sizes of their bodies. These distortions help to heighten the expressiveness of the work.

6.22 *Roettgen Pietà*. 1300–1325.
Painted wood, height 34½″.
LVR-Landesmuseum Bonn.

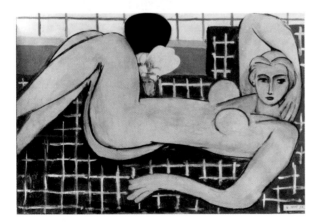

6.23 Henri Matisse (French, 1869–1954).
Photographs of three states of *Large Reclining Nude*.
a. State I, May 3, 1935.
b. State IX, May 29, 1935.
c. State XIII, September 4, 1935.
© 2012 Succession H. Matisse/Artists Rights Society (ARS), New York.

DESIGN SUMMARY

A finished work affects us because its design seems inevitable. However, design is not inevitable at all. Faced with a blank piece of paper, an empty canvas, a lump of clay, or a block of marble, an artist begins a process involving many decisions, false starts, and changes in order to arrive at an integrated whole. This chapter has presented some of the principles of design that guide the creation of artworks.

By photographing the progress of his painting *Large Reclining Nude*, Henri Matisse left us a rare record of the process of designing. He took twenty-four photographs over a period of four months; three of them are reproduced here.

The first version (State I) is by far the most naturalistic: the proportions of the model's body on the couch and the three-dimensional space of the room seem ordinary. This stage of the work shows the traditional rules of picture construction, but this is only the start of a fascinating journey.

By State IX, Matisse had introduced a number of bold changes. Because the model's head and crooked right arm did not give the proper weight to that side of the composition, he greatly enlarged the arm. He added more curves to the torso, and he put the legs together to provide a balancing element on the left side. The space of the room now has a new look because he removed the diagonal; this change flattened the composition, highlighting its two-dimensional design. The model's left arm is now closer to a ninety-degree angle, which makes it seem to support more weight; this is a stronger effect than that of the rubbery arm in the first photo. The boldest change regards the couch. Now it is far larger, with vertical white stripes in a rhythmic pattern. Because the stripes are parallel, they do not function as perspective lines; rather, the couch appears to be tipped toward us. Matisse kept the potted flowers and the chair, but he simplified the chair and placed the flowers on the couch.

By the time the artist took our third photograph (State XIII), he had introduced even more

6.24 Henri Matisse (French, 1869–1954).
Large Reclining Nude. 1935.
Oil on canvas. 26″ 3 36½″ (66 3 92.7 cm).
The Baltimore Museum of Art: The Cone Collection, formed by Dr. Claribel Cone and Miss Etta Cone of Baltimore,
Maryland. BMA 1950.258. © 2011 Succession H. Matisse/Artists Rights Society (ARS), New York.

changes, to compensate for some of the bold effects he had introduced earlier. The model's head is larger and placed upright, so that it fits better into the shape of the raised arm. He simplified the curves of the torso and created a new position for the left arm, a compromise between its position in the first photo and the second one. The legs are now almost a unit, their bulky mass balancing the verticals and diagonals on the right. He added horizontal lines to the couch, making a pattern of squares that parallel the framing edges of the painting. This netlike motif is repeated in the larger squares on the back wall of the room. The composition is already interesting, but Matisse did not stop here.

The final version shows further refinements and a few discoveries. Because the model's left arm probably still seemed weak, Matisse finally fixed it in the corner of the work at a strong angle aligned with the picture frame. The head is smaller, because the new position of the arms provides enough visual weight on that side of the work. He intensified the pattern on the back wall, so that it now serves as a variation of the motif on the couch. He gave new functions to the shapes and lines of the chair back and flowers by emphasizing their curves. They now echo the shapes of the body and balance the rigidity of the squares in the couch and wall. The position of the legs is the biggest change. By moving one of them down, he created a "pinwheel" effect that the arms carry through, adding a new circular element to the design of the whole. Finally, he repositioned the model's entire body at a slight angle from the horizontal.

Matisse's keen sense of design and restless experimentation produced a work in which powerful forces in the composition are balanced with seemingly simple means. He wrote that the expressiveness of a work does not rest merely on facial expressions or gestures of figures:

The entire arrangement of my picture is expressive: the place occupied by the figures, the empty spaces around them, the proportions, everything has its share.[4]

Notes

1. R. G. Swenson, "What Is Pop Art?" *Art News* (November 1963): 62.
2. Elizabeth McCausland, "Jacob Lawrence," *Magazine of Art* (November 1945): 254.
3. Jack D. Flam, *Matisse on Art* (New York: Dutton, 1978), 36; originally in "Notes d'un peintre," *La Grande Revue* (Paris, 1908).
4. Ibid.

Henri Matisse: Expression Is Foremost

IF HENRI MATISSE (1869–1954) had not had an attack of appendicitis, the history of art would have been different. After earning his law degree and working as a clerk, he fell gravely ill. During the long convalescence at his parents' home, his mother tried to amuse him with a gift of a box of paints, brushes, and a do-it-yourself book on painting. The result was extraordinary.

By the age of twenty-one, Matisse knew he wanted to be a painter. He returned to Paris and became a full-time art student. In the methodical manner of a lawyer, he began his artistic career by becoming thoroughly proficient in the traditional techniques of French art. Throughout his life he worked at adding to both his knowledge and his skills, while being careful to preserve his original freshness of vision.

For Matisse, a painting was a combination of lines, shapes, and colors before it was a picture of any object. His personal style was based on intuition, yet he acknowledged the importance of his years of study. He carefully assimilated influences from the arts of the Near East and Africa and from other painters.

Matisse's primary interest was to express his passion for life through the free use of visual form, with the human figure his main subject.

What interests me most is neither still life nor landscape but the human figure. It is through it that I best succeed in expressing the nearly religious feeling that I have towards life.[1]

His search for expressive means caused him to question or abandon many of the "rules" of art as it was then understood. For example, he often used colors that did not correspond to what the eye sees, but rather to what he felt inside. He also simplified and flattened his compositions, because he felt that adding too much detail took away feeling. For these and other innovations in painting style, he was once called a "wild beast"—*fauve* in French. The name stuck, and Fauvism took its place among the most important modern art movements.

Matisse sought to hide his own artistic struggles so that his work would appear effortless and light. He was concerned, however, that young people would think he had created his paintings casually—even carelessly—and would mistakenly conclude that years of disciplined work and study were unnecessary.

The dominant qualities in Matisse's art are lyric color and vitality. Behind the playful appearance lie radiant big-heartedness, grace, and wisdom. Although he lived through both world wars and was aware of acute suffering, Matisse chose to express joy and tranquility in his art.

What I dream of is an art of balance, of purity and serenity, devoid of troubling or depressing subject matter, an

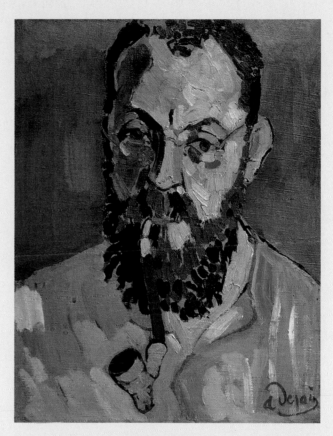

6.25 André Derain (1880–1954). *Portrait of Henri Matisse.* 1905. Oil on canvas. 46.0 34.9 cm. Tate Gallery, London, Great Britain. Art Resource, NY. © 2010 Artists Rights Society (ARS), New York/ADAGP, Paris; © 2010 Succession H. Matisse/Artists Rights Society (ARS), New York.

art which might be for every mental worker ... businessman or writer, like an appeasing influence, like a mental soother, something like a good armchair in which to rest from physical fatigue.[2]

Notes

1. Henri Matisse, "Notes of a Painter," translated by Alfred H. Barr, Jr., *Problems of Aesthetics,* edited by Eliseo Vivas and Murray Krieger (New York: Holt, 1953), 259–260; originally in "Notes d'un peintre."
2. Ibid., 260.

VISITING MUSEUMS

Museums can be intimidating places, but you should remember that the museum is, in fact, dedicated to your visit. Its mission is to help you understand and appreciate its collections and exhibits.

One of the primary functions of museums is to provide a *context* for works of art—that is, works are grouped together in such a way that they inform one another. They might be grouped by artist (all the sculptures of Rodin might be in a single room), by school or group (the French Cubists in one room, for instance, and the Italian Futurists in the next), by national and historical period (nineteenth-century British landscape), or by some critical theory or theme. Curators—the people who organize museum collections and exhibits—also guarantee the continued movement of people through their galleries by limiting the number of important or "star" works in any given room. The attention of the viewer is drawn to such works by positioning and lighting.

A good way to begin your visit to a museum is to quickly walk through the exhibit or exhibits that particularly interest you in order to gain an overall impression. Then return to the beginning and take your time. A set of worksheets that poses questions for you to consider as you look at the works in a museum can be found in the appendix to this book. Remember, this is your chance to look at the work close at hand, and, especially in large paintings, you will see details that are never visible in reproduction—everything from brushwork to the text of newsprint incorporated in a collage. Take the time to walk *around* sculptures and experience their full three-dimensional effects. You will quickly learn that there is no substitute for seeing works in person.

A DOS-AND-DON'TS GUIDE TO VISITING MUSEUMS

Do plan ahead. Most museums have Web sites that can be very helpful in planning your visit. The Metropolitan Museum of Art in New York, for instance, or the Louvre in Paris are so large that their collections cannot be seen in a single visit. You should determine in advance what you want to see.

Do help yourself to a museum guide once you are at the museum. It will help you find your way around the exhibits.

Do take advantage of any information about the collections—brochures and the like—that the museum provides. Portable audio tours can be especially informative, as can museum staff and volunteers—called *docents*—who often conduct tours.

Do look at the work *before you read about it.* Give yourself a chance to experience the work in a direct, unmediated way.

Do read the labels that museums provide for the artworks they display after you've looked at the work for a while. Almost all labels give the name of the artist (if known), the name and date of the work, its materials and technique (oil on canvas, for instance), and some information about how the museum acquired the work. Sometimes additional information is provided in a *wall text,* which might analyze the work's formal qualities, or provide some anecdotal or historical background.

Don't take photographs, unless cameras are explicitly allowed in the museum. The light created by flashbulbs can be especially damaging to paintings.

Don't touch the artwork. The more texture a work possesses, the more tempting it will be, but the oils in your skin can be extremely damaging to even stone and metal.

Do turn off your cell phone out of courtesy to others.

Don't talk loudly, and be aware that others may be looking at the same piece you are. Try to avoid blocking their line of sight.

Do enjoy yourself, don't be afraid to laugh (art can be funny), and if you get tired, take a break.

TIMELINE

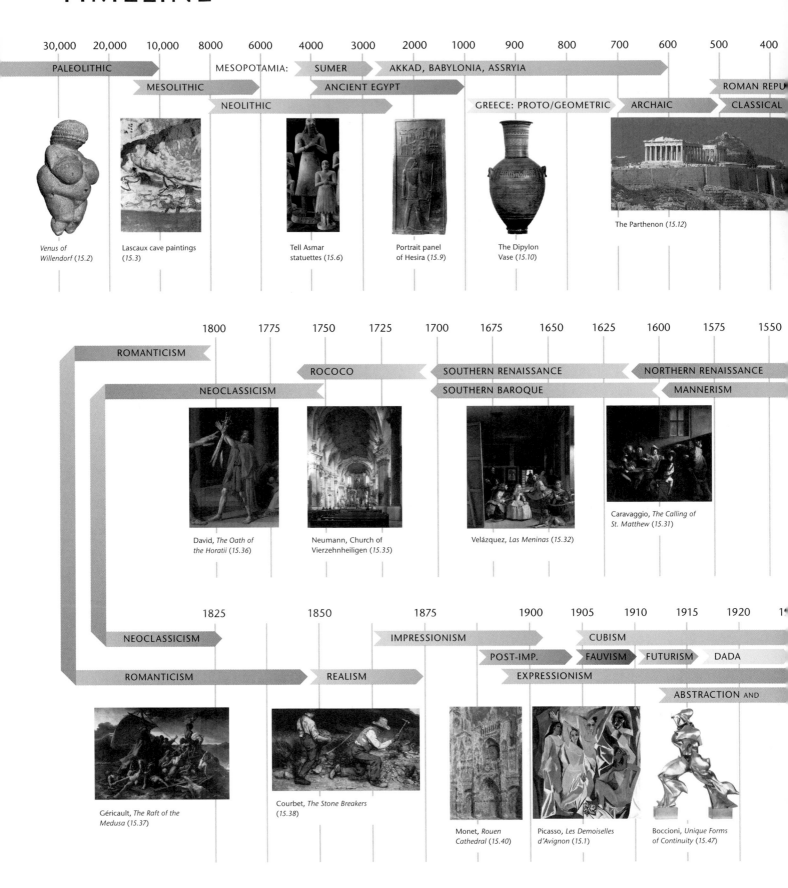

| 30,000 | 20,000 | 10,000 | 8000 | 6000 | 4000 | 3000 | 2000 | 1000 | 900 | 800 | 700 | 600 | 500 | 400 |

PALEOLITHIC

MESOPOTAMIA: SUMER   AKKAD, BABYLONIA, ASSRYIA

ROMAN REPU

MESOLITHIC   ANCIENT EGYPT

NEOLITHIC   GREECE: PROTO/GEOMETRIC   ARCHAIC   CLASSICAL

Venus of Willendorf (15.2)

Lascaux cave paintings (15.3)

Tell Asmar statuettes (15.6)

Portrait panel of Hesira (15.9)

The Dipylon Vase (15.10)

The Parthenon (15.12)

| 1800 | 1775 | 1750 | 1725 | 1700 | 1675 | 1650 | 1625 | 1600 | 1575 | 1550 |

ROMANTICISM

ROCOCO   SOUTHERN RENAISSANCE   NORTHERN RENAISSANCE

NEOCLASSICISM   SOUTHERN BAROQUE   MANNERISM

David, *The Oath of the Horatii* (15.36)

Neumann, Church of Vierzehnheiligen (15.35)

Velázquez, *Las Meninas* (15.32)

Caravaggio, *The Calling of St. Matthew* (15.31)

| 1825 | 1850 | 1875 | 1900 | 1905 | 1910 | 1915 | 1920 | 1 |

NEOCLASSICISM   IMPRESSIONISM   CUBISM

POST-IMP.   FAUVISM   FUTURISM   DADA

ROMANTICISM   REALISM   EXPRESSIONISM

ABSTRACTION AND

Géricault, *The Raft of the Medusa* (15.37)

Courbet, *The Stone Breakers* (15.38)

Monet, *Rouen Cathedral* (15.40)

Picasso, *Les Demoiselles d'Avignon* (15.1)

Boccioni, *Unique Forms of Continuity* (15.47)

Timeline was taken from *The Art of Seeing*, Eighth Edition by Paul Zelanski and Mary Pat Fisher.

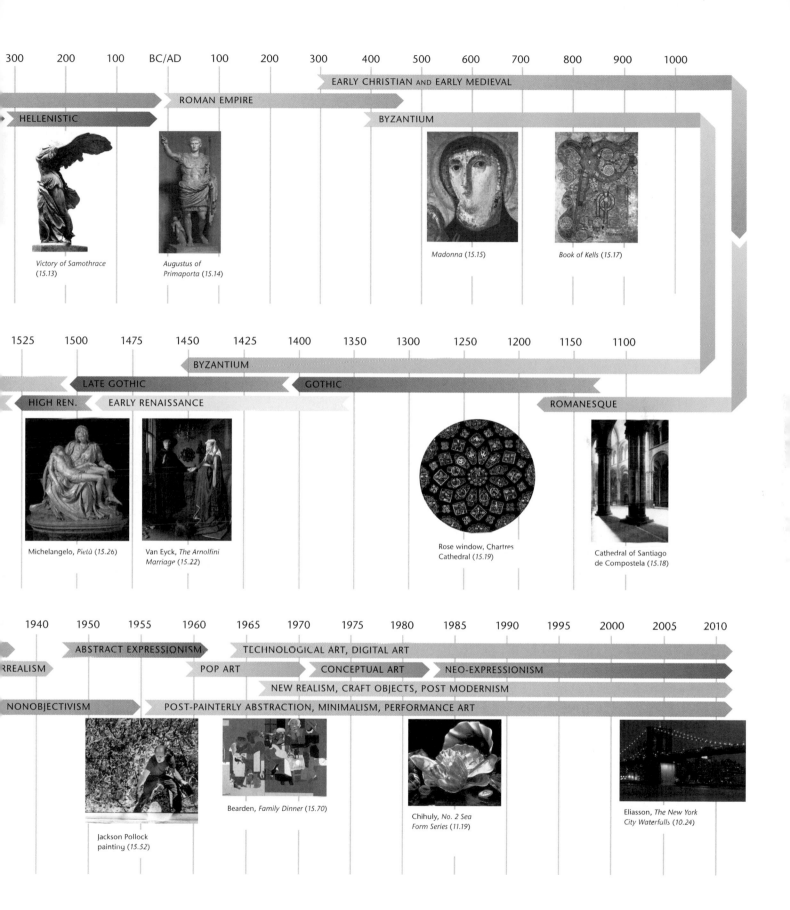

| 300 | 200 | 100 | BC/AD | 100 | 200 | 300 | 400 | 500 | 600 | 700 | 800 | 900 | 1000 |

EARLY CHRISTIAN AND EARLY MEDIEVAL

ROMAN EMPIRE

HELLENISTIC

BYZANTIUM

Victory of Samothrace (15.13)

Augustus of Primaporta (15.14)

Madonna (15.15)

Book of Kells (15.17)

| 1525 | 1500 | 1475 | 1450 | 1425 | 1400 | 1350 | 1300 | 1250 | 1200 | 1150 | 1100 |

BYZANTIUM

LATE GOTHIC

GOTHIC

HIGH REN.   EARLY RENAISSANCE

ROMANESQUE

Michelangelo, Pietà (15.26)

Van Eyck, The Arnolfini Marriage (15.22)

Rose window, Chartres Cathedral (15.19)

Cathedral of Santiago de Compostela (15.18)

| 1940 | 1950 | 1955 | 1960 | 1965 | 1970 | 1975 | 1980 | 1985 | 1990 | 1995 | 2000 | 2005 | 2010 |

ABSTRACT EXPRESSIONISM   TECHNOLOGICAL ART, DIGITAL ART

RREALISM   POP ART   CONCEPTUAL ART   NEO-EXPRESSIONISM

NEW REALISM, CRAFT OBJECTS, POST MODERNISM

NONOBJECTIVISM   POST-PAINTERLY ABSTRACTION, MINIMALISM, PERFORMANCE ART

Jackson Pollock painting (15.52)

Bearden, Family Dinner (15.70)

Chihuly, No. 2 Sea Form Series (11.19)

Eliasson, The New York City Waterfulls (10.24)

Differential timescales have been used, resulting in the relative compression of earlier periods. This apparent bias in favor of recency should be noted, although it is difficult to avoid: If this Timeline represented all periods on the timescale used for the twentieth century, it would measure 315 feet (96 m) in length.

FROM THE EARLIEST ART TO THE BRONZE AGE

Art history makes history visible and accessible. It is a record of how the people of the past—our ancestors—lived, felt, and acted in widely separated parts of the world at different periods of time.

Art history differs from other kinds of history because works of art from the past are with us in the present. One-to-one communication still occurs, even when artist and viewer are separated by thousands of years. This communicative power of art makes it possible for us to glimpse some of the experiences of those whose lives preceded ours, to better understand societies other than our own, and to see beyond our own cultural boundaries. Although interesting, old science has little practical use; but old art can be as life-enriching as new art.

There is no "better" or "best" when we compare the art of different societies, or even the art of different times within the same society. Rather, differences in art reflect differences in points of view. Pablo Picasso put the subject of art history in perspective in this way:

To me there is no past or future in art. If a work of art cannot live always in the present it must not be considered at all. The art of the Greeks, the Egyptians, the great painters who lived in other times, is not an art of the past; perhaps it is more alive today than it ever was.[1]

THE PALEOLITHIC PERIOD

Roughly two million years ago, in east-central Africa, early hominids made crude stonecutting tools. The making of these tools enabled our predecessors to extend their skills and thereby gain a measure of control over their surroundings. From such beginnings, human beings developed the abilities to reason and to visualize: to remember the past, to relate it to the present, and to imagine a possible future. As we became form-creating creatures, our ability to conceive mental images set us apart from other animals. Imagination is our special advantage.

About one million years ago in Africa, and more recently in Asia and Europe, people made more refined tools by chipping flakes from opposite sides of stones to create sharp cutting edges. It took another 250,000 years or so for human beings to develop choppers and hand axes that were symmetrical and refined in shape. An awareness of the relationship of form to function, and of form as enjoyable in itself, was the first step in the history of art.

Sprinkled powders and beads accompany many widely dispersed gravesites from about 100,000 years ago. These finds suggest to archaeologists that humans at that time practiced ritual burial, though the meaning of these decorative additions is unknown.

Chapter 7: From the Earliest Art to the Bronze Age was taken from *Prebles' Artforms: An Introduction to the Visual Arts,* Tenth Edition by Patrick Frank.

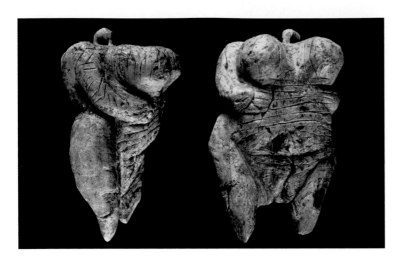

7.1 *Hohle Fels Figure.*
c. 35,000 B.C.E. Carved mammoth tusk. Front and side views of the recently discovered female figurine from the Aurignacian levels of Hohle Fels. Height 2½".
Photographer: H. Jensen. © University of Tübingen.

Sophisticated examples of Paleolithic art have been discovered at many locations around the world. Current scientific dating places the earliest of these findings at about 40,000 years ago, toward the end of the last ice age. As the southern edge of the European ice sheet slowly retreated northward, hunter-gatherers followed the animals that they hunted for food. They carved and painted images of these animals on cave walls deep in the earth.

The oldest surviving carved human figure was found in southwestern Germany in 2008; the *Hohle Fels Figure* is just over two inches high and at least 35,000 years old. Her female characteristics are highly exaggerated, and she shows carefully placed grooves at various points on her body. Her arms cling to her abdomen. In place of a head is a ring suitable for stringing the figure around a wearer's neck (the ring shows wearing marks). A similar figure about 10,000 years younger is the *Venus of Willendorf*, which was found in northern Austria. In both of these figures, the pointy legs, lack of facial detail, and exaggerated emphasis on hips and breasts implies a specific purpose that we can only guess at. These figures may

7.2 *Venus of Willendorf.*
Aurignacian (late Paleolithic).
c. 25,000–20,000 B.C.E.
Limestone. Height 4½".
Naturhistorisches Museum, Vienna, Austria. Copyright Erich Lessing/Art Resource, NY.

AT THE EDGE OF ART

Stones from Blombos

RECENT DISCOVERIES HAVE enlivened the debate about when art began. In 2002, archaeologists digging in the Blombos Cave in South Africa unearthed what may qualify as the earliest art that we know of. In a soil layer 77,000 years old, they found some pieces of Engraved Ochre bearing marks that appear to be symbols. The marks form an abstract pattern of parallel diagonal lines between horizontal bars. Any practical use for the markings is highly unlikely; rather, they seem symbolic or at least decorative, making these ochres the oldest embellished objects yet found. In 2010, researchers at a nearby site found ostrich egg shells with similar parallel scratch marks. Many archaeologists concluded that these African sites contain the first known instances of artistic creativity.

7.3 *Engraved Ochre.*
From Blombos Cave, South Africa. c. 75,000 B.C.E. Length 4".
Christopher Henshilwood © University of Bergen.

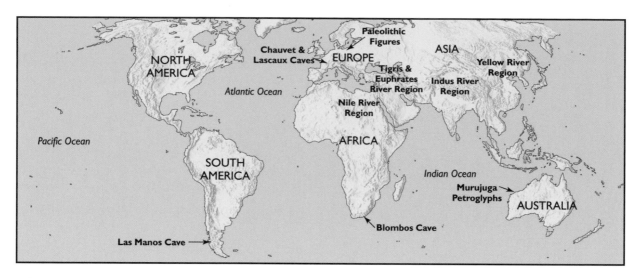

7.4 Earliest Centers of Civilization.

be the earliest known works of religious art, depicting the Paleolithic image of the Creator—the Great Mother Goddess. We refer to the Paleolithic period as the Stone Age, but that is mainly because only stone artifacts have survived. The *Hohle Fels Figure* was found near a three-hole flute carved of bone, indicating that music also existed in that remote age.

Paleolithic paintings have a different style from the copious bulges of the sculpture. Human beings rarely appear; those that do tend to be more simplified and abstract than the images of animals. Animals portrayed in sculpture and paintings of this period have an expressive naturalism. The oldest known paintings were found in 1994 in the Chauvet Cave in south central France. The *Wall Painting of Animals* is among dozens of 30,000-year-old images painted with charcoal and earthen pigments on the cave walls. The unknown artists

7.5 *Wall Painting of Animals.*
Chauvet Cave,
Pont d'Arc, France.
c. 28,000 B.C.E.
Photograph: Jean Clottes,
Conservateur général du patrimoine
(honoraire).

7.6 *Deer and Hands.*
Las Manos Cave, Argentina. c. 15,000 B.C.E.
Des & Jen Bartlett\Photoshot Holdings Ltd./Bruce Coleman.

depicted in a lifelike fashion horses, rhinoceroses, tigers, and other large animals, many of them now extinct. Explorers found a bear's skull in the middle of a flat stone slab nearby, which may have been an altar.

Scholars long believed that the purpose of naturalistic Paleolithic art was to bring the spirits of animals into rituals related to the hunt. Many authors accept this theory. However, careful study of footprints and other archaeological remains has recently led some experts to theorize that Chauvet and similar sites were used as sanctuaries where youth were initiated in ceremonies based on sym-

bolic and metaphysical associations with the portrayed animals.

Paleolithic people, in what is now southern Argentina, made paintings of their hands, probably by blowing earth colors as they placed their hands against the cave wall. *Deer and Hands* is similar to hand impressions and paintings of animals found on many continents.

Much of the world's Paleolithic art is found in caves, but large parts of this heritage are above ground, etched in stones in many locations around the world. These rock art carvings, also known as

petroglyphs, are made by scratching or pecking the surface of exposed stone. One of the largest petroglyph complexes is in the Dampier Archipelago off the northwest coast of Australia. There we see the *Murujuga Petroglyphs*, thousands of carvings that depict humans, animals, and mythic beings. Like the cave paintings, the purpose of the petroglyphs is a matter of conjecture. Their age is also difficult to determine because they are in exposed locations apart from soil sediments. A great deal of the world's rock art is also endangered for this reason; the *Murujuga Petroglyphs*, for example, have been eroded by acid rain, and economic development in the area threatens their outright destruction.

THE NEOLITHIC PERIOD

The transition from Old Stone Age to New Stone Age (Paleolithic to Neolithic) marked a major turning point in human history. The New Stone Age seems to have arisen first in what is now Iraq, between 9000 and 6000 B.C.E., when people made the gradual transition from the precarious existence of nomadic hunters and gatherers to the relatively stable life of village farmers and herders. The agricultural revolution—this major shift from nomadic groups to small agricultural communities—stabilized human life and produced early architecture and other technological developments. People learned new techniques for working with seasonal rhythms. Because food and seeds had to be stored, it is not surprising that clay storage pots are among the most significant artifacts of the period.

Neolithic art reflects the great shift in living patterns. The vigorous, naturalistic art of Paleolithic hunters was largely replaced by the geometric abstract art of Neolithic farmers. From about 10,000 to 3000 B.C.E., much art emphasized abstract designs used to embellish articles for daily use. The motifs, or dominant themes, used on clay pots were often derived from plant and animal forms.

7.7 *Murujuga Petroglyphs.*
Up to 10,000 years old.
Robert Bednarik.

The painted *Earthenware Beaker* is from Susa, the first developed city on the Iranian plateau. Solid bands define areas of compact decoration. The upper zone consists of a row of highly abstract long-necked birds, below which appears to be a band of dogs running in the opposite direction. The dominant image is an ibex or goat abstracted into triangular and circular shapes. The significant difference between the naturalism of Paleolithic animal art and the abstraction of Neolithic art becomes clear when we compare this goat with the naturalistic bulls of Chauvet.

Some of the finest Neolithic pottery was made in China. The well-preserved *Burial Urn* from Kansu Province is decorated with a bold interlocking design, which may have been abstracted from spirals observed in nature. The design in the center of the spirals is probably derived from the bottoms of cowrie shells.

Most Neolithic structures are primitive; one that shows real sophistication is *Stonehenge* in south-central England. Built in layers over more than a millennium, its oldest phase is the outermost circular ditch and bank; these date from about 3200 B.C.E. This bank is interrupted for a road (at lower right) that is aligned to the northernmost midwinter moonrise. Many archaeologists believe that this orientation was important in funeral rituals. Near the same time, wood structures were erected at the center of the circle.

Later phases involved replacing the wood structures with huge stones (weighing 25 tons) brought to the site from a quarry 19 miles away. These stones were fitted together using techniques borrowed from lumber construction; they form a semicircle surrounded by a ring of posts and lintels. Some of these stones have carvings of daggers and axes that resemble carvings found across the channel in France that accompany a female guardian of the afterlife. Many burials have been found nearby, most of them showing some sort of trauma or wound. An upright "heel stone" was placed on the road at a point beyond our photo that aligns with the midsummer sunrise. These indications make the function of *Stonehenge* a matter of debate: Was it a solar or a lunar temple? For coordinating agricultural rituals, for healing, or for honoring the dead? It may have had all of these functions at different times in its lengthy evolution.

7.10 *Stonehenge.*
c. 2000 B.C.E.
© English Heritage.NMR Aerofilms Collection.

THE BEGINNINGS OF CIVILIZATION

Artifacts indicate that early civilizations emerged independently, at different times, in many parts of the world. We use the term civilization to distinguish cultures, or composites of cultures, that have fairly complex social orders and relatively high degrees of technical development. Key elements are food production through agriculture and animal husbandry, occupational specialization, writing, and production of bronze by smelting lead and tin. All of these developments were made possible by the move to cooperative living in urban as well as agricultural communities. The rise of bronze also made possible better weapons, and thus larger empires.

Among the earliest major civilizations were those in four fertile river valleys: the Tigris and Euphrates Rivers in Iraq, the Nile River in Egypt, the Indus River in west Pakistan and India, and the Yellow River in northern China.

The ancient civilizations of Mesopotamia and Egypt were almost parallel in time, arising in the fourth millennium B.C.E. and lasting some three thousand years. Yet they were quite different from each other. Urban civilization developed earlier in Mesopotamia than it did in Egypt. The Nile Valley of Egypt was protected by formidable deserts, mak-

ing it possible for the Egyptians to enjoy thousands of years of relatively unbroken self-rule. The Tigris-Euphrates valley of Mesopotamia, however, was vulnerable to repeated invasion; the area was ruled by a succession of different peoples. Each civilization therefore developed its own distinctive art forms.

MESOPOTAMIA

The Greeks named the broad plain between the Tigris and Euphrates Rivers Mesopotamia, "the land between the rivers." Today, this plain is part of Iraq. The first Mesopotamian civilization arose in the southernmost part of the plain in an area called Sumer. The Sumerian people developed the world's first writing, the wheel, and the plow.

In the city-states of Sumer, religion and government were one; authority rested with priests who claimed divine sanction as they elected their rulers. The Sumerians worshiped a hierarchy of nature gods in temples set on huge platforms called **ziggurats**, which stood at the center of each city-state. Ruins of many early Mesopotamian cities are still dominated by eroding ziggurats, such as the *Ziggurat of Ur-Nammu*. The Tower of Babel mentioned in the Bible was probably a ziggurat.

Ziggurats embodied the concept of the "sacred mountain" that links heaven and earth. They were filled with sun-baked bricks, then faced with bricks colored with ceramic glazes and fired in kilns. Two or more successively smaller platforms stood on the solid base, with a shrine on the uppermost platform. On these heights, close to heaven, the city's deities might dwell, and there the ruling priests and priestesses had their sanctuaries. A lack of stone led to the use of brick and wood for building; consequently, very little Mesopotamian architecture remains.

We can imagine the splendor of Sumerian court life by studying the reconstruction of the

7.11 *Ziggurat of Ur-Nammu.*
Iraq. c. 2100 B.C.E.
Photograph: SuperStock, Inc.

7.12 *Lyre.*
Front plaque of recon-
structed lyre from "The
King's Grave" tomb RT
789. Ur. c. 2650–2550
B.C.E.
Wood with gold, lapis lazuli,
shell, and silver.
Penn Museum object B17694, image a.
#150888, image b. #150029.

elegant royal *Lyre* found in
the king's tomb in the ancient
city of Ur. The narrative panel
on the front and the bull's head
are original. The bearded bull's
head is a symbol of royalty often
seen in Mesopotamian art. In
contrast, the bulls and other
imaginary animals inlaid on the
harp's soundbox are depicted in

a. Front plaque.

a simplified narrative style. They take on human
roles, as do the animals in the later Greek fables
of Acsop. The upper panel, which shows a man
embracing two bearded bulls, is a type of heral-
dic design developed by the Sumerians that was to
influence the art of many later cultures. Both the
upper panel and the panel at the bottom—a goat
attending a scorpion-man—are believed to be
scenes from the great classic of Sumerian literature, the *Epic of Gilgamesh.*

The region of Mesopotamia north of Sumer was
called Akkadia. By about 2300 B.C.E., the scattered
city-states of Sumer had come under the authority
of a single Akkadian king. The magnificent *Head
of an Akkadian Rule* portrays such an absolute
monarch. Clearly, this highly sophisticated work
evolved from a long tradition. The elaborate hair-
style and rhythmic patterning show the influence of
Sumerian stylization. The handsome face expresses
calm inner strength. Such superb blending of
formal design with carefully observed naturalism
is a characteristic of both later Mesopotamian and
Egyptian art.

Mesopotamia was an area of continual local
rivalries, foreign invasions, and the rise and fall of

b. Soundbox.

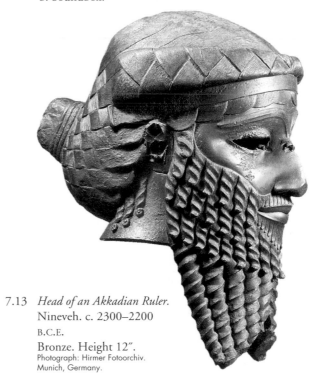

7.13 *Head of an Akkadian Ruler.*
Nineveh. c. 2300–2200
B.C.E.
Bronze. Height 12″.
Photograph: Hirmer Fotoorchiv.
Munich, Germany.

7.14 *The Great Pyramids.* Giza, Egypt. Pyramid of Mycerinus, c. 2500 B.C.E.; Pyramid of Chefren, 2650 B.C.E.; Pyramid of Cheops, c. 2570 B.C.E. Copyright SEF/Art Resource, NY.

military powers. Yet this disorder did not prevent the development and continuity of cultural traditions.

EGYPT

Deserts on both sides of the Nile diminished outside influences and enabled Egypt to develop distinctive styles of architecture, painting, and sculpture that remained relatively unchanged for 2,500 years—longer than the time from the birth of Christ to today. In our age of rapid cultural and technological change, such artistic stability is difficult to imagine.

Among the most impressive and memorable works of Egyptian civilization are *The Great Pyramids*, gigantic mountain-like structures built as burial vaults for pharaohs—rulers who were considered god-kings. Legions of workers cut huge stone blocks, moved them to the site, and stacked them, without mortar, to form the pyramidal structure. The interiors are mostly solid, with narrow passageways leading to small burial chambers.

Egyptian architects used a post-and-lintel system to create massive temples. Columns represent abstracted forms of plant life. These simplified stalks would later evolve into Greek columns.

Egyptian religious belief focused intently on life after death. Preservation of the body and care for the dead were considered essential for extending life beyond the grave. Upon death, bodies of royalty and nobility were embalmed; together with accompanying artifacts, tools, and furniture, they were then buried in pyramids or in hidden underground tombs. Architects put great effort into preventing access to these funerary structures. As a result, most of what we know about ancient Egypt comes from such tombs.

Names of many Egyptian architects are known in association with their buildings. A striking and well-preserved example is the *Funerary Temple of Queen Hatshepsut*, designed by Senmut, the queen's chancellor and architect. Complementing the majestic cliffs of the site, the ramps and colonnades provide an elegant setting for ritual pageantry. Wall paintings and reliefs at the site tell of an expedition that she funded to explore the legendary birthplace of the gods, and her own birth from

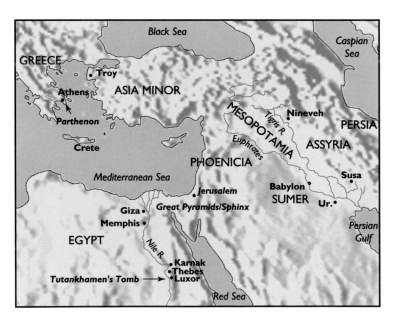

7.15 The Ancient Middle East.

the sun god Amen. This grandiose temple aided her effort to be taken seriously as a ruler in her own right, and the narrative art tells the first exploits of a famous woman in the history of art.

Egyptian sculpture is characterized by compact, solidly structured figures that embody qualities of strength and geometric clarity also found in Egyptian architecture. The final form of a piece of sculpture was determined by an underlying geometric plan that was first sketched on the surface of the stone block. The sculptor of *King Menkaura (Mycerinus) and Queen Khamerernebty* paid considerable attention to human anatomy yet stayed within the traditionally prescribed geometric scheme. The strength, clarity, and lasting stability expressed by the figures result from this union of naturalism and abstraction. With formal austerity, the couple stands in the frontal pose that had been established for royal portraits. Even so, the figures express warmth and vitality; the queen touches Mycerinus in a sympathetic, loving way. Typical of sculpture of this era are the formal pose with left foot forward, the false ceremonial beard, and figures that remain attached to the block of stone from which they were carved.

For a brief period, in the fourteenth century BCE, under the rule of the Emperor Akhenaten, the conventions of Egyptian art and culture were transformed. Akhenaten declared an end to traditional Egyptian religious practices, relaxing especially the longstanding preoccupation with the *ka,* and introducing a form of monotheism (the worship of a single god) into polytheistic Egypt. The sun god, manifested as a radiant sun disc—the Aten—embodied all the characteristics of the other Egyptian deities, and thus made them superfluous. Though the traditional standardized proportions of the human body were only slightly modified, artists seemed more intent on depicting special features of the human body—hands and fingers, the details of a face. Nowhere is this attention to detail more evident than in the famous bust of Akhenaten's queen, Nefertiti. Both the graceful curve of her neck and her almost completely relaxed look make for what seems to be a stunningly naturalistic arti-

7.16 *Funerary Temple of Queen Hatshepsut.* Deir el-Bahari, c. 1490–1460 B.C.E.
© Tom Till

7.17 *King Menkaura (Mycerinus) and Queen Khamerernebty.* Egyptian, Old Kingdom, Dynasty 4, reign of Menkaura, about 2490–2472 B.C. Egypt, Giza, Menkaure Valley Temple. Greywacke: 142.2 3 57.1 3 55.2 cm (56" 3 22½" 3 21¾").
Museum of Fine Arts, Boston. Harvard University-Boston Museum of Fine Arts Expedition, 1911. 11.1738. Photograph © 2006 Museum of Fine Arts, Boston.

fact, though it remains impossible to say if this is a true likeness or an idealized portrait.

Tutankhamen ("King Tut"), who died at age eighteen, is the best-known Egyptian ruler because his was the only Egyptian royal tomb discovered in modern times with most of its contents intact. The volume and value of the objects in the small tomb make it clear why grave robbers have been active in Egypt since the days of the first pharaohs. Tutankhamen's inlaid gold *Mask from Mummy Case* is but one of hundreds of extraordinary artifacts from the tomb. Its formal blend of naturalism and abstract idealism is distinctly Egyptian.

Egyptian artists in all media generally depicted the human figure either in a completely frontal position or in profile. Egyptian artists portrayed each object and each part of the human body from what they identified as its most characteristic angle, thus avoiding the ambiguity caused by random or chance angles of view (see also the *Pool in the Garden* on page 73).

In the *Wall Painting From the Tomb of Nebamun*, the painter of the hunting scene presented a wealth of specific information without making the painting confusing. Flat shapes portray basic elements of each subject in the clearest, most identifiable way. The head, hips, legs, and feet of the nobleman who dominates this painting are shown from the side, while his eye and shoulders are shown from the front. Sizes of human figures are determined by social rank, a system known as **hierarchic scale**; the nobleman is the largest figure, his wife is smaller, his daughter smaller still.

The family stands on a boat made of papyrus reeds; plants grow on the left at the shore. The entire painting is teeming with life, and the artist has even taken great care to show life below the water's surface. Attention to accurate detail lets us identify species of insects, birds, and fish. The hieroglyphics—the picture writing of ancient Egyptian priesthood—can be seen behind the figures.

Egyptian art greatly influenced that of early Greece, and the Greeks later developed one of the most important styles in Western art. To this period we now turn.

7.18   *Queen Nefertiti*, Tell el Amarna, c. 1365 BCE. Painted limestone, height 19⅝ in.
Agyptisches Museum, Berlin. Bildarchiv Preussischer Kulturbesitz / Art Resource, NY.
Figure 7.18 was taken from *A World of Art*, Sixth Edition by Henry M. Sayre.

7.19   *Mask from Mummy Case.*
Tomb of Tutankhamen. c. 1340 B.C.E. Gold inlaid with enamel and semiprecious stones. Height 21¼".
Photograph: SuperStock, Inc.

7.20 *Wall Painting from the Tomb of Nebamun.*
Thebes, Egypt. c. 1450 B.C.E.
Paint on dry plaster.
© The Trustees of the British Museum.

THE CLASSICAL AND MEDIEVAL WEST

If your definition of the word "beautiful" includes something ideal or perfect, then you have been influenced by classical Greece. Greece gave the West several concepts that we still value today. The classical cultures of Greece and Rome dominated Western civilization from the fifth century B.C.E. until the decline of Rome in the fifth century C.E. The later periods of Roman rule of Europe also saw the rise of Christianity, a faith that brought a wealth of new subjects to Western art.

The period between the fall of Rome and the beginning of the Renaissance is referred to as the Middle Ages or medieval period, a term that does little justice to the creativity of that era. If you attend a university, then you are at an institution that had its birth during the medieval period. Meanwhile, Eastern Europe was dominated by the Byzantine Empire, headquartered in Constantinople (today's Istanbul). Byzantine Christianity is today known as the Orthodox Church. Hence, Christianity of one form or another was a major force in the art of both Eastern and Western Europe for a thousand years.

GREECE

The Greeks distinguished themselves from other peoples of Europe and Asia by their attitude toward being human. They came to regard humankind as the highest creation of nature—the closest thing to perfection in physical form, coupled with the power to reason. Greek deities had human weaknesses, and Greek mortals had godlike strengths.

With this attitude came a new concept of the importance of the individual. The Greek focus on human potential and achievement led to the development of democracy and to the perfection of naturalistic images of the human figure in art. The philosopher Plato taught that behind the imperfections of transitory reality was the permanent, ideal form. Thus, to create the ideal individual (the supreme work of nature) became the goal of Greek artists.

Greek civilization passed through three broad stages: the Archaic period, the classical period, and the Hellenistic period. In the art of the Archaic period (from the late seventh to the early fifth centuries B.C.E.), the Greeks assimilated influences from Egypt and the Near East. Greek writers of the time tell us that Greek painters were often better known than Greek sculptors. Yet what we now see of Greek painting appears only on pottery because very few wall paintings survive. The elegant *Euphronios Krater* shows the level of achievement of Greek potters and painters. It is in the Archaic "red-figure" style and depicts a scene from Homer's *Odyssey*: the dead Trojan warrior Sarpedon, wounds gushing blood, is carried off to eternity by the gods of Sleep and Death. The painter Euphronios

Chapter 8: The Classical and Medieval West was taken from *Prebles' Artforms: An Introduction to the Visual Arts,* Tenth Edition by Patrick Frank.

8.1 *Euphronios Krater.* c. 515 B.C.E.
Terracotta. Height 18″, diameter 21¾″.
Scala/Ministero per i Beni e le Attività culturali/Art Resource, NY.

8.2 *Kouros.* Statue of standing youth. Greek, Attic.
c. 580 B.C. Said to be from the neighborhood of
anavyssos. Marble.
Height 76″ (193 cm).
Photograph © The Metropolitan Musuem of Art/Art Resource.

signed the work; the word **krater** refers to the vessel's handled shape, traditionally used for mixing
ceremonial beverages.

The Greeks honored individual achievement
by creating numerous life-size, freestanding statues of nude male and clothed female figures. The
Archaic-style *Kouros* has a rigid frontal position that
is an adaptation from Egyptian sculpture. (**Kouros**
is Greek for male youth; **kore** is the word for
female youth.) The Egyptian figure of *Mycerinus*
(page 131) and the *Kouros* both stand with arms
held straight at the sides, fingers drawn up, and left
leg forward with the weight evenly distributed on
both feet as they stare off into space.

In spite of the similarity of stance, however,
the character of Greek sculpture is already quite
different from that of Egyptian. The *Kouros* is freestanding, and it honors an individual who was not
a supernatural ruler. The *Kouros* thus reflects Greek
cultural values.

Within one hundred years after the making
of the *Kouros* figure, Greek civilization entered

its classical phase (480–323 B.C.E.). Greek aesthetic principles from this period provide the basis
for the concept of classicism. **Classical** art emphasizes rational simplicity, order, and restrained emotion. The rigid poses of Egyptian and early Greek
figures gave way to a greater interest in anatomy
and more relaxed poses. Sculpture became increasingly naturalistic and began to show the body as
alive and capable of movement, all within an overall program of idealism.

The statue known as the *Spear Bearer* is an
excellent example of Greek classicism. The sculp-

tor Polykleitos wrote a treatise on the perfect proportions of the human form and created this statue as an example. Neither the book nor the original statue survives, but both are known from documents and later copies. Polykleitos envisioned the human body as a harmonious set of divinely inspired ratios. By studying numerous models, he arrived at what he thought were the ideal proportions of the human body. Hence, the *Spear Bearer* combines actual observations with mathematical calculation.

The statue depicts an athlete who once held a spear on his left shoulder. Typical of classical art, the figure is in the prime of life, and blemish-free. It is not a portrait of an individual but rather a vision of the ideal. He bears most of his weight on one leg in a pose known as **contrapposto**, meaning counterpoised. The Greeks and then the Romans used this pose to give a lifelike quality to figures at rest. Centuries later, their sculpture would inspire Renaissance artists to use the same technique.

The city-state of Athens was the artistic and philosophical center of classical Greek civilization. Above the city, on a large rock outcropping called the Acropolis, the Athenians constructed one of the world's most admired structures, the *Parthenon*. Even in its current ruined state, the *Parthenon* continues to express the ideals of the people who created it.

The largest of several sacred buildings on the Acropolis, the *Parthenon* was designed and built as a gift to Athena Parthenos, goddess of wisdom, prudent warfare, and protector of the Athenian navy.

When Ictinus and Callicrates designed the *Parthenon,* they were follow-

8.3 Polykleitos of Argos. 5th century B.C.E. *Spear Bearer (Doryphoros).* Roman copy of Greek original. c. 440 B.C.E. Marble. Height 6′6″.
Courtesy of Scala/Ministero per I Beni e la Attivita culturali/Art Resource, NY.

ing Egyptian tradition of temple design based on the post-and-beam system of construction. Rites were performed on altars placed in front of the eastern entrance; the interior space held a forty-foot statue of Athena. The axis of the building was carefully calculated so that on Athena's birthday the rising sun coming through the east doorway would fully illuminate the towering (now lost) gold-covered statue.

The *Parthenon* exhibits the refined clarity, harmony, and vigor that are the basis of the Greek tradition. The proportions of the *Parthenon* are based on harmonious ratios. The ratio of the height to the widths of the east and west ends is approximately 4 to 9. The ratio of the width to the length of the building is also 4 to 9. The diameter of the columns relates to the space between the columns at a ratio of 4 to 9, and so on.

None of the major lines in the building are perfectly straight. The columns have an almost imperceptible bulge (called **entasis**) above the center, which causes them to appear straighter than if they were in fact straight-sided, and this gives the entire structure a tangible grace. Even the steps and tops of doorways rise slightly in perfect curves. Corner columns, seen against the light, are somewhat larger in diameter to counteract the diminishing effect of strong light in the background. The axis lines of the columns lean inward a little at the top. If extended into space, these lines would converge about a mile above the building. These unexpected variations are not consciously seen, but they

a. View from the northwest.
Photograph: Duane Preble.

b. View from the southwest.
Photograph: Duane Preble.

8.4 Ictinus and Callicrates.
Parthenon. Acropolis, Athens. 448–432 B.C.E.

c. *The Battle of the Lapiths and Centaurs.*
Metope from the Parthenon. c. 440 B.C.E.
Marble. Height 67¾".
Art Resource, NY.

are felt, and they help make the building visually appealing and correct optical illusions.

The sculptural program of the *Parthenon* shows specific aspects of the culture of that time. Athens had just concluded a successful war to resist a Persian invasion, and the costs of the *Parthenon* were paid from leftover war contributions collected from other Greek cities.

Surrounding the entire building just above the colonnade, the designers installed evenly spaced square panels called **metopes**; these,

too, promote Greek culture. The theme of the metopes is *The Battle of the Lapiths and Centaurs*: In an ancient myth, the Lapiths were ruled by reason, and the Centaurs were violent and unpredictable; when the Centaurs kidnapped the Queen of the Lapiths, the Lapiths went to war and defeated the Centaurs in battle. Just as order and reason triumphed in that ancient conflict, the democratic Greeks had defeated the despotic Persians. Thus, recent events confirmed the ultimate triumph of the Greek worldview.

The Battle of the Parthenon

THE PARTHENON MARBLES are among the world's most venerated artworks, but they are also among the most hotly contested. The majority of the sculptural decorations from the Parthenon, including many metopes and *The Three Goddesses* from the pediment, are in the British Museum; the Greeks have been seeking their return for many years. You could call it The Battle of the Parthenon.

The sculptures were removed between 1801 and 1810 by Lord Elgin, ambassador to the Ottoman Empire, which then controlled Greece. He claimed that the Ottoman sultan gave him permission to do so. Lord Elgin sold them to the British government in 1816, at which time they entered the British Museum collection.

The Greeks have been insisting with increasing urgency since 1965 that the marbles need to be reunited in Athens, where they were created, but the British have refused every request. According to a British Museum statement:

"The Museum is open seven days a week, free of charge, and attracts more than 6 million visitors a year from all parts of the world. The sculptures from the Parthenon constitute one of the greatest and best-loved of its treasures; and the fact that they exemplify, in a unique manner, the aesthetic genius of classical antiquity, which has exerted so profound an influence on the subsequent history of mankind, makes it all the more appropriate that they should find their setting in a Museum which is universal in its scope and designed to present as complete and integrated a picture as possible of the development of different, but related, cultures through the ages."

8.5 *Three Goddesses.*
Pediment sculpture from the Parthenon, Athens. 438–432 B.C.E.
Marble. Height 4'5".
Art Resource, NY.

The Greeks assert in response that Greece was under foreign domination when the marbles were removed, and thus the taking was illegal because no Greek government ever agreed to it.

Some British members of Parliament asserted that the Greeks had no facilities to care properly for the works. This objection was removed in mid-2009 with the opening of the new Acropolis Museum, a state-of-the-art facility where several rooms are reserved for just these pieces.

Many English people believe that because the British Museum cared for the works for almost 200 years, they have earned the right to possess them. The Greeks respond that British care was not always exemplary: Lord Elgin's ship ran aground and sank off the coast of France, causing untold damage. Moreover, the sculptures were scrubbed

with wire brushes in 1937, a grievous error that the Museum kept secret for sixty years.

The British position on returning the works hinges finally on legality: Having bought them, it claims legal right to the pieces. The Greeks question those legalities. Moreover, they assert moral claims that the works are fundamental to the Greek culture, and that the Parthenon sculptures are best viewed in one location as the architects of the Parthenon intended.

The Battle of the Parthenon is likely to continue, probably at the level of verbal salvos. This is because museum professionals generally believe that returning the Parthenon sculptures would set a bad precedent. Most of the world's major museums hold many works of art that were acquired under similar conditions that would not be permitted today.

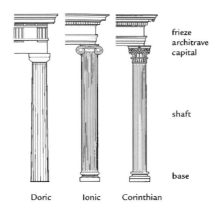

frieze
architrave
capital

shaft

base

Doric   Ionic   Corinthian

8.6 *Architectural Orders.*

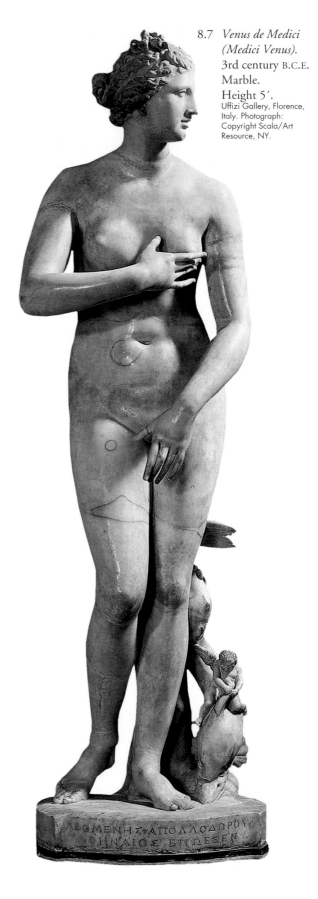

8.7 *Venus de Medici (Medici Venus).* 3rd century B.C.E. Marble. Height 5′. Uffizi Gallery, Florence, Italy. Photograph: Copyright Scala/Art Resource, NY.

On the **pediment** (the triangular area atop the narrow end) the designers set a large sculptural group that depicted the birth of Athena. The implication was that just as Wisdom was once born on Mount Olympus, Wisdom was reborn in Athens, the city of Athena. The sculptural group *The Three Goddesses* shows the news of the birth spreading: The leftmost goddess is about to stand, the central figure just beginning to notice, and the rightmost is still in repose. Even in their current fragmentary condition, the figures wonderfully convey three emotional states. Many of the Parthenon sculptures are the subject of a long-running international dispute, as the essay *The Battle of the Parthenon* shows.

The Greeks developed three *Architectural Orders:* Doric, Ionic, and Corinthian. Each order comprises a set of architectural elements and proportions. The most telling details for identification of the orders are the three types of **capitals** used at the tops of columns. Doric, which came first, is simple, geometric, and sturdy; Ionic is taller and more decorative than Doric; Corinthian is complex and organic. The *Parthenon* is in the Doric order, the first of the three to be developed.

During the latter part of the classical period (the late fourth century B.C.E.), Greek sculpture took a turn away from the noble and serious idealism of the *Three Goddesses* and the *Spear Bearer* toward a more sensuous vision. *Venus de Medici* is a Roman copy of a fourth-century B.C.E. Greek original by Praxiteles, the best-known sculptor of this time. Nude goddesses were unknown in previous periods. Its refined profile and modest pose are features of the Greek idealization of human figures. This figure came to represent a feminine ideal, and has strongly influenced many art works since that time, down to the feminists of the twentieth century who rejected it.

After the decline of the Greek city-states at the end of the fourth century B.C.E., the art of the Mediterranean changed. Though Greek art was still the strongest influence, the art was often produced for non-Greek patrons. Thus, Mediterranean art during this era is called *Hellenistic*, meaning Greek-like. The transition from classical to Hellenistic coincided with the decline of Athens as a city-state after it fought a useless war with the neighboring city of Sparta, and with the rise of an absolute monarchy in Macedonia that soon took over the entire peninsula. Most historians date the period

from approximately the death of Alexander the Great (323 B.C.E.) to the Roman conquest of Egypt (30 B.C.E.). Artists turned from the idealized restraint of the classical period to the subjective and imperfect aspects of life and humanity.

In the Hellenistic period, Greek art became more dynamic and less idealized. Everyday activities, historical subjects, and portraiture became more common subjects for art. Hellenistic Greek art contrasts with classical Greek art in that it is more expressive and frequently shows exaggerated movement.

The *Nike of Samothrace* is a masterpiece of Hellenistic realism. The goddess has been depicted as she alights on the prow of a victorious war galley, and one can almost feel the wind as it buffets her, and the surf spray that has soaked her garment so that it clings revealingly to her torso.

The *Laocoön Group* is a Roman copy of a Hellenistic work. In Greek mythology, Laocoön was the Trojan priest who warned against bringing the wooden horse into Troy during the Trojan War. Later,

8.8 *Nike of Samothrace,* c. 190 BCE.
Marble, height approximately 8 ft.
Courtesy of Réunion des Musées Nationaux/Art Resource, NY.

8.9 *The Laocoön Group.*
Roman copy of a 1st- or 2nd-century B.C.E. Greek original, perhaps after Agesander, Athenodorus, and Polydorus of Rhodes. c. 1st century C.E. Marble. Height 95¼″.
Vatican Museum, Vatican State, Rome. Photograph: Copyright Giraudon/Art Resource, NY.

Figure 8.8 was taken from *A World of Art,* Sixth Edition by Henry M. Sayre.

he and his sons were attacked by serpents, an act the Trojans interpreted as a sign of the gods' disapproval of Laocoön's prophecy. Laocoön is shown in hierarchic proportion to his sons.

The rationalism, clarity, and restraint of classical sculpture have given way to writhing movement, tortured facial expressions, and strained muscles expressing emotional and physical anguish. When this sculpture was unearthed in Italy in 1506, it had an immediate influence on the young Michelangelo.

ROME

The Hellenistic era saw the rise of Rome, a formidable new force in the Mediterranean. By the second century B.C.E., Rome had become the major power in the Western world. At its height, the Roman Empire would include Western Europe, North Africa, and the Near East as well as the shores of the Mediterranean. The governance of a multitude of unique peoples and cultures was a prime example of the Roman genius for order and practical politics. Roman culture has affected our lives in many areas: our systems of law and government, our calendar, festivals, religions, and languages. Roman art reflects this need to administer a huge empire.

The Romans were practical, less idealistic than the Greeks, and their art reflects these characteristics. They admired, collected, and copied Greek works, but their own art was not merely imitative. Roman portraiture of the Republican period, such as the *Portrait Head of an Old Man*, achieved a high degree of individuality rarely found in Greek sculpture. The warts-and-all style probably grew out of the Roman custom of making wax death masks of ancestors for the family shrine or altar. Later, these images were recreated in marble to make them more durable. Roman sculptors observed and carefully recorded those physical details and imperfections that give character to each person's face.

The Romans' greatest artistic achievements were in civil engineering, town planning, and architecture. They created utilitarian and religious structures of impressive beauty and grandeur that

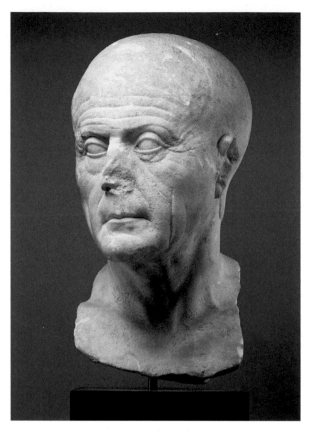

8.10 *Portrait Head of an Old Man.* Unknown. Italy. 25 B.C. – 10 A.D. Marble. Height 34.9 3 17.7 3 24.7 cm (13¾" 3 6¹⁵⁄₁₆" 3 9¾"). The J. Paul Getty Museum, Villa Collection, Malibu, California.

had a major influence on later Western architecture. The outstanding feature of Roman architecture was the semicircular arch, which the Romans utilized and refined in the construction of arcades, barrel vaults, and domes.

The most spectacular surviving example of a Roman public works project is the *Colosseum*. Built by the Flavian family between 68 and 80 C.E., it is sometimes known as the Flavian Amphitheater. The foundation of the *Colosseum* is an elliptical ring of concrete over 44 feet high. Brick, stone, and marble blocks complete the structure. The exterior is a three-story round-arch colonnade, with each level a different architectural order; each round arch on the lower floors opens to a concrete barrel vault. The principal use of the building was for amusements such as gladiatorial matches and wild game hunts. Its capacity was between 50,000 and 75,000 spectators, about as many as today's sports stadiums (a more accurate guess is impossible because much of the exterior marble was carried off during the middle ages). The Flavian family likely built the *Colosseum* to improve its public image and thus its legitimacy as rulers.

By developing the structural use of concrete combined with semicircular arch and vault construction, the Romans were also able to enclose large indoor spaces. In the *Pantheon*, a major temple dedicated to all the gods, Roman builders created a domed interior space of immense scale. The building is essentially a cylinder, capped by a hemispherical dome, with a single entrance framed by a columned porch, or **portico**. Because *The Interior of the Pantheon* is dimly lit and difficult to photograph, we see it in a famous 1734 painting (see fig. 8.13).

The Greeks had neither the need nor the technology to create buildings with huge interior spaces; their *Parthenon* was meant as a backdrop for outdoor ceremonies. In contrast, the *Pantheon* is a magnificent, awe-inspiring interior space that complemented its once opulent exterior. To meet their preference and need for spacious interiors, the Romans developed many other great domed and vaulted buildings.

8.11 *The Colosseum.*
Rome. 70–80 C.E.
Art Resource, NY.

The *Pantheon's* circular walls, which support the huge dome, are stone and concrete masonry, twenty feet thick and faced with brick. The dome diminishes in thickness toward the crown, and it is patterned on the interior surface with recessed squares called **coffers**, which both lighten and strengthen the structure. Originally covered with gold, the coffered ceiling symbolizes the dome

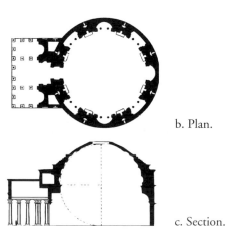

8.12 Pantheon. Rome. 118–125 C.E.
a. View of the entrance.
Photograph: Duane Preble.

b. Plan.

c. Section.

8.13 Giovanni Paolo Panini. *The Interior of the Pantheon, Rome.* c. 1734. Oil on canvas. 1.280 ⅹ .990 cm (50½" ⅹ 39").

8.14 Europe from 117 to 1400.

of heaven. The distance from the summit to the floor is equal to the 143-foot diameter, making the *Pantheon* a virtual globe of space. At the dome's crown, an opening called an **oculus**, or eye, thirty feet in diameter, provides daylight and ventilation to the interior. Neither verbal description nor views of the exterior and interior can evoke the awe many visitors experience on entering the *Pantheon.*

Wall paintings show the Roman love of luxury. The majority of surviving Roman paintings come from Pompeii, Herculaneum, and other towns buried—and thus preserved—by the eruption of Mt. Vesuvius in 79 C.E. In the first century, Roman artists continued the late Greek tradition of portraying depth in paintings of landscapes and urban views. The *Roman Painting* from a villa near Naples presents a complex urban scene painted with a form of perspective inherited from Hellenistic murals. As is typical of Roman painting, the receding lines are not systematically related to one another to create a sense of common space, nor is there controlled use of the effect of diminishing size relative to distance. (In other words, neither one-point perspective nor recession in space was practiced.) Perhaps the artist intended viewers simply to enjoy the pleasing interwoven shapes, patterns, colors, and varied scale. After the collapse of the Roman Empire, representation of the third dimension ceased to be of interest, and the knowledge was forgotten until it was rediscovered and developed as a scientific system during the Renaissance, more than one thousand years later.

EARLY CHRISTIAN AND BYZANTINE ART

The Romans first regarded Christianity as a strange cult and suppressed it through law. This forced the followers of Christ to worship and hide their art in private homes and underground burial chambers called **catacombs**. The earliest Christian art was a simplified interpretation of Greco-Roman figure painting, with a new emphasis on storytelling through images of Christ and other biblical figures, as well as through symbols. *Christ and the Apostles* shows a beardless Christ, dressed like a Roman senator, only slightly larger than the faithful who surround him.

8.15 *Roman Painting.*
1st century BC. Bedroom from the villa of P. Fannius Synistor at Boscoreale, Pompei. Detail #1: west wall, panel with ornate door to fantastic villa at Boscoreale. Fresco on lime plaster, height (average) 8′.
Photograph © The Metropolitan Musuem of Art/Art Resource.

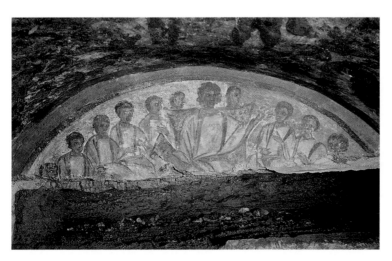

8.16 *Christ and the Apostles.*
Early Christian fresco. Catacomb of S. Domitilla, Rome, Italy. Mid-4th century C.E.
Photograph: Copyright Scala/Art Resource, NY.

By the time Emperor Constantine acknowledged Christianity in 313, Roman attitudes had changed considerably. The grandeur of Rome was rapidly declining. As confidence in the stability of the material world fell, more people turned toward the spiritual values that Christianity offered. Constantine pioneered a new type of imperial portrait, as we see in the *Head of Constantine*. It is beardless, colossal (eight feet high), and with bulging, oversized eyes. Constantine was the first Christian emperor; he attributed all of his successes to the Christian God, rather than to military genius as his predecessors had done.

In 330, Constantine moved the capital of the Roman Empire east from Rome to the city of Byzantium, which he renamed Constantinople (present-day Istanbul). Although he could not have known it, the move would effectively split the empire in two. In 395, the Roman Empire was officially divided, with one emperor in Rome and another in Constantinople. The latter city became known as Byzantium, capital of the Byzantine Empire. Over the course of the next century, the Western empire was repeatedly attacked by nomadic German tribes. They placed one of their own on the imperial throne in 476, a convenient marker for the end of the Roman Empire. Under attack from the tribes, and weakened from within by military rebellions and civil wars, the political unity of the Western Roman Empire decayed, ushering in the era in Europe known as the Middle Ages.

The eastern portion of the empire, however, did not collapse. Indeed, the Byzantine Empire survived well into the fifteenth century. Founded as a Christian continuation of the Roman Empire, Byzantium developed a rich and distinctive artistic style that continues today in the mosaics, paintings, and architecture of the Orthodox churches of Eastern Europe.

Not only did Constantine grant Christianity official recognition, he also sponsored an extensive building program. Thus, in the late Roman and early Byzantine empires, we find the first flowering of Christian art and architecture. For example, Christians adapted the Roman **basilica**, or assembly hall, for use in public worship. The original Roman basilica was a long hall flanked by columns with a semicircular **apse** at each end where government bodies and law courts met. One of the earliest Christian churches was *Old St. Peter's Basilica* in Rome. Its long central aisle, now called the **nave**, ends in an apse, as in a Roman building. Here, Christians placed an altar.

In contrast to the external grandeur of Greek and Roman temples, early Christian churches were built with an inward focus. Their plain exteriors gave no hint of the light and beauty that lay inside.

The rapid construction of many large churches created a need for large paintings or other decorations to fill their walls. Mosaic technique was perfected and widely used in early Christian churches. Although other cultures knew the art of attaching pieces of colored glass and marble (**tesserae**) to walls and floors, early Christians used smaller tesserae,

8.17 *Head of Constantine.*
c. 312 C.E. Marble. Height 8′.
Museo dei Conservatori, Rome. Photograph: Duane Preble.

8.18 Old St. Peter's Basilica. Rome. c. 320–335.

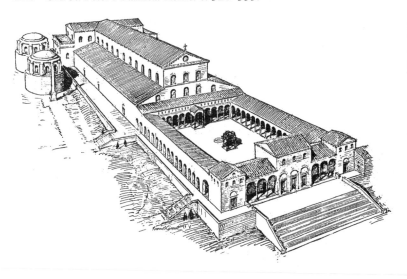

a. Reconstruction drawing.
Kenneth J. Conant, "Old St. Peter's Basilica, Rome." Restoration study. Courtesy of the Frances Loeb Library, Graduate School of Design, Harvard University.

b. Interior view of basilica of Old Saint Peter's.
Fresco. S. Martino ai Monti, Rome, Italy.
Photograph: Copyright Scala/Art Resource, NY.

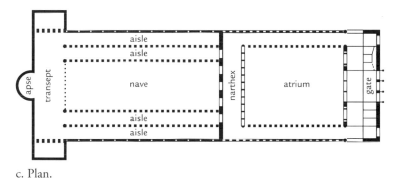

c. Plan.

with a greater proportion of glass, in a wider range of colors. Thus, they achieved a new level of brilliance and opulence.

We see the transition from Early Christian to Byzantine styles in the churches of Ravenna, an old Roman city about 80 miles south of Venice. Hoping to avoid the Germanic invasions, the Roman emperor moved his capital there in 404. When the Western empire fell in 476, Ravenna remained an important administrative center. However, emperor Justinian sent an army from his capital in Constantinople and reconquered it in 540, turning it into a showplace of Byzantine culture on the Italian peninsula.

The most important sixth-century Byzantine church is *San Vitale* in Ravenna. The glittering mosaic compositions that cover most of the interior surfaces depict the figures of Emperor Justinian and *Empress Theodora* in addition to religious figures and events. In a blending of religious and political authority, Justinian and Theodora are shown with halos, analogous to Christ and Mary, yet both are royally attired and bejeweled.

The elongated, abstracted figures provide symbolic rather than naturalistic depictions of the Christian and royal figures. Emphasis on the eyes is a Byzantine refinement of the stylized focus seen in the *Head of Constantine* (page 146). Figures are depicted with heavy outline and stylized shading. The only suggestion of space has been made by overlap. Background and figures retain a flat, decorative richness typical of Byzantine art.

a. Exterior.
Photograph: Copyright Scala/Art Resource, NY.

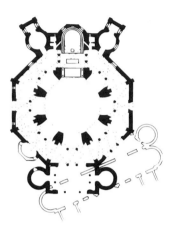

b. Plan.

c. *Empress Theodora.*
Mosaic detail.
Photograph: Copyright Scala/Art Resource, NY.

8.19 *San Vitale.*
Ravenna, Italy. 526–547.

d. Apse Mosaic.
Photograph: Copyright Scala/Art Resource, NY.

The arts of the Early Christian period were affected by an ongoing controversy between those who sought to follow the biblical prohibition against the making of images and those who wanted pictures to help tell the sacred stories. The Byzantine style developed as a way of inspiring the illiterate while keeping the biblical commandment that forbids the making of graven images. Byzantine theory held that highly stylized (abstract) and decorative images could never be confused with a real person, as a naturalistic work might be. As a result, the naturalism and sense of depth found in Roman painting gradually gave way to Byzantine **stylization**.

The apse mosaic in the interior of *San Vitale* shows Christ dressed in royal purple and seated on an orb that symbolizes the universe. He is beardless, in the fashion of classical gods. With his right hand, he passes a crown to San Vitale, who stands in a depiction of the biblical paradise along with other saints and angels. The appearance of all of these figures owes something to Roman art, but in keeping with Byzantine style, they stand motionless and stare straight ahead. In their heavenly majesty, they seem to soar above human concerns.

One of the most magnificent domes in the world was designed for the Byzantine cathedral of *Hagia Sophia* (Holy Wisdom) in Istanbul, Turkey. It was built in the sixth century as the central sanctuary of the Eastern Orthodox Christian Church. After the Islamic conquest of 1453, **minarets** (towers) were added and it was used as a mosque. It is now a museum. The dome of *Hagia Sophia* rests on curving triangular sections called **pendentives** over a square base.

Hagia Sophia's distinctive dome appears to float on a halo of light—an effect produced by the row of windows encircling its base. The huge dome is supported on what appears to be a larger dome with its top and sides removed. Pendentives carry the enormous weight from the circular base of the upper dome downward to a square formed by supporting walls.

In the eighth and ninth centuries, the Byzantine Empire was wracked by the Iconoclastic Controversy, a debate over religious images that at times turned violent. In 726, Byzantine Emperor Leo III ordered the destruction of all images of Christ, Mary, the saints, and the angels. He and his party believed that such images encouraged idolatry, or worship of the image rather than the divine being. They were soon termed **iconoclasts**, or image-breakers, and they punished persons who owned images by flogging or blinding them. (The iconoclasts did not resist all decoration; they permitted jeweled crosses and pictures of leafy paradises, for example.) Those who favored images (the iconophiles) argued that just as Christ was both god and human, an image of Christ combines the spiritual and the physical.

Although the Emperor's decree was not uniformly enforced, the controversy lasted for more than a hundred years, and it contributed to the split between the Roman Catholic and Eastern Orthodox churches. There was a political struggle as well: The iconoclasts favored the Emperor's power over that of local monasteries, which were wealthy with sumptuous images. The dispute finally came to an end in 843, when Empress Theodora officially overturned Leo's decree.

As the controversy subsided, the inside of the dome of Hagia Sophia was adorned with a new kind of image, Christ as ruler of the universe, or Pantocrator. This mosaic (now destroyed) became the inspiration for similar portrayals in

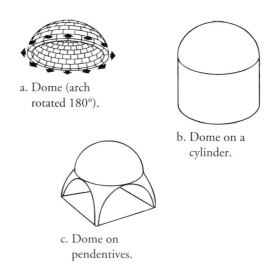

a. Dome (arch rotated 180°).

b. Dome on a cylinder.

c. Dome on pendentives.

8.20 *Dome.*

a. Exterior.

b. Interior.

8.21 *Hagia Sophia.* 532–535.
Istanbul, Turkey.
Copyright Erich Lessing/Art Resource, NY.

smaller Byzantine churches such as the Cathedral of Monreale, Sicily, where the mosaic of *Christ as Pantocrator with Mary and Saints* shows typical Byzantine style employing hierarchic scale to express the greater magnitude of Christ relative to Mary, the saints, and angels portrayed in rows below him.

By the tenth and eleventh centuries, Byzantine artists had created a distinct style that expressed Eastern Orthodox Christianity and also met the needs of a lavish court. The style had its roots in the Early Christian art of the late Roman Empire, as we have seen. But it also absorbed Eastern influences, particularly the flat patterns and nonrepresentational designs of Islam. Eastern influence continued with the hierarchical sizing and placement of subject matter in Byzantine church decoration.

The Byzantine style is still followed by painters and others working within the tradition of the Eastern Orthodox church. Clergy closely supervise the iconography and permit little room for individual interpretation. Artists of the Eastern Orthodox faith seek to portray the symbolic or mystical aspects of religious figures rather than their physical qualities. The figures are painted in conformity to a precise formula. Small paintings, referred to as **icons** (from the Greek *eikon*, meaning image), are holy images that inspire devotion but are not worshipped in themselves. The making of portable icon paintings grew out of mosaic and fresco traditions.

Even within the relatively tight stylistic confines of the Orthodox style, occasionally an artist is able to make icons that not only have the required easy readability but also communicate powerful feeling. Such an artist was Andrei Rublev, one of the most highly regarded painters in Russian history. His *Old Testament Trinity* depicts a story in which Jewish patriarch Abraham entertained three strangers who later turned out to be angels: Christians have seen this story as foreshadowing their doctrine of the trinity. Rublev gave the scene a sweetness and tenderness through subtle facial expressions and elongation of bodies. The bright colors add intensity to the work, even in its present poor state.

8.22   *Christ as Pantocrator with Mary and Saints.*
Apse mosaic. Cathedral of Monreale, Sicily. Late 12th century.
Photograph: Copyright Scala/Art Resource, NY.

8.23   Andrei Rublev.
Icon of the Old Testament Trinity. c. 1410.
Tempera on panel. 55½" 3 44½".
Tretyakov Gallery, Moscow. Photograph: Copyright Scala/
Art Resource, NY.

The design of the icon painting *Madonna and Child on a Curved Throne* is based on circular shapes and linear patterns. Mary's head repeats the circular shape of her halo; circles of similar size enclose angels, echoing the larger circle of the throne. The lines and shapes used in the draped robes that cover the figures give scarcely a hint of the bodies beneath. Divine light is symbolized by the gold background that surrounds the throne in which the Virgin Mary sits. The large architectural throne symbolizes Mary's position as Queen of the City of Heaven. Christ appears as a wise little man, supported on the lap of a heavenly, supernatural mother.

In order that they be worthy of dedication to God, icons are usually made of precious materials. Gold leaf was used here for the background and costly lapis lazuli for the Virgin's robe.

8.24 Byzantine School.
Madonna and Child on a Curved Throne.
Byzantine, 13th century.
Tempera on panel. .815 3 .490 cm (32⅛″ 3
19⅜″); framed: .908 3 583 3 .076 cm (35¾″ 3
22¹⁵⁄₁₆″ 3 3″).

THE MIDDLE AGES IN EUROPE

The one thousand years that followed the fall of the Western Roman Empire have been called the medieval period, or the Middle Ages, because they came between the fall of the Roman Empire and the rebirth, or renaissance, of Greco-Roman ideas in the fifteenth century. The age that gave us transcendent cathedrals also gave birth to memorable art works in many media.

Early Medieval Art

The art of the early Middle Ages took shape as Early Christian art absorbed a new influence: the art of the invaders. Many nomadic peoples traveled across the Eurasian grasslands, which extend from northwest China to central Europe. Their migrations occurred over a long period that began in the second millennium B.C.E. and lasted well into the Middle Ages. The Greeks called these nomads (and other non-Greeks) "barbarians." What little we know about them is derived from artifacts and records of literate cultures of the Mediterranean, Near East, and China, to whom the nomads were a menace. Both the Great Wall of China and Hadrian's Wall in Britain were built to keep out such invaders.

Eurasian nomads created a distinctive style known as the **animal style.** Because of their migrant way of life, their art consisted of small, easily portable objects such as personal adornments, weapons, and fittings for saddles and harnesses. The style is characterized by active, intertwining shapes. The art of the animal style rarely depicts human beings; when it does, they play subordinate roles to animals.

Nomadic metalwork often exhibits exceptional skill. Because of frequent migrations and the durability and value of the art objects, the style was diffused over large geographic areas. Among the best-known works of nomadic art are small gold and bronze ornaments such as the *Scythian Animal.* The Scythian culture flourished between the eighth and fourth centuries B.C.E. across a wide area from the northern Black Sea to western China. Their abstracted animal forms influenced groups in the British Isles and Scandinavia. Two animal forms dominate the composition of this piece; we see their heads near the top and bottom.

The gold and enamel *Purse Cover* found in a grave at Sutton Hoo belonged to a seventh-century East Anglian king. The distinct variations of its motifs indicate that they are derived from several sources. The motif of a man standing between confronting animals appeared first in Sumerian art over three thousand years earlier (see page 129).

8.25 *Scythian Animal.*
(Bridle Plaque with a Beast of Prey Curved Round).
Scythian culture. 5th century B.C. Bronze.
10.5 3 9.7 cm.
Kulakovsky Barrow No. 2; Crimea. The State Hermitage Museum,
St. Petersburg, Russia.

The meeting of decorative nomadic styles with
Christianity can be seen most clearly in the illustrated holy books created in Ireland. The Irish had
never been part of the Roman Empire, and in the
fifth century they were Christianized without first
becoming Romanized. During the chaotic centuries that followed the fall of Rome, Irish monasteries became the major centers of learning and the
arts in Europe, and they produced numerous hand-
lettered copies of religious manuscripts.

The initial letters in these manuscripts were
increasingly embellished over time, moving first
into the margin and then onto a separate page.
This splendid initial page is the opening of St.
Matthew's account of the Nativity in the *Book of
Kells,* which contains the Latin Gospels. It is known
as the *Chi-Rho Monogram* because it is composed
of the first two letters of Christ in Greek (*XP*) and
is used to represent Christ or Christianity. Except
for *XP* and two Latin words beginning the story of
Christ's birth, most of the page is filled with a rich
complexity of spirals and tiny interlacings. If we
look closely at the knots and scrolls we see angels
to the left of the X, a man's head in the P, and cats
and mice at the base.

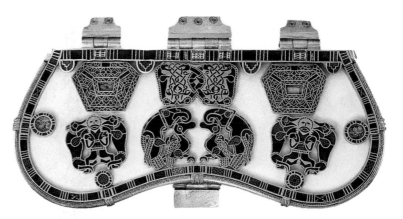

8.26 Purse Cover.
From the Sutton Hoo Ship Burial, Suffolk, England.
Before 655. Gold and enamel. Length 7½″.

8.27 *Chi-Rho Monogram (XP).*
TCD MS 58. Page from the *Book of Kells.* FOL 34 r. Late
8th century. Inks and pigments on vellum. 12¾″ 3 9½″.

Romanesque

The stylistic term **Romanesque** was first used to designate European Christian architecture of the mid-eleventh to the mid-twelfth centuries, which revived Roman principles of stone construction, especially the round arch and the barrel vault. This term is now applied to all medieval art of Western Europe during that period.

Romanesque art developed in a Western Europe dominated by feudalism and monasticism. Feudalism involved a complex system of obligations to provide services through personal agreements among local leaders of varying ranks. In addition to accommodating religious practices, monasteries provided shelter from a hostile world and served as the main sources of education.

Churches continued to have wooden roofs, but stone vaults gradually replaced fire-prone wooden ceilings, giving the new structures a close resemblance to Roman interiors. Consistent throughout the variety of regional styles was a common feeling of security provided by massive, fortress-like walls.

Romanesque churches feature imaginative stone carvings that are an integral part of the architecture.

Subjects and models came from miniature paintings in illuminated texts, but sculptors gradually added a degree of naturalism not found in earlier medieval work. In addition to stylized and at times naive figures from biblical stories, relief carvings include strange beasts and decorative plant forms. The largest and most elaborate figures were placed over the central doorways of churches. Such figures were the first large sculpture since Roman times.

Deviation from standard human proportions enabled sculptors to give appropriately symbolic form to figures such as *Christ of the Pentecost*. The mystical energy and compassion of Christ are expressed in this relief carving above the doorway of Saint Madeleine Cathedral at Vézelay, France. As worshippers enter the sanctuary, the image above them depicts Christ at the time he asked the apostles and all Christians to take his message to the world. The image of Christ is larger in scale than the other figures, showing his relative importance. The sculptor achieved a monumental quality by making the head smaller than normal and by elongating the entire figure. Swirling folds of drapery are indicated with precise curves and spirals that show the continuing influence of the

8.28 *Christ of the Pentecost.*
Saint Madeleine Cathedral, Vézelay, France.
1125–1150. Stone. Height of the tympanum 35½".
Courtesy of the Bridgeman Art Library.

linear energy of the animal style and the *Chi-Rho Monogram.* Surrounding Christ and the apostles are depictions of the peoples of the world; in the round medallions we see the signs of the zodiac and the monthly tasks associated with each.

Gothic

The Romanesque style had lasted barely a hundred years when the **Gothic** style began to replace it in about 1145. The shift is seen most clearly in architecture, as the Romanesque round arch was superseded by the Gothic pointed arch. This new advance, coupled with the flying buttress, made possible some of the most spectacular religious buildings ever seen.

Gothic cathedrals were expressions of a new age of faith that grew out of medieval Christian theology and mysticism. The light-filled, upward-reaching structures symbolize the triumph of the spirit over the bonds of earthly life, evoking a sense of joyous spiritual elation. Inside, the faithful must have felt they had actually arrived at the visionary Heavenly City.

Gothic cathedrals such as *Notre Dame de Chartres* (Our Lady of Chartres) were the center of community life. In many cases, they were the only

8.29 *Notre Dame de Chartres.*
Chartres, France. 1145–1513. Cathedral length 427´; facade height 157´; south tower height 344´; north tower height 377´.
a. View from the southeast.
© John Elk, III.

b. *West Front.*
Photograph: Duane Preble.

c. *"Rose de France" Window.* c. 1233.
Photograph: Duane Preble.

indoor space that could hold all the townspeople at once; thus, they were used for meetings, concerts, and religious plays. But most of all, they were places of worship. Above the town of Chartres, the cathedral rises, its spires visible for miles around.

The entire community cooperated in the building of *Notre Dame de Chartres*, although those who began its construction never saw its final form. The cathedral continued to grow and change for more than three hundred years. Although the basic plan is symmetrical and logically organized, the architecture of *Chartres* has a rich, enigmatic complexity that is quite different from the easily grasped totality of the classical *Parthenon*.

One of the first cathedrals based on the full Gothic system, it helped set the standard for Gothic architecture in Europe. In its *West Front*, Chartres reveals the transition between the early and late phases of Gothic architecture. The massive lower walls and round arch portals were built in the mid-twelfth century. The north tower (on the left) was rebuilt with the intricate flamelike or **flamboyant** curves of the late Gothic style early in the sixteenth century, after the original tower collapsed in 1506.

The principal goal of the Gothic structural advances was to allow more churches to be filled with light, a metaphor for the presence of God. Stained glass windows fulfill this transcendent function in a specifically Christian fashion, in imagery that transforms the nave with showers of color, changing hour by hour. At Chartres, the brilliant north rose window, known as the *Rose de France*, is dedicated to the Virgin Mary, who sits in majesty, surrounded by doves, angels, and royal figures of the celestial hierarchy.

The statues of the *Old Testament Prophet, Kings, and Queen* to the right of the central doorway at the west entrance of *Chartres* are among the most impressive remaining examples of early Gothic sculpture. The kings and queen suggest Christ's royal heritage and also honor French monarchs

d. *Old Testament Prophet, Kings, and Queen.* c. 1145–1170. Doorjamb statues from West (or Royal) Portal.
Photograph: Duane Preble.

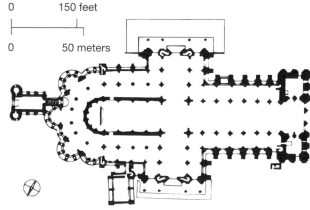

e. Plan based on Latin cross.

of the time. The prophet on the left depicts Christ's mission as an apostle of God. In contrast to active, emotional Romanesque sculpture, the figures are passive and serene. Their elongated forms allow them to blend readily with the vertical emphasis of the architecture.

Although they are part of the total scheme, the figures stand out from the columns behind them. Their draped bodies, and especially their heads, reveal a developing interest in portraying human features. Such interest eventually led again to full portraiture and freestanding figures.

The cathedral expresses an idea of Abbot Suger, the man credited with starting the Gothic style. At the Abbey church of St. Denis, where Suger began the Gothic style, he had an inscription placed on the entrance door stating his idea of the church's spiritual purpose:

Whoever you may be, if you are minded to praise this door,

Wonder not at the gold, nor at the cost, but at the work.

The work shines in its nobility; by shining nobly,

May it illumine the spirit, so that, through its trusty lights,

The spirit may reach the true Light in which Christ is the Door.

The golden door proclaims the nature of the Inward:

Through sensible things, the heavy spirit is raised to the truth;

From the depths, it rises to the light.[1]

Note

1. Titus Burckhardt, *Chartres and the Birth of the Cathedral* (Bloomington, IN: World Wisdom Books, 1996), 47.

RENAISSANCE AND BAROQUE EUROPE

Many works generally regarded as masterpieces were created during the Renaissance, when ambitious artists joined technical advances with profound subject matter to create works that still resonate today. Then in the following Baroque period, an exceptionally dynamic time in Western history, artists expanded the means and subjects available. The techniques and attitudes developed in those periods remained in force until the twentieth century.

THE RENAISSANCE

A shift in attitude occurred in Europe as the religious fervor of the Middle Ages was increasingly challenged by logical thought and the new philosophical, literary, and artistic movement called **humanism**. Leading humanist scholars did not discard theological concerns, yet they supported the secular dimensions of life, pursued intellectual and scientific inquiry, and rediscovered the classical culture of Greece and Rome. The focus gradually shifted from God and the hereafter to humankind and the here and now. For many Europeans, the Renaissance was a period of achievement and worldwide exploration—a time of discovery and rediscovery of the world and of the seemingly limitless potential of individual human beings. The period was foreshadowed in the fourteenth century, reached its clear beginning in the early fifteenth century, and came to an end in the early seventeenth century. However, Renaissance thinking continues to influence our lives today, not only in Western countries but in all parts of the world where individualism, modern science, and technology influence the way people live. In art, new and more scientific approaches were brought to the quest for representational accuracy. The resulting naturalism defined the Western tradition for more than four hundred years.

The intellectuals of the time were the first in European history to give their own era an identifying name. They named their period the **Renaissance**—literally, "Rebirth"—an apt description for the period of revived interest in the art and ideas of classical Greece and Rome. Fifteenth-century Italians believed they were responsible for the rebirth of "the glory of ancient Greece," which they considered the high point of Western civilization. Muslim and European scholars of the thirteenth and fourteenth centuries then recovered Greek and Roman books and made them available in Latin. In essence, the Renaissance was a period of new and renewed understanding that transformed the medieval European world, and laid the foundation for modern society.

Chapter 9: Renaissance and Baroque Europe was taken from *Prebles' Artforms: An Introduction to the Visual Arts,* Tenth Edition by Patrick Frank.

9.1 Giotto di Bondone.
Lamentation.
Scrovegni Chapel, Padua, Italy.
c. 1305. Fresco. 72″ 3 78″.
Photograph: Alinori/Art Resource, NY.

We see the beginnings of the new humanistic art in Italian painter Giotto di Bondone, known as Giotto. He departed from the abstract, Byzantine style by portraying the feelings and physical nature of human beings. His innovative depictions of light, space, and mass gave a new sense of realism to painting. In *Lamentation*, Giotto depicted physical as well as spiritual reality. His figures are shown as individuals within a shallow, stagelike space, and their expressions portray personal feelings of grief rarely seen in medieval art.

In retrospect, Giotto is considered not only a precursor of the Renaissance, but also the reinventor of naturalistic painting, which had not been seen in Europe since the decline of Rome a thousand years earlier. This "realism" is still an important current in Western painting.

The ancient Greeks had been concerned with idealized physical form; Roman artists had emphasized physical accuracy; and artists of the Middle Ages had focused on spiritual concerns rather than physical existence. In the Renaissance, as attention shifted from heaven to earth, artists portrayed Christian subjects in human terms. Italian civic leaders expressed a desire to equal or surpass the glory of ancient Greece and Rome and to imbue their achievements with the light of Christian understanding.

Italy was the principal homeland of the Renaissance. In time the movement spread northward, but it did not flourish everywhere in Europe; it came late to Spain and Portugal, and it barely touched Scandinavia.

The Renaissance in Italy

Artistic and intellectual developments in the Italian city-states were aided by a flourishing economy set against a chaotic political background. The wealth of Italian merchants enabled them to compete with one another, and with church officials and nobility, for the recognition and power that came with art patronage.

Italian architects, sculptors, and painters sought to integrate Christian spiritual traditions

New values combined with technological advances brought forth a new style of art in the fourteenth century. Painting and sculpture were liberated from their medieval roles as supplements to architecture. Artists, who considered themselves anonymous workers in the Middle Ages, came to be seen as individuals of creative genius.

The art of the Renaissance evolved in different ways in northern and southern Europe because the people of the two regions had different backgrounds, attitudes, and experiences. The Gothic style reached its high point in the north while Byzantine and Greco-Roman influences remained strong in the south. Italian Renaissance art grew from classical Mediterranean traditions that were human-centered and often emphasized the ideal. In contrast, the art of the northern Renaissance evolved out of pre-Christian, nature-centered religions that became God-centered through conversion to Christianity.

with the rational ordering of physical life in earthly space. Artists began an intense study of anatomy and light, and they applied geometry to the logical construction of implied space through the use of linear perspective (see page 74). In turn, the careful observation of nature initiated by Renaissance artists aided the growth of science.

About one hundred years after the foreshadowings of Giotto, Masaccio became the first major painter of the Italian Renaissance. In his fresco *The Holy Trinity*, the composition is centered on an open chapel in which we see the Trinity; God the father, Christ the son, and between their heads a white dove symbolizing the Holy Spirit. Within the niche, Mary the mother of Jesus stands, gesturing to Christ; opposite her is St. John. Kneeling outside are the donors who paid for the painting, a husband and wife who headed a powerful banking family of that time. He is wearing the red robe that marks him as a member of the Florence city council. Below, a skeleton is lying on a sarcophagus beneath the inscription, "I was what you are, and what I am you shall become." If we view the painting from top to bottom, we move from the spiritual to the physical.

The Holy Trinity was the first painting based on the systematic use of linear perspective. Although perspective was known to the Romans in a limited way, it did not become a consistent science until architect Filippo Brunelleschi rediscovered and developed it in Florence early in the fifteenth century. Masaccio used perspective to construct an illusion of figures in three-dimensional space. The single vanishing point is below the base of the cross, about five feet above ground, at the viewer's eye level. Masaccio's perspective is so precise that we can see the interior of the illusionary chapel as a believable extension of the space we occupy. The setting also reveals Masaccio's knowledge of the new Renaissance architecture developed by Brunelleschi, which he based on Roman prototypes.

The figures in *The Holy Trinity* have a physical presence that shows what Masaccio learned from

9.2 Masaccio.
The Holy Trinity.
Santa Maria Novella, Florence, Italy. 1425.
Fresco. 21′10½″ 3 10′5″.
Photograph: Copyright Scala/Art Resource, NY.

the work of Giotto. In Giotto's work, however, body and drapery still appear as one; Masaccio's figures are clothed nudes, with garments draped like real fabric.

During the Italian Renaissance, the nude became a major subject for art, as it had been in Greece and Rome. Unclothed subjects are rare in medieval art and appear awkward, their bodies graceless. In contrast, sculpted and painted figures by Italian Renaissance artists appear as strong and natural as the Greek and Roman nudes that inspired them.

As Masaccio was in painting, Donatello was in sculpture. Donatello brought the Greek ideal of what it means to be human into the Christian context. As a young adult, he made two trips to Rome, where he studied medieval and Roman art.

Donatello shows himself as an ambitious artist even in his early work. His bronze figure of *David* was the first life-size, freestanding nude statue since ancient Roman times. To Florence, where the work was located, *David* was not only a biblical figure; his resistance to foreign domination of the Jews inspired the Florentines, who were surrounded by stronger enemy cities.

Although he was greatly attracted to the classical ideal in art, Donatello's sculpture was less idealized and more naturalistic than that of ancient Greece. He chose to portray the biblical shepherd, David—slayer of the giant Goliath and later king of the Jews—as an adolescent youth rather than as a robust young man. The sculptor celebrated the sensuality of the boy's body by clothing him only in hat and boots. It is not so much the face, but every shift in the figure's weight and angle that is expressive. The youth's position is derived from classical contrapposto. The few nudes that appeared in medieval art showed little sensual appeal and often portrayed shame and lust. Under the influence of humanist scholars who sought to surpass the Greeks and Romans in the nobility of form, the nude became a symbol of human worth and divine perfection, a representation of the "immortal soul."

During the Renaissance, artists received growing support from the new class of wealthy merchants and bankers, such as the Medici family, who, with great political skill and a certain ruthlessness, dominated the life of Florence and Tuscany. It is likely that Donatello created his bronze *David* as a private commission for Cosimo de Medici, for the courtyard of the Medici palace.

A major influence on Donatello and other Renaissance artists was the renewal of Neoplatonist philosophy, embraced by the Medici family and their circle of philosophers, artists, historians, and humanists. These intellectuals believed that all sources of inspiration or revelation, whether from the Bible or classical mythology, are a means of ascending from earthly existence to mystical union with the divine. In this context, Donatello's *David* was intended to be a symbol of divine beauty.

Donatello's work displayed a wide range of expression, from lyric joy to tragedy. In contrast to the youthful and somewhat brash *David*, Donatello's *Mary Magdalene* is haggard and withdrawn—a forcefully expressive figure of old age and repentance. For this late work, Donatello chose painted wood, the favorite medium of northern Gothic sculptors.

9.3 Donatello.
David. c. 1425–1430.
Bronze. Height 62¼".
Museo Nazionale del Bargello, Florence.
Photograph: Copyright Scala/Art Resource, NY.

9.4 Donatello.
Mary Magdalene (La Madellena). c. 1455.
Wood, partially gilded. Height 74".
Battistero, Florence.
Photograph: Copyright Scala/Art Resource, NY.

Another Medici commission is Sandro Botticelli's *Birth of Venus*, the first large mythological painting since antiquity. Completed about 1480, this work depicts the Roman goddess of love just after she was born from the sea. She is blown to shore by a couple symbolizing the wind. As she arrives, Venus is greeted by a young woman who represents Spring. The lyric grace of Botticelli's lines shows Byzantine influence. The background is decorative and flat, giving almost no illusion of deep space. The figures appear to be in relief, not fully three-dimensional.

The posture and gestures of modesty were probably inspired by a third-century B.C.E. Greco-Roman sculpture of Venus that Botticelli must have seen in the Medici family collection (see page 140). In her posture of introspection and

repose, Botticelli's Venus combines the classical Greek idealized human figure with a Renaissance concern for thought and feeling.

To place a nude "pagan" goddess at the center of a large painting, in a position previously reserved for the Virgin Mary, was revolutionary. Botticelli's focus on classical mythology was, like Donatello's, based on Neoplatonist philosophy, a central preoccupation of the business-oriented, secular art patrons who commissioned most Renaissance art.

The High Renaissance

Between about 1490 and 1530—the period known as the High Renaissance—Italian art reached a peak of accomplishment in the cities of Florence, Rome, and Venice. The three artists who epitomized the period were Leonardo, Michelangelo, and Raphael.

9.5 Sandro Botticelli.
Birth of Venus. c. 1480.
Tempera on canvas. 5′8⅞″ 3 9′1⅞″.
Uffizi Gallery, Florence, Italy. Courtesy of Erich Lessing/Art Resource, NY.

They developed a style of art that was calm, balanced, and idealized, combining Christian theology with Greek philosophy and the science of the day.

Leonardo da Vinci was motivated by strong curiosity and belief in the human ability to understand the fascinating phenomena of the physical world. He believed that art and science are two means to the same end: knowledge.

Leonardo showed his investigative and creative mind in his journals, where he documented his research in notes and drawings. His notebooks are filled with studies of anatomy and ideas for mechanical devices, explorations that put him in the forefront of the scientific development of his time. His study of *The Babe in the Womb* has a few errors, yet much of the drawing is so accurate that it could serve as an example in one of today's medical textbooks.

So frequently has Leonardo's world-famous portrait of *Mona Lisa* been reproduced that it has become a cliché and the source of innumerable spoofs. Despite this overexposure, it still merits our attention. We can still be intrigued by the mysterious mood evoked by the faint smile and the strange, other-worldly landscape. The ambiguity is heightened by the hazy light quality that gives a sense of atmosphere around the figure. This soft blurring of the edges—in Leonardo's words, "without lines or borders in the manner of smoke"—achieved through subtle value gradations, is a special type of chiaroscuro invented by Leonardo. Most important for the history of art, this work is a portrait of an individual, a type of art fairly common in ancient Rome and almost unknown in the medieval period.

9.6 Leonardo da Vinci.
The Babe in the Womb. c. 1510.
Pen and ink. 11⅞″ 3 8⅜″.
The Royal Collection © 2009 Her Majesty Queen Elizabeth II.
Photograph: EZM. RL19102r.

9.7 Leonardo da Vinci.
Mona Lisa. c. 1503–1506.
Oil on wood. 30¼″ 3 21″.
Musée du Louvre, Paris, France. Photograph: Copyright Scala/Art Resource, NY.

The impact of Renaissance humanism becomes apparent when we compare *The Last Supper* by Leonardo with the Byzantine mosaic *Christ as Pantocrator* on page 151. In the Byzantine painting, Christ is portrayed as a lofty being of infinite power, the King of Heaven. In Leonardo's painting, Jesus sits across the table from us—an accessible person who reveals his divinity in an earthly setting, among disciples who look like us.

The naturalist style of the work contains a hidden geometry, which structures the design and strengthens the painting's symbolic content. The interior is based on a one-point linear perspective system, with a single vanishing point in the middle of the composition, behind the head of Christ. Leonardo placed Christ in the center, at the point of greatest implied depth, associating him with infinity. Over Christ's head an architectural pediment suggests a halo, further setting him off from the irregular shapes and movements of the surprised disciples on either side. In contrast to the anguished figures surrounding him, Christ is shown with his arms outstretched in a gesture of acceptance, his image a stable triangle.

9.8 Leonardo da Vinci.
The Last Supper.
Santa Maria delle Grazie, Milan, Italy. c. 1495–1498. Experimental paint on plaster. 14′5″ 3 28′¼″.
Photograph: Copyright Scala/Art Resource, NY.

a. Perspective lines as both organizing structure and symbol of content.

b. Christ's figure as stable triangle, contrasting with active turmoil of the disciples.

Leonardo da Vinci on Chiaroscuro

LEONARDO DA VINCI (1452–1519) was one of the major figures of the Italian High Renaissance. His subtle *Mona Lisa* (**Fig. 9.7**) is perhaps the world's most famous painting. The mysterious smile of his model has fascinated viewers for centuries.

Leonardo was an inventor, sculptor, and architect as well as a painter, and he had far-reaching curiosity about all natural phenomena. His intensive studies of human anatomy involved dissection of corpses, from which he created detailed drawings of musculature, bones, and joints. He also wrote extensively on art, anatomy, machinery, and natural history, but his voluminous writings were never published during his lifetime. His statements about the use of lights and darks in painting help us to understand why the boundaries of Mona Lisa's facial features are soft and undefined, though undoubtedly the darkened dirty state of the varnish now obscures the original colors of the painting:

"The first intention of the painter is to make a flat surface display a body as if modeled and separated from this plane, and he who most surpasses others in this skill deserves most praise. This accomplishment, with which the science of painting is crowned, arises from light and shade, or we may say chiaroscuro."

"Shadow is the privation of light. Shadows appear to me to be supremely necessary in perspective, since without them opaque and solid bodies will be ill defined. Those features that are located within their boundaries—and their boundaries themselves—will be ill defined if they do not end against a background of a color different from that of the body. In addition to this, these shadows are in themselves of varying degrees of darkness because they represent the loss of varying quantities of luminous rays, and these I term original shadows, because, being the first shadows, they clothe the bodies to which they are attached. From these original shadows there arise shadowy rays which are transmitted throughout the air, and these are of a quality corresponding to the variety of the original shadows from which they are derived. And on this account I will call these shadows derived shadows, because they have their origins in other shadows."

"Shadow shares the nature of universal things, which are all more powerful at their beginning and become enfeebled towards their end. When I speak about the beginning of every form and quality, discernible or indiscernible, I do not refer to things arising from small beginnings that become greatly enlarged over a period of time, as will happen with a great oak which has a modest start in a little acorn. Rather, I mean that the oak is strongest at the point at which it arises from the earth, that is to say, where it has its greatest thickness. Correspondingly, darkness is the first degree of shadow and light is the last. Therefore, painter, make your shadow darker close to its origin, and at its end show it being transformed into light, that is to say, so that it appears to have no termination."

"That body will exhibit the greatest difference between its shadows and its lights that happens to be seen under the strongest light, like the light of the sun or the light of a fire at night. And this should be little used in painting because the works will remain harsh and disagreeable.

"There will be little difference in the lights and shadows in that body which is situated in a moderate light, and this occurs at the onset of evening or when there is cloud, and such works are sweet and every kind of face acquires grace. Thus in all things extremes are blameworthy. Too much light makes for harshness; too much darkness does not allow us to see. The medium is best."[1]

Note

1. Quoted in Martin Kemp and Margaret Walker, eds., *Leonardo on Painting,* Yale University Press, New Haven and London, 1989, pp. 15, 97, 98, 162. [Reprinted by kind permission of the publisher.]

Artists on Art: Leonardo da Vinci on Chiaroscuro was taken from *The Art of Seeing,* Eighth Edition by Paul Zelanski and Mary Pat Fisher.

Michelangelo Buonarroti: Temperamental Genius

MICHELANGELO BUONARROTI (1475–1564) is probably the prototype of the brilliant artist of complicated temperament. He was such a celebrity that two biographies of him were published in his lifetime. His noble if difficult character and his mistrust of human nature—including his own—make his life one of the most interesting known to us from the sixteenth century.

Michelangelo's father was a member of the minor nobility of Florence, who lived off the remains of the family fortune. Michelangelo's mother was of poor health, so the future artist was principally raised by a stonecutter and his wife, a fateful situation. Michelangelo's mother died when he was six. Before he could read or write, he had learned to use a hammer and chisel.

When he was ten, his father remarried, and Michelangelo returned home and was enrolled in school for the first time. He learned to read and write in Italian but absorbed little else; rather, he drew whenever he could and neglected his other studies. He decided to leave school to become an artist, starting as an apprentice to the painter Ghirlandaio. His father and uncles looked down on artists and thought it a disgrace to have one in the house. Michelangelo's later career did much to change the status of "artist" from manual laborer to cultural leader.

After a year, Michelangelo transferred to the school in the Medici gardens, where he was inspired by the Medici collection of contemporary Italian and ancient Greco-Roman art. He studied there from age fifteen to seventeen, in the company of the lead-ing artists and scholars of the time. During the turmoil following the death of his patron, Lorenzo de Medici, Michelangelo left Florence for Rome. In Rome he completed the first of his major sculptures, the *Pietà*, at the age of twenty-four (see page 110). His handling of the difficult subject and the beautiful finish of the work established his reputation and led to important commissions, including *David*, when he returned to Florence. For the rest of his life, he divided his career between Florence and Rome.

Although he considered himself primarily a sculptor, Michelangelo's painting on *The Sistine Chapel* ceiling is one of the Western world's most acclaimed works of art. The project was made enormous by Michelangelo himself; although the original plan called for twelve figures, Michelangelo expanded the program to depict the creation of the world.

No other artist has left such worthy accomplishments in four major art forms: sculpture, painting, architecture, and poetry. Perhaps the most revealing writings are his poems, which express his innermost feelings about his mind and soul as well as his art.

Michelangelo was very different from Leonardo, who was twenty-three years older. Michelangelo saw human beings as unique, almost godlike, whereas Leonardo saw them as one

9.9 Daniele da Volterra.
Michelangelo Buonarroti (Busto di Michelangelo). 1565.
Detail of bronze bust. Height of entire work 32".
Accademia, Florence. Photograph: Alinari/Art Resource, NY.

more part of nature, which he viewed with the cool eye of a scientist. For Michelangelo, sculpture and the process of its creation reflected people's struggle with their imperfect selves—souls in turmoil, bound in their bodies.

Michelangelo's life spanned nearly a century. From the time he was apprenticed at age thirteen until six days before his death at eighty-nine, he worked continuously. His last words were, "I regret that I have not done enough for the salvation of my soul and that I am dying just as I am beginning to learn the alphabet of my profession."[1]

Note

1. *The World of Michelangelo* (New York: Time-Life Books, 1966), 192.

Artists on Art: Michelangelo Buonarroti: Temperamental Genius was taken from *Prebles' Artforms: An Introduction to the Visual Arts,* Tenth Edition by Patrick Frank.

Michelangelo's *Libyan Sibyl*

ON MAY 10, 1506, Michelangelo received an advance payment from Pope Julius II to undertake the task of frescoing the ceiling of the Sistine Chapel at the Vatican in Rome. By the end of July, a scaffolding had been erected. By September 1508, Michelangelo was painting, and for the next four and a half years, he worked almost without interruption on the project.

According to Michelangelo's later recounting of events, Julius had originally envisioned a design in which the central part of the ceiling would be filled with "ornaments according to custom" (apparently a field of geometric ornaments) surrounded by the 12 apostles in the 12 spandrels. Michelangelo protested, assuring Julius that it would be "a poor design" since the apostles were themselves "poor too." Apparently convinced, the pope then freed Michelangelo to paint anything he liked. Instead of the apostles, Michelangelo created a scheme of 12 Old Testament prophets alternating with 12 sibyls, or women of classical antiquity said to possess prophetic powers. The center of the ceiling would be filled with nine scenes from Genesis.

As the scaffolding was erected, specially designed by the artist so that he could walk around and paint from a standing position, Michelangelo set to work preparing hundreds of drawings for the ceiling. These drawings were then transferred to full-size cartoons, which would be laid up against the moist surface of the fresco as it was prepared, their outlines traced through with a stylus. None of these cartoons, and surprisingly few of Michelangelo's drawings, have survived.

One of the greatest, and most revealing, of the surviving drawings is a *Study for The Libyan Sibyl* (**Fig. 9.10**).

9.10   Michelangelo Buonarroti.
Study for the Libyan Sibyl, c. 1510.
Red chalk on paper, 11³/₈ 3 8⁷/₁₆ in. Metropolitan Museum of Art, New York. Purchase, Joseph Pulitzer Bequest, 1924 (24.197.2).
Photograph © The Metropolitan Musuem of Art/Art Resource.

Each of the sibyls holds a book of prophecy—though not Christian figures, they prophesy the revelation of the New Testament in the events of the Old Testament that they surround. *The Libyan Sibyl* (**Fig. 9.11**) is the last sibyl that Michelangelo would paint. She is positioned next to the *Separation of Light from Darkness*, the last of the central panels, which is directly over the altarpiece. The Libyan Sibyl herself turns to close her book and place it on the desk behind her. Even as she does so, she steps down from her throne, creating a stunning opposition of directional forces, an exaggerated, almost spiral *contrapposto*. She abandons her book of prophecy as she turns to participate in the celebration of the Eucharist on the altar below.

The severity of this downward twisting motion obviously came late in Michelangelo's work on the figure. In the drawing, the sibyl's hands are balanced evenly, across an almost hori-

Works in Progress: Michelangelo's *Libyan Sibyl* was taken from *A World of Art*, Sixth Edition by Henry M. Sayre.

9.11 Michelangelo Buonarroti. *The Libyan Sibyl*, 1511–12. Fresco, detail of the Sistine Ceiling, Sistine Chapel, Vatican City.
Canali Photobank, Capriolo, Italy.

zontal plane. But the idea of dropping the left hand, in order to emphasize more emphatically the sibyl's downward movement, came almost immediately, for just below her left arm is a second variation, in which the upper arm drops perceptively downward and the left hand is parallel to the face instead of the forehead, matching the positions of the final painting. In the drawing, the sibyl is nude, and apparently Michelangelo's model is male, his

musculature more closely defined than in the final painting. Furthermore, in the drawing, the model's face is redone to the lower left, her lips made fuller and feminized, the severity of the original model's brow and cheek softened. The magnificently foreshortened left hand is redone in larger scale, as if in preparation for the cartoon, and so is the lower-left foot. There are, in fact, working upward from the bottom of the drawing, three versions of the big

toe, and, again, the second and third are closer to the final painted version than the first, more fully realized foot, the second toe splaying more radically backward, again to emphasize downward pressure and movement. It is upon this foot that, in the final painting, Michelangelo directs our attention, illuminating it like no other portion of the figure, the fulcrum upon which the sibyl turns from her pagan past to the Christian present.

9.12 Michelangelo Buonarroti.
David. 1501–1504.
Marble. Height of figure 14′3″.
Accademia, Florence. Photograph: Duane Preble.

Like the *Last Supper*, Michelangelo's *David* is an important work that expresses many Renaissance ideas. The biblical hero David was an important symbol of freedom from tyranny for Florence, which had just become a republic. Other Renaissance artists such as Donatello had already given the city images of the young David, but Michelangelo's figure gave the most powerful expression to the idea of David as hero, the defender of a just cause.

Michelangelo took *David*'s stance, with the weight of the body on one foot, from the contrapposto of Greek sculpture. But the positions of the hands and tense frown indicate anxiety and readiness for conflict. Through changes in proportion and the depiction of inner feeling, Michelangelo humanized, then made monumental, the classical Greek athlete.

Michelangelo worked for three years on this sculpture. When it was finished and placed in the town square, most citizens of Florence greeted it with approval. With this achievement, Michelangelo became known as the greatest sculptor since the Greeks.

When Pope Julius II decided to redecorate the ceiling of his private prayer chapel, he begged, cajoled, and eventually ordered the unwilling sculptor to take on the painting commission. Michelangelo began work on *The Sistine Chapel* ceiling in 1508 and finished it four years later. The surface is divided into three zones. In the highest are nine panels of scenes of the creation of the world from Genesis, including *The Creation of Adam*. The next level contains prophets and sibyls (female prophets). The lowest level consists of groups of Old Testament figures, some of them Christ's biblical ancestors. *The Last Judgment*, painted later, fills the end wall above the altar.

The most-admired composition on the ceiling is the majestic portrayal of *The Creation of Adam*, in which God reaches out to give life to the first man. Eve, not yet mortal, stares at Adam from behind God's left arm.

The work powerfully expresses the Renaissance humanist concept of God: an idealized, rational

9.13 Michelangelo Buonarroti.
Frescoes on the ceiling of The Sistine Chapel. Vatican, Rome. 1508–1512.
a. *The Creation of Adam.*
Vatican Museums, Rome, Italy.

b. *The Sistine Chapel.*
Vatican Museums, Rome, Italy. © Reuters NewMedia Inc./Corbis.

man who actively tends every aspect of creation, and has a special interest in humans. Michelangelo invented this powerful image, which does not exist in the Bible, to tell the story of the relationship between God and people from a Renaissance point of view.

Raphael was the third major artist of the High Renaissance. His warmth and gentleness were in sharp contrast to Leonardo's solitary, intellectual nature and Michelangelo's formidable moodiness. Of these three major creators, Raphael was the most expressive of the clarity and balance that marked the art of the period. His paintings present his awareness of the divine in human beings, the insight that was the driving enthusiasm of Italian Renaissance.

In *The School of Athens* (page 76), we see one of the clearest summations of Renaissance beliefs. He organized the complex composition into symmetrical sub-groups, all revolving around the central figures of Plato and Aristotle under the arch. Perspective lines help to frame our focus on them. Most of the figure poses in this work

Raphael's *Alba Madonna*

IN A SERIES OF STUDIES for *The Alba Madonna* (**Fig. 9.15**), the great Renaissance draughtsman Raphael demonstrates many of the ways that artists use drawings to plan a final work. It is as if Raphael, in these sketches, had been instructed by Leonardo himself. We do know, in fact, that when Raphael arrived in Florence in 1504, he was stunned by the freedom of movement and invention that he discovered in Leonardo's drawings. "Sketch subjects quickly," Leonardo admonished his students. "Rough out the arrangement of the limbs of your figures and first attend to the movements appropriate to the mental state of the creatures that make up your picture rather than to the beauty and perfection of their parts."

In the studies illustrated here, Raphael worked on both sides of a single sheet of paper (**Fig. 9.14**). On one side he has drawn a male model from life and posed him as the Madonna. In the sweeping cross-hatching below the figure in the sketch, one can already sense the circular format of the final painting, as these lines rise and turn up the arm and shoulder and around to

9.14 Raphael
Studies for The Alba Madonna *(recto and verso),* c. 1511.
Left: red chalk; right: red chalk and pen and ink, both 16⁵/₈ 3 10³/₄ in.
Courtesy of Réunion des Musées Nationaux / Art Resource, NY. (left); © Bridgeman Art Library/private collection/Giraudon (right).

Works in Progress: Raphael's *Alba Madonna* was taken from *A World of Art,* Sixth Edition by Henry M. Sayre.

the model's head. Inside this curve is another, rising from the knee bent under the model up across his chest to his neck and face. Even the folds of the drapery under his extended arm echo this curvilinear structure.

On the other side of the paper, all the figures present in the final composition are included. The major difference between this and the final painting is that the infant St. John offers up a bowl of fruit in the drawing and Christ does not yet carry a cross in his hand. But the circular format of the final painting is fully realized in this drawing. A hastily drawn circular frame encircles the group (outside this frame, above it, are first ideas for yet another Madonna and Child, and below it, in the bottom-right corner, an early version of the Christ figure for this one). The speed and fluency of this drawing's execution is readily apparent, and if the complex facial expressions of the final painting are not yet indicated here, the emotional tenor of the body language is. The postures are both tense and relaxed. Christ seems to move away from St. John even as he turns toward him. Mary reaches out, possibly to comfort the young saint, but equally possibly to hold him at bay. Raphael has done precisely as Leonardo directed, attending to the precise movements and gestures that will indicate the mental states of his subjects in the final painting.

9.15 Raphael.
The Alba Madonna, c. 1510.
Oil on panel transferred to canvas, diameter 37^{1}/4 in.; framed: 54 3 53^{1}/2 in.
National Gallery of Art, Washington, D.C. Andrew W. Mellon Collection. © 1999 Board of Trustees, National Gallery of Art. Photo: José A. Naranjo.

are based in Classical antiquity. More important, *The School of Athens* elevates human reason by presenting a philosophical discussion among learned people as an ideal. The Pope commissioned this work for the wall of a meeting room, so that persons discussing church business could be inspired by an ideal meeting of great people from the past. Rarely has humanism been so clearly embodied.

For Pope Leo X (a Medici descendant), Raphael made a series of cartoons for tapestries that would decorate the walls of the Sistine Chapel, below Michelangelo's ceiling. The tapestries have faded, but the cartoons retain most of the original vivid colors. Leo wished to glorify the early church by commissioning illustrations of important events in the Acts of the Apostles, and Raphael responded by creating memorable and dramatic works. *Paul Preaching at Athens* is a diverse yet well-organized composition, as Paul preaches to the philosophically inclined Athenians. Among the audience is the Pope, just to the left of Paul. The message of this work, that reason can transmit religious truth, perfectly expresses Renaissance beliefs.

The Renaissance in Northern Europe

As the Early Renaissance was unfolding in Italy, a parallel new interest in realism arose in northern Europe, where artists were even more concerned than the Italians with depicting life in the real world. Jan van Eyck was a leading painter in Flanders, the region of present-day Belgium and adjacent parts of France and The Netherlands. He was one of the first to use oil as a painting **medium**. The fine consistency and flexibility of the new oil medium made possible a brilliance and transparency of color that were previously unattainable. His oil paintings remain in almost perfect condition, attesting to his skill and knowledge of materials. Later Italian artists admired and imitated the innovations of van Eyck and other Flemish artists.

On the same type of small wooden panels previously used for tempera painting, van Eyck painted in minute detail, achieving an illusion of depth, directional light, mass, rich implied textures, and the physical likenesses of particular people. Human figures and their interior settings took on a new, believable presence.

9.16 Raphael (Raffaello Sanzio).
Paul Preaching at Athens.
1515–1516.
Watercolor on paper mounted on canvas. 11′5½″ 3 14′6¾″.
Victoria and Albert Museum, London. Art Resource, NY.

9.17 Jan van Eyck.
The Arnolfini Portrait. 1434.
The Portrait of Giovanni, Arnolfini
and his Wife Giovanna Cenami. Oil
on panel. 33½″ 3 23½″.
National Gallery, London, U.K. Photograph:
Bridgeman Art Library.

His most famous work, *The Arnolfini Portrait*, is discussed in detail in Chapter 3.

In the early sixteenth century in Germany, Albrecht Dürer further developed the practice of combining instructive symbolism with detailed realism. His engraving *The Knight, Death, and the Devil* combines Christian symbols with familiar subjects in the Flemish tradition of van Eyck.

A major factor that conditioned art production in northern Europe was the Protestant Reformation, which began in approximately 1521 when the rebellious monk Martin Luther was excommunicated from the Roman Catholic Church. Clergy allied with the burgeoning Protestant movement discouraged elaborate church interiors, and this led to a sharp drop in commissions for altarpieces and religious decorations. Therefore, a great deal of Renaissance art in the North was destined for private possession in homes.

Pieter Bruegel developed a new artistic vision of the northern European landscape. As a young man, he traveled extensively in France and Italy.

The Isenheim Altarpiece

CREATED FOR THE HOSPITAL of a monastery in Isenheim, the altarpiece was normally closed, revealing only the crucifixion on the outer panel, apparently to help patients deal with their own sufferings by seeing the greater sufferings of Jesus on behalf of humanity. On Sundays, the altarpiece was opened, revealing the annunciation, nativity, and resurrection, all of them full of sacred mysteries and celebration, culminating in the risen Christ's brilliant resurrection from the life of the flesh to the life of the spirit. Such a visionary work was made possible by the attacks of the northern Christian humanists on what they regarded as the corrupt authority of the Catholic Church.

9.18 Matthias Grünewald.
The Isenheim Altarpiece. 1506–1515, First view.
a. Courtesy of Mansell/Getty Images.

Works in Progress: The Isenheim Altarpiece was taken from *The Art of Seeing*, Eighth Edition by Paul Zelanski and Mary Pat Fisher.

The Isenheim Altarpiece, Second view.
b. Courtesy of Scala/Art Resource

The Isenheim Altarpiece, Third view.
c. Courtesy of Photolibrary.

9.19 Pieter Bruegel. *Hunters in the Snow (Jager im Schnee).* 1565. Oil on panel. 46½" 3 63¾". Kunsthistorisches Museum, Vienna, Austria.

Under the influence of Italian Renaissance painting, Bruegel developed a broad sense of composition and spatial depth. The focus of Bruegel's paintings was the lives and surroundings of common people. Such works that dignify everyday life are still beloved today and are called **genre paintings**.

Toward the end of his life, he did a series of paintings representing the activities of the twelve months of the year. The work corresponding to January, *Hunters in the Snow*, is among the most highly regarded. Following the precedent set by manuscript painters (illuminators) of medieval calendars, who depicted each month according to the agricultural labor appropriate to it, Bruegel shows peasants augmenting their winter diet by hunting. New here is the emphasis on nature's winter mood rather than on human activity. The illusion of deep space, so important to this image, came from the innovations of the Italians and was also inspired by Bruegel's journey over the Alps.

Compare Bruegel's painting with an illuminated page for *February: Winter* from a late Gothic book of hours painted by the Limbourg brothers in the early fifteenth century, before the Renaissance

influence reached the North. Notice how far landscape painting evolved in 150 years. Although there is a huge difference in the way space is depicted, in both paintings there is attention to nature and the details of everyday life. Bruegel achieved greater naturalism by portraying what he might see from one vantage point at a particular time; the Limbourg brothers implied various moments in time by creating an imaginary composite view.

Late Renaissance in Italy

During the later sixteenth century, architects made a deliberate effort to rethink and extend classical rules even as they used classical forms. The most learned and influential architect was the Venetian Andrea Palladio. His famous *Villa Rotonda* is a free reinterpretation of the Roman Pantheon (see pages 143–144). It has four identical sides, complete with porches resembling ancient temple façades, built around a central domed hall. The villa's design hardly satisfies the architectural goal of livability, but it was not intended for family living; it was designed for a retired nobleman as a kind of open summer house for social occasions. From its

9.20   The Limbourg Brothers.
February: Winter from Très Riches Heures du Duc de Berry.
15th century.
Ink and colors on parchment. Ms. 65/1284,
fol. 71v. 8⅞″ 3 5⅜″.
Musée Condé, Chantilly, France. Photograph: Giraudon/Art Resource, NY.

hilltop site, visitors standing in the central rotunda could enjoy four different views of the countryside.

Palladio's designs were published in books that were widely circulated throughout the Western world. For the next two centuries, architects and builders from Russia to Pennsylvania often used motifs that he developed, and his designs have even reappeared on postmodern buildings in our generation.

Palladio's Venice became the scene of the last great flowering of Renaissance art. Using the newly developed oil paints on canvas supports, Venetian painters experimented with figure poses, compositions, and subjects. Responding to a clientele made wealthy from trading across the Mediterranean world, Venetian painting was rich and lavish, less idealized than the work of central Italian artists such as Raphael and Michelangelo.

9.21   Andrea Palladio.
Villa Rotonda.
Vicenza, Italy. 1567–1570.
Photograph: Cameraphoto/AKG Images.

9.22 Paolo Veronese.
Feast in the House of Levi. 1573.
Oil on canvas. 18′4″ 3 16′7″.
Accademia Gallery, Venice/Canali PhotoBank, Milan/SuperStock.

We see an example of Venetian opulence in one of its most celebrated paintings, *Feast in the House of Levi* by Paolo Veronese. This large work depicts a sumptuous banquet described in the New Testament that Jesus attended (we see him seated at the center). The artist set the scene under a Venetian arcade, using features borrowed from Palladio's buildings. Servants rush about, waiting on persons of various nationalities (including a German in stripes at the right center). Not everyone in the work is sober. The atmosphere is one of elegant yet boisterous wealth.

Today, the work is called *Feast in the House of Levi,* but it was commissioned by the monks of a monastery for their dining hall as a Last Supper. Veronese took such liberties with the traditional subject of Christ bidding farewell to his disciples (compare to Leonardo's *Last Supper*), that the religious authorities called Veronese before the Inquisition on a charge of impiety. This led to one of the first important trials of artistic freedom in the Western world.

Why, they asked Veronese, did he include depictions of "buffoons, drunkards, Germans, dwarfs, and similar vulgarities" when none were present at the actual Last Supper? The artist's defense was one that most Western artists have eagerly embraced ever since: The artist should be free to interpret subjects as he wishes. Or, as Veronese said: "I paint pictures as I see fit and as well as my talent permits." The Inquisitors ordered him to alter the painting and bring it more in line with what viewers of a Last Supper could expect. But instead of changing the work, the artist merely retitled it to reflect the lively party in the house of Levi. The controversy had no discernible impact on Veronese's reputation in otherwise liberal-minded Venice.

Another work by an important Venetian artist is the *Pietà* by Titian on page 22.

THE MANNERIST STYLE IN EUROPE

Shortly after the Spanish conquest of separatist states within Spain in 1519 and the death of Raphael in 1520, many Italian painters embarked on a stylistic course that came to be known as **Mannerism**. Highly individualistic and *mannered*, or consciously artificial, this Mannerist style was dedicated to

The Mannerist Style in Europe section was taken from *A World of Art,* Sixth Edition by Henry M. Sayre.

9.23 Tintoretto.
The Miracle of the Slave, 1548.
Oil on canvas, approximately 14 3 18 ft. Gallerie dell'Accademia, Venice.
Courtesy of Scala/Ministero per I Beni e la Attivita culturali/Art Resource, NY.

"invention," and the technical and imaginative virtuosity of the artist became of paramount importance. Each Mannerist artist may, therefore, be identified by his own "signature" style. Where the art of the High Renaissance sought to create a feeling of balance and proportion, quite the opposite is the goal of Mannerist art. In the later work of Michelangelo, for example, particularly the great fresco of *The Last Judgment* on the altar wall of the Sistine Chapel (Fig. 4.9), executed in the years 1534 to 1541, we find figures of grotesque proportion arranged in an almost chaotic, certainly athletic, swirl of line. Mannerist painters represented space in unpredictable and ambiguous ways, so that bodies sometimes seem to

fall out of nowhere into the frame of the painting, as in Tintoretto's *The Miracle of the Slave* (**Fig. 9.23**). The drama of Tintoretto's painting is heightened by the descent of the vastly foreshortened St. Mark, who hurtles in from above to save the slave from his executioner. The rising spiral line created by the three central figures—the slave, the executioner holding up his shattered instruments of torture, and St. Mark—is characteristic of Mannerism, but the theatricality of the scene, heightened by its dramatic contrast of light and dark, anticipates the Baroque style which soon followed.

Often, the space of a Mannerist painting seems too shallow for what is depicted, a feeling emphasized by the frequent use of radical fore-shortening, as in the Tintoretto (Fig. 9.23). Or the figure itself may be distorted or elongated, as in Bronzino's *Venus, Cupid, Folly, and Time (The Exposure of Luxury)* (**Fig. 9.24**). The colors are often bright and clashing. At the upper right of Bronzino's painting, Time, and, at the upper left, Truth, part a curtain to reveal the shallow space in which Venus is fondled by her son, Cupid. Folly is about to shower the pair in rose petals. Envy tears her hair out at center left. The Mannerist distortion of space is especially evident in the distance separating Cupid's shoulders and head.

As in El Greco's *The Burial of Count Orgaz* (**Fig. 9.25**), Mannerist painting often utilizes more than one focal point, and these often seem contradictory. Born in Crete and trained in Venice and Rome, where he studied the works of Titian,

Tintoretto, and the Italian Mannerists, El Greco moved to Toledo, Spain, in 1576, and lived there for the rest of his life. In the painting we see here, the realism of the lower ensemble, which includes local Toledo nobility and clergy of El Greco's day (even though the painting represents a burial that took place more than 200 years earlier, in 1323), gives way in the upper half to a much more abstract and personal brand of representation. El Greco's elongated figures—consider St. Peter, in the saffron robe behind Mary on the upper left, with his long piercing fingers on a longer, almost drooping hand, to say nothing of the bizarrely extended arm of Christ himself—combine with oddly rolling clouds that rise toward an astonishingly small representation of Christ. So highly eclectic and individual is this painter's style that it is difficult to label it even as Mannerist.

9.24 Bronzino.
Venus, Cupid, Folly, and Time (The Exposure of Luxury), c. 1546.
Oil on wood, approximately 61 3 56³/₄ in.
© National Gallery, London/Art Resource, NY.

9.25 El Greco.
The Burial of Count Orgaz, 1586.
Oil on canvas, 16 ft. 3 11 ft. 10 in.
Church of Santo Tomé, Toledo, Spain.
Scala / Art Resource, NY.

BAROQUE

During the Baroque period, which ran from about 1600 to 1770, artists used the Renaissance techniques to move art in the direction of drama, emotion, and splendor. The Baroque period had more varied styles than the Renaissance, yet much of the art shows great energy and feeling, and a dramatic use of light, scale, and composition. Baroque artists set aside the balanced harmony achieved by Renaissance artists such as Raphael in his *School of Athens* (page 76) and Michelangelo in his *David*, as they explored more innovative uses of space and more intense ranges of light and shadow. Their art, with its frequent use of curves and countercurves, often appeals to the emotions first. Also, we can see a new degree of vivid realism in compositions using sharp diagonals and extreme foreshortening.

Many of the characteristics of the Baroque style were spawned and promoted by the Counter-Reformation, the Roman Catholic Church's response to the Protestant Reformation. In a series of decrees that emanated from the Council of Trent, the Church reaffirmed the mysteries of the sacraments, glorified the saints, and encouraged the arts as aids to prayer. Much Baroque religious art places a new emphasis on personal and mystical types of faith.

Michelangelo Merisi da Caravaggio's down-to-earth realism and dramatic use of light broke from Renaissance idealism and became the leading influences on other Baroque painters, north and south. Caravaggio created the most vivid and dramatic paintings of his time, using directed light and strong contrasts to guide the attention of the viewer and intensify the subject matter.

In *The Conversion of Saint Paul*, Caravaggio used light to imply a blinding flash, symbolizing the

9.26   Michelangelo Merisi da Caravaggio. The Conversion of Saint Paul. 1600–1601. Oil on canvas. 100½″ 3 69″.
Santa Maria del Popolo, Rome, Italy.
Photograph: Scala/Art Resource, NY.

evangelist's sudden and soul-shattering conversion. The figure of Paul, in Roman dress, is foreshortened and pushed into the foreground, presenting such a close view that we feel we are right there. In keeping with the supernatural character of the spiritual events he portrayed, Caravaggio evoked a feeling for the mystical dimension within the ordinary world. Here we see a Baroque figure far removed from Raphael's logical, reasonable Paul who preached at Athens. Some of the Roman clergy rejected his style; his emotional realism was too strong for people accustomed to idealized aristocratic images that demonstrated little more than gestures of piety.

9.27 Gian Lorenzo Bernini.
David. 1623.
Marble. Life-size.
Galleria Borghese, Rome/Canali PhotoBank, Milan/SuperStock.

9.28 Gian Lorenzo Bernini.
The Ecstasy of Saint Teresa.
1645–1652. Detail of the altar. Marble. Life-size.
Cornaro Chapel, Santa Maria della Vittoria, Rome, Italy.
Photograph: Scala/Art Resource, NY.

Emotional realism and use of extreme chiaroscuro, especially in Caravaggio's night effects, influenced later Baroque painters. Displayed in a dark chapel, Caravaggio's paintings take on a vivid, lifelike quality intended to heighten the religious experience.

Caravaggio's influence in painting was equaled in sculpture by Gian Lorenzo Bernini. Because Bernini's *David* is life-size rather than monumental, viewers become engaged in the action. Rather than capture an introspective moment, as Michelangelo did, Bernini depicted David in the midst of his backswing, as he prepares to fling the stone at Goliath.

Bernini's elaborate orchestrations of the visual arts are the climax of Italian Baroque expression. The emotional intensity of his art is vividly apparent in his major work *The Ecstasy of Saint Teresa*. It features a life-size marble figure of the saint and

depicts one of her visions as she recorded it in her diary. In this vision, she saw an angel who seemed to pierce her heart with a flaming arrow of gold, giving her great pain as well as pleasure and leaving her "all on fire with a great love of God."[2] Bernini made the visionary experience vivid by portraying the moment of greatest feeling, revealing spiritual passion through physical expression. Turbulent drapery heightens the emotional impact. His departure from the naturalistic, classical norm soon influenced artists throughout Europe.

Flemish painter Peter Paul Rubens, a renowned diplomat and humanist, was the most influential Baroque artist in northern Europe. He studied painting in Antwerp, then traveled to Italy in 1600. During a stay of several years, he carefully studied the work of Michelangelo and the Venetians. When Rubens returned north, he won increasing acclaim and patronage; being a sophisticated businessman, he enjoyed an aristocratic lifestyle. His work came to be in such demand by the nobility and royalty of Europe that he established a large studio with many assistants. Although Rubens was noted for the exuberant quality of his nudes, there was a tendency for everything in his paintings to take on a similar sensuality. His free brushwork influenced many painters.

In *The Raising of the Cross*, we see his interpretation of a religious subject, painted for an important Roman Catholic cathedral in his homeland. The composition is arranged along a diagonal anchored at the bottom right by the well-muscled figure. This and other taut bodies in the work show the results of the artist's recent visit to Italy, where he saw works by Michelangelo and Caravaggio. At the same time, there is a high degree of realis-

tic detail in the foliage and the dog at the bottom left that show Rubens's Flemish heritage from Jan van Eyck and others. The action and drama in the work seem to burst out of the frame, led by the upward glance of Christ. This visual dynamism, extending the action of the work into the viewer's space, marks this work as a Baroque painting.

Many artists worked on behalf of the church; some worked in the service of the nobility. The most innovative of these was the Spaniard Diego Velázquez, who worked all his life in the court of Philip IV, King of Spain. Philip was a broad-minded monarch who took delight in his chief painter's sometimes adventurous works. Such a painting is *The Maids of Honor*, in which Velázquez plays an elaborate game. At first it is unclear who is the subject, because the artist himself stares out from

9.29   Peter Paul Rubens.
The Raising of the Cross. 1610–1611.
Oil on panel. 462 3 339 cm.
Onze Lieve Vrouwkerk, Antwerp Cathedral, Belgium.
Photograph: Peter Willi/Bridgeman Art Library International Ltd.

9.30   Diego Velázquez de Silva.
The Maids of Honor (Las Meninas). 1665.
Oil on canvas. 138 3 276 cm.
Museo del Prado, Madrid, Spain.
Photograph: Erich Lessing/Art Resource, NY.

9.31 Sebastián Salcedo.
Virgin of Guadalupe. 1779.
Oil on copper. 25″ 3 19″.
Denver Art Museum Collection: Funds contributed by Mr. and Mrs. George G. Anderman and
an Anonymous Donor, 1976.56. Photograph courtesy of the Denver Art Museum.

behind a canvas, brush in hand. The maids of honor encircle the king's daughter, who stares coquettishly at us, as if expecting something. She seems to be the center of the composition, as she stands in the brightest light. Another courtier stands in an illuminated doorway in the background. Only when we see the mirror on the far wall, with the faces of the royal couple reflected in it, do we realize that this is a court portrait changed into a visual riddle. Velázquez painted a portrait of himself making a royal portrait! Like other Baroque works, this painting reaches out beyond its frame in a subtle dynamism of glance and image in which light and shadow play a major role.

In the Spanish colonies of Latin America, most painting and sculpture remained strongly bound to the ideas of the Counter-Reformation. *The Virgin of Guadalupe* by Sebastián Salcedo glorifies a miracle that took place in 1531 when Mary appeared on a hilltop, in native skin and speaking the indigenous language of the Aztecs. Mexicans took this apparition as proof that God cared as much for the native races as for the Europeans. The work shows the influence of Rubens in the fleshy babies, and of engraved banknote imagery in the decorations. Surrounding the central figure of Mary are other scenes connected with her appearance. The Church certified the apparition in 1754; this work was done about 25 years later.

We have seen that Baroque characteristics are found in art that depicts both religious and secular subjects. This was primarily because artists no longer relied wholly on the church for their support; many worked for nobles and aristocrats. In The Netherlands, the major patrons of art were middle-class merchants and bankers, most of them Protestants.

As the result of recently won independence and booming international trade, Holland became a new type of society in the seventeenth century: predominantly middle class, wealthy, mercantile, and Protestant. The middle and upper classes enjoyed and invested in contemporary art. Favored subjects were the same ones enjoyed to this day: landscape, still life, genre scenes, and portraits. Through Dutch painters, art became accessible and understandable in everyday terms.

We can see why Rembrandt remains one of the Western world's most revered artists in his large work *Return of the Prodigal Son*. The story comes from the Bible: A disobedient son cuts himself off from his family, demands his inheritance early, wastes it in disorderly living, and ends up in dire poverty. When he reaches the end of his rope, he returns to his wealthy father and asks for a job feeding the hogs. The father is not scornful or judgmental, rather the opposite. He tenderly welcomes the haggard and forlorn young man. Rembrandt portrays this touching scene with great reserve and economy. We see the prodigal son's ragged clothing, and the father's gentle embrace. We also see standing at the right, hanging back guardedly, the father's other son.

Rembrandt's composition shows the influence of the Italian Baroque painters in its dramatic contrasts of light and dark. The story, however, is not of the miraculous vision of a saint, as in Caravaggio's *Conversion of St. Paul*, but rather a miraculous restoration of affection between estranged people.

Rembrandt also created a long series of *Self-Portraits* that show deepening introspection. In the early works he is full of youthful optimism and bravado; in the later ones, we see an older, wiser person who refuses to glamorize himself.

9.32 Rembrandt van Rijn.
Return of the Prodigal Son. c. 1668–1669.
Oil on canvas. 8′8″ 3 6′8″.
The State Hermitage Museum, St. Petersburg, Russia.

Jan Vermeer, another seventeenth-century Dutch painter, created monumental genre paintings that raise daily life to the level of religious mysticism. Unlike Caravaggio and Rembrandt, who used light for dramatic emphasis, Vermeer concentrated on the way light reveals each color, texture, and detail of the physical world. No one since Jan van Eyck demonstrated such passion for seeing, or such love for the visual qualities of the physical world.

Vermeer's understanding of the way light defines form enabled him to give his images a clear, luminous vitality. Much of the strength of

9.33 Jan Vermeer.
The Kitchen Maid. c. 1658.
Oil on canvas. 18″ 3 16⅛″.
Rijksmuseum, Amsterdam.

The Kitchen Maid comes from a limited use of color: yellow and blue accented by red-orange, surrounded by neutral tones. The light has a mystical quality in this work; the act of pouring milk takes on the air of solemn ritual.

We can glimpse a clear view of Baroque aristocratic splendor in the architecture and garden design of the French royal palace of *Versailles*, built for King Louis XIV. The main palace and its gardens exemplify French Baroque architecture and landscape design. Throughout the palace and gardens, cool classical restraint and symmetry balance the romance of Baroque opulence and grand scale.

Versailles expressed the king's desire to surpass all others in the splendor of his palace. It is an example of royal extravagance, set in fifteen thousand acres of manicured gardens, twelve miles south of Paris. The vast formal gardens, with their miles of clipped hedges, proclaimed the king's desire to

9.34 Pierre Patel.
Versailles. c. 1665.
Chateau de Versailles et de Trianon, Versailles, France.
Photograph: Copyright Giraudon/Art Resource, NY.

9.35 Germain Boffrand.
Salon de la Princesse, Hôtel de Soubise.
Paris. Begun 1732.
Photograph: Hirmer Fotoarchiv, Munich, Germany.

rule over nature itself. This palace, which was also a governmental center, played an important role in the program of absolute monarchy that Louis XIV personified. Never more than here is the Baroque style allied with aristocracy.

In the middle years of the eighteenth century in France, the heavy, theatrical qualities of Italian Baroque art gradually gave way to the decorative **Rococo** style, a light, playful version of the Baroque. Designers copied the curved shapes of shells for elegantly paneled interiors and furniture, and they influenced the billowing shapes later found in paintings. The arts moved out of the marble halls of palaces such as *Versailles* and into fashionable town houses (called hotels) such as the *Hôtel de Soubise*.

The enthusiastic sensuality of the Rococo style was particularly suited to the extravagant and often frivolous life of the French court and aristocracy. Some of the movement, light, and gesture of the Baroque remained, but now the effect was one of lighthearted abandon rather than dramatic action or quiet repose. Rococo paintings provided romantic visions of life free from hardships, in which courtship, music, and festive picnics filled the days.

We clearly see the aristocratic life of ease and dalliance in Jean-Honoré Fragonard's painting *Happy Accidents of the Swing*. A well-dressed and idle young woman, attended by a dimly visible bishop, swings in a garden. At the lower left, a youth hides in the bushes and admires her. The story line of the work is provided by her flying shoe, which has come off and will soon land in the young man's lap. Fragonard learned the lessons of the Baroque well, as we can see in the off-balance composition arranged along the diagonal, and the contrasts of light and dark visible in the lush garden. But Baroque drama

gives way here to the sensual abandon and light-as-air subject matter of the Rococo at its best.

Or worst. The next generation of French artists and intellectuals would rebel against the social irresponsibility portrayed in this type of art, which they saw as merely fluffy. The Enlightenment was already breaking out across Western Europe, and its new ideas of social equality and scientific inquiry would soon shake European culture to its core.

9.36   Jean-Honoré Fragonard.
Happy Accidents of the Swing. 1767.
Oil on canvas. 31⅞" 3 25¼".
The Wallace Collection, London.

Engendering It

THE CONDITIONS FOR producing great art—or for excelling in any discipline—include family support, educational opportunity, community support, and patronage, as well as aptitude. Many artists now considered "great" benefited from most of these advantages. Yet the situation has been and still is discouraging, even hostile at times, for anyone who is not born white, moderately affluent, and male. Obstacles begin with the attitudes of parents, teachers, and others in power. What is amazing is that so many women have achieved so much in the face of gender-based discrimination.

During the Renaissance in Italy, it became socially and politically acceptable for aristocrats to educate daughters as well as sons in the social arts. Although the idea was simply to produce women who could write poetry, dance, sing, paint, and excel in the art of conversation so that they would make good companions for aristocratic men, some women became highly accomplished artists. However, most were denied access to the training necessary for professional careers.

Sofonisba Anguissola was the first female artist of the Renaissance to achieve recognition throughout Europe. Anguissola studied with a portrait painter, and her well-publicized success led other male artists to accept female students. While still in her twenties, she became court painter to King Philip II of Spain. Her *Self-Portrait* of 1556 shows her solemnly at work.

Women artists were somewhat more numerous and better known during the Baroque period. Among the most remarkable was Artemisia Gentileschi, daughter of well-known artist Orazio Gentileschi. Although some of today's art historians consider Artemisia a better painter than her father, until recently her work received limited recognition because she was a woman.

Her painting *Judith and the Maidservant with the Head of Holofernes* tells the Bible story of the heroic Judith who beheaded an enemy general. The intensity of the moment is communicated clearly in this Baroque work. The drama is intensified by bold use of theatrical light, sweeping curves, dramatic gestures, and warm colors.

Because women were not allowed to study from the nude in art academies, most of the women who achieved distinction in the visual arts depended on the help of fathers or close male friends who were artists. A list of such women includes Rosa Bonheur (see Chapter 10) and Marietta Robusti, both daughters of artists; Berthe Morisot, an Impressionist who was closely associated with Edouard Manet; and Mary Cassatt (see pages 211–212), who was a close friend of Edgar Degas.

The art world made great strides toward gender equality in the twentieth century, but the goal has not yet been achieved.

9.37 Sofonisba Anguissola (Italian, 1527–1625). *Self-Portrait.* 1556. Oil on canvas. 66 3 57 cm. Museum Zamek, Lancut, Poland. © The Bridgeman Art Library International Ltd.

9.38 Artemisia Gentileschi. *Judith and the Maidservant with the Head of Holofernes.* c. 1625. Oil on canvas. 6'½" 3 4'7¾". Gift of Mrs. Leslie H. Green. Photograph © 1984 The Detroit Institute of Arts/The Bridgeman Art Library, NY.

LATE EIGHTEENTH AND NINETEENTH CENTURIES

The period of great social and technological change we call the modern age was launched by three revolutions: the Industrial Revolution, which began in Britain about 1760; the American Revolution of 1776; and the French Revolution of 1789. The Industrial Revolution caused the most significant shift in the way people lived since the Neolithic agricultural revolution ten thousand years earlier. The American and French revolutions implanted the ideas of the Enlightenment in government and public affairs.

The Enlightenment, or Age of Reason, as the late eighteenth century has been called, was characterized by a shift to a more rational and scientific approach to religious, political, social, and economic issues. Belief in the importance of liberty, self-determination, and progress caused renewed interest in democracy and secular concerns. Consistent belief systems that tended to unify earlier societies became increasingly fragmented. Traditional values were challenged by the new atmosphere of independent investigation, by technological changes, and by increased contact between peoples and cultures. Artists both expressed and abetted these changes.

A new self-consciousness regarding styles led to increasing uncertainty about the place of art and artists in society. In earlier periods, artists generally adhered to a dominant style. Following the French Revolution and the subsequent break with traditional art patronage in France, a variety of styles developed simultaneously. The traditional sources of art patronage (royalty, aristocracy, the church) gradually withered away, leaving artists to hope for commercial galleries and business-class collectors to fill the gap.

NEOCLASSICISM

With the beginning of the French Revolution in 1789, the luxurious life that centered on the French court ended abruptly, and French society was disrupted and transformed. As the social structure and values changed, tastes also changed.

One of the artists who led the way to revolutions in both art and politics was painter Jacques-Louis David. Believing that the arts should serve a beneficial social purpose in a time of social and governmental reform, he rejected what he saw as the frivolous immorality of the aristocratic Rococo style. When he painted *Oath of the Horatii*, David pioneered an austere style called **Neoclassicism**. The term refers to the emulation of classical Greek and Roman art; much of the subject matter in Neoclassical art was Roman because Rome represented a republican, or non-hereditary, government.

Chapter 10: Late Eighteenth and Nineteenth Centuries was taken from *Prebles' Artforms: An Introduction to the Visual Arts,* Tenth Edition by Patrick Frank.

10.1　Jacques-Louis David.
Oath of the Horatii. 1784.
Oil on canvas. 10′10″ 3 14′.
Musée du Louvre, Paris, France. Photograph: Copyright Scala/Art Resource, NY.

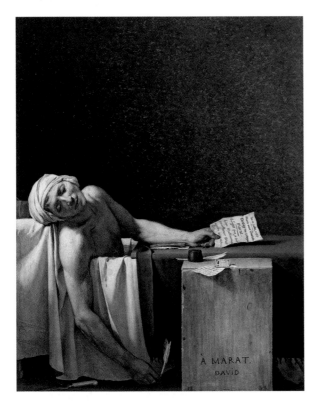

10.2　Jacques Louis David.
The Death of Marat, 1793.
Oil on canvas, 65 3 50½ in. Musées Royaux des
Beaux-Arts de Belgique, Brussels.

Figure 10.2 was taken from *A World of Art,* Sixth Edition by Henry M. Sayre.

The subject of *Oath of the Horatii* is a story of virtue and the readiness to die for liberty: The three brothers pledge to take the swords their father offers in order to defend Rome. With such paintings, David gave revolutionary leaders an inspiring image of themselves rooted in history. "Take courage," was the painting's message, "your cause is a noble one, and it has inspired heroes of the past."

David's Neoclassicism, seen in the rational, geometric structure of his composition, provides strong contrast to the lyrical softness of Rococo designs (see *Happy Accidents of the Swing* on page 189). *The Oath of the Horatii* has the quality of classical (Greco-Roman) relief sculpture, with strong side light emphasizing the figures in the foreground. Even the folds in the garments are more like carved marble than soft cloth. The background arcade gives strength to the design and provides a historically appropriate setting for the Roman figures. The two center columns separate the three major parts of the subject. Vertical and horizontal lines parallel the edges of the picture plane, forming a stable composition that resembles a stage set.

The women at the right of *The Oath of the Horatii* seem overcome by emotion, unable to participate in the serious decisions required of men who would defend their homeland. This painting reflects the common belief at that time that women were unfit for public life. Their exclusion from most professions was also true of the art world, where women were banned from academy classes in which unclothed models were used. If a woman did succeed as an artist, it was because she either could afford private study or came from an artistic family.

David's *Death of Marat* celebrates a fallen hero of the Revolution. Slain in his bath by a Monarchist—a sympathizer with the overthrown king—Marat is posed by David as Christ is traditionally posed in the Deposition, his arm draping over the edge of the tub. A dramatic Caravaggesque light falls over the revolutionary hero, his virtue embodied in the Neoclassical simplicity of David's design.

In the works of the Neoclassicist Angelica Kauffmann, who overcame such obstacles, we see a different vision of woman's abilities. Born in Switzerland and trained by her father, Kauffmann spent six years in Italy before settling in London in 1768. She was elected a full member of the British Royal Academy two years later, the last woman to be so honored until the 1920s. She created *Cornelia, Pointing to Her Children As Her Treasures* a year after David's *Oath of the Horatii*. Cornelia is at the center of the work, talking with a friend seated at the right. The friend shows a string of jewels as if boasting about them, to which Cornelia replies that her children are her jewels. Indeed, to a student of Roman history, this was true: Cornelia's children adopted her well-known democratic beliefs and went on to become important figures in the development of the Roman republic.

The new classical (that is, Neoclassical) spirit also infected architecture. After the American statesman-architect Thomas Jefferson spent five years in Europe as minister to France (1784–1789), he redesigned his home, *Monticello*, in accordance with classical ideals. *Monticello* is based on Palladio's Renaissance reinterpretation of Roman country-style houses (see the *Villa Rotonda* on page 179). The Greco-Roman portico, topped by a dome, makes the entire design reminiscent of the *Pantheon* (see pages 143–144) by way of contemporary French Neoclassical architecture.

Both *Monticello* and Jefferson's designs for the University of Virginia show the Roman phase of Neoclassical American architecture, often called the Federal Style. Jefferson advocated this Neoclassical style as an embodiment of the values of the new American republic where Roman civic virtues of courage and patriotism would be reborn. Jefferson's Neoclassical style is reflected in much of American architecture before the Civil War. Neoclassical architecture can be found in practically every city in the United States, and it dominated government buildings in Washington, D.C., into the twentieth century.

10.3 Angelica Kauffmann.
Cornelia, Pointing to Her Children as Her Treasures. c. 1785.
Oil on canvas. 40″ 3 50″ (101.6 3 127.0 cm).
Virginia Museum of Fine Arts, Richmond. The Adolph D. and Wilkins C. Williams Fund. Photograph: Ann Hutchison. © Virginia Museum of Fine Arts. 75.22/50669.2.

10.4 Thomas Jefferson.
Monticello. Charlottesville, Virginia. 1793–1806.
Monticello/Thomas Jefferson Foundation, Inc.

ROMANTICISM

The Enlightenment celebrated the power of reason; however, an opposite reaction, **Romanticism**, soon followed. This new wave of emotional expression motivated the most creative artists in Europe from about 1820 to 1850. The word Romanticism comes from *romances*, popular medieval tales of adventure written in romance languages.

Neoclassicism and Romanticism agree on the importance of individual liberty, but little else. Romantic artists, musicians, and writers believed that imagination and emotion are more valuable than reason, that nature is less corrupt than civilization, and that human beings are essentially good. Romantics celebrated nature, rural life, common people, and exotic subjects in art and literature. They asserted the validity of subjective experience and sought to escape Neoclassicism's fixation on classical forms.

Spanish artist Francisco Goya was a groundbreaking Romantic painter and printmaker. A contemporary of David, he was aware of the French Revolution, and he personally experienced some of the worst aspects of the ensuing Napoleonic era, when French armies invaded Spain and much of the rest of Europe. Goya at first welcomed Napoleon's invading army because his sympathies lay with the French Revolution and its democratic values. But he soon discovered that the occupying army was destroying rather than defending the ideals he associated with the Revolution. Napoleon's troops occupied Madrid in 1808; on May 2, a riot broke out against the French in the central square. Officers fired from a nearby hill, and the cavalry was ordered to cut down the crowds. The following night, firing squads were set up to shoot anyone suspected of causing the disturbance. Later, Goya vividly and bitterly depicted these brutalities in his powerful indictment of organized murder, *The Third of May 1808*.

10.5 Francisco Goya.
The Third of May, 1808. 1814.
Oil on canvas. 8′9″ 3 13′4″ (2.67 3 4.06 m).

His print series *The Disasters of War* makes similar statements in etching. *The Third of May 1808* is enormous, yet so well conceived in every detail that it delivers its message instantly. A structured pattern of light and dark areas organizes the scene, giving it impact and underscoring its meaning. Mechanical uniformity marks the faceless firing squad, in contrast to the ragged group that is the target. From the soldiers' dark shapes, we are led by the light and the lines of the rifles to the central figure in white. The focal point is this man, raising his arms in a gesture of helpless defiance. This work is more than a mere reconstruction of history; it is a universal protest against the brutality of tyrannical governments.

Goya's painting deals with events that took place only seven years before the artist took up the brush; a preoccupation with current events (rather than a mythological past) is an important characteristic of the Romantic movement. Another Romantic artist who painted current events was Théodore Géricault. On July 2, 1816, the French frigate *Medusa* was wrecked on a reef off the African coast. The overloaded ship had been carrying soldiers and settlers to Senegal. The captain and other senior officers escaped in lifeboats, leaving 150 behind to fend for themselves on a makeshift wooden raft. After 12 harrowing days on the raft, only 15 survived. The incident infuriated Géricault. The captain's appointment had depended on his connections with the French monarchy, which had been restored after Napoleon's defeat at Waterloo. Here, therefore, was clear evidence of the nobility's decadence. To illustrate his beliefs and feelings, Géricault planned a giant canvas, showing the raft just at the moment that the rescue ship, the *Argus*, was spotted on the horizon. He went to the Normandy coast to study the movement of water. He visited hospitals and morgues to study the effects of illness and death on the human body. He had a model of the raft constructed in his studio and arranged wax figures upon it. His student, Delacroix, posed face down for the central nude. The final painting positions the raft on a diagonal axis, creating two contradictory pyramidal points of tension. On the left, the mast not only suggests the crucifix but also reveals that the raft is sailing away from its rescuers, while on the right, the survivors climb desperately in their attempt to be seen. Géricault's horrifying picture, exhibited only a few months after it was conceived, fueled the Romantic movement with the passion of its feelings.

In his own journal, Delacroix wrote, "[The poet] Baudelaire . . . says that I bring back to painting . . . the feeling which delights in the terrible. He is right." It was in the face of the sublime

10.6 Théodore Géricault. *The Raft of the Medusa*, 1819. Oil on canvas, 16 ft. 1¼ in. 3 23 ft. 6 in.

Figure 10.6 was taken from *A World of Art*, Sixth Edition by Henry M. Sayre.

that this enjoyment of the terrible was most often experienced. Theories of the **sublime** had first appeared in the seventeenth century, most notably in Edmund Burke's *Inquiry into the Origin of Our Ideas of the Sublime and the Beautiful* (1756). For Burke, the sublime was a feeling of awe experienced before things that escaped the ability of the human mind to comprehend them—mountains, chasms, storms, and catastrophes. The sublime exceeded reason; it presented viewers with something vaster than themselves, thereby making them realize their smallness, even their insignificance, in the face of the infinite. The sublime evokes the awe-inspiring

forces of Nature, as opposed to the Beautiful, which is associated with Nature at her most harmonious and tranquil. A pastoral landscape may be beautiful; a vast mountain range, sublime.

When the British houses of Parliament burned in a disastrous fire one night in 1834, another Romantic, Joseph Mallord William Turner, witnessed the event and made several sketches that soon became paintings. His work *The Burning of the Houses of Lords and Commons* typifies the Romantic movement in several ways.

The brushwork is loose and expressive, as if he created the painting in a storm of passion. The

10.7   Joseph Mallord William Turner.
The Burning of the Houses of Lords and Commons. 1834.
Oil on fabric. 36¼″ 3 48½″ (92 3 123.2 cm).
© Cleveland Museum of Art, Bequest of John L. Severance.

colors are bright and vivid. Although the work depicts an event that happened only a few months before, the artist introduced distortions and exaggerations. According to contemporary reports, the flames did not leap up into the night as the artist shows them. Moreover, the Thames River has a curve that would partially block the view; Turner "straightened" the river to afford a wide horizon.[1] Turner made these departures from factual accuracy in order to convey the feeling of the event, as an English national symbol burned. This emphasis on feeling over fact is Romantic. Turner's loose painting style influenced the later Impressionist movement, but there are important differences between them, as we shall see.

Many Romantic artists also painted the landscape, finding there a reflection of their own emotional states. Romantic landscape painting flourished especially in the United States, where Thomas Cole founded the Hudson River School in the 1830s.

Like Turner, Cole began with on-site oil and pencil sketches, then made his large paintings in his studio. The broad, panoramic view, carefully rendered details, and light-filled atmosphere of paintings such as *The Oxbow* became the inspiration for American landscape painting for several generations. See also Asher Durand's *Kindred Spirits* (see page 77).

In nineteenth-century America it was difficult to obtain the education necessary to become a professional artist; for an African-American it was almost impossible. Nevertheless, with the help of antislavery sponsors, a few succeeded.

Robert S. Duncanson was one of the first African-American artists to earn an international reputation. As the son of a Scots-Canadian father and an African-American mother, he may have had an easier time gaining recognition as an artist than those who did not straddle the color line. Prior to settling in Cincinnati, he studied in Italy, France, and England, and he was heavily influenced by European

10.8 Thomas Cole.
The Oxbow. 1836.
Oil on canvas. 51½" 3 76" (130.8 3 193 cm).
The Metropolitan Museum of Art. Gift of Mrs. Russell Sage, 1908. (08.228) Photograph: © 1995 The Metropolitan Museum of Art/Art Resource, NY.

10.9 Robert S. Duncanson.
Blue Hole, Little Miami River. 1851.
Oil on canvas. 29¼″ 3 42¼″.
Cincinnati Art Museum. Gift of Norbert Heermann and Arthur Helwig.

Romanticism. With *Blue Hole, Little Miami River*, Duncanson reached artistic maturity. He modified the precise realism of the Hudson River School with an original, poetic softening. He orchestrated light, color, and detail to create an intimate and engaging reverie of a person in nature.

In France, the leading Romantic painter was Eugène Delacroix, previously mentioned as a student of Géricault. Delacroix's painting *The Death of Sardanapalus* is based on the life of an ancient Assyrian king who may or may not have existed. In the play *Sardanapalus* by Lord Byron, Sardanapalus is an Assyrian king in a hopeless military situation. Rather than surrender, he takes poison and orders all of his favorite possessions brought before him

10.10 Eugène Delacroix.
The Death of Sardanapalus. 1827.
Oil on canvas. 12′1½″ 3 16′2⅞″.
Photograph: Copyright Kevaler/Art Resource, NY.

and destroyed in an orgy of violence. Delacroix composed this writing work along a diagonal and lit it using strong chiaroscuro in a way that recalls certain Baroque paintings (see page 183). His brushwork is loose and open, or **painterly**, not at all like the cool precision of Neoclassicism. Delacroix used all of these devices in order to enhance the viewer's emotional response to a horrifying, if imagined, event. The Romantic painters in general stressed strong viewer involvement, use of color in painterly strokes, and dramatic movement, in contrast to the detached rationality and clear idealism of the Neoclassicists.

PHOTOGRAPHY

Landscape and portrait painters initially saw photography as a threat to their livelihood. In fact, the camera freed painters from the roles of narrator and illustrator, allowing them to explore dimensions of visual experience that were largely out of reach in Western art since the Renaissance. At the same time, photography offered new opportunities to infuse images of objective reality with personal visions.

In its first two generations, the new medium was put to many uses. The perfection of glass-plate negatives in the 1850s made possible reproductions of photographs, though the technology was still quite cumbersome to use. Photographers had to smear glass plates with just the right amount of toxic chemicals, expose the plate for the correct number of seconds, and develop the image almost immediately.

Carleton Watkins in 1861 journeyed into the Sierra Nevada to photograph *The Three Brothers* in Yosemite Valley. This image is part of a portfolio of landscape photographs that he made for sale, signing each one as if it were a painting. These photographs were widely circulated, and they influenced the U.S. Congress to set aside Yosemite as a national park.

Delacroix was one of the first to recognize the difference between camera vision and human vision. He believed that photography was potentially of great benefit to art and artists. In an essay for students, Delacroix wrote:

A daguerreotype is a mirror of the object; certain details almost always overlooked in drawing from nature

10.11 Carleton E. Watkins.
The Three Brothers. 1861.
Photograph.
Courtesy of the Library of Congress.

take on in it characteristic importance, and thus introduce the artist to complete knowledge of construction as light and shade are found in their true character.[2]

Félix Tournachon, called Nadar, first gained fame as a balloonist, and from a hot air balloon he made the first aerial photographs. He even took the first underground photographs in the sewers and catacombs of Paris, using artificial lighting techniques and long exposures.

Nadar recognized that photography was primarily a mechanical process, and that the photographer had to be intelligent and creative in order to make significant works of art with a camera. The most notable artists, writers, and intellectuals of Paris went to him to have their portraits made. His photograph of French actress *Sarah Bernhardt* is an evolutionary link between Romantic painted portraits and the glamour photography of today. Another pioneer portrait photographer was Julia Cameron, who began photographing at age forty-eight and created an impassioned body of work.

10.12 Nadar (Félix Tournachon).
Sarah Bernhardt. 1855.
Photograph printed from a collodion negative. International Museum of Photography of George Eastman House, Rochester, New York.

As both a tool and a way of seeing, photography influenced the next major stylistic development.

REALISM

Both Neoclassicism and Romanticism had their beginnings in rebellion. But by mid-century each had become institutionalized, functioning as a conservative force in French artistic life. At the state-sponsored École des Beaux Arts, or School of Fine Arts, students were taught by members of the Academy of Fine Arts (an organization of government-approved artists) that "great painting" demanded "classical" technique and "elevated" subject matter found in history, mythology, literature, or exotic locations.

Delacroix accused Academy members of teaching beauty as though it were algebra. Today, we still use the term **academic art** for generally unimaginative works that follow stale formulas laid down by an academy or school, especially the French Academy of the nineteenth century.

French Academy members played a major role in selecting artists for a huge annual exhibition known as the **Salon**. Participating in the Salon was virtually the only way an artist might become known to the public in those days. The history of the rest of the nineteenth century is largely one of rebellion against such institutions and authority figures. Vast changes in art and the artist's role in society were about to topple the dominance of the French Academy.

Realism describes a style of art and literature that depicts ordinary existence without idealism, exoticism, or nostalgia. We have seen it before the nineteenth century, notably in Roman portrait sculpture and Flemish and Dutch painting. By mid-century, a growing number of artists were dissatisfied with both the Neoclassicists' and the Romantics' attachment to mythical, exotic, extraordinary, and historical subjects. They believed that art should deal with human experience and observation. They knew that people in the nineteenth century were living a new kind of life, and wanted art to show it.

In the 1850s, French painter Gustave Courbet revived Realism with new vigor by employing a direct, painterly technique for the portrayal of the dignity of ordinary things and common life. In doing so, he laid the foundation for a rediscovery of the extraordinary visual qualities of everyday experience.

The Stone Breakers shows Courbet's rejection of Romantic and Neoclassical formulas. His subject is neither historical nor allegorical, neither religious nor heroic. The men breaking stones are ordinary road workers, presented almost life-size. Courbet did not idealize the work of breaking stones or dramatize the struggle for existence; he simply said, "Look at this."

Courbet's detractors were sure that he was causing artistic and moral decline by painting what they considered unpleasant and trivial subjects on a grand scale. They accused him of raising "a cult of ugliness" against cherished concepts of Beauty and the Ideal. Conservative critics and most of the public saw Realism as nothing less than the enemy of art, and many believed that photography was the source and the sponsor of this disaster. When *The Stone Breakers* was exhibited in Paris in the Salon of 1850, it was attacked as inartistic, crude, and socialistic. The latter charge actually had some

10.13   Gustave Courbet.
The Stone Breakers. 1849 (destroyed in 1945).
Oil on canvas. 5′5″ 3 7′10″.
The Bridgeman Art Library International Ltd.

validity: Courbet was in fact a lifelong radical who espoused anarchist philosophies. He believed that most governments were oppressive institutions that only served the wealthy, and that average people could better meet their needs by banding together in voluntary associations for such functions as public works, banking, and policing. Beginning in 1855, Courbet practiced what he preached and set up his own exhibits.

Courbet was one of the first to finish his paintings outdoors, working directly from nature. Previously, most landscape painting had been done in the artist's studio from memory, sketches, and reference materials such as rocks and plants brought in from outside. When portable tubes of oil paint became available in 1841, oil painting outdoors became practical. By working directly from subjects outdoors, painters were able to capture first impressions. This shift in practice opened up whole new ways of seeing and painting.

Of his own work, Courbet said: "To be able to represent the customs, the ideas, the appearance of my own era . . . to create living art; that is my aim."[3] An example of Realism in printmaking is *Transnonain Street* by Honore Daumier.

Realism of a more popular sort was practiced by Rosa Bonheur, who specialized in painting rural scenes with animals. In *The Horse Fair*, she captured the surging energy of a group of horses offered for sale, some of them untamed. Many scholars believe that the riding figure in the blue-green coat near the center of the picture is a portrait of the artist wearing men's clothing. If so, it was one of several unconventional personal characteristics that she adopted in order to help her career (see accompanying essay).

The Realist paintings of American artist Thomas Eakins are remarkable for their humanity and insight into the everyday world. A comparison of the paintings of Eakins and those of his teacher, Jean-Léon Gérôme, shows the contrast between Realism and officially sanctioned academic art. Both *Pygmalion and Galatea* by Gérôme and *William Rush Carving His Allegorical Figure* take up the theme of the sculptor and his model; Gérôme created a painting based on classical and academic ideals, while Eakins showed respect for the beauty

10.14 Rosa Bonheur.
The Horse Fair. 1853–1855.
Oil on canvas. 96¼″ 3 199½″ (244.5 3 506.7 cm).
Image copyright © The Metropolitan Museum of Art. Image Source: Art Resource, NY.

10.15 Jean-Léon Gérôme.
Pygmalion and Galatea. c. 1860.
Oil on canvas. 35″ 3 27″ (88.9 3 68.6 cm).
The Metropolitan Museum of Art. Gift of Louis C. Raegner, 1927.
(27.200) Photograph: © 1989 The Metropolitan Museum
of Art/Art Resource, NY.

10.16 Thomas Eakins.
William Rush Carving His Allegorical Figure of the Schuylkill River. 1876–1877.
Oil on canvas on masonite. 20⅛″ 3 26⅛″.
Philadelphia Museum of Art. Gift of Mrs. Thomas Eakins and Miss Mary A. Williams, 1929-184-27. Photograph: Graydon Wood, 2000.

Rosa Bonheur: Flouting Social Conventions

THE LIST OF awards that Rosa Bonheur (1822–1899) earned in her lifetime was impressive by any standard: First Medal at the Paris Salon; Grand Cross of the French Legion of Honor; Commander of the Order of Isabella the Catholic; Member of the Order of King Leopold of Belgium. She was the first woman ever to receive most of these honors. Yet Rosa Bonheur also led an unusual personal life that showed the difficulties that a woman of her day had to face if she wanted a career.

Her most important early influence was her father, Raymond, a drawing teacher. He was a Saint-Simonian Socialist—that is, he believed all wealth should be shared because everybody was equal; girls were as worthy as boys and should be raised the same way. These beliefs are somewhat radical even today, but he took them even further. He believed that a new savior would come to the human race, as Christ had done in ancient times, and that this new Messiah would be a woman. Hence, he took special pains to educate his daughters, an unusual step for that period.

Rosa Bonheur decided as a teenager to become an artist, and benefited from her father's teaching; in fact, she soon surpassed him. Because the Academy forbade women from studying the nude model, she decided to specialize in painting country scenes with animals. There was a ready market for such works, partly because France was industrializing and people from the country were moving to the city in great numbers. People wanted to remember country life, and Bonheur became their painter. A few Parisian artists had already specialized in this subject, but she soon surpassed them, too.

The main problem inherent in her career choice was that she would have to do things that women simply did not do: spend a lot of time on farms and ranches, become an expert rider, and sketch animal anatomy in slaughterhouses. All of these she did, apparently with pleasure.

She found that she could do her work with more ease and comfort if she cut her hair short and wore trousers. Cutting the hair was not a problem, but for a woman to wear trousers in public was illegal. She had to obtain a permit from the local police and renew it every six months.

She was not the first woman to adopt a male appearance as a career move. The novelist Amandine Dupin, eighteen years older than Bonheur, had scandalized Paris by wearing men's clothing and using the pen name George Sand; Bonheur admired her.

How else might a woman advance her career in a male-dominated society? Bonheur always insisted that her only goals were convenience and career advancement: "If, however, you see me dressed as I am, it is not in the least in order to make me into an original, but simply in order to facilitate my work. Consider that, at a certain period in my life, I spent whole days at the slaughterhouse."[1]

She never married, regarding it as a hindrance. Rather, she lived most of her life with her friend Natalie Micas in a home filled with pets. The two of them were active in the Society for the Prevention of Cruelty to Animals. Her favorite males, she said, were the bulls that she painted.

Meanwhile, her work kept selling and gaining honors. She bought a country estate next to the emperor's family home. When Empress Eugenie arrived at her door to present her with the Legion of Honor, the artist kept Her Majesty waiting while she threw a robe on over her pants.

To the end of her life, Bonheur lived the dichotomy of the successful

10.17 W. H. Mote.
Rosa Bonheur. 1856.
Engraving after R. Buckner.
Picture Collection, The New York Public Library, Astor, Lenox and Tilden Foundations.

and honored career woman forced into an unconventional personal life. Accused of seeming unfeminine, she defended herself in a way that rings as a call for women's equality:

Why wouldn't I be proud of being a woman? My father, that enthusiastic apostle of humanity, repeated to me many times that woman's mission was to uplift the human race, that she was the Messiah of future centuries. I owe to his doctrines the great and proud ambition that I conceived for the sex to which I take glory in belonging, and whose independence I will uphold until my last day. Moreover, I am persuaded that the future belongs to us.[2]

Notes

1. From *Reminiscences of Rosa Bonheur*, published in 1910 and quoted in Wendy Slatkin, ed., *The Voices of Women Artists* (Englewood Cliffs, NJ: Prentice Hall, 1993), 132.
2. Ibid.

of the ordinary human being. Eakins's insistence on painting people the way they actually look led him to escape the bondage of stylization imposed by the rules of the academy; it also led to shock and rejection by the public and much of the art world.

In the academic painting *Pygmalion and Galatea*, Gérôme placed the woman, Galatea, on a pedestal, both literally and figuratively. The Greek myth of Pygmalion tells of a sculptor who carved a statue of a woman so beautiful that he fell in love with it. Pygmalion prayed to Aphrodite, goddess of love, who responded by making the figure come to life. The sentimental approach (note the cupid at right), smooth finish, and mild eroticism are typical of academic art. In his painting *William Rush Carving His Allegorical Figure*, Eakins presented a Realist view of the sculptor's trade: A model poses as the artist chisels away at the left; nineteenth-century custom demanded that a chaperone be present. Eakins selected this subject because William Rush was the first American artist to use nude models, bringing controversy on himself in the 1820s.

We can see Eakins's influence in the work of his student and friend Henry Ossawa Tanner, who was the best known African-American painter before the twentieth century. At the age of thirteen, Tanner watched a landscape painter at work and decided to become an artist. While studying with Eakins at the Academy of Fine Arts in Philadelphia, Tanner changed his subject matter from landscapes to scenes of daily life. In 1891, after an exhibition of his work was largely ignored, Tanner moved to France, where he remained for most of the rest of his life. He found less racial prejudice in Paris than in the United States. His paper "The American Negro in Art," presented at the 1893 World's Congress on Africa in Chicago, voiced the need for dignified portrayals of Blacks, and he offered his painting *The Banjo Lesson* as a model.

The lively realism of *The Banjo Lesson* reveals Tanner's considerable insight into the feelings of his subjects, yet he avoids the sentimentality that was common in many late nineteenth-century American paintings. This painting shows the influence of Eakins in its detail and its humanistic content.

The most important predecessor of Impressionism in French art is without a doubt Edouard Manet, who was the most controversial artist in Paris in the 1860s. He studied with an academic master, but soon broke away from traditional teaching in an effort to update the art of the old masters (Veronese, Velázquez, and Rembrandt, for example) by infusing painting with a dose of realism inherited from Gustave Courbet. In addition, Manet often flattened out the figures in his paintings under the influence of the Japanese prints that he knew and

10.18   Henry Ossawa Tanner.
The Banjo Lesson. 1893.
Oil on canvas. 49" 3 35½".
Hampton University Museum, Hampton, Virginia.

10.19 Edouard Manet.
Luncheon on the Grass (Le Déjeuner Sur l'Herbe). 1863.
Oil on canvas. 7′ 3 8′10″ (2.13 3 2.6 m).
Musée d' Orsay, Paris. RMN Reunion des Musees Natioaux/Art Resource, NY.

admired. His loose, open brushwork and sometimes commonplace subjects were an inspiration to younger painters who led the Impressionist movement. Manet's painting *Luncheon on the Grass* scandalized French critics and the public—because of the way it was painted as well as the subject matter. Manet painted the female figure without shading, employed flat patches of color throughout the painting, and left bare canvas in some places. He concentrated on the interplay among the elements of form that make up the composition: light shapes against dark, cool

colors accented by warm colors, directional forces, and active balance. Manet's concern with visual issues over content or storytelling was revolutionary.

The juxtaposition of a female nude with males dressed in clothing of the time shocked viewers, but such a combination was not new. Nude and clothed figures were combined in landscape paintings going back to the Renaissance and even Roman compositions that depicted ancient myths or stories from the Bible. However, in Manet's painting, there is no allegory, no history, no mythology, and not even a significant title to suggest morally redeeming values. Manet based his composition (but not his meaning) on the figures in an engraving of a Renaissance drawing by Raphael (Fig. 4.6), who in turn had been influenced by Roman relief sculpture.

It is ironic that Manet, who had such reverence for the art of the past, would be attacked by the public and the critics for his radical innovations. Simultaneously, he was championed by other artists as a leader of the avant-garde. Manet became the reluctant leader of an enthusiastic group of young painters who later formed the group known as the Impressionists.

IMPRESSIONISM

In 1874, a group of painters who had been denied the right to show in the Salon of 1873 organized an independent exhibition of their work. These artists, opposing academic doctrines and Romantic ideals, turned instead to the portrayal of contemporary life. They took their canvases outdoors and sought to paint "impressions" of what the eye actually sees, rather than what the mind knows. This is no simple goal; we usually generalize what we think we see from the most obvious fragments. A river may become a uniform blue-green in our minds, whereas direct, unconditioned seeing shows a rich diversity of colors.

Landscape and ordinary scenes painted outdoors in varied atmospheric conditions, seasons, and times of day were among the main subjects of these artists. For example, in 1877 Claude Monet took his easel to the St. Lazare railroad station and painted a series of works in the train shed, among them *Arrival of the Normandy Train, Gare St. Lazare*. Rather than focus on the human drama of arrival and departure, he was fascinated by the play of light amid the steam of the locomotives and the clouds glimpsed through the

10.20 Claude Monet.
Arrival of the Normandy Train, Gare St. Lazare.
1877. Oil on canvas. 59.6 3 80.2 cm.
Mr. and Mrs. Martin A. Ryerson Collection, 1933.1158, The Art Institute of Chicago. Photograph: © The Art Institute of Chicago.

10.21   Claude Monet.
         Impression: Sunrise. 1872.
         Oil on canvas. 49.5 3 64.8 cm.
         Musée Marmottan–Monet, Paris. The Bridgeman Art Library International Ltd.

glass roof. He made his paintings quickly under the constantly shifting conditions, painting as traditional artists might make sketches.

Monet and his colleagues were dubbed **Impressionists** by a critic who objected to the sketchy quality of their paintings. The term was suggested by one of Monet's versions of *Impression: Sunrise*. Although the critic's label was intended to be derogatory, the artists adopted the term as a fitting description of their work. Monet had seen the extremely fluid paintings of Turner (page 196), but he used Turner's techniques in a more objective and less emotional manner

From direct observation and from studies in physics, the Impressionists learned that we see light as a complex of reflections received by the eye and reassembled by the mind during the process of per-

ception. Therefore, they used small dabs of color that appear merely as separate strokes of paint when seen close up, yet become lively depictions of subjects when seen at a distance. Monet often applied strokes of pure color placed next to each other, rather than colors premixed or blended on the palette. The viewer perceives a vibrancy that cannot be achieved with mixed color alone. The effect was startling to eyes accustomed to the muted, continuous tones of academic painting.

The Impressionists enthusiastically affirmed modern life, as Monet's paintings in the railroad station show. They saw the beauty of the world as a gift and the forces of nature as aids to human progress. Although misunderstood by their public, the Impressionists made visible a widely held optimism about the promise of the new technology.

Claude Monet: Guided by Light

CLAUDE MONET (1840–1926) grew up in Le Havre, a bustling port town on the north coast of France. In high school, he developed a reputation for drawing caricatures. A local picture framer exhibited them in his shop, and there they caught the eye of the painter Eugène Boudin.

Monet's senior by sixteen years, Boudin was a pioneer in the new practice of painting outdoors, working directly from nature. He encouraged Monet to pursue art seriously and invited him along on a painting excursion. The experience started Monet on the path he would follow all his life. "Boudin set up his easel and began to paint," Monet later recalled. "I looked on with some apprehension, then more attentively, and then suddenly it was as if a veil was torn from my eyes; I had understood. I had grasped what painting could be."[1]

Monet continued his studies in Paris, where he immersed himself in the lively artistic debates of the day. He met and admired the controversial painters Courbet and Manet. He met other art students, Renoir among them, who shared his passion for painting nature and modern life. In time, they would become famous as leading Impressionists.

Fame was long in coming, however; Monet was over forty before his paintings sold well enough to guarantee a living for himself and his family. In the meantime, life was difficult. From dawn to dusk he painted; in the evening, by lamplight, he wrote letters — letters asking for money, letters stalling creditors, letters trying to arrange for his work to be seen and sold.

As Monet's artistic vision deepened, he realized that every shift in light and atmosphere created a new subject. He would arrive at a site with as many as a dozen blank canvases, working on each one in turn as the light changed. His painting grew increasingly subjective in later years, as he strove to express not only light but his feelings about the changing qualities of light. Relentlessly self-critical, he was often driven to despair by his work, and he destroyed dozens of canvases he considered failures.

In back of his house at Giverny, the small town outside Paris where he finally settled, Monet created a water lily pond that became the favorite subject of his final years. In old age, he embarked on one of his most ambitious projects: a series of huge paintings of the water surface, its shimmering reflections of sky and clouds punctuated with floating flowers. Shown end to end, they form dazzling panoramas over six feet tall and twenty-eight feet long.

10.22 *Claude Monet.*
On his eightieth birthday. 1920.
The Bridgeman Art Library International.

Monet intended them as a gift to the French government, and one of his last acts before he died was to send a letter declaring them finished.

Note

1. William Seitz, *Claude Monet* (New York: Abrams, 1982), 13.

10.23   Pierre-Auguste Renoir.
Le Moulin de la Galette. 1876.
Oil on canvas. 51½″ 3 68⅞″.
Musée d'Orsay, Paris. Photograph: Art
Resource, NY.

Impressionism was at its most creative between about 1870 and 1880. After 1880, Claude Monet continued for more than forty years to advance Impressionism's original premise.

Pierre-Auguste Renoir's *Le Moulin de la Galette* ("The Pancake Mill") depicts a popular Impressionist theme: contemporary middle-class people enjoying outdoor leisure activities. The young men and women depicted are conversing, sipping wine, and generally enjoying the moment at the popular outdoor café that served up pancakes and dance music with equal liberality. The Industrial Revolution had created an urban middle class with leisure, respect for the new technol-ogy, and a taste for fashion, and the Impressionists chronicled their lives. Renoir was more interested in the human drama than Monet—we sense the mood of some of the people in this work—but he was also very interested in how the light, filtered by leaves of the trees, hits the bodies and clothing in the crowd.

Edgar Degas exhibited with the Impressionists, although his approach differed somewhat from theirs. He shared with the Impressionists a direct-ness of expression and an interest in portraying contemporary life, but he combined the immediacy of Impressionism with a highly inventive approach to pictorial composition. Degas, along with the

Impressionists, was influenced by the new ways of seeing and composing that he saw in Japanese prints and in unposed, street-scene photography.

Conventional European compositions placed subjects within a central zone. Degas, however, used surprising, lifelike compositions and effects that often cut figures at the edge. The tipped-up ground planes and bold asymmetry found in Japanese prints inspired Degas to create paintings filled with intriguing visual tensions, such as those in *The Ballet Class*, in which two diagonal groups of figures appear on opposite sides of an empty center.

Degas depicted ballet classes in ways that showed their unglamorous character. Often, as here, he was able to turn his ability to the task of defining human character and mood. The painting builds from the quiet, disinterested woman in the foreground, up to the right, then across to the cluster of dancing girls, following the implied sightline of the ballet master.

American painter Mary Cassatt was born into Philadelphia high society, and when she went to Paris in the late 1860s to further her artistic development she did not seek out Academy teachers. Rather, she was independent-minded enough to befriend Manet and Degas, and soon she joined and exhibited with the Impressionists. She was among the many European and American artists who were influenced by Japanese prints and casual compositions of late nineteenth-century do-it-yourself photography. A resemblance to Japanese prints is readily apparent in the simplicity and bold design of *The Boating Party* (on the following page). Cassatt refined her subject in sweeping curves and almost flat shapes.

There is, in addition, subtle feminist content in this work. The difference in clothing styles between the woman and the man shows that she has hired him to take her and the child out for a boat ride. This was an unusually assertive thing for a woman to do for herself in those days, and the glances between all three persons in the painting show some of the social tension that would have accompanied this event. The work is typical of

10.24 Edgar Degas.
The Ballet Class. c. 1879–1880.
Oil on canvas. 32⅜″ 3 30¼″.
Philadelphia Museum of Art. Purchased with the W. P. Wilstach Fund. W1937-2-1.

Cassatt in its focus on the world of women and their concerns.

The Impressionist group disbanded after its exhibition in 1886, but its influence was immeasurable—in spite of the fact that Impressionist paintings were looked upon with indifference or hostility by most of the public until the turn of the twentieth century.

Auguste Rodin was at least as innovative in sculpture as his contemporaries were in painting. Rodin became the first sculptor since Bernini (see page 184) to return sculpture to the status of a major art form, renewed with emotional and spiritual depth.

In 1875, after training as a sculptor's helper, Rodin traveled to Italy where he carefully studied the work of the Renaissance masters Donatello

10.25   Mary Cassatt.
The Boating Party. 1893–1894.
Oil on canvas. .900 3 1.173 cm (35⅞″ 3 46⅛″).
Chester Dale Collection. Photograph: © 2001 Board of Trustees, National
Gallery of Art, Washington, DC. 1963.10.94.(1758)PA.

and Michelangelo. Rodin was the first to use Michelangelo's unfinished pieces as an inspiration for making rough finish an expressive quality. In contrast to Michelangelo, however, Rodin was primarily a modeler in plaster and clay, rather than a carver in stone.

His best-known work, *The Thinker*, shows his expressive style to good advantage. He wrote that at first he was inspired by a figure of the medieval poet Dante, but he rejected the idea of a thin, ascetic figure:

Guided by my first inspiration I conceived another thinker, a naked man, seated upon a rock, his feet drawn under him, he dreams. The fertile thought slowly elaborates itself within his brain. He is no longer dreamer, he is creator.[4]

In *The Thinker*, Rodin projected the universal artist/poet as creator, judge, and witness, brooding over the human condition. Rodin combined a superb knowledge of anatomy with modeling skill to create the fluid, tactile quality of hand-shaped clay. He restored sculpture as a vehicle for personal expression after it had lapsed into mere decoration and heroic monuments. Another work of his is *The Kiss* on page 36.

10.26 Auguste Rodin.
The Thinker. c. 1910.
Bronze. Life-size.
Christie's Images. SuperStock.

THE POST-IMPRESSIONIST PERIOD

Post-Impressionism refers to trends in painting starting in about 1885 that followed Impressionism. The Post-Impressionist painters did not share a single style; rather, they built on or reacted to Impressionism in different ways. Some felt that the Impressionists' focus on sketchy immediacy had sacrificed solidity of form and composition. Others felt that Impressionism's emphasis on the objective observation did not leave enough room for personal expression or spiritual content.

Georges Seurat and Paul Cézanne were interested in developing formal structure in their paintings. Each in his own way organized visual form to achieve structured clarity of design, and their paintings influenced twentieth-century formalist styles.

Seurat's large painting *A Sunday on la Grande Jatte* has the subject matter, light, and color qualities of Impressionism, but this is not a painting

10.27 Georges Seurat.
A Sunday on la Grande Jatte. 1884–1886.
Oil on canvas. 81″ 3 120⅜″.
Helen Birch Bartlett Memorial Collection.
Photograph: © 2005 The Art Institute of Chicago. All rights reserved.

of a fleeting moment; it is a carefully constructed composition of lasting impact. Seurat set out to systematize the optical color mixing of Impressionism and to create a more solid, formal organization with simplified shapes. He called his method divisionism, but it is more popularly known as **pointillism**. With it, Seurat tried to develop and apply a "scientific" technique. He arrived at his method by studying the principles of color optics that were being formulated at the time. Through the application of tiny dots of color, Seurat achieved a vibrant surface based on **optical color mixture**. Seurat preceded *A Sunday on la Grande Jatte* with more than fifty drawn and painted preliminary studies in which he explored the horizontal and vertical relationships, the character of each shape, and the patterns of light, shade, and color. The final painting shows the total control that Seurat sought through the application of his method. The frozen formality of the figures seems surprising, considering the

casual nature of the subject matter; yet it is precisely this calm, formal grandeur that gives the painting its strength and enduring appeal.

Like Seurat, Cézanne sought to achieve strength in the formal structure of his paintings. "My aim," he said, "was to make Impressionism into something solid and enduring like the art of the museums."[5]

Cézanne saw the planar surfaces of his subjects in terms of color modulation. Instead of using light and shadow in a conventional way, he relied on carefully developed relationships between adjoining strokes of color to show solidity of form and receding space. He questioned, then abandoned, linear and atmospheric perspective and went beyond the appearance of nature, to reconstruct it according to his own interpretation.

Landscape was one of Cézanne's main interests. In *Mont Sainte-Victoire*, we can see how he flattened space yet gave an impression of air and depth with some atmospheric perspective and the

10.28 Paul Cézanne. *Mont Sainte-Victoire.* 1902–1904. Oil on canvas. 27½″ 3 35¼″. Philadelphia Museum of Art. The George W. Elkins Collection. E1936-1-1.

use of warm advancing and cool receding colors. The dark edge lines around the distant mountain help counter the illusion of depth. Cézanne simplified the houses and trees into patches of color that suggest almost geometric planes and masses. This entire composition uses color and brushstroke to orchestrate nature to a degree then unprecedented in Western art. His rhythm of parallel brushstrokes and his concept of a geometric substructure in nature offered a new range of possibilities to later artists.

Among Post-Impressionists of an expressive bent, Vincent van Gogh and Paul Gauguin brought to their work emotional intensity and a desire to make their thoughts and feelings visible. They often used strong color contrasts, shapes with clear contours, bold brushwork, and, in van Gogh's case, vigorous paint textures. Their art greatly influenced twentieth-century Expressionist styles.

With Vincent van Gogh, late nineteenth-century painting moved from an outer impression of what the eye sees to an inner expression of what the heart feels.

From Impressionism, van Gogh learned the expressive potential of open brushwork and relatively pure color, but the style did not provide him enough freedom of expression. Van Gogh intensified the surfaces of his paintings with textural brushwork that recorded each gesture of his hand and gave an overall rhythmic movement to his paintings. He also began to use strong color in an effort to express his emotions more clearly. In letters to his brother Theo, he wrote,

. . . instead of trying to reproduce exactly what I have before my eyes, I use color more arbitrarily so as to express myself forcibly . . .

I am always in hope of making a discovery there to express the love of two lovers by a marriage of two complementary colors, their mingling and their opposition, the mysterious vibrations of kindred tones. To express the thought of a brow by the radiance of a light tone against somber background.[6]

As did other artists of the period, van Gogh developed a new sense of design from studying Japanese prints, as we see in *Japonaiserie: Flowering Plum Tree*. In *The Sower*, the Japanese influence led van Gogh to adopt bold, simplified shapes and flat

10.29 Vincent van Gogh.
Japonaiserie: Flowering Plum Tree. 1887.
After Hiroshige. Oil on canvas. 21½″ 3 18″.
Vincent van Gogh Foundation. Van Gogh Museum, Amsterdam.

10.30 Vincent van Gogh.
The Sower. 1888.
Oil on canvas. 17⅜″ 3 22⅛″.
Vincent van Gogh Foundation. Van Gogh Museum, Amsterdam.

10.31 Vincent van Gogh.
The Starry Night. 1889.
Oil on canvas. 29″ 3 36¼″.
Acquired through the Lillie P. Bliss Bequest. (472. 1941). Digital Image
© The Museum of Modern Art/Licensed by Scala-Art Resource, NY.

color areas. The wide band of a tree trunk cuts diagonally across the composition; its strength balances the sun and its energy coming toward us with the movement of the sower.

Van Gogh was driven by a strong desire to share personal feelings and insights. In *The Starry Night*, a view of a town at night became the point of departure for a powerful symbolic image. Hills seem to undulate, echoing tremendous cosmic forces in the sky. The small town nestled into the dark forms of the ground plane suggests the small scale of human life. The church's spire reaches toward the heavens, echoed by the larger, more dynamic upward thrust of the cypress trees in the left foreground. (The evergreen cypress is traditionally planted beside graveyards in Europe as a symbol of eternal life.) All these elements are united by the surging rhythm of lines that express van Gogh's passionate spirit and mystical vision. Many know of van Gogh's bouts of mental illness, but few realize that he did his paintings between seizures, in moments of great clarity. See the biography on page 217.

French artist Paul Gauguin was highly critical of the materialism of industrial society. He experienced that business world firsthand during the several years that he worked as a stockbroker to support

Vincent van Gogh: A Life's Work in Ten Years

TODAY THE ART of Vincent van Gogh (1853–1890) is internationally known and admired, but it is hard to believe that van Gogh worked as an artist for only ten years. During his lifetime his art was known only to a few; in fact, he sold only one painting.

Van Gogh was born in the Netherlands to a middle-class family: His father was a minister, his grandfather a famous preacher; three uncles, and later his brother, were art dealers—a background that paved the way for Vincent's lifelong concern with both art and religion.

After six years working in the art business in Paris and London, he returned to the Netherlands to study theology. In 1878, at age twenty-five, he became a lay preacher among impoverished miners in Belgium. Although not successful at preaching, van Gogh was effective at aiding the victims of mining disasters and disease. When his compassion spurred him to give most of his possessions to the poor, the missionary society that had hired him dismissed him because they thought he interpreted Christ's teachings too literally.

He then decided to take up art, not because he possessed any obvious talent, but because he saw art as the means through which he could communicate with others. Although determined to be a painter, van Gogh believed that he had to master drawing before he allowed himself to use color. The miners and farm laborers that he helped with his social work were his first models. As he developed his skill, Vincent was supported by his brother Theo, who regularly sent money and provided encouragement through his letters.

Van Gogh studied briefly at the art academy in Antwerp, Belgium, but he was largely self-taught. In 1886 he joined his brother in Paris, where he met the leading French Impressionist and Post-Impressionist painters. Under their influence van Gogh's paintings, which had been limited to the somber tones of traditional Dutch painting, became much lighter and brighter in color, as we see in *Self-Portrait with Gray Hat*.

In 1888 he moved to southern France, where in less than two years he produced most of the paintings for which he is known. There, armed with the Impressionists' bright, free color, and inspired by the intense semitropical light, van Gogh took color even further. He developed a revolutionary approach to color based on the way colors and color combinations symbolize ideas and emotional content. His new understanding of expressive color led him to write that "the painter of the future will be a colorist such as has never existed."[1]

Van Gogh's use of pure colors and his bold strokes of thick paint created images of emotional intensity that had a great impact on artists of the twentieth century. Before van Gogh, most Western painters used color to describe the appearance of their subjects. After van Gogh, painters began to realize that color and brushwork could make visible feelings and states of mind.

Beginning in his teenage years, van Gogh suffered episodes of mental breakdown. With passing years, these increased in duration. Spells of fervent painting were interrupted by periods of illness and depression. Contrary to popular belief, these episodes contributed nothing to his development as an artist.

Increasing illness led him voluntarily to enter a mental hospital for several months. After leaving the hospital,

10.32   Vincent van Gogh.
Self-Portrait with Gray Hat, 1887.
Oil on canvas. $17\frac{1}{2}" \times 14\frac{3}{4}"$.
Amsterdam, Van Gogh Museum (Vincent van Gogh Foundation).

he returned to Paris, then settled in a nearby town under the watchful eye of a doctor known to be a friend of artists. However, his increasing despair over his mental state drove him to suicide at age thirty-seven.

An emphasis on the tragic aspects of van Gogh's now legendary life has produced a popular view of the man that tends to obscure his great contribution to art. In spite of his difficulties, van Gogh produced almost two thousand works of art within a mere ten years. Although most of his contemporaries could not see the value of his art, his paintings and drawings are displayed today in major museums worldwide, and exhibitions of his works attract record crowds.

Note

1. Robert Wallace. *The World of Van Gogh* (New York: Time-Life, 1969), 90.

Vincent van Gogh's *The Sower*

WE KNOW MORE about the genesis and development of *The Sower* than of almost all of Vincent van Gogh's other paintings, and we can follow the work's progress in some detail. There are four different descriptions of it in his letters, the first on June 17, 1888, in a letter to Australian painter John Russell (**Fig. 10.33**) that includes a preliminary sketch of his idea. "Am working at a Sower," van Gogh writes in the letter, "the great field all violet the sky & sun very yellow. It is a hard subject to treat."

The difficulties he was facing in the painting were numerous, having particularly to do with a color problem. At sunset, he wrote in a letter to the painter Emile Bernard on the very next day, June 18, Van Gogh was faced with a moment when the "excessive" contrast between the yellow sun and the violet shadows on the field would necessarily "irritate" the beholder's eye. He had to be true to that contrast and yet find a way to soften it. For approximately eight days he worked on the painting. First, he tried making the sower's trousers white in an effort to create a place in the painting that would "allow the eye to rest and distract it." That strategy apparently failing, he tried modifying the yellow and violet areas of the painting. On June 26, he wrote to his brother Theo: "Yesterday and today I worked on the sower, which is completely recast. The sky is yellow and green, the ground violet and orange." This plan succeeded (**Fig. 10.34**). Each area of the painting now contained color that connected it to the opposite area, green to violet and orange to yellow.

10.33   Vincent van Gogh.
Letter to John Peter Russell, June 17, 1888.
Ink on laid paper, 8 3 10¼ in.
Solomon R. Guggenheim Museum, New York. Thannhauser Collection, Gift, Justin K. Thannhauser, 1978. 78.2514.18. Photo by Robert E. Mates. © The Solomon R. Guggenheim Foundation, New York.

Works in Progress: Vincent van Gogh's *The Sower* was taken from *A World of Art*, Sixth Edition by Henry M. Sayre.

10.34 Vincent van Gogh.
The Sower, 1888.
Oil on canvas, 25¼ 3 31¾ in. Signed, lower left: Vincent.
Collection Kröller-Müller Museum, Otterlo, The Netherlands.

The sower was, for van Gogh, the symbol of his own "longing for the infinite," as he wrote to Bernard, and having finished the painting, he remained, in August, still obsessed with the image. "The idea of the Sower continues to haunt me all the time," he wrote to Theo. In fact, he had begun to think of the finished painting as a study that was itself a preliminary work leading to a drawing (**Fig. 10.35**). "Now the harvest, the Garden, the Sower . . . are sketches after painted studies. I think all these ideas are good," he wrote to Theo on August 8, "but the painted studies lack clearness of touch. That is [the] reason why I felt it necessary to draw them."

In the drawing, sun, wheat, and the sower himself are enlarged, made more monumental. The house and tree on the left have been eliminated, causing us to focus more on the sower himself, whose stride is now wider and who seems more intent on his task. But it is the clarity of van Gogh's line that is especially astonishing. Here we have a sort of anthology of line types: short and long, curved and straight, wide and narrow. Lines of each type seem to group themselves into bundles of five or ten, and each bundle seems to possess its own direction and flow, creating a sense of the tilled field's uneven but regular furrows. It is as if, wanting to represent his longing for the infinite, as it is contained at the moment of the genesis of life, sowing the field, van Gogh himself returns to the most fundamental element in art—line itself.

10.35 Vincent van Gogh.
The Sower, 1888.
Drawing. Pencil, reed pen, and brown and black ink on wove paper, 9⅝ 3 12½ in.
Amsterdam, Van Gogh Museum, Vincent van Gogh Foundation.

10.36   Paul Gauguin.
The Vision After the Sermon (Jacob Wrestling with the Angel). 1888.
Oil on canvas. 28¾″ 3 36½″.
National Gallery of Scotland, Edinburgh.

his family, painting on the weekends. He exhibited occasionally with the Impressionists, but he longed to escape what he called "the European struggle for money." This attitude led Gauguin to admire the honest life of the Brittany peasants of western France. In 1888, he completed *The Vision After the Sermon*, the first major work in his new, expressive version of Post-Impressionism. The large, carefully designed painting shows Jacob and the angel as they appear to a group of Brittany peasants in a vision inspired by the sermon in their village church.

The symbolic representation of unquestioning faith is an image that originated in Gauguin's mind rather than in his eye. With it, Gauguin took a major step toward personal expression. In order to avoid what he considered the distraction of implied deep space, he tipped up the simplified background plane and painted it an intense vermilion. The entire composition is divided diagonally by the trunk of the apple tree, in the manner of Japanese prints. Shapes have been reduced to flat curvilinear areas outlined in black, with shadows minimized or eliminated.

Both van Gogh's and Gauguin's uses of color were important influences on twentieth-century painting. Their views on color were prophetic. The subject of a painting, Gauguin wrote, was only a pretext for symphonies of line and color.

In painting, one must search rather for suggestion than for description, as is done in music. . . . Think of the highly important musical role which color will play henceforth in modern painting.[7]

Gauguin retained memories of his childhood in Peru that persuaded him that the art of ancient and non-Western cultures had a spiritual strength that was lacking in the European art of his time. He wrote:

Keep the Persians, the Cambodians, and a bit of the Egyptians always in mind. The great error is the Greek, however beautiful it may be.[8]

A great thought system is written in gold in Far Eastern art.[9]

Gauguin's desire to rejuvenate European art and civilization with insights from non-Western traditions would be continued in the early twentieth century by Matisse, Picasso, and the German Expressionists. They adopted Gauguin's vision of the artist as a spiritual leader who could select from the past, and from various world cultures, anything capable of releasing the power of self-knowledge and inner life.

At the age of 43, Gauguin tried to break completely with European civilization by going to Tahiti, leaving behind his wife and their five children. In *Day of the God*, he summarized the results of several years of painting. At the top center of this beach scene is a god figure from a book about Southeast Asia (not Tahiti). The women at the left

10.37   Paul Gauguin.
        Day of the God (Mahana no Atua). 1894.
        Oil on canvas. 26⅞″ 3 36″ (68.3 3 91.5 cm).
        The Art Institute of Chicago. Helen Birch Bartlett Memorial Collection, 1926.198.

Paul Gauguin: Struggling Idealist

"I WANT TO establish the right to dare everything," Gauguin wrote on the eve of his death.[1] Battered by bronchitis, neuralgia, syphilis, and a series of strokes, alone, impoverished, and halfway around the world from France, Gauguin had indeed dared everything—not only in his art, but in his life.

Paul Gauguin (1848–1903) was twenty-three when a family friend introduced him to the world of art and artists. Immersing himself in the new art of his day, he collected works by Cézanne, Degas, and others, and he began to paint in his spare time. By 1879, he was exhibiting with the Impressionist artists he so admired. His job as a stockbroker had become an unbearable distraction, and when he lost it in the aftermath of a financial crash a few years later, he decided not to look for another: He would be an artist. He was then thirty-five, with a pregnant wife and four children. It quickly became clear that he could not support his family as an artist, and after two years of arguments and compromises, his wife moved back to her family, taking the children with her.

Gauguin sought a place to paint that would nourish his vision of an art in touch with the primal mysteries of life. He moved first to Brittany, drawn to the primitive lives of the Breton peasants. In 1887, he painted on the Caribbean island of Martinique, but he fell ill, ran out of money, and had to return to France. The following year he joined van Gogh in the south of France, but their idealistic plans for an artists' commune disintegrated in disastrous quarrels.

Convinced that he had to escape the "disease of civilization," Gauguin voyaged to Tahiti in 1891. He left its Westernized capital, Papeete, for a grass hut in a remote village, where he took a teenage bride, fathered a child, and steeped himself in the island's myths and legends. Despite the pressure of constant poverty, Gauguin transformed the raw material of Tahiti into a dream of earthly paradise, where a sensual people lived in harmony with their gods.

The world that Gauguin painted in *Day of the God* and other works was not the one that actually existed in Tahiti when he lived there. Gauguin idealized the "primitive" nature of life and left out the Western clothing, the missionaries, and the towns.

In 1893, Gauguin returned to France, confident that his Tahitian work would bring him success. It did not come. Lonely and disillusioned, he returned to Tahiti in 1895 and found it more Westernized than before. Frustrated and angry, he fought with the colonial authorities and railed against the missionaries. His health was failing rapidly, he was desperate for money, and he grew so despondent that he attempted suicide. Again he set off in search of a simpler life, sailing in 1901 to the Marquesas Islands, where he died two years later.

"It is true that I know very little," Gauguin wrote to a friend. "But who can say if even this little, worked on by others, will not become something great?"[2] In Paris, in 1906, a large retrospective of Gauguin's work made the extent of his achievement clear for the first time. His achievement was considerable, and, built on by Picasso, Matisse, and many others, his "little" did indeed become something great.

10.38 Paul Gauguin.
Portrait of the Artist with the Idol. c. 1893.
Oil on canvas. 17¼" 3 12⅞".
© McNay Art Museum / Art Resource, NY.

Notes

1. Jean Leymarie, "Paul Gauguin," *Encyclopedia of World Art* (London: McGraw-Hill, 1971), vol. 6, 42.
2. Yann Le Pichon, *Gauguin: Life, Art, Inspiration* (New York: Abrams, 1987), 240.

10.39 Henri de
Toulouse-Lautrec.
*At the Moulin
Rouge.* 1893–1895.
Oil on canvas.
123 3 141 cm.
The Art Institute of
Chicago, Helen Birch
Bartlett Memorial
Collection, 1928.610.

bring offerings as the two on the right dance. In the foreground, three other women sit or lie on the edge of the sea, but the colors of this body of water are nothing like reality; rather, Gauguin here used colors as "the language of dreams," as he put it. Where we might expect to see the statue reflected, we get a mysterious ooze of organic shapes in acidic hues. The seated figure just above stares back at us with a mysterious look.

For Gauguin, art had become above all a means of communicating through symbols, a synthesis of visual form carrying memory, feelings, and ideas. These beliefs link him to **Symbolism**, a movement in literature and the visual arts that developed around 1885.

Reacting against both Realism and Impressionism, Symbolist poets and painters sought to lift the mind from the mundane and the practical. They employed decorative forms and symbols that were intentionally vague or open-ended in order to create imaginative suggestions. The poets held that the sounds and rhythms of words were part of their poems' deeper meaning; the painters recognized that line, color, and other visual elements were expressive in themselves. Symbolism, a trend rather than a specific style, provided the ideological background for twentieth-century abstraction; it has been seen as an outgrowth of Romanticism and a forerunner of Surrealism.

Henri de Toulouse-Lautrec painted the gaslit interiors of Parisian nightclubs and brothels. His quick, long strokes of color define a world of sordid gaiety. Toulouse-Lautrec was influenced by Degas (see pages 210–211), but Toulouse-Lautrec plunged

10.40   Edvard Munch.
The Scream. 1893.
Casin on paper. 91 3 73 cm.
National Gallery, Oslo. © 2010 The Munch Museum/The Munch-Ellingsen
Group/Artists Rights Society (ARS), NY.

and prints explore depths of emotion—grief, loneliness, fear, love, sexual passion, jealousy, and death.

In *The Scream*, Munch takes the viewer far from the pleasures of Impressionism and extends considerably van Gogh's expressive vision. In this powerful image of anxiety, the dominant figure is caught in isolation, fear, and loneliness. Despair reverberates in continuous linear rhythms. Munch's image has been called the soul-cry of that age.

The Impressionists had staged their own exhibitions that competed with the official Salons; the following generation of Post-Impressionists and Symbolists gave up on even that level of recognition. The most creative artists worked outside the normal channels of advancement in the art world, giving rise to the term **avant-garde** to describe their social group. The term comes from military theory: It describes the most courageous soldiers who attack in advance of the main body of troops. The analogy held that the most creative artists similarly work well ahead of the general public's ability to comprehend, pioneering new ideas in taste and thought that will eventually take hold in society at large. This model aptly symbolized the social structure of artistic innovation far into the twentieth century.

Notes

1. Katherine Solender, *Dreadful Fire! The Burning of the Houses of Parliament* (Cleveland: Cleveland Museum of Art, 1984), 42–56.
2. Beaumont Newhall, "Delacroix and Photography," *Magazine of Art* (November 1952): 300.
3. Margaretta Salinger, *Gustave Courbet, 1819–1877, Miniature Album XH* (New York: Metropolitan Museum of Art, 1955), 24.
4. Albert E. Elsen, *Rodin* (New York: Museum of Modern Art, 1963), 53; from a letter to critic Marcel Adam, published in an article in *Gil Blas* (Paris: July 7, 1904).
5. John Rewald, *Cézanne: A Biography* (New York: Abrams, 1986), 208.
6. Vincent van Gogh, *Further Letters of Vincent van Gogh to His Brother, 1886–1889* (London: Constable, 1929), 139, 166.
7. Ronald Alley, *Gauguin* (Middlesex, England: Hamlyn, 1968), 8.
8. Paul Gauguin, *Lettres de Paul Gauguin à Georges-Daniel de Monfried* (Paris: Georges Cres, 1918), 89.
9. John Russell, *The Meanings of Modern Art* (New York: HarperCollins, 1974), 35.

more deeply into nightlife. In *At The Moulin Rouge*, Toulouse-Lautrec used unusual angles, cropped images, such as the face on the right, and expressive, unnatural color to heighten feelings about the people and the world he painted. His paintings, drawings, and prints of Parisian nightlife influenced twentieth-century Expressionist painters, just as his posters influenced graphic designers. Norwegian painter Edvard Munch traveled to Paris to study the works of his contemporaries, especially Gauguin, van Gogh, and Toulouse-Lautrec. What he learned from them, particularly from Gauguin's works, enabled him to carry Symbolism to a new level of expressive intensity. Munch's powerful paintings

EARLY TWENTIETH CENTURY

11

During the first decade of the last century, Western views of the nature of reality changed radically. In 1900, Sigmund Freud published *The Interpretation of Dreams*, a vast work that explored the power and influence of the subconscious mind on all of us. In 1903, the Wright brothers flew the first power-driven aircraft, and Marie and Pierre Curie isolated the radioactive element radium for the first time. In 1905, Albert Einstein changed our concepts of time, space, and substance with his theory of relativity. Matter could no longer be considered solid; rather, it was a form of energy.

The industrial revolution had changed life in myriad ways. Thousands of new jobs opened in city-based factories, drawing rural people into a new, crowded, and impersonal urban environment. Business-oriented capitalism moved the workplace farther from family life than it had ever been before, and most wage work became much more unpleasant. The most violent revolutions of the century—in Russia, Mexico, and China—sprang from class tensions. At the same time, the industrial system created vast amounts of wealth that engendered a middle class and gave millions a financial floor. Better vaccines and public health led to longer life expectancies and a lower birth rate. A steady stream of inventions made business more productive and made scientists into heroes. Government functions expanded into new areas such as factory inspection, education, regulation of currency, and product safety.

Simultaneously, great changes occurred in art, and some of them were inspired by scientific discoveries. In 1913, Russian artist Wassily Kandinsky described how deeply he was affected by the discovery of subatomic particles:

A scientific event cleared my way of one of the greatest impediments. This was the further division of the atom. The crumbling of the atom was to my soul like the crumbling of the whole world.[1]

The art of the twentieth century came from a series of revolutions in thinking and seeing. Its characteristics are those of the century itself: rapid change, diversity, individualism, and exploration—accompanied by abundant discoveries. Twentieth-century artists, as well as scientists, have helped us see the world in new ways and revealed new levels of consciousness.

The explosion of new styles of art at the beginning of this century grew from Impressionist and Post-Impressionist innovations. Yet in their search for forms to express the new age, European artists often looked to ancient and non-Western cultures for inspiration and renewal. In so doing, they overturned the authority of the Renaissance, which had

Chapter 11: Early Twentieth Century was taken from *Prebles' Artforms: An Introduction to the Visual Arts,* Tenth Edition by Patrick Frank.

11.1 Henri Matisse.
Harmony in Red (The Red Room). 1908–1909.
Oil on canvas. 70⅞" 3 86⅝".
Hermitage Museum, St. Petersburg, Russia. © 2011 Succession H. Matisse/Artists Rights
Society (ARS), New York.

dominated Western artistic thought for five hundred years.

The merest glance at *Harmony in Red* by Henri Matisse will show that a new world is dawning in art. The rich maroon of the tablecloth shows a deep blue vine pattern that also claws its way up the wall. The colors of the fruit are bold and flat. The window with its bright golden edge looks out to a radically simplified, yet intensely colored scene. Matisse was a leader in the early twentieth-century movement known as **Fauvism**, which expanded on the innovations of the Post-Impressionists.

THE FAUVES AND EXPRESSIONISM

At the turn of the century, the most creative young painters in France carefully studied Post-Impressionist works. Some drew inspiration from the rationalizing tendencies of Cézanne; others wanted to move farther down the expressive path that Vincent van Gogh and Paul Gauguin had charted.

Matisse was in the latter camp. He saw a large collection of Gauguin's Tahitian works in 1905 and soon he extended the older artist's innovations.

He also led a faction of painters who experimented with vigorous brushwork and large flat areas of highly expressive color. Their first group exhibition shocked the public. A critic of that show derisively called them "les fauves" (the wild beasts).

However, Matisse was not as rebellious as his detractors claimed; rather, he was a thoughtful person who tried merely to express his enthusiasm for life. Every part of a painting by Matisse is expressive: the lines, the colors, the subject, and the composition itself. He frequently reduced his subjects to a few outlines, rather than fill in all of their details. He did this to better preserve the original impulse of feeling. More detail in a work would merely overburden the viewer and distract attention from the immediate burst of emotion.

Matisse's painting *Joy of Life* (on the following page) is another early Fauvist work that shows Matisse's degree of enthusiasm. Pure hues vibrate across the surface; lines, largely freed from descriptive roles, align with simplified shapes to provide a lively rhythm in the composition. The seemingly careless depiction of the figures is based on Matisse's knowledge of human anatomy and drawing. The intentionally direct, childlike quality of the form serves to heighten the joyful content. Asked if he was religious, he replied, "Only when I am painting." (See the biographical essay on page 117.) Matisse defined his aim: "What I am after, above all, is expression."

Matisse had befriended fellow Fauve member André Derain while the two were still in art school. In Derain's *London Bridge*, brilliant, invented color is balanced by some use of traditional composition and perspective. Derain spoke of intentionally using discordant color. It is an indication of today's acceptance of strong color that Derain's painting does not appear disharmonious today. Note also the pure touches of yellow, blue, and green in the lower left; these are expanded versions of the pointillist dots of Georges Seurat.

The Fauve movement lasted little more than two years, from 1905 to 1907, yet it was one of the most influential developments in early twentieth-century painting. The Fauves took the decisive step

11.2 Henri Matisse.
*The Joy of Life
(Le bonheur
de vivre).*
1905–1906.
Oil on canvas.
69⅛" 3 94⅞".
The Barnes Foundation,
Merion, Pennsylvania.
© 2011 Succession H.
Matisse/Artists Rights
Society (ARS), New York.
Photograph: Bridgeman Art
Library.

11.3 André Derain.
London Bridge.
1906.
Oil on canvas.
26" 3 39"
(66 3 99.1 cm).
The Museum of Modern
Art/Licensed by Scala-Art
Resource, NY. Gift of Mr.
and Mrs. Charles Zadok.
Photograph: © 2002 The
Museum of Modern Art,
New York. © 2010 Artists
Rights Society (ARS), New
York, ADAGP, Paris.

in freeing color from its traditional role of describing the natural appearance of an object. In this way, their work led to an increasing use of color as an independent expressive element.

We can categorize Fauvism as an expressive style. **Expressionism** is a general term for art that emphasizes inner feelings and emotions over objective depiction (Expressionism has also enlivened works of music and literature). In Europe, romantic or expressive tendencies can be traced from seventeenth-century Baroque art to the early nineteenth-century painting of Delacroix, who in turn influenced the

11.4 Ernst Ludwig Kirchner.
Street, Berlin. 1913.
Oil on canvas. 47½" 3 35⅞" (120.6 3 91.1 cm).
The Museum of Modern Art/Licensed by Scala-Art Resource, NY. Purchase.
Photograph: © 2002 The Museum of Modern Art, New York.

expressive side of Post-Impressionism (particularly van Gogh).

A few German artists at the beginning of the century shared the expressionist goals of the Fauves. Their desire to express attitudes and emotions was so pronounced and sustained that we call their art German Expressionism. They developed imagery characterized by vivid, often angular simplifications of their subjects, dramatic color contrasts, with bold, at times crude finish. These techniques added emotional intensity to their works. Like their Fauve counterparts, the German Expressionists built on the achievements of Gauguin and van Gogh and the soul-searching paintings of Munch. They felt compelled to use the power of Expressionism to address the human condition, often exploring such themes as natural life, sorrow, passion, spirituality, and mysticism. As their art developed, it absorbed formal influences from medieval German art and some non-Western art from Africa and Oceania.

Two groups typified the German Expressionist movement of the early twentieth century: The Bridge (*Die Brücke*) and The Blue Rider (*Der Blaue Reiter*). Ernst Ludwig Kirchner, architecture student turned painter, was the founder of The Bridge. They appealed to artists to revolt against academic painting and establish a new, vigorous aesthetic that would form a bridge between the Germanic past and modern experience. They first exhibited as a group in 1905, the year of the first Fauve exhibition.

Kirchner's concern for expressing raw emotion gave his work an intensity similar to that of Munch. Kirchner's early paintings employed the flat color areas of Fauvism; by 1913, he had developed a style that incorporated the angularities of Cubism (discussed presently), African sculpture, and German Gothic art. In *Street, Berlin*, elongated figures are crowded together. Repeated diagonal lines create an urban atmosphere charged with energy. Dissonant colors, chopped-out shapes, and rough, almost crude, brushwork heighten the emotional impact.

Paula Modersohn-Becker developed an Expressionist language apart from either group.

Trips to Paris in 1903 and 1905 exposed her to the art of Cézanne and Gauguin, and she combined their influences in self-revealing paintings such as *Self-Portrait with an Amber Necklace*. She reduced the curves of her head to flat regions, and used color for expressive rather than representational purposes. The oversized eyes seem to tell us something, but they remain mysterious.

The Blue Rider group was led by Russian painter Wassily Kandinsky, who lived in Munich between 1908 and 1914 and who shared with his German associates a concern for developing an art that would turn people away from false values, toward spiritual rejuvenation. He believed that a painting should be "an exact replica of some inner emotion": In *Blue Mountain*, he created a "choir

11.5   Paula Modersohn-Becker.
Self-Portrait with an Amber Necklace. 1906.
Oil on canvas. 24″ 3 19¾″.
AKG-Images.

of colors" influenced by the vivid, freely expressive color of the Fauves.[2]

Kandinsky's paintings evolved toward an absence of representational subject matter. In *Blue Mountain*, subject matter had already become secondary to the powerful effect of the visual elements released from merely descriptive roles.

By 1910, Kandinsky overturned one of the most important rules of Western art. He made the shift to totally nonrepresentational imagery in order to concentrate on the expressive potential of pure form, freed from associations with recognizable subjects. After Kandinsky, art need not be a "picture" of anything. A person of mystical inclinations, Kandinsky hoped to create art only in response to what he called "inner necessity," or the emotional stirrings of the soul, rather than in response to what he saw in the world. He said that art should transcend physical reality and speak directly to the emotions of viewers without intervening subject matter. He sought a language of visual form comparable to the sound language we experience in music. The rhythms, melodies, and harmonies of music please or displease us because of the way they affect us. To exploit this relationship between painting and music, Kandinsky often gave his paintings musical titles, such as *Composition IV* (on the following page). Here we see colors and shapes that only vaguely correspond to things in the world. Rather, the artist painted out of inner necessity to make visible his personal mood at that time. Just as a composer uses harmony and melody, Kandinsky used color and form to (as he put it) "set the soul vibrating."

Kandinsky said that the content of his paintings was "what the spectator *lives* or *feels* while under the effect of the *form and color combinations* of the picture." He was an important innovator in the history of art, and his revolutionary nonfigurative works played a key role in the development of later non-

11.6 Wassily Kandinsky.
Blue Mountain (Der blaue Berg).
1908–1909.
Oil on canvas. 41¾" 3 38"
(106 3 96.6 cm).
The Solomon R. Guggenheim Museum, New York.
Gift, Solomon R. Guggenheim, 1941. 41. 505.
Photograph by David Heald. © The Solomon R.
Guggenheim Foundation, New York. © 2010 Artists
Rights Society (ARS), New York/ADAGP, Paris.

11.7 Wassily
Kandinsky.
Composition IV.
1911.
Oil on canvas.
62¹³⁄₁₆" 3 98⅝".
Kunstsammlung
Nordrhein-Westfalen,
Düsseldorf.
Photograph: Walter
Klein, Düsseldorf.
© 2010 Artists Rights
Society (ARS), New
York/ADAGP, Paris.

representational styles. His purpose was not simply aesthetic: He saw his paintings as leading a way through an impending period of catastrophe to a great new era of spirituality. Kandinsky hoped that abstract art could provide spiritual nourishment for the modern world.

CUBISM

While living in Paris, Spanish artist Pablo Picasso shared ideas and influences with French artist Georges Braque. Together they pursued investigations that led to **Cubism**, another principal innovation in painting before World War I. Generally speaking, Cubist painters emphasized picto-rial composition over personal expression through color or brushstroke. Cubism heavily influenced the basic visual structure of many of the notable paintings and sculptures of the century. Through its indirect influence on architecture and the arts, Cubism has become part of our daily lives.

Picasso absorbed influences quickly, keeping only what he needed to achieve his objectives. His break-through painting, *Les Demoiselles d'Avignon* (Young Ladies of Avignon; see also pages 12–13), shows a radical departure from traditional composition. Picasso created a new vocabulary of form influenced by Cézanne's faceted reconstructions of nature and by the inventive abstraction and power he admired

11.8 Pablo Picasso. *Les Demoiselles d'Avignon.* Paris. June-July 1907. Oil on canvas. 8′ 3 7′8″ (243.9 3 233.7 cm). The Museum of Modern Art/ Licensed by Scala-Art Resource, NY. Acquired through the Lillie P. Bliss Bequest. Photograph: © 2002 The Museum of Modern Art, New York. © 2010 Estate of Pablo Picasso/Artists Rights Society (ARS), New York.

in African sculpture such as the *Kota Reliquary Figure* and the *Mask from Ivory Coast*. While the meanings and uses of African sculpture held little interest for him, their form revitalized his art.

11.9   *Kota Reliquary Figure.*
Bakota Funerary Figure, French Equatorial Africa, probably 20th century. Brass sheeting over wood. Length 27½".
Department of Anthropology, Smithsonian Institution. Cat. No. 323686, Neg. No 36712A.

11.10   *Mask from Ivory Coast.*
Wood. 9¾" 3 6½".
Collection Musée de l'Homme, Paris.
Photograph: D. Ponsard.

In *Les Demoiselles d'Avignon*, the fractured, angular figures intermingle with the sharp triangular shapes of the background, activating the entire picture surface. This reconstruction of image and ground, with its fractured triangulation of forms and its merging of figure and ground, was the turning point. With this painting, Picasso shattered the traditional window of Renaissance perspective. *Les Demoiselles* thus set the stage and provided the impetus for the development of Cubism. Though some art historians decry the work's negative depiction of women, viewers are challenged by the painting's hacked-out shapes and overall intensity.

A comparison of two paintings—Cézanne's *Gardanne*, completed in 1886, and Braque's *Houses at l'Estaque*, completed in 1908—shows the beginning of the progression from Cézanne's Post-

11.11   Paul Cézanne.
Gardanne. 1885–1886.
Oil on canvas. 31½" 3 25¼" (80 3 64.2 cm).
The Metropolitan Museum of Art. Gift of Dr. and Mrs. Franz H. Hirschland, 1957. (57.181). Photograph: © 1991 The Metropolitan Museum of Art/Art Resource, NY.

Impressionist style to the Cubist approach that Braque and Picasso developed.

Picasso made the first breakthrough, but Braque did more to develop the vocabulary of Cubism. In a series of landscapes painted in the south of France (where Cézanne had worked), Braque took Cézanne's faceted planar constructions a step further.

Instead of the regular perspective that had been common in European painting since the Renaissance, Braque's shapes define a rush of forms that pile up rhythmically in shallow, ambiguous space. Buildings and trees seem interlocked in an active space that pushes and pulls across the picture surface.

Houses at l'Estaque provided the occasion for the movement's name: When Matisse saw this paint-

ing, he declared it to be nothing but a bunch of little cubes. (His somewhat dismissive attitude indicates the widely varying goals of the Cubists and the Expressionistic Fauves.) From 1908 to 1914, Braque and Picasso were jointly responsible for bringing Cubism to maturity. They worked for a time in increasingly neutral tones, in an effort to achieve formal structure devoid of the emotional distractions of color.

By 1910, Cubism had become a fully developed style. During the Analytical phase of Cubism (1910 to 1911), Picasso, Braque, and others analyzed their subjects from various angles, then painted abstract, geometric references to these views. Because mental concepts of familiar objects are based on experiences of seeing many sides, they aimed to show objects as the mind, rather than the eye, perceives

11.12　Georges Braque.
Houses at l'Estaque. 1908.
Oil on canvas. 28½″ 3 23″.
Foundation RUPF, Bern, Switzerland. Giraudon.
Copyright Giraudon/Art Resource, NY.
© 2010 Artists Rights Society (ARS), New York/
ADAGP, Paris.

them. Georges Braque's *The Portuguese* is a portrait of a man sitting at a café table strumming a guitar. The subject is broken down into facets and recombined with the background. Figure and ground thus collapse into a shallow and jagged pictorial space.

Cubism was a rational, formalist counterpart to the subjective emphasis of the Fauves and other Expressionists. Above all, it was a reinvention of pictorial space. The Cubists realized that the two-dimensional space of the picture plane was quite different from the three-dimensional space we occupy. Natural objects were points of departure for abstract images, demonstrating the essential unity of forms within the spaces that surround and penetrate them. Cubism is thus a reconstruction of objects based on geometric abstraction. By looking first at Cézanne's *Gardanne*, then at Braque's *Houses at l'Estaque*, and finally at *The Portuguese*, we see a progression in which forms seem to build, then spread, across the surface in overlapping planes.

Picasso extended the Cubist revolution to sculpture when he assembled his *Guitar* from pieces of sheet metal; the flat pieces in this work overlap in

11.13 Georges Braque.
The Portuguese. 1911.
Oil on canvas. 46″ 3 32″.
Kunstmuseum, Basel, Switzerland. Copyright Giraudon/Art Resource, NY. © 2010 Artists Rights Society (ARS), New York/ADAGP, Paris.

11.14 Pablo Picasso.
Guitar. Paris, winter. 1912–1913.
Construction of sheet metal and wire. 30½″ 3 13¾″ 3 7⅞″ (77.5 3 35 3 19.3 cm).
The Museum of Modern Art/Licensed by Scala-Art Resource, NY. Gift of the artist. Photograph: © 2002 The Museum of Modern Art, New York. © 2010 Estate of Pablo Picasso/Artists Rights Society (ARS), New York.

Pablo Picasso: Restless Creativity

EVEN BEFORE HE could talk, Pablo Picasso (1881–1973) showed skill in drawing. Years later, he could remember the colors of things he saw in early childhood.

Born in the southern Spanish town of Málaga to artistic parents, Picasso first studied art with his father, a drawing teacher. At the age of ten, he moved with his family to La Coruña on the Atlantic coast, then to Barcelona four years later, when the future Cubist was fourteen. Such was his skill at drawing, that upon arrival he passed the entrance examinations for the School of Fine Arts. He won his first gold medal at an exhibition in his hometown in 1897.

At the age of sixteen, he entered the Royal Academy in Madrid, but attended only briefly because he regarded the teaching methods as oppressive. Returning to Barcelona in 1899, he began to frequent the advanced art circles where modern art was practiced and hotly debated. His own work evolved rapidly through Symbolism and Post-Impressionism to expressive portraits of social outcasts and poor people.

From 1904 to 1945 he lived in Paris. His early work shows his ability to assimilate varied influences and his interest in exploring new modes of expression.

Picasso became fascinated with art from outside Western traditions. He was particularly interested in the African and Oceanic sculpture that Gauguin and later the Fauves had "discovered." Picasso's own paintings of the period certainly show a familiarity with sculpture and masks of the Ivory Coast and the metal-covered figures of the Gabon. By 1909 Picasso had become a serious collector of African art.

In the 1920s, Picasso's style reverted toward a more orthodox mode of representation, influenced by classical art. In the following decade, he became increasingly involved with the political unrest in Europe as Fascist regimes gained power in Italy, Germany, and his native Spain. Picasso produced a series of drawings and paintings that expressed his anguish over the growing violence that led to World War II (See *Guernica*, page 259, which many regard as his greatest work.)

11.15 *Picasso in His Studio at Cannes.* c. 1965.
© Arnold Newman/Getty Images.

Any written biography of Picasso is only a footnote to the autobiographical content of much of his art. In his many variations on the themes of the artist at work and the artist with his model, we recognize that Picasso is commenting on his own experience. Within his images there is the ebb and the flow of Picasso's turbulent love life. Five different women, who shared his life, appear again and again in his art.

His later work included ceramics and huge numbers of prints and drawings in addition to many paintings. Hardworking and prolific until the end of his life, he gave expression to the essential character of his time. In its diversity, Picasso's art relates to most of the twentieth century's art movements. With his prodigious imagination and many changes in style and media, Picasso inspired generations of younger artists.

Picasso's stature in the twentieth century is comparable to Michelangelo's during the Renaissance: Both artists lived nearly a century, both became famous early in life, both lived during periods of rapid change, and both were at the forefront of the artistic developments of their times.

a way similar to a Cubist painting. This work began a dominant trend toward sculptural construction: Before *Guitar*, most sculpture was carved or modeled. Since *Guitar*, a great deal of contemporary sculpture has been constructed.

In 1912, Picasso and Braque modified Analytical Cubism with color, textured and patterned surfaces, and the use of cutout shapes. The resulting style came to be called Synthetic Cubism. Artists used pieces of newspaper, sheet music, wallpaper, and similar items, not represented but actually *presented* in a new way. The newspaper in *Violin, Fruit and Wineglass* is part of a real Paris newspaper. The shapes, which in ear-

lier naturalistic, representational paintings would have been "background," have been made equal in importance to foreground shapes. Picasso chose traditional still-life objects; but rather than paint the fruit, he cut out and pasted printed images of fruit. Such compositions, called "papier collé" in French, or pasted paper, became known as **collage** in English. Analytical Cubism involved taking apart, or breaking down, the subject into its various aspects; Synthetic Cubism was a process of building up or combining bits and pieces of material.

TOWARD ABSTRACT SCULPTURE

The comparison in Chapter 3 of two works of sculpture, both titled *The Kiss* (page 36), illustrates the transition from nineteenth- to twentieth-century thinking in sculpture. Rodin, the leading sculptor of the nineteenth century, created a naturalistic work. Constantin Brancusi led the way toward abstraction.

A sequence of Brancusi's early work shows his radical, yet gradual, break with the past. *Sleep* of 1908 appears similar to Rodin's romantic naturalism. With *Sleeping Muse I* in 1911, Brancusi simplified the subject as he moved from naturalism to abstraction. *Newborn [I]* of 1915 is stripped to essentials. Brancusi said, "Simplicity is not an end in art, but one arrives at simplicity in spite of oneself, in approaching the real sense of things."[3]

11.16   Pablo Picasso.
Violin, Fruit and Wineglass. 1913.
Charcoal colored papers, gouache, painted paper collage.
25¼" 3 19½".
Philadelphia Museum of Art; A.E. Gallatin Collection,
1952-61-106. © 2010 Estate of Pablo Picasso/Artists Rights Society (ARS), New York.

11.17   Constantin Brancusi.
Sleep. 1908.
White marble. 111.5 3 35 3 120 cm.
Musee National d'Art Moderne, Centre National d'Art et de Culture
Georges Pompidou. © VISARTA (The Romanian Visual Arts Copyright
Collecting Society), Bucharest, Romania. © 2010 Artists Rights
Society (ARS), New York/ADAGP, Paris.

11.18 Constantin Brancusi.
Sleeping Muse I. 1909–1911.
Marble. 6¾" 3 10⅝" 3 8⅜".
Hirschhorn Museum and Sculpture Garden, Smithsonian Institution. Gift of Joseph H. Hirschhorn (1966). © 2010 Artists Rights Society (ARS), New York/ADAGP, Paris.

11.19 Constantin Brancusi.
Newborn [I]. 1915.
White marble. 5¾" 3 8¼" 3 5⅞".
Philadelphia Museum of Art. The Louise and Walter Arensberg Collection, 1950. (1950–134–10) © 2010 Artists Rights Society (ARS), New York/ADAGP, Paris.

11.20 *Cycladic II.*
From Naxos. 2700–2300 B.C.E. Head from a large female statuette. 2700–2300 B.C.E. Marble. Height 10½".
Louvre Museum, Paris, France. Photograph: Herve Lewandowski. Reunion des Musees Nationaux/Art Resource, NY.

Brancusi's journey toward abstraction was also a journey back to a pre-classical style of carving. Ancient sculpture from the Cyclades (islands of the Aegean Sea) has a distinctive, highly abstract elegance similar to Brancusi's, as the *Cycladic II* head shows. Just as the Cubists studied African art, Brancusi spent time in the Louvre sketching works in the Ancient Art department where *Cycladic II* is located.

Brancusi sought to go beyond surface embellishments to make viewers conscious of form. Brancusi achieved expressive strength by carefully reducing forms to their essence. As a result, his sculpture invites contemplation.

With *Bird in Space*, Brancusi transformed inert mass into an elegant, uplifting form. The implied soaring motion of the "bird" embodies the idea of

11.21 Constantin Brancusi.
Bird in Space. 1928.
Bronze (unique cast).
54" 3 8½" 3 6½"
(137.2 3 21.6 3 16.5 cm).
The Museum of Modern Art/Licensed by Scala-Art Resource, NY.
© 2010 Artists Rights Society (ARS), New York/ADAGP, Paris.

flight. The highly reflective polish Brancusi applied to the bronze surface contributes to the form's weightless quality. Brancusi started working on this visual concept about a decade after the Wright brothers initiated the age of human flight, but long before the world was filled with streamlined consumer goods. Brancusi said, "All my life I have sought the essence of flight."[4] *Bird in Space* seems to express it.

THE MODERN SPIRIT IN AMERICA

As Picasso and Braque took the steps that led to Cubism, American photographer Alfred Stieglitz was turning photography into an art form. When Picasso saw Stieglitz's photograph *The Steerage*, he said, "This photographer is working in the same spirit as I am."[5] By that he meant that Stieglitz had a similar eye for abstract composition.

The Steerage looked "chopped up" to many people; some of the artist's friends felt that it should have been two photographs rather than one. Stieglitz, however, saw the complex scene as a pattern of interacting forces of light, shade, shape, and direction. Aboard a ship headed for Europe, he saw the composition of this photograph as "a round straw hat, the funnel leaning left, the stairway leaning right, the white drawbridge with its railings made of circular chains, white suspenders crossing on the back of a man on the steerage below, round shapes of iron machinery, a mast cutting into the sky, making a triangular shape. . . . I saw a picture of shapes and underlying that, the feeling I had about life."[6] He rushed to his cabin to get his camera, and he made the photograph he considered his best.

Stieglitz also played a key role in introducing the new European painting and sculpture to Americans. In 1907, he opened a gallery in New York and began showing the work of the most progressive European artists, including photographers. He was the first in America to show works by Cézanne, Matisse, Brancusi, Picasso, and Braque. Following the exhibition of art by these European pioneers, Stieglitz began to show work of American modernists, including Georgia O'Keeffe. O'Keeffe's work from the time of World War I was innovative, consisting mostly of abstractions based on nature. In 1917, while teaching in the Texas Panhandle, she took frequent walks in the lonely, windswept prairie. Finding its emptiness immensely stimulating, she made a series of pioneering abstract watercolors entitled *Evening Star*, based on her sightings of the planet Venus in the darkening sky. Venus is the small unpainted circle that the yellow orb encloses, and this empty spot seems to radiate ever wider sweeps of rich, saturated color. The grandiosity of the Texas landscape inspired her; she wrote to a friend, "It is absurd how much I love this country."

11.22 Alfred Stieglitz.
The Steerage. 1907.
From *Camera Work, New York, No. 34*, October 1911.
Photogravure. 7¾" 3 6½" (19.7 3 16.5 cm).

Georgia O'Keeffe on Abstraction

GEORGIA O'KEEFFE (1887–1986), an austere, strong-minded woman who painted until her death at the age of ninety-nine, is considered one of the greatest American artists of the twentieth century. She is particularly famous for her large abstractions of flowers, as shown in *Lily—White with Black*, animal bones, mysterious organic forms, and landscapes of the New Mexico desert, where she spent her later years as a near-recluse. For her, painting was a way of communicating about experiences and sensations that could not be expressed in any other way. And, although she had studied and practiced previous artists' methods, she was also determined to use her skills to communicate in a different way. She explains in her letters:

"It was in the fall of 1915 that I first had the idea that what I had been taught was of little value to me except for the use of my materials as a language—charcoal, pencil, pen and ink, watercolor, pastel, and oil. I had become fluent with them when I was so young that they were simply another language that I handled easily. But what to say with them? I had been taught to work like others, and after careful thinking I decided that I wasn't going to spend my life doing what had already been done .... I decided I was a very stupid fool not to at last paint as I wanted to and say what I wanted to when I painted."[1]

Among her letters are these comments:

"The large White Flower with the golden heart is something I have to say about White—quite different from what White has been meaning to me. Whether the flower or the color is the focus I do not know. I do know that the flower is painted large to convey to you my expe-

11.23 Georgia O'Keeffe.
Evening Star No. VI. 1917.
Watercolor on paper. 8⅞" 3 12".
1997.18.03. Gift of the Burnett Foundation. Photograph: Malcolm Varon 2001. The Georgia O'Keeffe Museum, Santa Fe, New Mexico, U.S.A. Georgia O'Keeffe Museum, Santa Fe/Art Resource, NY. © 2010 Georgia O'Keeffe Museum/Artists Rights Society (ARS), New York.

rience of the flower—and what is my experience of the flower if it is not color?

"I know I cannot paint a flower. I cannot paint the sun on the desert on a bright summer morning but maybe in terms of paint color I can convey to you my experience of the flower or the experience that makes the flower significant to me at that particular time.

"Color is one of the great things in the world that makes life worth living to me and as I have come to think of painting it is my effort to create an equivalent with paint color for the world—life as I see it."

November 1, 1930

"From experiences of one kind or another shapes and colors come to me very clearly—sometimes I start in very realistic fashion and as I go on from one painting after another of the same thing it becomes simplified till it can be

nothing but abstract—but for me it is my reason for painting it, I suppose.

"At the moment I am very annoyed—I have the shapes—on yellow scratch paper—in my mind for over a year—and I cannot see the color for them—I've drawn them again—and again—it is from something I have heard again and again till I hear it in the wind—but I cannot get the color for it—only shapes."[2]

April 22, 1957

Notes

1. Georgia O'Keeffe, "Some Memories of Drawing," Atlantis Editions, New York, 1974. Quoted in *Georgia O'Keeffe*, Viking Press, New York, 1976, p. 1. Copyright © 2004 The Georgia O'Keeffe Foundation/Artists Rights Society (ARS), New York.
2. Quoted in Jack Coward and Juan Hamilton, *Georgia O'Keeffe: Art and Letters*, letters selected by Sarah Freenough, National Gallery of Art, Washington, D.C., 1987, pp. 200, 266, 242–43. Copyright © 2004 The Georgia O'Keeffe Foundation/Artists Rights Society (ARS), New York.

Artists on Art: Georgia O'Keeffe on Abstraction was taken from *The Art of Seeing*, Eighth Edition by Paul Zelanski and Mary Pat Fisher.

Frank Lloyd Wright: Radical Innovator

FRANK LLOYD WRIGHT (1867–1959), the most influential twentieth-century American architect, was born in Wisconsin, the son of a Baptist minister.

At age eighteen, Wright took a job with a local builder while studying civil engineering part-time at the University of Wisconsin. In 1887, he went to Chicago, where he worked as an apprentice in the newly formed architectural firm of Adler & Sullivan. When Louis Sullivan was designing the *Wainwright Building*, Wright was his chief draftsman. Eager to do his own work, Wright began designing houses on his own at night. Sullivan took offense at this practice, and Wright left the firm. Wright, however, was strongly influenced by Sullivan and continued throughout his life to refer to him as Lieber Meister (beloved master).

By 1893, Wright had opened his own office in the rapidly growing community of Oak Park, Illinois, where he designed a series of houses with low horizontal lines that echoed the flat prairie landscape. This distinctive approach became known as his Prairie Style.

That same year, at the Columbian Exposition in Chicago, Wright saw a Japanese tea house. The encounter led to a deep interest in Japanese architecture and long stays in Japan. He found the asymmetrical balance, large extended eaves, and flexible open plan (with sliding doors and walls) of traditional Japanese houses more sensitive to nature and to human life than the often static symmetry of traditional American homes.

Wright brought his own poetic sense of nature into harmony with the new materials and the engineering technology of the machine age. In terms of both structure and aesthetics, Wright was a radical innovator. He used poured reinforced concrete and steel cantilevers in houses at a time when such construction was usually confined to commercial structures. His *Kaufmann Residence* is dramatically cantilevered over a waterfall, and two of his major buildings were designed with flowing interior spaces and spiral ramps. Among his many notable buildings was the structurally innovative Imperial Hotel in Tokyo, built between 1916 and 1922. His use of the cantilever in this hotel was criticized as a violation of sound construction—until the devastating quake of 1923, when it remained one of the few undamaged buildings in the city.

In his later years, Wright continued his large practice and devoted considerable time to writing and to teaching apprentices in his workshop-homes. Throughout his career Wright was guided by his awareness that buildings have a profound, life-shaping influence on the people who inhabit them.

Among Wright's many unrealized projects was a plan for a mile-high skyscraper. His last major work was the controversial Solomon R. Guggenheim Museum, built in the late 1950s. Its immense spiraling ramp enables viewers to see exhibitions in a clearly defined continuous path, but the sloping, eye-filling space tends to overpower the presentation of other works of art.

Wright's guiding philosophy is most apparent in his houses, where his concern for simplicity and his sensitivity to the character of space and materials express what he defined as an organic ideal for architecture. According to Wright, the word *organic* goes beyond its strictly biological meaning to refer to the integration of all aspects of a form, the part to the whole and the whole to the part. Thus, in architecture, one should determine the form of a building by designing in terms of the

11.24 Frank Lloyd Wright. 1936.
Photo by Edmund Teske. © The Frank Lloyd Wright Fdn, AZ/Art Resource, NY.

unique qualities of the site, proceeding from the ground up, and honoring the character of the natural conditions as well as the materials and purposes of the structure. Wright spoke of organic architecture as having a meaning beyond any preconceived style:

Exalting the simple laws of common sense—or of super-sense if you prefer—determining form by way of the nature of materials, the nature of purpose so well understood that a bank will not look like a Greek Temple, a university will not look like a cathedral, nor a fire-engine house resemble a French château. . . . Form follows function? Yes, but more important now [with organic architecture] form and function are one.[1]

Note

1. Frank Lloyd Wright, *The Future of Architecture* (New York: Horizon Press, 1953), 227.

11.25 Guggenheim Museum, interior.
Courtesy of Robert Harding Picture Libary Ltd/ Alamy.

11.26 Guggenheim Museum, exterior.
Courtesy of Roger Wood/CORBIS.

Frank Lloyd Wright's *Fallingwater*

FALLINGWATER (**Fig. 11.28**), Frank Lloyd Wright's name for the house he designed for Edgar and Lillian Kaufmann in 1935, is arguably the most famous modern house in the world. Edgar Kaufmann was owner of Kaufmann's Store in Pittsburgh, the largest ready-made men's clothing store in the country, and his son had begun to study with Wright in 1934. In November of that year, Wright first visited the site. There are no known design drawings until the following September. Writing a few years before about his own design process,

Wright stated that the architect should "conceive the building in the imagination, not on paper but in the mind, thoroughly—before touching paper. Let it live there—gradually taking more definite form before committing it to the draughting board. When the thing lives for you, start to plan it with tools. Not before. . . . It is best to cultivate the imagination to construct and complete the building before working on it with T-square and triangle."

The first drawings were done in two hours when Kaufmann made a surprise call to Wright and told him he

was in the neighborhood and would like to see something. Using a different colored pencil for each of the house's three floors on the site plan, Wright completed not only a floor plan, but a north-south cross-section and a view of the exterior from across the stream (**Fig. 11.27**). The drawings were remarkably close to the final house.

Wright thought of the house as entirely consistent with his earlier Prairie Houses. It was, like them, wedded to its site, only the site was markedly different. The reinforced concrete cantilevers mirrored the natural cliffs of

11.27   Frank Lloyd Wright.
drawing for *Fallingwater*, Kaufmann House, Bear Run, Pennsylvania, 1936.
15³/₈ 3 27¹/₄ in. The Frank Lloyd Wright Archives.
© 2011 Frank Lloyd Wright Foundation, Scottsdale, AZ / Artists Rights Society (ARS), NY.

Works in Progress: Frank Lloyd Wright's *Fallingwater* was taken from *A World of Art*, Sixth Edition by Henry M. Sayre.

11.28 Frank Lloyd Wright.
Fallingwater, Kaufmann House,
Bear Run, Pennsylvania, 1936.
© 2011 Frank Lloyd Wright Foundation,
Scottsdale, AZ/Artists Rights Society (ARS),
NY. Courtesy of Western Pennsylvania
Conservancy/ Art Resource, NY.

the hillside down and over which the stream, Bear Run, cascades. By the end of 1935, Wright had opened a quarry on the site to extract local stone for the house's construction.

Meanwhile, the radical style of the house had made Kaufmann nervous. He hired engineers to review Wright's plan, and they were doubtful that reinforced concrete could sustain the 18-foot cantilevers that Wright proposed. When Kaufmann sent the engineers' reports to Wright, Wright told him to return the plans to him "since he did not deserve the house." Kaufmann apologized for his lack of faith, and work on the house proceeded.

Still, the contractor and engineer didn't trust Wright's plans for reinforcing the concrete for the cantilevers, and before the first slab was poured, they put in nearly twice as much steel as Wright had called for. As a result,

the main cantilever droops to this day. Wright was incensed that no one trusted his calculations. After the first slab was set, but still heavily braced with wooden framing (**Fig. 11.29**), Wright walked under the house and kicked a number of the wooden braces out.

The house, finally, is in complete harmony with its site. "I came to see a building," Wright wrote in 1936, as the house was nearing completion, "primarily . . . as a broad shelter in the open, related to vista; vista without and vista within. You may see in these various feelings, all taking the same direction, that I was born an American, child of the ground and of space."

11.29 Frank Lloyd Wright.
Fallingwater scaffolding, from the Fallingwater Collection at the Avery Architectural and Fine Arts Library, Columbia University, New York.
© 2005 Frank Lloyd Wright Foundation, Scottsdale, AZ / Artists Rights Society (ARS), New York.

11.30 Frank Lloyd Wright.
Robie House. 1909.
Chicago, Illinois.

Between 1905 and 1910, architects began to challenge traditional concepts of form in space just as painters and sculptors had done. While Cubism was developing in painting, leading American architect Frank Lloyd Wright was designing "prairie houses," in which he often omitted or minimized walls between living and dining rooms, and between interior and exterior spaces. Wright's concept of open plans changed the way people design living spaces. In many contemporary homes, kitchen, dining room, and living room now join in one continuous space, and indoors often intermingles with outdoors.

In the *Robie House* of 1909, a striking cantilevered roof reaches out and unifies a fluid design of asymmetrically interconnected spaces. Through Wright's influence, the open flow of spaces became a major feature of contemporary architecture. To get a feeling of how far ahead of his time Wright was, imagine the incongruity of a new 1909 automobile that could have been parked in front of the *Robie House* the year it was completed. The American public had its first extensive look at leading developments in European art during the Armory Show, held in New York in 1913. In this show of over sixteen hundred works, American artists were able to see key works by Impressionists, Post-Impressionists, and Fauves—particularly Matisse, who was much maligned by critics. Also shown were paintings by Picasso and Braque, and sculpture by Brancusi. As a result, Cubism and other forms of abstract art spread to America.

FUTURISM AND THE CELEBRATION OF MOTION

The Italian **Futurists** were among the many artists who gained their initial inspiration from Cubism. To the shifting planes and multiple vantage points of Cubism, Futurists such as Giacomo Balla and Umberto Boccioni added a sense of speed and motion and a celebration of the machine.

11.31 Giacomo Balla.
Abstract Speed—The Car Has Passed. 1913.
Oil on canvas. 19¾" 3 25¾".
Copyright Tate Gallery, London/Art Resource, NY
© 2010 Artists Rights Society (ARS), New York/SIAE, Rome.

By multiplying the image of a moving object, Futurists expanded the Cubist concepts of simultaneity of vision and metamorphosis. In 1909, the poet Filippo Tommaso Marinetti proclaimed in the *Initial Manifesto of Futurism*: "the world's splendor has been enriched by a new beauty; the beauty of speed . . . a roaring motorcar . . . is more beautiful than the Victory of Samothrace."[7]

The Futurists translated the speed of modern life into works that captured the dynamic energy of the new century. Giacomo Balla intended his work *Abstract Speed—The Car Has Passed* to depict the rushing air and dynamic feeling of a vehicle passing. This "roaring motorcar" is passing at about 35 miles an hour, but at that time this was the pinnacle of speed.

An abstract sculpture of a striding figure climaxed a series of Umberto Boccioni's drawings, paintings, and sculpture. Boccioni insisted that sculpture should be released from its usual confining outer surfaces in order to open up and fuse the work with the space surrounding it. In *Unique Forms of Continuity in Space*, muscular forms seem to leap outward in flamelike bursts of energy. During this period, the human experience of motion, time, and space was transformed by the development of the automobile, the airplane, and the movies. Futurist imagery reflects this exciting period of change.

11.32 Umberto Boccioni.
Unique Forms of Continuity in Space. 1913.
Bronze (cast in 1931). 43⅞" 3 34⅞" 3 15¾"
(111.2 3 88.5 3 40 cm).
The Museum of Modern Art/Licensed by Scala-Art Resource, NY.
Acquired through the Lillie P. Bliss Bequest. Photograph: © 2002 The
Museum of Modern Art, New York.

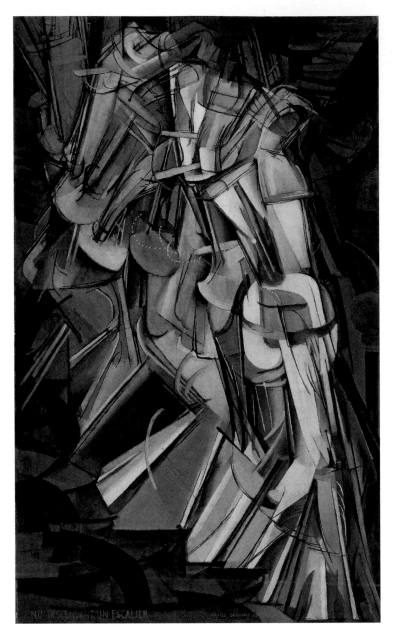

11.33 Marcel Duchamp.
Nude Descending a Staircase, No. 2. 1912.
Oil on canvas. 58″ 3 35″.
Philadelphia Museum of Art. The Louise and Walter Arensberg
Collection. 1950-134-59. Photo by Graydon Wood, 1994.
© 2010 Artists Rights Society (ARS), New York/ADAGP,
Paris. Succession Marcel Duchamp.

French artist Marcel Duchamp, working independently of the Futurists, brought the dimension of motion to Cubism. His *Nude Descending a Staircase, No. 2* was influenced by stroboscopic photography, in which sequential camera images show movement by freezing successive instants (see page 49 for an example). Through sequential, diagonally placed, abstract references to the figure, the painting presents the movement of a body through space, seen all at once, in a single rhythmic progression. Our sense of gravity intensifies the overall feeling of motion. When the painting was displayed at the Armory Show in New York in 1913, it caused cries of dismay and was seen as the ultimate Cubist madness. The painting, once described as "an explosion in a shingle factory," has remained an inspiration to artists who use repetition and rhythm to express motion.

Notes

1. Wassily Kandinsky, "Reminiscences," *Modern Artists on Art,* ed. Robert L. Herbert (Englewood Cliffs, NJ: Prentice Hall, 1964), 27.
2. William Fleming, Art, *Music and Ideas* (New York: Holt, 1970), 342.
3. Alfred H. Barr, Jr., ed., *Masters of Modern Art* (New York: Museum of Modern Art, 1955), 124.
4. H. H. Arnason, *History of Modern Art,* rev. ed. (New York: Abrams, 1977), 146.
5. Nathan Lyons, ed., *Photographers on Photography* (Englewood Cliffs, NJ: Prentice Hall, 1966), 133.
6. Beaumont Newhall, *The History of Photography* (New York: Museum of Modern Art, 1964), 111.
7. Joshua C. Taylor, *Futurism* (New York: Museum of Modern Art, 1961), 124.

BETWEEN WORLD WARS 12

In 1914, enthusiasm for grand patriotic solutions to international tensions led citizens of many countries into World War I, an intense and protracted conflict that involved most European countries and eventually the United States. But the war turned out to be far more devastating than the people of the time expected: Over ten million were killed and twice that number wounded. The promise of a whole new generation was lost in the world's first experience with mechanized mass killing.

As a result of the war, the political and cultural landscape changed forever. The war set the stage for the Russian Revolution and sowed grievances that the Nazis of Germany and the Fascists of Italy later exploited. Governments assumed new powers to mobilize people and material, to dictate economic life, to censor public expression, and, by controlling information, to manipulate the way people thought. Dissent was denounced as unpatriotic.

Many artists in the interwar period consciously linked their creations to their hopes for a better world. Some expressed those hopes by angrily denouncing present conditions; others offered Utopian visions. This tendency to use art as a tool for social betterment is a prominent marker for this period. Another marker is the spread of modernist innovations to non-European populations, as variations on modern styles arose in many places.

DADA

Dada began in protest against the horrors of World War I. The artists and writers who began the movement in Zurich chose the ambiguous word **Dada** as their rallying cry. According to some accounts, they arrived at the name by inserting a knife into a dictionary. The two-syllable word was well suited for expressing the essence of what was more a rebellious attitude than a cohesive style. In the eyes of the Dadaists, the destructive absurdity of war was caused by traditional values, which they set out to overturn. According to artist Marcel Janco:

Dada was not a school of artists, but an alarm signal against declining values, routine, and speculation, a desperate appeal on behalf of all forms of art, for a creative basis on which to build a new and universal consciousness of art.[1]

French artist and poet Jean Arp said:

While the thunder of guns rolled in the distance, we sang, painted, glued, and composed for all our worth. We were seeking an art that would heal mankind from the madness of the age.[2]

The insanity of the war proved to Dadaists that European culture had lost its way. To make a new beginning, the Dadaists rejected most moral, social, political, and aesthetic values. They thought it was pointless to try to find order and meaning

Chapter 12: Between World Wars was taken from *Prebles' Artforms: An Introduction to the Visual Arts,* Tenth Edition by Patrick Frank.

in a world in which so-called rational behavior had produced only chaos and destruction. They aimed to shock viewers into seeing the absurdity of the Western world's social and political situation.

The Dadaists protested, in part, through play and spontaneity. Their literature, art, and staged events were often based on chance rather than premeditation. Poets shouted words at random; artists joined elements into startling and irrational combinations.

Marcel Duchamp was the most radical of the Dadaists, and perhaps the most radical artist of the twentieth century. He had the audacity to offer mass-produced objects as artworks, calling them **readymades**. For example, he once signed a snow shovel and titled it *In Advance of the Broken*

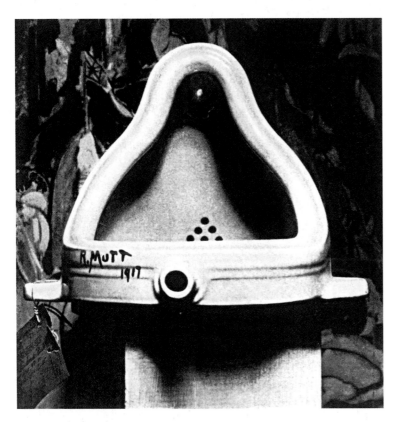

12.1 Marcel Duchamp.
The Fountain, 1917.
Fountain by R. Mutt. Glazed sanitary china with black print.
Photo by Alfred Stieglitz in *The Blind Man,* No. 2 (May 1917); original lost.
© Philadelphia Museum of Art. The Louise and Walter Arensberg Collection, 1950. 1998-74-1.
© 2007 Artists Rights Society (ARS), New York / ADAGP, Paris / Succession Marcel Duchamp.
© 2011 Georgia O'Keeffe Museum / Artists Rights Society (ARS), New York.

Arm. In New York, Duchamp submitted a common urinal to the Independents Exhibition in 1917, titled it *Fountain,* signed it R. Mutt, and claimed for it the status of sculpture (**Fig. 12.1**). At first it was rejected, but when Duchamp let it be known that he and R. Mutt were one and the same, it was accepted. Thus, whether something was art depended on who made it—or found it, in this case. It also depended on where it was seen—in the museum it was one thing, in the plumbing store, quite another. Furthermore, on its pedestal, in the context of the museum, Duchamp's "fountain" looked to some as if it were indeed sculpture. Duchamp did not so much invalidate art as authorize the art world to consider all manner of things in aesthetic terms. His logic was not without precedent. Cubist collage had brought "real things" like newspaper clippings into the space of painting, and photography, especially, often revealed aesthetic beauty in common experience. But Duchamp's move, like Dada generally, was particularly challenging and provocative. "I was interested," he explained, "in ideas—not merely in visual products."

In a purposeful slap at traditional standards of beauty, Duchamp bought a picture postcard reproduction of Leonardo da Vinci's *Mona Lisa* and drew a mustache and beard on her face. He signed the work with his own name and titled it *L.H.O.O.Q.* The title is a vulgar pun in French, comprehensible to those who can hear the sentence in the sound of the letters pronounced aloud quickly in French. Translated into English, it means, "She has a hot tail." Duchamp's outrageous irreverence toward one of the world's most revered paintings was an attempt to shake people out of their unthinking acceptance of dominant values.

Man Ray, an American, was a friend of Duchamp. His Dada works include paintings, photographs, and assembled objects. In 1921, he saw an iron displayed in front of a shop selling housewares. He purchased the iron, a box of tacks, and a tube of glue. After gluing a row of tacks to the smooth surface of the iron, he titled his assemblage *Gift*—thus creating a useless and dangerous object.

12.2 Marcel Duchamp.
L.H.O.O.Q. From "Boite-en-Valise". Paris. 1919.
Pencil on reproduction of Leonardo's *Mona Lisa*.
7¾" 3 4¾".
Philadelphia Museum of Art: Louise and Walter Arensburg Collection.
© 2010 Artists Rights Society (ARS), New York/ADAGP, Paris/Estate of
Marcel Duchamp.

12.3 Man Ray.
Cadeau (Gift). c. 1958.
Replica of 1921 original. Painted flatiron, with
row of thirteen tacks, heads glued to the bottom.
6⅛" 3 3⅜" 3 4½" (15.3 3 9 3 11.4 cm).
The Museum of Modern Art/Licensed by Scala-Art Resource, NY. James
Thrall Soby Fund. Photograph: © 2001 The Museum of Modern Art, New
York. © 2010 Man Ray Trust/Artists Rights Society (ARS), New York/
ADAGP, Paris.

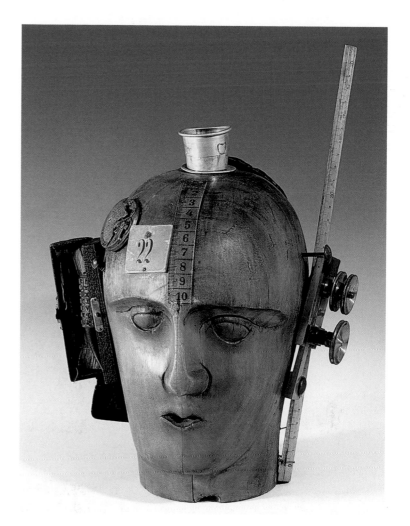

12.4 Raoul Hausmann.
The Spirit of Our Time. 1919.
Mixed media. Combine, Height 12¾".
Musée National d'Art Moderne, Georges Pompidou Centre, Paris.
© 2010 Artists Rights Society (ARS), New York/ADAGP, Paris.
© CNAC/MNAM/Dist. Reunion de Musées Nationaux/
Art Resource, NY

One memorable Dada sculpture, Raoul
Hausmann's *The Spirit of Our Time*, continues to
express a truth about our culture. We would like to
know ourselves, yet we succumb to the playthings
of our technology. Have the artifacts of our mass
production turned us into hollow-headed robots
who simply receive and transmit information and
are unable to think for ourselves? Hausmann seems
to have anticipated the world of artificial intelli-
gence, headset radios, and mp3 players.

Dadaists expanded on the Cubist idea of collage with **photomontage**, in which parts of photographs are combined in thought-provoking ways.

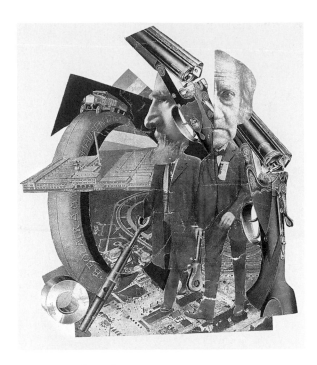

12.5 Hannah Höch.
The Multi-Millionaire. 1923.
Photomontage. 14″ 3 12″.
© 2010 Artists Rights Society (ARS), New York. VG Bild-Kunst, Bonn.

12.6 Max Ernst.
The Horde. 1927.
Oil on canvas. 44⅞″ 3 57½″ (114 3 146.1 cm).
Stedelijk Museum, Amsterdam.

In *The Multi-Millionaire*, by Dadaist Hannah Höch, industrial-age man stands as a fractured giant among the things he has produced. At the time she created this work, the artist was attacked for lacking originality because she merely combined already existing things. But now we see how original she was.

Some Dadaists maintained that art was dead. By this they meant that it was useless to try to create beauty in a world that could destroy itself. They often intended to be anti-aesthetic, but ironically, they created a new aesthetic of lasting influence.

SURREALISM

In the 1920s, a group of writers and painters gathered to protest the direction of European culture. They thought that the modern emphasis on science, rationality, and progress was throwing the consciousness of Europeans out of balance. In response, they proclaimed the importance of the unconscious mind, of dreams, fantasies, and hallucinations. They were indebted to the irrationality of Dadaism, and they also drew heavily on the new psychology of Sigmund Freud.

The new movement, **Surrealism**, was officially launched in Paris in 1924 with the publication of its first manifesto, written by poet-painter André Breton. He defined the movement's purpose as:

the future resolution of these two states, dream and reality, which are seemingly so contradictory, into a kind of absolute reality, a surreality, if one may so speak.[3]

One of the first converts to the movement was the former Dadaist Max Ernst, who had fought in the war and was still haunted by its nightmares. To allow freer play to fantasy, he laid his canvases over textured surfaces such as asphalt pavement. In this way he could be surprised by the patterns that emerged for fertilization in his imagination. In the 1927 work *The Horde*, we see a gaggle of silhouetted monsters who tumble over one another in a violent scene. The artist's combat experience in World War I most likely influenced the chaotic nature of this work.

The Spanish artist Salvador Dalí dealt more directly with his nightmares. He teamed with filmmaker Luis Buñuel on the anti-rational film *The Andalusian Dog*. In painting, he simply re-created his nightmares in a highly illusionistic fashion based on academic techniques. *The Persistence of Memory* evokes the eerie quality of some dreams. Mechanical time wilts in a deserted landscape of infinite space. The warped, headlike image in the foreground may be the last remnant of a vanished humanity. The artist called it a self-portrait.

Dalí's illusionary deep space and representational techniques create near-photographic dream images that make the impossible seem believable. The startling juxtaposition of unrelated objects creates a nightmarish sense of a super reality beyond the everyday world. This approach has been called Representational Surrealism. In contrast, Joan Miró's Abstract Surrealism provides suggestive elements that give wide play to the viewer's imagination, and emphasize color and design rather than storytelling content.

To probe into the unconscious, Miró and others used automatic processes, sometimes called **automatism**, in which chance was a key factor. They scribbled, doodled, and poured paint in order to cultivate the chance accident that might prove revealing. With the adoption of such spontaneous and "automatic" methods, the Surrealists sought

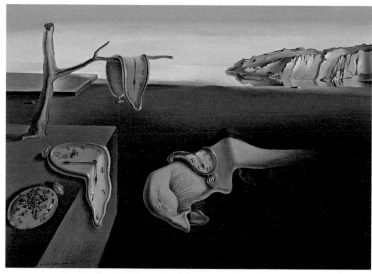

12.7 Salvador Dalí.
The Persistence of Memory (Persistance de la memoire). 1931.
Oil on canvas. 9½″ 3 13″ (24.1 3 33 cm).

to expand consciousness by transcending limits of rational thought.

Miró's evocative paintings often depict imaginary creatures. He made them by scribbling on the canvas and then examining the results to see what the shapes suggested. The bold, organic shapes in *Woman Haunted by the Passage of the Bird-Dragonfly Omen of Bad News* are typical of his mature work.

12.8 Joan Miró.
Woman Haunted by the Passage of the Bird-Dragonfly Omen of Bad News. 1938.
Oil on canvas. 31½″ 3 124″ (80 3 315 cm).

The wild, tormented quality, however, is unusual for Miró and reflects his reaction to the times. Miró pointed out that this painting was done at the time of the Munich crisis that helped precipitate World War II. Even though there is a sense of terror here, Miró's underlying playful optimism is apparent. He loved the art of children so much that he tried to paint like one.

Belgian Surrealist René Magritte used an illogical form of realism, similar to Dalí's in surface appearance but quite different in content. Magritte's paintings engage the viewer in mind-teasing mystery and playful humor. Everything depicted in *Portrait* is ordinary; the impact comes from the unsettling placement of an eye staring back at us from a plate of ham. Perhaps his best-known work is *The Treason of Images*, pictured on page 27.

EXPANDING ON CUBISM

Cubism makes possible many ambiguities between presence and absence, representation and abstraction, figure and ground. Far from presenting the world as stable and predictable, Cubism suggests constant change and evolution. An art historian wrote, "By devaluing subject matter, or by monumentalizing simple, personal themes, and by allowing mass and void to elide, the Cubists gave effect to the flux and paradox of modern life and the relativity of its values."[4] Thus, Cubism makes visible some important characteristics of modern life.

Russian artists took Cubism toward complete abstraction. A leader there was Kazimir Malevich, who branded his style Suprematism. His painting *Suprematist Composition: Airplane Flying* shows in

12.9   René Magritte.
Portrait (Le Portrait). 1935.
Oil on canvas. 28⅞″ 3 19⅞″ (73.3 3 50.2 cm).
The Museum of Modern Art/Licensed by Scala-Art Resource, NY. Gift of Kay Sage Tanguy. Photograph: © 2002 The Museum of Modern Art, New York. © 2010 C. Herscovici, London/Artists Rights Society (ARS), New York.

12.10   Kazimir Malevich.
Suprematist Composition: Airplane Flying. 1915.
Oil on canvas. 22⅞″ 3 19″ (58.1 3 48.3 cm).
The Museum of Modern Art/Licensed by Scala-Art Resource, NY. Acquisition confirmed in 1999 by agreement with the Estate of Kazimir Malevich and made possible with funds from the Mrs. John Hay Whitney Bequest (by exchange). Photograph: © 2002 The Museum of Modern Art, New York.

its title that the artist was familiar with Futurism: its subject is a speeding modern airplane. Yet Malevich so simplified the Cubist pictorial language that we are left with a succession of flat irregular rectangles against a pure background.

Malevich believed that shapes and colors in a painting always communicate, no matter what the subject of the work. Ideally, he thought, art should not need subject matter. This is why he named his movement Suprematism, because he wanted to focus on the supremacy of shape and color in art over representation or narrative. He shared some points of view with his fellow Russian Wassily Kandinsky, whom he knew (see page 229). But while Kandinsky (who worked in Germany) painted brash, expressive works, Malevich's constant urge to simplify makes him the more radical painter.

In his large painting *The City*, Fernand Léger crushed jagged shapes together, collapsing space in a composition reminiscent of a Cubist portrait or still life. The forms in his paintings look machine-made, rounded and tubular; this is in keeping with the urban bustle that is the work's subject.

12.11 Fernand Léger.
The City. 1919.
Oil on canvas. 91″ 3 177½″.
Philadelphia Museum of Art. A. E. Gallatin Collection, 1952-61-58.
© 2010 Artists Rights Society (ARS), New York/ADAGP, Paris.

Léger soon took Cubist composition into film when he made *Ballet Mecanique*, a 17-minute cinematic collage in which churning machines alternate with a swinging pendulum, a smiling woman, and shifting geometric shapes. Sometimes these forms are distorted with a kaleidoscopic mirror, which mashes them up and flattens them in the manner of a Cubist still life. Léger intended the film to have a score by the American George Antheil, but practicalities prevented this. (Antheil composed an unforgettably riotous work for seventeen player pianos, various percussion instruments, and a siren, but because it ran twice as long as the film, the two could not be synchronized.) Léger's film follows no obvious logic, but it seems to argue that machines and humans are about equally rhythmic if not equally graceful.

BUILDING A NEW SOCIETY

Several art movements that emerged between the wars had the goal of improving the world somehow. Surrealists, for example, hoped to liberate human consciousness. Pioneer abstractionists felt that the nonrepresentational language of form they were creating would provide an ideal basis for the utopian society they sought. Constructivism, in Russia, focused on developing a new visual language for a new industrial age. De Stijl, in Holland, advocated the use of basic forms, particularly rectangles, horizontals, and verticals. Both movements spread throughout Europe and strongly influenced many art forms.

Constructivism

Constructivism was a revolutionary movement that began in Russia, inspired in part by the Suprematism of Malevich and others. Seeking to create art that was relevant to modern life in form, materials, and content, Constructivists made the first nonrepresentational constructions out of such modern materials as plastic and electroplated metal.

The Constructivists were in concert with the Cubists in rejecting the traditional view of space

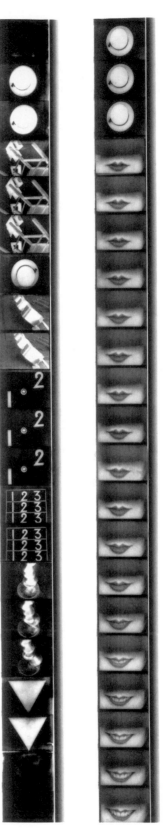

12.12 Fernand Léger.
Ballet Mecanique. 1924. Film.
© 2010 Artists Rights Society (ARS), New York/
ADAGP, Paris.

as regular and static. The name of the movement came from their preference for constructing planar and linear forms that suggested a dynamic quality and, whenever possible, contained moving elements.

The painter Lyubov Popova pioneered many of these effects in nonrepresentational works that she called *Architectonic Compositions*. Planes intersect in a shallow space that derives from Cubism (see her earlier Cubist work *The Pianist* on page 107). Though the work seems to resemble a mechanical contrivance of unknowable function, nothing is pictured here except forms and colors. Popova combined her painting with teaching in workers' schools, and she helped to found the First Working Group of Constructivists in 1921.

One of her Constructivist colleagues was Aleksandr Rodchenko, who is among the century's most innovative multi-media artists. He began as a painter, working with compass and ruler in true Constructivist fashion. Soon he renounced painting in favor of more useful arts: He designed the poster *Give Me Sun At Night*, as he also worked on furniture, photography, and stage set design.

12.13 Lyubov Popova
Architectonic Composition. 1918
Oil on canvas
45 3 53 cm.

12.14 Aleksandr Rodchenko. View of *The Workers' Club*. Exhibited at the International Exposition of Modern Decorative and Industrial Arts, Paris. 1925.

He created *The Workers' Club* as a training ground for the new Soviet mind. Rodchenko envisioned every aspect of this installation to educate workers in the new historical dynamic that would lead to a future classless society. The chairs, shelves, and desks are all made of simple, mass-produced parts, and designed to facilitate sitting upright.

De Stijl

A group of Dutch artists took Cubism toward Utopian speculation when they formed the movement called **De Stijl** (The Style). Led by painter Piet Mondrian, this group began to employ nonrepresentational geometric elements in a group style that involved both two- and three-dimensional art forms. Their goal was the creation of a world of universal harmony. Using the newly independent vocabulary of abstract visual form, they created an inventive body of work in painting, architecture, furniture, and graphic design.

Mondrian's evolution as an artist represents the origin and essence of De Stijl. Working to free

painting completely from both the depiction of real objects and the expression of personal feelings, he developed an austere style based on the expressive potential of simple visual elements and their relationships. He created a new aesthetic that would provide a poetic vitality capable of setting standards of harmony for the new technological age.

From 1917 until his death in 1944, Mondrian was the leading spokesperson for an art reflecting universal order. For Mondrian, the universal elements were straight lines, the three primary colors, and rectangular shapes. He reduced painting to four elements: line, shape, color, and space. His painting *Tableau 2* exemplifies his nonrepresentational work. Mondrian hoped that the rhythms and forms of his works paralleled those of nature itself, which he viewed as rational and orderly.

International Style Architecture

The search for a new visual language engaged architects as well as painters. Ideas about form developed by the Constructivists, the De Stijl art-

12.16 Gerrit Rietveld.
Schröder House. 1924.
Centraal Museum Utrecht, The Netherlands. © 2010 Artists Rights
Society (ARS), New York/Pictoright, Amsterdam.

ists, and previously by American architect Frank Lloyd Wright, were carried further by architects who were stimulated by the structural possibilities of modern materials including steel, plate glass, and reinforced concrete.

About 1918, a new style of architecture emerged simultaneously in Germany, France, and the Netherlands and came to be called the **International Style**. Steel-frame, curtain-wall construction methods made it possible to build structures with undecorated rectilinear planes. Extensive use of glass in non-load-bearing exterior walls brought abundant light and flexible space to interiors. In many International Style buildings, asymmetrical designs created dynamic balances of voids and solids. Unlike Frank Lloyd Wright, who blended houses with their natural surroundings, architects working in the International Style deliberately created a visual contrast between natural and manufactured forms.

Dutch architect and furniture designer Gerrit Rietveld joined de Stijl in 1919. His *Schröder House* in Utrecht was an early classic of the International Style. Its design of interacting planes, spaces, and primary colors are closely related to Mondrian's paintings.

The International Style buildings designed by Walter Gropius for the **Bauhaus** clearly reflect the concepts of both De Stijl and Constructivism. Today, the spare style that Mondrian and the Bauhaus helped to initiate can be seen in the design not only of buildings, but of books, interiors, clothing, furnishings, and many other articles of daily life.

Architect and designer Ludwig Mies van der Rohe was one of the most influential figures associated with the Bauhaus and the International Style. For the Barcelona World's Fair in 1929, he designed the *German Pavilion* in marble, glass, and steel. Like the *Schröder House*, the *German Pavilion*

12.17 Ludwig Mies van der Rohe.
German Pavilion. 1929.
International Exposition, Barcelona.
Guggenheim. © 2010 Artists Rights Society
(ARS), New York/VG Bild-Kunst, Bonn.

is an abstract composition similar to a De Stijl painting. Mies designed the pavilion with flowing spaces so that the visitor never feels "boxed in." An attached rectangular pool on the left reflects the elegant design on the water's surface. In 1938, Mies immigrated to the United States. There, his ideas and works potently influenced the post–World War II development of the steel-frame skyscraper.

POLITICAL PROTEST

Many artists in the interwar period focused their art on political life. Protesting against fascism and dictatorship was a dominant theme.

Throughout the 1920s and into the 1930s, Spanish-born Pablo Picasso continued to produce innovative drawings, paintings, prints, posters, and sculptures. In 1937, while the Spanish Civil War was in progress, Picasso was commissioned by the doomed Spanish democratic government to paint a mural for the Paris Exposition. On April 26 of that year, he was shocked into action by the "experimental" mass bombing of the defenseless Basque town of Guernica. To aid his bid for power, General Franco had allowed Hitler to use his war machinery on the town as a demonstration of military power. The bombing, which leveled the fifteen-square-block city center, was the first incidence of saturation bombing in the history of warfare. Hundreds died, and more were strafed with machine gun fire from German aircraft as they fled the city into neighboring fields.

Picasso, appalled by this brutality against the people of his native country, responded by creating the mural-size painting *Guernica*. Although this work stems from a specific incident, it is a statement of protest against the brutality of all war.

Guernica covers a huge canvas more than 25 feet long. It is painted in the somber black, blue-blacks, whites, and grays of newspapers before the days of color printing. A large triangle embedded under the smaller shapes holds the whole scene of chaotic destruction together as a unified composition. *Guernica* combines Cubism's intellectual restructuring of form with the emotional intensity of earlier forms of Expressionism and Abstract Surrealism. In dream symbolism, a horse often represents a dreamer's creativity. Here the horse is speared and is dying in anguish. Beneath the horse's feet a soldier lies in pieces; near his broken sword a faint flower suggests hope. Above, a woman reaches out from an open window, an oil lamp in hand. Near the old-fashioned lamp and above the horse's head is an eyelike shape with an electric light bulb at the center. Jagged rays of light radiate out from the bottom edge. Sometimes an eye representing the eye of God was painted on the ceiling of medieval churches. The juxtaposition between old and new sources of illumination could be a metaphor relating to enlightenment.

Interviewed during the war, Picasso remarked that "painting is not done to decorate apartments. It is an instrument of war for attack and defense against the enemy."[5] Unfortunately, the type of aerial bombardment that he decried in *Guernica* soon became a common strategy that all sides adopted.

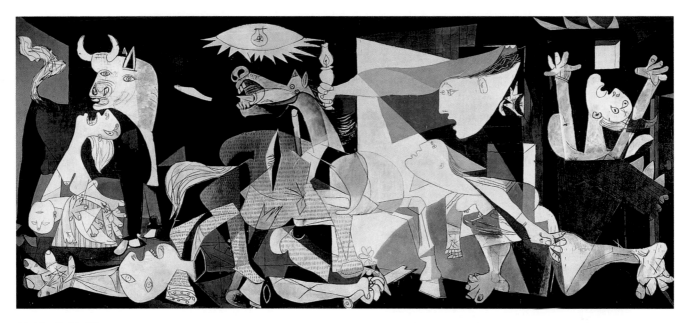

12.18 Pablo Picasso.
Guernica. 1937.
Oil on canvas. 11'5½" 3 25'5¼".
Museo Nacional Centro de Arte Reina Sofía. Copyright Giraudon/Art Resource, NY. © 2010 Estate of Pablo Picasso/Artists Rights Society (ARS), New York.

Between the world wars, a socially and politically committed form of art called **social realism** became common in many countries. This style took many forms, but they all include a retreat from the radical innovations of modern art and a desire to communicate more readily with the public about social causes and issues. In Nazi Germany and in Communist Russia, this style became an officially sponsored "norm" for art, which artists could ignore only if they did not care to have a successful career. A good example of Russian social realism is Vera Mukhina's *Monument to the Proletariat and Agriculture.* Her huge statue, which depicts a male factory worker and a female farm worker in stainless steel 78 feet high, was first exhibited at the Paris World's fair of 1937. Later set up in Moscow, it expresses the hopes and ideals of the workers' state, which came crashing down in 1991 with the fall of the Communist regime.

Mexican social realism took the form of mural paintings that embodied the ideals of the revolution of 1910–1917, when a popular

12.19 Vera Mukhina.
Monument to the Proletariat and Agriculture. 1937.
Stainless steel. 78' high.
All-Russia Exposition Grounds, Moscow. © Estate of Vera RAO, Moscow/Licensed by VAGA, New York.

uprising overthrew a long-entrenched dictatorship. The Mexican government in 1921 embarked on a program to pay artists an hourly wage to decorate public buildings with murals that spoke to the people about the recent revolution and about their long history. Inspired by the murals of the Italian Renaissance and by pre-Columbian wall paintings of ancient Mexican cultures, the muralists envisioned a national art that would glorify the traditional Mexican heritage and promote the new

post-revolutionary government. Diego Rivera's fresco *The Liberation of the Peon* is a good example that deals with a common event of the revolution: The landlord's house burns in the background, while revolutionary soldiers untie the peon from a stake and cover his naked body, which is scarred by repeated lashings. This work is a variation of a large painting on a wall of the Ministry of Education in Mexico City. Both Diego Rivera and fellow muralist José Clemente Orozco visited the

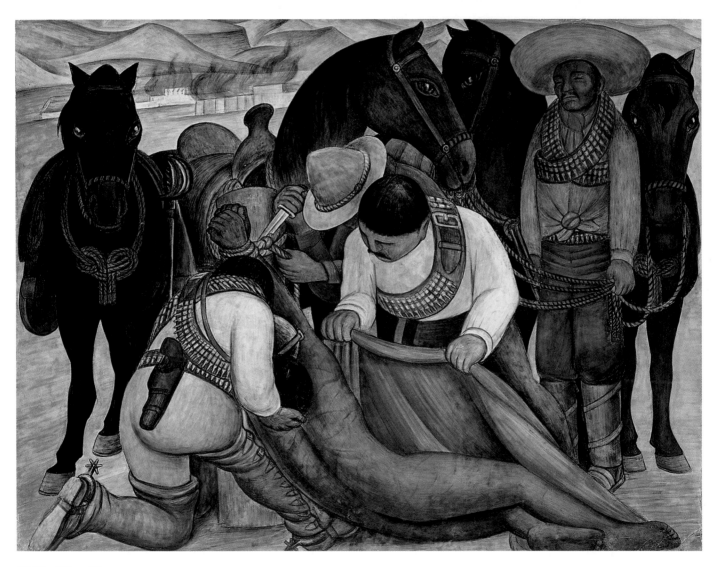

12.20   Diego Rivera.
The Liberation of the Peon. 1931.
Fresco. 73" 3 94¼".

United States, where they influenced American mural painting (a work by Orozco is pictured on page 108).

During the Depression years of the 1930s, the United States government maintained an active program of subsidy for the arts. The Works Progress Administration (WPA) commissioned painters to paint murals in public buildings, and the Farm Security Administration (FSA) hired photographers and filmmakers to record the eroding dustbowl and its workworn inhabitants. With government support, the art of documentary filmmaking reached a peak of achievement.

Photographer Dorothea Lange documented the helplessness and hopelessness of the urban unemployed. Her sensitive study, *White Angel Bread Line, San Francisco*, is a powerful image of a difficult period.

LATIN AMERICAN MODERNISM

Modern art showed distinctive characteristics when it bloomed across Latin America in the 1920s. Art movements were often interdisciplinary, allying painters with poets or composers. A case in point was Modern Art Week in São Paulo, Brazil, in 1922: Artists showed works influenced by Cubism and abstraction, poets read lyrics denouncing their elders, and musicians played new work that reflected Afro-Brazilian traditions. The crucial question that they all faced was how to relate to European culture, and Brazilian modernists came up with a perfectly logical but also rebellious answer: cannibalism. Brazilians would "ingest" European culture and let it nourish their own self-expression.

Tarsila do Amaral embodied this cannibalism in her work when she created *Abaporu*. The style shows her study of Fernand Legér's Cubism and the abstract sculpture of Brancusi (see pages 236–238). But the composition has "tropical" clichés

12.21 Dorothea Lange.
White Angel Bread Line, San Francisco. 1933.
Photograph.
The Oakland Museum of California, City of Oakland. © The Dorothea Lange Collection. Gift of Paul S. Taylor. A67.137.33001.1.

12.22 Tarsila Do Amaral.
Abaporu. 1928.
Oil on canvas. 34″ 3 29″.
Museo de Arte Latinoamericano, Buenos Aires (Malba).
Courtesy of Guilherme Augusto do Amaral.

12.23   Xul Solar.
Dragon. 1927.
Watercolor on paper. 10″ 3 12⅝″.
Fundación Pan Klub, Museo Xul Solar, Buenos Aires.
© Pan Klub Foundation–Xul Solar Museum.

like the lemon-slice sun and the cactus. Thus, she slyly affirmed Brazilian culture. The solitary figure is the cannibal, or, translating the title from the native Brazilian language, "the one who eats." One of the poets of that period wrote in a Cannibalistic Manifesto that Brazilians have a dual heritage: the jungle and the school. Tarsila's art shows both of these.

In Argentina, painters and poets banded together in order to combat the public's ignorance about modern art. Their journal, *Martín Fierro,* extolled the most creative artists, among them Xul Solar. Xul—pronounced shool—is the Latin word for "light" spelled backward. The artist thus named himself after sunlight! He spent many years in Europe, and when he returned in 1924 he began exhibiting fantasy-based watercolors such as *Dragon.* Here a figure in an elaborate headdress (a priest?) rides a giant serpent pierced with fifteen protruding flagpoles. The head of this dragon is adorned with a cross, a star, and a moon, symbols of Christianity, Judaism, and Islam. The work embodies Xul's hopes for a universal spiritualism, a union of religions and nations. Author Jorge Luis Borges wrote that being Argentine gives artists a uniquely detached perspective on the rest of the Western world; Xul seems to want to embrace all of it.

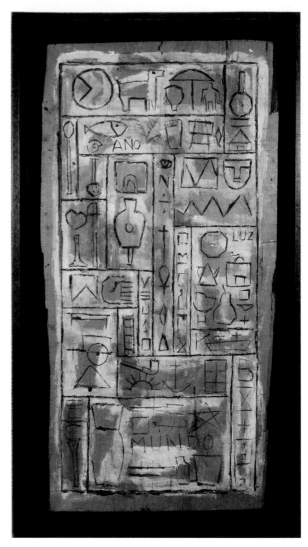

12.24   Joaquín Torres-García.
Universal Constructivism. 1930.
Oil on wood. 23¼″ 3 11⅜″.
Museo Nacional Centro de Arte Reina Sofía, Madrid. © Artists Rights Society (ARS), New York/VEGAP, Madrid.

Uruguayan artist Joaquín Torres-García developed a uniquely American version of Constructivism (and here we refer to all of the Americas, as the artist did). The rectangular blocks in his work *Universal Constructivism* refer both to Mondrian's paintings and to the stone architecture of pre-Conquest indigenous Peru. Over that framework, he drew symbols that refer both to modern life and to the pottery designs of ancient Americans. Thus, he aimed at a cross-cultural synthesis of modern and ancient that he hoped would have universal appeal. A few words in Spanish (year, light, world) are all that mark this as a specifically Latin American work.

The Surrealists adopted Mexican painter Frida Kahlo, even though her sources were closer to the folk arts of her native country. Her painting *The Two Fridas* shows herself as a split personality, divided between her European and Mexican heritage. As each stares back at us, we see their hearts plainly visible, joined by blood vessels. This is an allusion both to ancient Aztec human sacrifice and to the artist's own surgical traumas. Her many self-portraits provide insight to an exceptional person who lived life with passionate intensity in spite of incredible physical problems, as the accompanying essay shows.

AMERICAN REGIONALISM

In the 1930s, the spread of the Depression, along with political upheaval, helped motivate artists in America (and here we mean the United States) to search for both national and personal identity. American artists were caught between a public largely indifferent to art and a feeling, both at home and abroad, that American art was merely provincial. In this atmosphere of relative cultural isolation, an American regionalism developed, based on the idea that artists in the United States could find their identity by focusing attention on the subject matter that was local and American.

Edward Hopper made several trips to Europe between 1906 and 1910, but he remained apart

12.25 Frida Kahlo.
The Two Fridas. 1939.
Oil on canvas. 5′8½″ square.

from European avant-garde movements as he portrayed the loneliness of much of American life. *Nighthawks* shows Hopper's fascination with the mood of people in a particular place and time. The haunting effect of his paintings comes largely

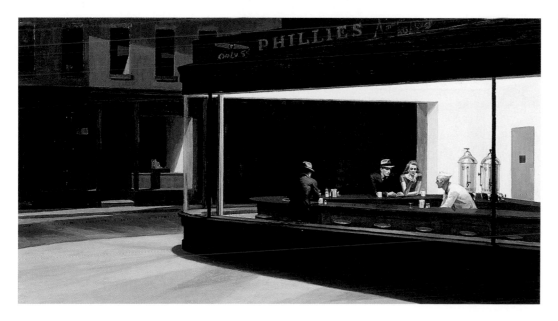

12.26 Edward Hopper.
Nighthawks. 1942.
Oil on canvas.
33⅛″ 3 60″.
84.1 3 152.4 cm.

Frida Kahlo: Compelling Autobiographer

FRIDA KAHLO (1907–1954) WAS a strong-willed, determined woman in a society that taught women to be passive.

Born in a suburb of Mexico City, she was the child of a photographer of German descent and a part-Spanish, part-Indian mother. When she was six years old, she was stricken with polio. The painful disease quarantined her for nine months and left her with one leg shorter and thinner than the other. At age eighteen she was in a trolley car accident that was followed by ineffective orthopedic treatments and thirty-two operations over the course of her life.

Chronic physical suffering caused by her illness and the accident led to a preoccupation with her severely damaged body—often the central subject in her paintings. In spite of her pain, her art reveals deep feelings of connection with nature and with the creative energy that flows through all life. In her paintings, details of nature are integrated with elements of dreams and fantasies.

When her work was shown in Paris in 1938, it received favorable attention from leading Surrealists. However, Kahlo's unique style is probably more indebted to Mexican narrative folk painting than to European Surrealism. Her paintings contain a mixture of folk art motifs, Surrealist elements, and autobiographical elements.

Her life was as unconventional as her art: She had two stormy marriages to the muralist Diego Rivera, numerous affairs, and friendships with leading international leftist and Surrealist leaders.

After her divorce from Diego Rivera in 1940, she painted *Self-Portrait with Cropped Hair*, a declaration of independence from his infidelities. She sits staring back at us after putting on an oversized man's suit and snipping at her hair. The inscription above quotes a Mexican folk song ("Look, if I loved you

12.27   Frida Kahlo.
Self-Portrait with Cropped Hair. 1940.
Oil on canvas. 15¾" 3 11".
The Museum of Modern Art/Licensed by Scala-Art Resource, NY. © 2010 Banco de México Diego Rivera
Frida Kahlo Museums Trust, Mexico, D.F./Artists Rights Society (ARS), New York.

it was because of your hair; since you no longer have hair I no longer love you"), reflecting the Mexican folk tradition of inscribing painting with lines of verse.

The work also shows the artist turning herself into a man, an image that hints at her bisexuality. She once said that she did not care if her works

reflected Surrealist beliefs, as long as they reflected her life. She remarried Rivera the next year.

In the 1980s her psychologically loaded self-portraits found an appreciative new audience. Kahlo has become the heroine of the Mexican avant-garde and the subject of several books and a feature-length movie.

from his carefully organized compositions and his emphasis on controlled use of light and shadow areas. Both Hopper and the Impressionists were interested in light, but for different purposes: Hopper employed it to clarify and organize structure, whereas the Impressionists used light in ways that seemed to dissolve structure.

Regional painter Grant Wood studied art in Paris in the early 1920s. Although he never worked with Cubist or Expressionist ideas, he did identify with modern trends and began making freely brushed paintings derived from Impressionism. After years of little success, Wood returned to his birthplace in rural Midwestern America and dedicated himself to memorializing the unique character of the land, the people, and their way of life.

Wood's personal style of crisp realism was inspired by the paintings of the Northern Renaissance masters such as van Eyck and Dürer. He also drew on American folk painting and the characteristically stiff, long-exposure portraits taken by late nineteenth-century photographers. Wood, like van Eyck, calculated every aspect of design and all details of the subject matter to enhance the content of his paintings.

The idea for the famous painting *American Gothic* came to Wood when he saw a modest farmhouse built in a local carpenter's version of the Gothic style. The restrained color, simplification of round masses such as trees and people, and the high detail are typical of Wood's paintings. The two figures (the artist's sister and his dentist) are echoed in the pointed-arch window shapes. Vertical lines and paired elements dominate. For example, the lines of the pitchfork are repeated in the man's overalls and shirt front. The upright tines of the fork seem to symbolize the pair's firm, traditional stance and hard-won virtue. Wood's *American Gothic* has become a national icon that speaks clearly to many; it continues to spark a wealth of responses.

The most forceful spokesperson for American regional art was Thomas Hart Benton, son of a

12.28   Grant Wood.
American Gothic. 1930.
Oil on beaverboard. 29¼" 3 24⅞". 74.3 3 62.4 cm.
Friends of American Art Collection. 1930.934. © The Art Institute of Chicago/© Figge Art Museum, successors to the Estate of Nan Wood Graham/Licensed by VAGA, New York, NY.

Missouri United States senator. Benton worked to create a style that was American in both form and content—a realistic style that would be easily understood by all, based on the depiction of American themes. Some of the strength for both figures and composition came from the influence of Michelangelo's muscular bodies. But Benton transformed Renaissance and modern influences into a highly personal style in which all forms are conditioned by strong curvilinear rhythms. The push and pull of shapes in shallow space, emphasized by contrasting light and dark edges, shows what Benton learned from Cubism.

12.29 Thomas Hart Benton.
Palisades, from the series *American Historical Epic.*
c. 1919–1924.
Oil on cotton duck on aluminum
honeycomb panel. 66⅛″ 3 72″ (168.0 3 182.9 cm).

Palisades was part of a series of paintings titled *American Historical Epic.* In contrast to conventional histories that feature great men, Benton wanted to create a people's history, one that depicted the actions of ordinary people on the land. Here, the European colonizers are staking out and dividing up the land, while the Indians, in contrast, are sharing their knowledge of growing corn, which the newcomers will need for survival.

AFRICAN-AMERICAN MODERNISTS
Philosopher Alain Locke wrote in the 1925 book *The New Negro* that African-American artists should reconnect with their roots in the "ancestral arts of Africa." They should not seek to paint or sculpt in highly polished academic styles; neither should they explore Parisian modern movements. Rather, they should attune themselves to their own cultural heritage and express themselves through recognizably African-based styles.

This book was a major force behind the cultural flowering known as the Harlem Renaissance, which included poets, musicians, and novelists along with visual artists. Some important figures associated with the Renaissance include Langston Hughes, Paul Robeson, Zora Neale Hurston, and many others both in Harlem and elsewhere in the United States. Visual artists were an integral part of the movement; they illustrated books, designed interior spaces, and photographed the teeming life around them.

The principal vehicle for displaying the painting and sculpture of African Americans at that time was the annual traveling exhibition sponsored by the Harmon Foundation. One artist who was repeatedly honored in that show was Sargent Johnson. A resident of California, he produced painted wood sculptures such as *Forever Free* that expressed

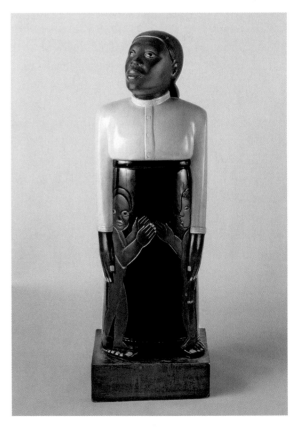

12.30 Sargent Johnson.
Forever Free. 1933.
Wood with lacquer on cloth. 36″ 3 11½″ 3 9½″
(91.44 3 29.21 3 24.13 cm).

his view of the Black identity. A motherly woman shelters two smaller figures, all of whom show pronounced African characteristics. The title of the work comes from the Emancipation Proclamation of 1863, which ended slavery in the Confederate states. He wrote of this expression of cultural roots: "I am producing strictly a Negro Art, studying not the culturally mixed Negro of the cities, but the more primitive slave type as existed in this country during the period of slave importation."[6]

During the Depression of the 1930s, the Works Progress Administration (WPA) set up community art centers in one hundred cities. Jacob Lawrence was a product of one of these centers in Harlem, where he met most of the leaders of the Renaissance. In 1938, he made a series of forty-one paintings on the life of Toussaint l'Ouverture, the Black leader of the revolt that made Haiti the first independent nation in Latin America in 1804. *General Toussaint l'Ouverture Defeats the English at Saline* shows his style, which he called "dynamic Cubism." Lawrence was not practicing the French Cubism of Braque and Picasso, however; he made his own investigation of African art and reinterpreted it in his own way.

12.31 Jacob Lawrence.
General Toussaint l'Ouverture Defeats the English at Saline.
1937–1938.
Gouache on paper. 19″ 3 11″.
48.3 3 27.9 cm.
Aaron Douglas Collection, The Amistad Research Center, Tulane University, © 2010 The Jacob and Gwendolyn Lawrence Foundation, Seattle/Artists Rights Society (ARS), New York.

12.32 Archibald Motley, Jr.
Barbeque. 1934.
Oil on canvas. 36¼″ 3 40⅛″.
Chicago History Museum and Valerie Gerrard.

12.33 Barbara Hepworth.
Forms in Echelon. 1938.
Wood. Height 42½″.
Tate Gallery, London, Great Britain. Photograph: Tate, London/
Art Resource, NY. Copyright Bowness, Hepworth Estate.

Archibald Motley of Chicago took a realist view of African-American culture. His painting *Barbeque* of 1934 is ebullient and full of motion, and also shows an interest in how figures look under artificial light. Motley specialized in depicting all aspects of the urban Black experience, including on occasion gamblers and drinkers during Prohibition. Such subject matter did not endear him to pretentious art patrons, but Motley replied, "I have tried to paint the Negro as I have seen him and as I feel him, in my self without adding or detracting, just being frankly honest."[7]

ORGANIC ABSTRACTION

The Fascist and Communist regimes in Germany and Russia suppressed most modern art, especially abstract art; European artists in opposition to this stance formed the group Abstraction-Creation in 1931. Their second manifesto proclaimed "total opposition to all oppression, of whatever kind it may be." Abstract art thus became a statement on behalf of personal freedom. Many abstract artists adopted organic shapes that resemble life forms.

An early member of Abstraction-Creation was the English sculptor Barbara Hepworth. Her *Forms in Echelon* consists of two pieces of mahogany, carved into shapes that suggest growing plant forms. She was the first to put holes in her sculpted works, opening the shape to light and air. Viewers who apply a little imagination to the arrangement of *Forms in Echelon* can visualize a conversation, or perhaps mutual nurturing, between the two forms.

Hepworth's colleague and friend Henry Moore took her invention in a more figural direction. After serving in World War I, Moore used a veteran's grant to study art in London. While there, he spent long hours studying the collections of non-Western

12.34   Henry Moore.
Recumbent Figure. 1938.
Green Hornton stone. 35″ 3 52¼″ 3 29″. 89.9 3 132.7 3 73.7 cm.
© Henry Moore Foundation, Tate Gallery, London/Art Resource, NY.

arts in the British Museum and the Victoria and Albert Museum. His *Recumbent Figure* from 1938 is an elaboration of the reclining Toltec *Chacmool.* Moore smoothed the stone into an organic abstract shape that suggests the human form without exactly depicting it. Moore's carving of the stone also preserves its origins in sedimentary geological deposits, and the label ("Green Hornton Stone"), specified at Moore's insistence, identifies its source where he quarried it.

The outbreak of World War II in Europe in 1939 took humanity to the brink of destruction yet again. Besides the suffering that it created, the war also redrew the world map of artistic innovation. Many European artists migrated to the Americas and fertilized modern movements there.

Notes

1. Hans Richter, *Dada 1916–1966* (Munich: Goethe Institut, 1966), 22.
2. Paride Accetti, Raffaele De Grada, and Arturo Schwarz, *Cinquant'annia Dada— Dada in Italia 1916–1966* (Milan: Galleria Schwarz, 1966), 39.
3. André Breton, *Manifestos of Surrealism,* translated by Richard Seaver and Helen R. Lane (Ann Arbor: University of Michigan Press, 1972), 14.
4. Sam Hunter and John Jacobus, *Modern Art* (New York: Harry N. Abrams, 1985), 148.
5. Herbert Read, *A Concise History of Modern Painting* (New York: Praeger, 1959), 160.
6. *San Francisco Chronicle,* October 6, 1935; quoted in Evangeline Montgomery, "Sargent Claude Johnson," *Ijele: Art Journal of the African World* (2002), 1–2.
7. Romare Bearden and Harry Henderson, *A History of African American Artists from 1792 to the Present* (New York, 1993), 152.

Henry Moore on Form and Space

WHEN HENRY MOORE (1898–1986) was a student at the Royal College of Art in London, he visited the British Museum twice a week to explore the riches of the world's sculptural traditions. The work that spoke to him the most was the sculpture of ancient Mexico, with its powerful closed forms. He also had a lifetime interest in organic forms, such as weatherworn bones and watersmoothed pebbles. From these and other elements, he evolved a distinctive personal sculptural style that was characterized by abstract, rounded contours interwoven with shapely voids, as in his *Sheep Piece* around which sheep cluster at his homestead (**12.35**). Whether he was working in stone, wood, or bronze castings, Moore was consistently interested in the interplay between positive form and negative space, and in how a piece looks from all sides:

"Appreciation of sculpture depends upon the ability to respond to form in three dimensions. That is perhaps why sculpture has been described as the most difficult of all arts …. Many more people are 'form-blind' than colour-blind. The child learning to see first distinguishes only two-dimensional shape; it cannot judge distances, depths. Later, for its personal safety and practical needs, it has to develop (partly by means of touch) the ability to judge roughly three-dimensional distances. But having satisfied the require ments of practical necessity, most people go no farther …. They do not make the further intellectual and emotional effort needed to comprehend form in its full spatial existence.

"This is what the sculptor must do. He must strive continually to think of, and use, form in its full spatial completeness. He gets the solid shape, as it were, inside his head—he thinks of it, whatever its size, as if he were holding it completely enclosed in the hollow of his hand. He mentally visualises a complex form from all round itself; he knows while he looks at one side what the other side is like; he identifies himself with its centre of gravity, its mass, its weight."[1]

"At one time the holes in my sculpture were made for their own sakes. Because I was trying to become conscious of spaces in the sculpture—I made the hole have a shape in its own right, the solid body was encroached upon, eaten into, and sometimes the form was only the shell holding the hole. Recently I have attempted to make the forms and the spaces (not holes) inseparable, neither being more important than the other."[2]

"If you hold your hand as I am doing now, the shape that those fingers could enclose if I were holding an apple would be different from the shape if I were holding a pear. If you can tell what that is, then you know what space is. That is space and form. You can't understand space without being able to understand form and to understand form you must be able to understand space. If I can really grasp in my mind the shape of your head, I must know what distance there is from your forehead to the back of your head, and I must know what shape the air is between your eyebrows and your nostrils, or down to the cheeks. The idea that space is something new in sculpture is only spoken of by people who can't know what space and form are."[3]

Notes

1. Henry Moore, "The Sculptor Speaks," article in *The Listener*, vol. XVIII, no. 449, August 18, 1937, pp. 338–40. Quoted in *Henry Moore on Sculpture*, ed. Philip James, Viking Press, New York, 1967, p. 62. [Reprinted by kind permission of the Henry Moore Foundation.]
2. Henry Moore in H. Felix Man, *Eight European Artists*, Heinemann, London, 1954. Quoted in James, op. cit., p. 118. [Reprinted by kind permission of the Henry Moore Foundation.]
3. Henry Moore in Donald Hall, "An Interview with Henry Moore," article in *Horizon, A Magazine of the Arts*, November 1960, vol. iii, no. 2, American Horizon, New York, 1960. Interview quoted without omissions in James, op. cit., p. 119. [Reprinted by kind permission of the Henry Moore Foundation.]

Artists on Art: Henry Moore on Form and Space was taken from *The Art of Seeing*, Eighth Edition by Paul Zelanski and Mary Pat Fisher.

12.35 Henry Moore
Sheep Piece, 1971–72, Hoglands, Hertfordshire.
Bronze, length 19 ft (5.8 m).
Courtesy of the Henry Moore Foundation, Hertfordshire, England.

POSTWAR MODERN MOVEMENTS IN THE WEST

In the years following World War II, modern artists made a frontal assault on the rules of art. The conventions and customs that had governed artistic creation since the Renaissance were gradually overturned, rejected, or ignored. In 1945, even the most innovative artists still worked in traditional media; but thirty years later they were also scratching lines in the desert, copying boxes of laundry soap, gluing themselves to trees, and selling kisses for money. Whatever an artist did, or whatever a gallery exhibited, became art. It was a restless and wildly creative period.

THE NEW YORK SCHOOL

At the end of World War II, Europe lay in ruins—financially, emotionally, and physically. The war took the lives of a quarter million English people, six hundred thousand French, five million Germans, and twenty million Russians. The Nazi Holocaust counted for six million of these deaths. Refugees and displaced persons numbered forty million. England's wartime Prime Minister Winston Churchill in 1947 described Europe as "a rubble heap, a charnel house, a breeding ground for pestilence and hate." Many prominent European artists had fled from Nazi oppression to the United States, which emerged from the war economically strong and optimistic.

Among the artists who settled in New York were Mondrian, Léger, Duchamp, Dalí, and André Breton. They worked, taught, exhibited, and generally stirred things up, opening new possibilities for American artists. This immigration made modernism no longer a distant, European phenomenon; many of its leading practitioners came to the United States. Mexican muralists Diego Rivera and David Siqueiros also exhibited and taught in New York during the 1930s, encouraging artists away from traditional easel painting.

War had altered the consciousness of the developed world in subtle but profound ways. The Nazi genocide machine had taken human cruelty to a new low, and the atomic bomb gave humankind terrifying new powers: People were now living in a world they had the power to destroy in minutes.

The horrors of World War II led artists to rethink the relationship between art and life. The dislocations caused by war led artists to explore visual realms other than the representational and narrative. One result was **Abstract Expressionism**, a culmination of the expressive tendencies in painting from Fauvism, German Expressionism, and the automatic methods of Surrealism.

The new émigrés influenced many American painters, leading them to move away from realist styles dominant in the 1930s, and to experiment with more expressive and inventive ways of creating. The unparalleled crisis of the World War also led them to move away from public issues of history and social comment that Depression-era painting emphasized. As a result, they began to paint in styles that were both stylistically innovative and personal.

Chapter 13: Postwar Modern Movements in the West was taken from *Prebles' Artforms: An Introduction to the Visual Arts,* Tenth Edition by Patrick Frank.

Arshile Gorky on Art Elements Conveying Life's Intensity

ARSHILE GORKY'S WORK revolves around lines, shapes, and fields of color. At first glance, they may seem fanciful, spontaneous, playful, but his own life and words correct this impression. Born in Armenia in 1904 as Vosdanik Adoian, Gorky experienced the terrible sufferings of the Armenian people. The Turks killed all his grandparents, six uncles, and three aunts, in some cases before his eyes. His family residence was shelled, and his people were forced to undertake a 150-mile (240-km) death march. That year, 1915, two million Armenians were massacred by the Turks. During a Turkish blockade when he was fifteen, his beloved mother died of starvation in his arms.

In 1920, Gorky emigrated to America, where he faced hunger and poverty but gradually achieved recognition as an artist, only to see some of his best works destroyed in a barn fire. In 1948, his father died, his neck was broken and his painting arm paralyzed in an automobile crash, and his wife left him, taking their two children with her. He ended this life of suffering that year by hanging himself. Gorky's words about art therefore ring with the intensity of his personal experience:

"We have been made privy to mankind's evil secrets as well as its glorious achievements. And the living, sensitive, thinking man cannot help but respond with greater than normal intensity. And the remembrance of Armenia's beauty prior to the bloodshed. The art and accomplishments of our unfortunate people. Great art's problem, that is to say my goal, is to enable those who have not experienced certain elements of reality to experience them through the power of my work on their mind and eyes and imagination. To enable them to come as close to realization of reality as possible, simply through my work.

"To be alive is to feel, to be sensitive, and above all to be aware. Art must always remain earnest. Great art contains great topics. What do I mean by great? Not kings, rich men, and clerics, not publicized political scoundrels. I mean love of man, love of nature, love of beauty, love of progress in the well-being of man. Sarcasm has no place in art because it verges on cynicism, which is weakness and the inability to face reality, to master reality.

"The history of our Armenian people has shown us the secret of creativity. The secret is to throw yourself into the water of life again and again, not to hang back, no reservations, risk everything, but, above all, strike out boldly with all you have."[1]

Note

1. Arshile Gorky (Vosdanik Adoian), interviewed by Malcolm Johnson, "Café Life in New York," *New York Sun*, August 22, 1941, as quoted in *Arshile Gorky: Drawings to Paintings*, The University of Texas at Austin, Austin, Texas, p. 67.

13.1 Arshile Gorky.
Making the Calendar, 1947.
Oil on canvas.
The Munson-William-Proctor Institute, Utica, New York. Edward W. Root Bequest.

Artists on Art: Arshile Gorky on Art Elements Conveying Life's Intensity was taken from *The Art of Seeing*, Eighth Edition by Paul Zelanski and Mary Pat Fisher.

13.2 Hans Namuth.
Jackson Pollock. 1950.
Gelatin silver print.
National Portrait Gallery, Smithsonian Institution. Hans Namuth/
Hans Namuth Ltd.

Jackson Pollock, the leading innovator of Abstract Expressionism, studied in the 1930s with both Thomas Hart Benton and the Mexican muralist David Siqueiros. The rhythmic structure of Benton's style and the mural-scale art of the Mexicans influenced Pollock's poured paintings of the late 1940s and early 1950s. Searching for ways to express primal human nature, Pollock also studied Navajo sand painting and psychologist Carl Jung's theories of the unconscious. His belief that he was painting for the age of the "atom bomb and the radio" led Pollock to innovative techniques. He created *Autumn Rhythm* by dripping thin paint onto the canvas rather than brushing it on. Working on huge canvases placed on the floor, Pollock was able to enter the space of the painting physically and psychologically. The huge format allowed ample room for his sweeping gestural lines. Pollock dripped, poured, and flung paint, yet he exercised control and selection by the rhythmical, dancing movements of his body. A similar

13.3 Jackson Pollock.
Autumn Rhythm. (Number 30). 1950.
Oil on canvas. 105" 3 207" (266.7 3 525.8 cm).
The Metropolitan Museum of Art, George A. Hearn Fund, 1957. (57.92). Photograph: © 1998 The Metropolitan Museum of Art/Art Resource, NY. © 2010. The Pollock-Krasner Foundation. Artists Rights Society (ARS), New York.

Jackson Pollock's *No. 29, 1950*

WHILE NOT AS LARGE as Monet's paintings at the Orangerie, Jackson Pollock's works are still large enough to engulf the viewer. The eye travels in what one critic has called "galactic" space, following first one line, then another, unable to locate itself or to complete its visual circuit through the web of paint. Work such as this has been labeled "Action Painting," not only because it prompts the viewer to become actively engaged with it, but also because the lines that trace themselves out across the sweep of the painting seem to chart the path of Pollock's own motions as he stood over it. The drips and sweeps of paint record his action as a painter and document it, a fact captured by Hans Namuth in October of 1950 in a famous series of photographs (**Fig. 13.4**) of Pollock at work on the painting *Autumn Rhythm*, and then in two films, one shot in black-and-white and the other in color. The second of these was shot from below through a sheet of glass on which Pollock was painting (**Fig. 13.5**), vividly capturing the motion embodied in Pollock's work. The resulting work, *No. 29, 1950* (**Fig. 13.6**), was completed over the course of five autumn weekends, with Namuth filming the entire event. After a false start on the painting, which Pollock wiped out in front of the camera, he created a collage web of paint, containing pebbles, shells, sand, sections of wire mesh, marbles, and pieces of colored plastic.

Namuth's photographs and films teach us much about Pollock's working method. Pollock longed to be completely involved in the process of painting. He wanted to become wholly

13.4 Jackson Pollock painting *Autumn Rhythm,* 1950.
Center for Creative Photography, Tucson.
Photo: Hans Namuth. © 2001 Pollock-Krasner Foundation / Artists Rights Society (ARS), New York.

13.5 Jackson Pollock painting on glass, 1951. Still from a color film by Hans Namuth and Paul Falkenberg.
The Museum of Modern Art, New York, NY, U.S.A. Digital Image © The Museum of Modern Art/Licensed by SCALA/Art Resource, NY. Courtesy of Hans Numuth ltd.

Works in Progess: Jackson Pollock's *No. 29, 1950* was taken from *A World of Art,* Sixth Edition by Henry M. Sayre.

13.6 Jackson Pollock.
No. 29, 1950, 1950.
Oil on canvas, expanded steel, string, glass, and pebbles on glass, 48 3 72 in. National Gallery of Canada, Ottawa. Purchased 1968.
© 2007 Pollock-Krasner Foundation / Artists Rights Society (ARS), New York.

absorbed in the work. As he had written in a short article called "My Painting," published in 1947, "When I am in my painting, I'm not aware of what I'm doing . . . the painting has a life of its own. I try to let it come through. It is only when I lose contact with the painting that the result is a mess. Otherwise there is pure harmony, an easy give and take, and the painting comes out well."

In Namuth's photographs and films, we witness Pollock's absorption in the work. We see the immediacy of his gesture as he flings paint, moving around the work, the paint tracing his path. He worked on the floor, in fact, in order to heighten his sense of being in the work. "I usually paint on the floor," he says in Namuth's film. "I feel more at home, more at ease in a big area, having a canvas on the floor, I feel nearer, more a part of a painting. This way I can walk around it, work from all four sides and be in the painting." We also see in Namuth's images something of the speed with which Pollock worked. According to Namuth, when Pollock was painting, "his movements, slow at first, gradually became faster and more dancelike." In fact, the traceries of line on the canvas are like choreographies, complex charts of a dancer's movement. In Pollock's words, the paintings are

energy and motion
made visible—
memories arrested in space.

Namuth was disturbed by the lack of sharpness and the blurred character in some of his photographs, and he did not show them to Pollock. "It was not until years later," Namuth admitted, "that I understood how exciting these photographs really were." At the time, though, his inability to capture all of Pollock's movement led him to the idea of making a film. "Pollock's method of painting suggested a moving picture," he would recall, "the dance around the canvas, the continuous movement, the drama."

13.7 Mark Rothko.
Blue, Orange, Red. 1961.
Oil on canvas. 90¼″ 81¼″.
Hirschhorn Museum and Sculpture Garden, Smithsonian Institution, Washington, DC. Gift of Joseph H. Hirschhorn Foundation (1966). Photograph: Lee Stalsworth. © 1998 Kate Rothko Prizel and Christopher Rothko. Artists Rights Society (ARS), New York. HMSG 66.4420.

13.8 Helen Frankenthaler.
Mountains and Sea. 1952.
Oil and charcoal on canvas. 86⅝″ 3 117¼″.
Collection: Helen Frankenthaler Foundation, Inc. (on extended loan to the National Gallery of Art, Washington, D.C.). © 2011 Helen Frankenthaler / Artists Rights Society (ARS), New York.

approach in the work of many of his colleagues led to the term **action painting**.

A related painting style that evolved at about the same time was **color field**, a term for painting that consists of large areas of color, with no obvious structure, central focus, or dynamic balance. The canvases of color field painters are dominated by unified images, images so huge that they engulf the viewer.

Mark Rothko is now best known as a pioneer of color field painting, although his early works of the 1930s were urban scenes. By the 1940s, influenced by Surrealism, he began producing paintings inspired by myths and rituals. In the late 1940s, he gave up the figure and began to focus primarily on color. In works such as *Blue, Orange, Red*, Rothko used color to evoke moods ranging from joy and serenity to melancholy and despair. By superimposing thin layers of paint, he achieved a variety of qualities from dense to atmospheric to luminous. Rothko's paintings have sensuous appeal and monumental presence.

Helen Frankenthaler's work also evolved during the height of Abstract Expressionism. In 1952, she pioneered staining techniques as an extension of Jackson Pollock's poured paint and Mark Rothko's fields of color. Brushstrokes and paint texture were eliminated as she spread liquid colors across a horizontal, unprimed canvas. As the thin pigment soaked into the raw fabric, she coaxed it into fluid, organic shapes. Pale, subtle, and spontaneous, *Mountains and Sea* marked the beginning of a series of paintings that emphasize softness and openness and the expressive power of color. The twenty-three-year-old Frankenthaler painted it in one day, after a trip to Nova Scotia.

Robert Motherwell's series of paintings titled *Elegy to the Spanish Republic* is permeated with a tragic sense of history. His elegies brood over the destruction of the fragile Spanish democracy by General Franco in the bloody Spanish Civil War of the 1930s. Heavy black shapes crush and obliterate the lighter passages behind them. Motherwell began with a specific subject as his starting point and expressed its inner mood through abstract means.

13.9 Robert Motherwell. *Elegy to the Spanish Republic.* No. 34. 1953–1954. Oil on canvas. 80″ 3 100″. Albright-Knox Art Gallery, Buffalo, New York. Gift of Seymour H. Knox, Jr. (1957). © Dedalus Foundation, Inc. Licensed by VAGA, New York.

The influence of Expressionist and Surrealist attitudes on Willem de Kooning's work is evident in his spontaneous, emotionally charged brushwork and provocative use of shapes. Throughout his career, de Kooning emphasized abstract imagery, yet the human figure underlies many of his paintings. After several years of working without subjects, he began a series of large paintings in which ferocious female figures appear. These canvases, painted with slashing attacks of the brush, have an overwhelming presence. In *Woman and Bicycle*, the toothy smile is repeated in a savage necklace that caps tremendous breasts. While it explodes with the energies of Abstract Expressionism, this work is controversial for the monstrous image of women that it presents.

Norman Lewis was an African-American artist who participated in Abstract Expressionism from its inception. Like most of the Abstract Expressionists, during the 1930s Lewis painted in a Social Realist style, depicting urban poverty that

13.10 Willem de Kooning (1904–1997). *Woman and Bicycle.* 1952–1953. Oil on canvas. 78¼″ 3 50⅜″ 3 2″ (198.8 3 128.6 3 5.1 cm). Whitney Museum of American Art, New York; Purchase 55.35. Photograph: © 2011 The Willem de Kooning Foundation/Artists Rights Society (ARS), New York.

13.11 Norman Lewis.
Untitled. c. 1947.
Oil on canvas. 30″ 3 36″.
Private Collection, New York. Courtesy of Michael Rosenfeld Gallery, New York, and Landor Fine Arts, NJ.

he observed in his Harlem neighborhood. During and after World War II, he was increasingly influenced by modern art. His *Untitled* work from 1947 documents his shift toward a more spontaneous and improvisational style. Lewis's art differs from other Abstract Expressionists in that it seems more poetic and reserved. In addition, his painting at times shows traces of nature or, as we see in this work, city life.

David Smith, for many critics the most important American sculptor of the postwar period, took the formal ideas of Cubism and gave them an American vigor. His assembled metal sculpture balanced formal qualities with the elemental energy of Abstract Expressionist painting. His use of factory methods and materials provided new options for the next generation of sculptors. Smith's late work included the stainless steel *Cubi* series, based on cubic masses and planes balanced dynamically above the viewer's eye level. The scoured surfaces of the steel reflect light in ways that seem to dissolve their solidity. Smith intended the sculpture to be viewed outdoors in strong light, set off by green landscape.

13.12 David Smith.
Cubi XVII. 1963.
Polished stainless steel. 107¾″ 3 64⅜″ 3 38⅛″.
The Dallas Museum of Art. The Eugene and Margaret McDermott Fund. © Estate of David Smith. Licensed by VAGA, New York.

13.13 BBDR.
Velasca Tower.
Milan, Italy. 1954–56.
Courtesy of Vincenzo Lombardo/
Getty Images.

ARCHITECTURE AT MID-CENTURY

In the immediate post-war years, the International Style represented the leading edge of architecture. Its clean masses and sleek exteriors spoke across the Western world of efficiency, cosmopolitanism, and future-oriented thinking.

A few European architects looked for ways to integrate the International Style with their own local history. One of the most notable of these projects in the middle 1950s was the *Velasca Tower* in central Milan. The building follows most of the teachings of the International Style: It lacks decoration, uses modern materials, and plainly shows its structure. But the building's mushroom shape is meant to recall watchtowers of the Renaissance period. When the architects were attacked for making that historical reference, they replied that they were only making the most efficient use of a narrow building site. The *Velasca Tower* was for many years a symbol of modern Italy, forward-looking yet aware of the past. Its heavy use of cement and its overall brooding appearance, though, were soon dubbed Brutalist, a somewhat unflattering style name often applied to later, similar office buildings.

Most American architects at mid-century also used the International Style, but in a more elegant way. *Lever House* in New York City heralded the future of office buildings for the next twenty-five

13.14 Skidmore, Owings, and Merrill.
Lever House. 1952.
New York City.
Courtesy of Mark Fiennes/Arcaid/CORBIS.

years: It is a steel-and-glass box that looks slick, convenient, and modern. Most American cities have such buildings. Later architects would revolt against it, but for a generation this ultra-clean look represented the image of the American corporation. Following the words of American architect Louis Sullivan ("Form follows function"), International Style architects built practical buildings that clearly showed structural supports and banished all ornament. While many such buildings (such as *Lever House*) looked elegant and distinguished, the glass-box regularity of the style began to seem limiting. For example, Brazilian architect Oscar Niemeyer seized the opportunity that his country presented when it commissioned a new capital city to open in 1960.

His *Planalto Palace* participates in the glass box style yet departs from it in important ways. The entrance ramp hardly looks practical, and the sweeping, curved struts of the external skeleton take on a decorative life of their own. Such imaginative building soon became a hallmark of the postmodern movement, as we shall see in Chapter 14.

ASSEMBLAGE

Most leading artists of the 1940s and 1950s chose not to deal with recognizable subject matter. They mostly avoided referring to the world in which they lived. In the mid-1950s, a few young artists began to acknowledge, confront, and even celebrate the visual diversity of the urban scene; they wanted to move beyond the exclusive, personal nature of Abstract Expressionism. In their effort to re-engage art with ordinary life, these artists created loose conglomerations of seemingly random objects, often called **assemblages**. The art of assemblage took the Dada collage of Hannah Höch (see page 250) into three dimensions.

Under the influence of avant-garde composer John Cage, who urged artists to make art from the lives they were living, Robert Rauschenberg began combining ordinary objects and collage materials

13.15   Oscar Niemeyer.
Planalto Palace.
Presidential Residence, Brasília, Brazil. 1960.
Photograph: Bernard Boutrit/Woodfin Camp & Associates, Inc.

13.16 Robert Rauschenberg.
Monogram. 1955–1959.
Freestanding combine. 42″ 3 64″ 3 64½″.
Moderna Museet, Stockholm. © Estate of Robert Rauschenberg.
Licensed by VAGA, New York.

with Abstract Expressionistic brushwork in what he called "combine-paintings." The essence of creative thinking involves combining elements of the world in order to make an unexpected, previously unthinkable new thing. Such is the startling presence of Rauschenberg's *Monogram.* What is a stuffed, long-haired angora goat with a tire around its middle doing, standing in the middle of a collage-painting? The artist is acting as a prankster, in the spirit of the Surrealist artists such as Magritte (see page 27).

This strange assemblage offers glimpses of seemingly unrelated objects and events and acts as a symbol for the wild juxtapositions of modern life. Instead of blocking out the chaotic messages of city streets, TV, and magazines, Rauschenberg incorporated the trash of urban civilization in his art.

In the early 1960s, with the aid of the new technique of photographic screenprinting, Rauschenberg brought together images from art history and documentary photographs. In *Tracer* he combined Expressionist paint strokes with modified parts of art reproductions and news photographs so that art history, the Vietnam War, and street life interact with one another. Just as we can move from sports to dinner to televised wars and sitcoms, Rauschenberg's work assembles the unrelated bits and pieces of everyday experience.

13.17 Robert Rauschenberg (American, b. 1925).
Tracer. 1963.
Oil and silkscreen on canvas. 84⅛″ 3 60″
(213.7 3 152.4 cm).
Photograph: Jamison Miller. © 2002 The Nelson Gallery Foundation.
The Nelson-Atkins Museum of Art, Kansas City, MO, (Purchase) F84-70. © Estate of Robert Rauschenberg. Licensed by VAGA, New York.

Assemblage artists on the West Coast made more direct social comments. For example, *John Doe* by Edward Kienholz makes the average American into an outrageous caricature. Half of a store mannequin rides on a baby stroller with his chest blown out (revealing a cross). Paint drips add to the ridiculous effect. An inscription below adapts a sarcastic riddle: "How is John Doe like a piano? Because he is square, upright, and grand." Kienholz was friendly with many writers of the Beat movement, who similarly despaired over the blandness of middle-class life.

Rauschenberg often discussed art making with Jasper Johns during their formative years in the 1950s. Whereas Rauschenberg's work is filled with visual complexity, Johns's work is deceptively simple. His large early paintings were based on common graphic forms such as targets, maps, flags, and numbers. He was interested in the difference between signs (emblems that carry meaning) and art. In Johns's work, common signs play a dual role: They have the power of Abstract Expressionist forms in their size, bold design, and painterly surface qualities, yet they represent familiar objects and thus bring art back to everyday life. In his *Target with Four Faces*, a target becomes a painting, while the faces (sculpture) are perceived as a sign.

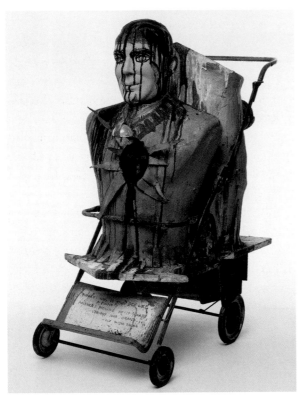

13.18 Edward Kienholz.
John Doe. 1959.
Free-standing assemblage. Oil and paint on mannequin parts; perambulator, toy, wood, metal, plaster, plastic, rubber.
39½" 3 19" 3 31¼"
(100.2 3 48.3 3 79.4 cm).
The Menil Collection, Houston. Acc. #86-27 DJ. Photographer: George Hixson, Houston. Videographer: Laurie McDonald.

13.19 Jasper Johns.
Target with Four Faces. 1955.
Assemblage: encaustic on newspaper and collage on canvas with objects, surmounted by four tinted plaster faces in wood box with hinged front.
Overall dimensions with box open,
33⅜" 3 26" 3 3" (85.3 3 66 3 7.6 cm).
The Museum of Modern Art, New York. Licensed by Scala-Art Resource, NY. Gift of Mr. and Mrs. Robert C. Scull. Photograph: © 2002 The Museum of Modern Art, New York. © Jasper Johns. Licensed by VAGA, New York.

As with Man Ray's *Gift* (page 249), Johns's common subjects are now objects of contemplation. His irony relates back to Dada and forward to Pop Art. The Neo-Dada works of Johns and Rauschenberg provided a bridge between Abstract Expressionism and later Pop Art. Johns and Rauschenberg are champions of art in an environment saturated with media-promoted icons of popular culture.

The Neo-Dada spirit also broke out in Europe, where in 1958 Yves Klein greeted visitors at an empty gallery, in a show he called "The Void." Italian artist Piero Manzoni turned people into "works of art" by signing their bodies and clothing. Niki de Saint Phalle made paintings and collages and then symbolically killed them by piercing them

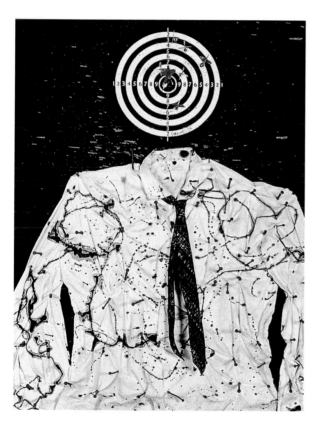

13.20   Niki de Saint Phalle.
St. Sebastian, or the Portrait of My Love. 1960. Oil, fabric, darts, and nails on wood and dartboard. 28½″ 3 21¾″ 3 2¾″.

with nails, darts, or even gunshots. In *St. Sebastian, or the Portrait of My Love*, we see one of her husband's shirts and neckties below a dartboard. The artist drove dozens of nails into the shirt, and then threw darts at the board. These works by Saint Phalle and others continue the irreverent aspects of the spirit of Dada. Saint Phalle's target carries a far more direct meaning than that of Jasper Johns in his *Target with Four Faces*.

EVENTS AND HAPPENINGS

Artists have continued to extend the boundaries of the visual arts until they can no longer simply be defined as stable aesthetic objects. Some artists in the late 1950s and early 1960s began to create living, moving art events.

For Swiss sculptor Jean Tinguely, life was play, movement, and perpetual change. Tinguely made machines that do just about everything except work in the manner we expect. Although much kinetic art has celebrated science and technology, Tinguely enjoyed a mocking yet sympathetic relationship to machines and machine fallibility. "I try to distill the frenzy I see in the world, the mechanical frenzy of our joyful, industrial confusion," he said.[1]

In 1960, Tinguely built a large piece of mechanized sculpture that he put together from materials gathered from junkyards and stores in and around New York City. The result was a giant assemblage designed to destroy itself at the turn of a switch—which it did in the courtyard of the Museum of Modern Art in New York City on March 17, 1960. The environmental sculpture was titled *Homage to New York: A Self-Constructing, Self-Destructing Work of Art*. Tinguely's *Homage to New York* was an event, similar in its effect to a **happening**.

Happenings are cooperative events in which viewers become active participants in partly planned, partly spontaneous performances that combine scripted scenarios with considerable improvisation. One critic defined happenings as drama with "structure but no plot, words but no dialogue, actors but no characters, and above all, nothing logical or continuous."[2]

13.21 Jean Tinguely. *Homage to New York: A Self-Constructing, Self-Destructing Work of Art.* 1960. Photograph: 2010 Artists Rights Society (ARS), New York/ ADAGP, Paris.

AT THE EDGE OF ART

Decoy Gang War Victim

TO ONLOOKERS IN a strife-torn portion of Los Angeles, it looked like dead body in the street, but in reality it was an artwork. The art collective Asco in 1975 laid one of their members down in the street and set out cautionary flares, titling the event *Decoy Gang War Victim*. The event took place in a strife-torn zone of East Los Angeles where gangs had indeed been in conflict. The collective photographed the event and presented it to the media as the last victim of a gang war. Not realizing that it was a hoax, television news channels broadcast the image as another example of gang violence. The work drew attention to an urban social problem as it pushed out the boundaries of art.

13.22 Asco (Willie Herrón III, Humberto Sandoval, Gronk, Patssi Valdez, Harry Gamboa Jr.). *Decoy Gang War Victim.* 1976. Photograph: © 1976 Harry Gamboa Jr.

13.23 Allan Kaprow.
Household.
Happening commissioned by Cornell University,
performed May 1964.
Photograph: Solomon A. Goldberg.
© Allan Kaprow Estate and Houser & Wirth

The term "happening" was first used by Allan
Kaprow in the late 1950s. There were no spectators
at Kaprow's happening, *Household*. At a preliminary meeting, participants were given parts. The
action took place at an isolated rural dump, amid
smoldering piles of refuse. The men built a wooden
tower on a trash pile while the women constructed
a nest on another mound. During the course of a
series of interrelated events, the men destroyed the

nest and the women retaliated by pulling
down the men's tower. In the process,
participants gained a new perspective on
the theater of life in our time.

POP ART

Pop artists use real objects or mass-pro-
duction techniques in their art. Like the
Dadaists before them, Pop artists wanted
to challenge cultural assumptions about
the definition of art; they also made ironic
comments on contemporary life.

Commercial art, long denigrated by
fine artists, became a source of inspiration. Pop painters used photographic
screenprinting and airbrush techniques
to achieve the surface characteristics of
such anonymous mass-produced imagery
as advertising, food labels, and comic
books. The resulting slick look and
ironic attitude separates Pop Art from
Assemblage.

Pop Art flowered most brilliantly in
the United States, but it first appeared
in London, where a group of young artists made collages with images cut from
popular magazines. In 1957, English artist Richard Hamilton published a list of
characteristics of Pop Art for the London
artists who were beginning to work in
this vein. The list includes qualities of
contemporary mass culture these artists addressed.
Hamilton wrote that Pop Art should be:

Popular (designed for a mass audience)
Transient (short-term solution)
Expendable (easily forgotten)
Low-cost
Mass-produced
Young (aimed at youth)
Witty
Sexy
Gimmicky
Glamorous
Big business[3]

Pop Art's media sources include the comic strip, the advertising layout, the famous-name-brand package, and the visual clichés of billboard, newspaper, movie theater, and television. Elements from all these mass media are included in Hamilton's collage *Just What Is It That Makes Today's Homes So Different, So Appealing?* Hamilton's work is a hilarious parody of the superficiality and materialism of modern popular culture. The word "pop" on the giant sucker gave the movement its name.

American artist James Rosenquist worked as a billboard painter after attending art school. Later, he incorporated his billboard experiences in a mature style that presents impersonally rendered montages of contemporary American popular culture. He drew on the techniques and imagery of sign painting, rendering outsized close-up details of faces, natural forms, and industrial objects with a mechanical airbrush.

Rosenquist's huge mural *F-111* filled all four walls of the Leo Castelli Gallery in New York City when it was first presented in 1965. The image of an F-111 fighter jet sweeps across his wall-to-wall environment of 1960s Americana. Rosenquist mixed symbols of affluence and destruction in his billboard-sized painting, which includes—in addition to a jet fighter plane—a chain-link fence, a child under a hair dryer, a tire, light bulbs, a beach umbrella, and a mushroom cloud from a nuclear bomb.

No American artist in the 1960s sparked more public indignation than Andy Warhol. He did not invent Pop Art, but he was its most visible and controversial exponent. Like Rosenquist, Warhol began his career as a commercial artist. Warhol's art shows us, in new ways, the effect of mass media and mass marketing on all of us.

13.24 Richard Hamilton.
Just What Is It That Makes Today's Homes So Different, So Appealing? 1956.
Collage. 10¼" 3 9¾".
The Bridgeman Art Library International © 2010 Artists Rights Society (ARS), New York/DACS, London.

13.25 James Rosenquist.
F-111. 1965.
Oil on canvas with aluminum, four parts. 10′ 3 86′.
Private collection. © James Rosenquist/Licensed by VAGA, New York.

Among his most common subjects were consumer products such as Coca-Cola and Campbell's soup. He blew up images of these products, silkscreened them onto canvas, and presented them as art. He made these works at a time when nationally standardized brands were just becoming the norm, as Americans began to prefer them to locally produced goods. If multiple rows of identical cans in a store make us happy, then why not make them into art?

Celebrities are consumer products, and Warhol's *Marilyn Diptych* is his meditation on celebrity status. The work gives us the actress's face fifty times over, in smudged black-and-white and garish color. The work seems to be telling us that a

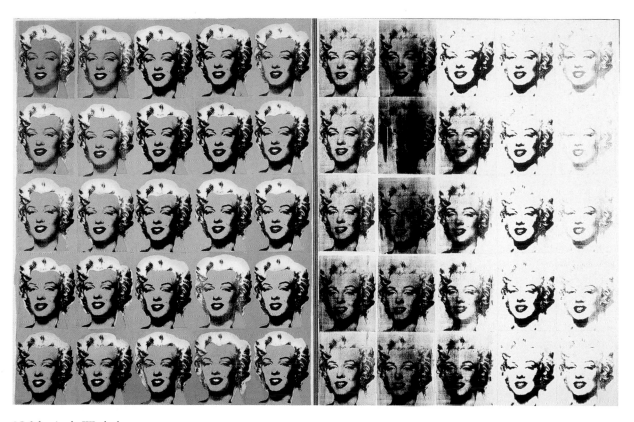

13.26 Andy Warhol.
Marilyn Diptych. 1962.
Synthetic polymer paint and silkscreen ink on canvas, 6′10″ 3 57″ (205.4 3 144.8 cm).
© Tate Gallery, London. Art Resource, NY. © 2010 Andy Warhol Foundation for the Visual Arts. Artists Rights Society (ARS),
New York.™ 2002 Marilyn Monroe LLC under license authorized by CMG Worldwide Inc., Indianapolis, IN 46256. www.MarilynMonroe.com.

Andy Warhol: The Pope of Pop

PROBABLY NO ARTIST of the twentieth century foreshadowed today's culture more than Andy Warhol (1928–1987). His treatment of themes such as celebrities, consumerism, and the mass media of the 1960s has become part of most people's standard way of thinking today.

His work functioned in the same way that his *Self-Portrait* does. His cool and detached face stares blankly back at us, just as his art reflects in a straightforward fashion our culture of celebrities, consumer products, and the media. Taking these phenomena wholesale into the art gallery raises our awareness of how they function.

He should be as famous for his philosophical pronouncements as for his art. Here are a few examples: "In the future everyone will be world famous for fifteen minutes." "When you see a gruesome picture over and over again, it doesn't really have any effect." "Being good in business is the most fascinating kind of art." "Department stores are kind of like museums." "I don't know where the artificial stops and the real starts." "Hollywood films are just planned-out commercials."

His early life gave little hint of his later importance: Born in Pittsburgh to a family of Ukrainian immigrants, he studied commercial art at the Carnegie Institute. Upon graduation in 1949, he moved to New York City, where he began to rise in the ranks of designers, making advertising layouts. His first paintings in 1960 served as backdrop for a department store display.

Following the lead of early Pop artists such as Richard Hamilton and Robert Rauschenberg, Warhol began to borrow the media's popular imagery and mass production for his own art. Most art critics in the early sixties panned his work, deeming it insincere, lacking in craftsmanship, and boring. But Warhol's defenders replied that he is only showing us our culture, where most of our public life is staged to look good in the media, craftsmanship vanished with the dawn of mass production, and boredom is common even in households with 250 TV channels. If contemporary culture is obsessed with celebrities and spectacles, Warhol foreshadowed this in works that isolate those phenomena in a memorable way.

He gave up painting in 1962 because it was, he said, too much work; instead, he favored silkscreen, which yields hundreds of identical copies. His assistants made these works in a studio that he ironically called The Factory; it became a gathering place for the glamorous and the avant-garde.

Warhol was active in many realms besides the visual arts: He made several notorious movies on the theme of boredom. His first film in 1963 was *Sleep*, a six-hour film of a man sleeping. He promoted rock concerts featuring The Velvet Underground, a band that influenced many later groups. He also started the magazine *Interview*, which still functions today.

He reduced his activities somewhat after a disaffected member of The

13.27 Andy Warhol.
Self-Portrait. 1966.
Silkscreen on silver coated paper. 23⅟₁₆″ 3 23″.
The Art Archive/Musee d'Art et d'Industrie Saint-Etienne/Gianni Dagli Orti. © 2010 Andy Warhol Foundation for the Visual Arts/Artists Rights Society (ARS), New York.

Factory crew shot him in 1968. This was Valerie Solanas, the subject of the documentary film *I Shot Andy Warhol*.

In the seventies, Warhol devoted himself mostly to making portraits of the rich and famous, who lined up to sit for him. The portraits were not based on the sitter's individual personality but rather on how they appeared in the media. Warhol apparently doubted that an individual's deeper soul even existed. Here is how he described himself: "If you want to know all about Andy Warhol, just look at the surface of my paintings and films and there I am. There's nothing behind it." His influence outlasted modern art, as we shall see in Chapter 14.

13.28 Andy Warhol.
Little Race Riot. 1964.
Synthetic polymer paint and silkscreen
on canvas. 30" 3 33".
© 2010 The Andy Warhol Foundation for the Visual Arts/
ARS, NY. Photograph: The Andy Warhol Foundation, Inc./
Art Resource, NY.

celebrity is a packaged commodity. This was news in the 1960s; today most people seem to realize it. Warhol's work called attention to the pervasive and insistent character of our commercial environment. The repetition of mass imagery has become our cultural landscape and our mythology.

For his treatment of mass media, Warhol borrowed headline-generating images from news photographs and re-created them, singly or in identical rows. *Little Race Riot* (see also Fig. 1.22 on page 20) shows police dogs attacking non-violent civil rights protesters in the South. His works take no position on the event pictured; rather, they repackage for us their sensational aspect. He discovered that repeated exposure to events in the media desensitizes us to them, and his works re-enact the boredom. Indeed, boredom was one of his major themes, because it seems to characterize so much of modern life.

In *Drowning Girl* and other paintings, Roy Lichtenstein used comic book images with their bright primary colors, impersonal surfaces, and characteristic printing dots. His work is a commentary on a world obsessed with consumer goods and spectacles.

13.29 Roy Lichtenstein.
Drowning Girl. 1963.
Oil and synthetic polymer paint on canvas.
67⅜" 3 66¾" (171.6 3 169.5 cm).
The Museum of Modern Art, New York. Licensed by Scala-Art
Resource, New York. Philip Johnson Fund and gift of Mr. and Mrs.
Bagley Wright. Photograph: © 2002 The Museum of Modern Art,
New York.

13.30 Claes Oldenburg.
Two Cheeseburgers with Everything (Dual Hamburgers). 1962.
Burlap soaked in plaster, painted with enamel.
7" 3 14¾" 3 8⅝" (17.8 3 37.5 3 21.8 cm).

He saw Pop Art as "involvement with what I think to be the most brazen and threatening characteristics of our culture, things we hate, but which are also powerful in their impingement on us."[4]

For several decades, Claes Oldenburg has been finding inspiration in the common, mass-produced artifacts of American society. His lumpy and gross *Two Cheeseburgers with Everything* (also known as *Dual Hamburgers*) needs no explanation. There it is! Oldenburg enjoys taking mundane objects and remaking them into icons; see another project on page 109. Oldenburg embraced and transformed the most mundane commercial items. He said:

I am for Kool-Art, 7-UP art, Pepsi-art, Sunshine art, 39 cents art . . . Menthol art . . . Rx art . . . Now art . . . I am for U.S. Government Inspected Art, Grade A art, Regular Price art, Yellow Ripe art, Extra Fancy art, Ready-to-eat art.[5]

MINIMAL ART

In the late 1950s and early 1960s, a number of artists aimed to create art that would exclude subject matter, symbolic meanings, personal content, and hidden messages of any kind. Was it possible to have art that referred to nothing outside itself, told no story except for its own shapes and colors? The artists who went on this quest were called **Minimalists**.

13.31 Donald Judd.
Untitled. 1967.
Stainless steel and plexiglass, ten units.
9⅛" 3 40" 3 31".

Among the leaders of this movement was Donald Judd. He worked with industrial materials such as sheet metal, aluminum, and molded plastics, which had not previously been used for art; his *Untitled* combines stainless steel and plexiglass. Judd was the major spokesman for the Minimalist

13.32 Ellsworth Kelly.
Blue, Green, Yellow, Orange, Red. 1966.
Oil on canvas, 5 panels. Overall: 60″ 3 240″ (152.4 3 609.6 cm).
Solomon R. Guggenheim Museum, New York. Photograph by Ellen Labenski. © The Solomon R. Guggenheim Foundation, New York. (FN 67.1833).

movement. In his essay "Specific Objects," he wrote about the aims of his art:

It isn't necessary for a work to have a lot of things to look at, to compare, to analyze one by one, to contemplate. The thing as a whole, its quality as a whole, is what is interesting. . . . In the new work the shape, image, color, and surface are single, and not partial and scattered.[6]

Judd never titled his works, because he did not want viewers to infer any meaning beyond the colors and shapes that he used. His 1967 *Untitled* work tells no story, has no personal expression, no symbolic content; he wants it to be seen as only color and form.

Some painters shared an interest in what they saw as the essence of painting: a flat surface covered with colors. Quick-drying acrylic paints, which were developed at this time, lend themselves to uniform application and to the use of tape to obtain shapes with precise edges. Brushstrokes were suppressed, because they told a story of the work's creation. Minimalist painters urged viewers to see their paintings as objects, not as pictures.

Ellsworth Kelly's bold paintings are richly hued studies in color and form. *Blue, Green, Yellow, Orange, Red* is self-explanatory in at least a superficial sense. At a deeper level, Minimalism is a quest to see if art can still be art without representation, storytelling, or personal feeling. If the work had curved lines, modeled color, or paint strokes, it would not be as pure. Rather, the subject seems to be color itself: how we respond to it, and how different colors interact with each other in our field of view. It is an optical experiment that throws away a great many of the traditional rules. Such quests for the essence of art motivated many in those years.

Frank Stella's paintings of the 1960s emphasize the flatness of the picture plane and its boundaries. He used shaped canvases because a rectangular work might still be seen as a picture. In *Agbatana III*, Stella used a distinctive outer profile to further extend the concept of the surface as an object in its own right rather than as a field for pictorial allusions. External boundaries of the overall shape are arrived at from the

13.33 Frank Stella.
Agbatana III. 1968.
Fluorescent acrylic on canvas. 120″ 3 180″
(305 3 457 mm).
© Allen Memorial Art Museum, Oberlin College, OH. Ruth C. Roush Fund for Contemporary Art and National Foundation for the Arts and Humanities Grant, 1968. © 2010 Frank Stella. Artists Rights Society (ARS), New York.

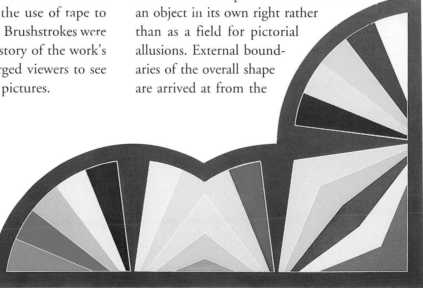

internal shapes. There is no figure–ground relationship; within the painting, everything is figure. Interwoven bands of both muted and intense colors pull together in a tight spatial weave. He summarized the minimal movement with this statement: "What you see is what you see."

CONCEPTUAL ART

During the 1960s and 1970s, artists reacted ever more quickly to each successive aesthetic movement. Pushing back the limits, the next step after Minimalism became art about only an idea. **Conceptual art**, in which an idea takes the place of the art object, was an outgrowth of Minimalism. The Conceptual movement was heavily indebted to Marcel Duchamp, the first champion of an art of ideas.

Joseph Kosuth, the most rigorous early Conceptualist, was perplexed by the materialism of the art market and Pop Art's embrace of commercialism. In 1965, he produced *One and Three*

Chairs, which consisted of a wooden chair, a photograph of the same chair, and a photographic enlargement of a dictionary definition of the word "chair." The work is about how we apprehend things, images, and words; it shows that we process each version of the chair differently.

Conceptual art is based on the fact that a work of art usually begins as an idea in the artist's mind. A great work of art is a great idea first, and its creator merely carries out the idea. If this is true, then art can still be art without a unique, artist-made object. If we "get the idea," then we have understood the piece. Creativity is, after all, a mental process.

Rather than making things, Conceptual artists present us with enough information so that we grasp the concept they have in mind. Another early leader in the movement was Yoko Ono, whose pieces are generally instructions to viewers. One example: Take 15 minutes to pronounce the word *south*. The best way to illustrate this work is to try it yourself and see what happens.

SITE WORKS AND EARTHWORKS

Minimal and Conceptual works are radical, but they are still seen in art galleries. Several artists in the late 1960s and 1970s began creating works that are inseparable from the sites for which they were designed. In site-specific works, the artist's response to the location determines the composition, scale, medium, and even the content of each piece. See page 55 for a site-specific work by Richard Serra.

Bulgarian artist Christo, a leader in the site-specific movement, first made his living as a portrait painter. Later, his work was exhibited with the "New Realists" in Paris who were presenting common objects as art, rather than making painted or sculpted representations of objects. He often used fabric in his early works at this time, and in 1961, he and Jeanne-Claude began creating temporary works of art, often using fabric as well. They began wrapping objects ranging in size from a motorcycle to a mile of Australian sea cliffs.

One of Christo and Jeanne-Claude's most ambitious projects was *Running Fence*, a temporary environmental artwork that was as much a process and an event as it was sculpture. The

13.34 Joseph Kosuth.
One and Three Chairs. 1965.
Wooden folding chair, photographic copy of a chair, and photographic enlargement of dictionary definition of a chair. Chair, 32⅜″ 3 14⅞″ 3 20⅞″. Photo panel, 36″ 3 24⅛″ (91.5 3 61.1 cm). Text panel, 24″ 3 24⅛″ (61 3 61.3 cm).

eighteen-foot-high white nylon fence ran from the ocean at Bodega Bay in Sonoma County, California, through 24.5 miles of agricultural and dairy land. *Running Fence* stood for two weeks and ultimately involved thousands of people. The project required eighteen public hearings, the agreement of landowners, and the help of hundreds of workers. They paid the workers and raised the funds for this project by selling early works, preparatory drawings and collages.

The seemingly endless ribbon of white cloth made the wind visible and caught the changing light as it stretched across the gently rolling hills, appearing and disappearing on the horizon. The simplicity of *Running Fence* relates it to Minimalist art, but the fence itself was not presented as an art object. Rather, it was the focal point for a work that involved people, process, object, and place.

Walter De Maria's *The Lightning Field* consists of four hundred stainless-steel poles arranged in a rectangular grid over an area measuring one mile

13.35 Christo and Jeanne-Claude.
Running Fence. Sonoma and Marin Counties, California, 1972–1976. Nylon fabric and steel poles. 18 feet 3 24½ miles (5.48 m 3 39.4 km).
Courtesy of Wolfgang Volz/Laif/Redux.

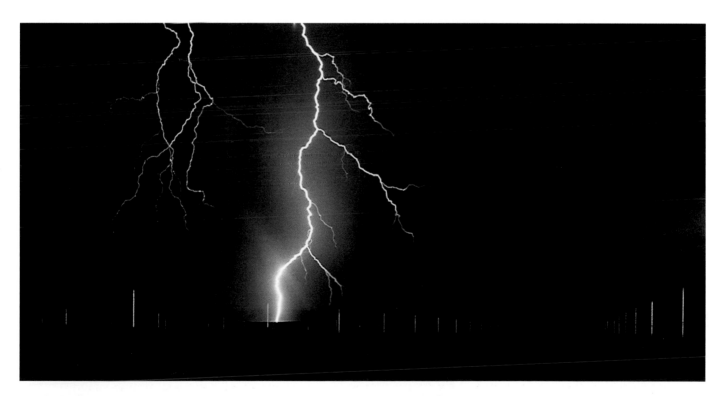

13.36 Walter De Maria.
The Lightning Field. 1977.
Quemado, New Mexico. 400 stainless-steel poles, average height 20′7″; land area 1 mile 3 1 kilometer.
Photograph: John Cliett. © Dia Art Foundation, New York.

by one kilometer (0.6 mile) in west-central New Mexico. The sharpened tips of the poles form a level plane, a kind of monumental bed of nails. Each of the poles can act as a lightning conductor during the electrical storms that occur frequently over the desert. Early and late in the day, the poles reflect the sun, creating accents of technological precision in sharp contrast to the otherwise natural landscape. Purposely isolated from the art-viewing public, *The Lightning Field* combines aspects of both Conceptual and Minimalist art. Viewers must arrange their visits through the Dia Foundation, which commissioned the piece. Once there, they are left to study the work and make their own interpretations.

Site works are environmental constructions, frequently made of sculptural materials, designed to interact with, but not permanently alter, the environment. **Earthworks** are sculptural forms made of materials such as earth, rocks, and sometimes plants. They are often very large, and they may be executed in remote locations. Earthworks are usually designed to merge with or complement the landscape. Many site works and earthworks show their creators' interest in ecology and in the earthworks of ancient America.

Robert Smithson was one of the founders of the earthworks movement. His *Spiral Jetty*, com-pleted at Great Salt Lake, Utah, has since gone in and out of view several times with changes in the water level. Its natural surroundings emphasize its form as willful human design. Although our society has little agreed-upon symbolism or iconography, we instinctively respond to universal signs like the spiral, which are found in nature and in ancient art.

Although site-specific works can be commissioned, they are almost never resold unless someone buys the land they occupy. Artists who create Conceptual art, earthworks, site works, and performance art share a common desire to subvert the gallery-museum-collector syndrome, to present art as an experience rather than as a commodity.

INSTALLATIONS AND ENVIRONMENTS

While some artists were creating outdoor earthworks and site works, others were moving beyond the traditional concepts of indoor painting and sculpture. Since the mid-1960s, artists from diverse backgrounds and points of view have fabricated interior installations and environments rather than portable works of art. Some installations alter the entire spaces they occupy; others are experienced as

13.37 Robert Smithson.
Spiral Jetty. 1970.
Great Salt Lake, Utah. Earthwork.
Length 1500′, width 15′.
© Gianfranco Gorgoni Art. © Estate of Robert Smithson. Licensed by VAGA, New York.

large sculpture; most of them assume the viewer to be a part of the piece.

James Turrell's installations challenge assumptions about the truth of what we see. By manipulating light and space, Turrell creates environments that intensify viewers' perceptions. His work goes beyond the lean physical structures of Minimalism, and beyond Conceptualism's reliance on words and ideas, to dwell on the mysterious and at times awe-inspiring interaction of light, space, and time. Light becomes a tangible physical presence in works such as *Amba*, where viewers are coaxed into paying attention to their own perceptions.

What really interests me is having the viewer make discoveries the same way the artist does . . . instead of having the viewer participate vicariously, through someone else. . . . You determine the reality of what you see. The work is the product of my vision, but it's about your seeing. The poles of the realm in which I operate are the physical limitations of human vision and the learned limits of perception, or what I call "prejudiced perception." Encountering these prejudices can be an amazing experience, and if someone can come to these discoveries directly, the way the artist does, the impact is greater and so is the joy.[7]

Turrell has also created what he calls "sky-spaces," windowless rooms with a portion of the ceiling removed to expose the sky. He encourages viewers to visit them near sunset, when the daylight is changing to evening.

As San Francisco's de Young Museum was moving into its new building in 2005, the directors engaged British artist Andy Goldsworthy to create an installation at the entrance. For his creation *Drawn Stone*, the artist broke off huge blocks of paving stones to make benches. He then pierced

13.38 Andy Goldsworthy.
Drawn Stone. 2005.
Appletone Greenmoor sandstone. Site-specific stone installation at the de Young Museum, San Francisco.
Fine Arts Museums of San Francisco, museum purchase. Gift of Lonna and Marshall Wais, 2004–2005. De Young Museum, San Francisco.

the courtyard with a long, thin crack that meanders crazily from the sidewalk to the front door, passing through some of the benches. This crack is a subtle reference to the earthquake that ruined the museum's previous building. Goldsworthy said:

Holes and cracks have always been for me a way of reaching below the surface of a material—a way of entering a stone, and a release of the energy contained within. These ideas inevitably take on greater significance and meaning in California.[8]

EARLY FEMINISM

In the late 1960s, many women artists began to speak out against the discrimination they faced in their careers. It was rare for women to be taken seriously in artists' groups; galleries were more willing to exhibit the work of men than of women; and museums collected the work of men far more often than that of women. Moreover, it seemed to the early **feminists** that making art about their experience as women might doom them to obscurity in a male-dominated art world. In the early 1970s

in New York and California, they began to take action.

Lucy Lippard, an art critic and feminist, wrote, "The overwhelming fact remains that a woman's experience in this society—social and biological—is simply not like that of a man. If art comes from the inside, as it must, then the art of men and women must be different, too."[9] The work of some women artists definitely is influenced by their gender and their interest in feminist issues.

California feminists tended to work collaboratively, and to make use of media that have been traditionally associated with "craft work" and with women: ceramics and textiles. *The Dinner Party* was a collaboration of many women (and a few men), organized and directed by Judy Chicago over a period of five years. This cooperative venture was in itself a political statement about the supportive nature of female experience, as opposed to the frequently competitive nature of the male.

A large triangular table contains place settings for thirty-nine women who made important contribu-

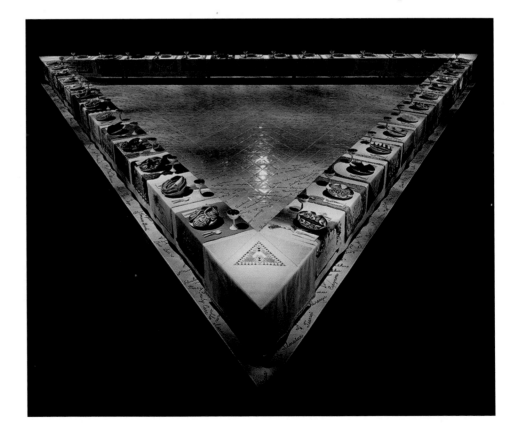

13.39 Judy Chicago.
The Dinner Party. 1979.
Mixed media. 48′ 3 42′ 3 3′.
Triangular table on white tile floor.
Collection of the Brooklyn Museum of Art, Gift of the Elizabeth A. Sackler Foundation. Photograph: Donald Woodman. © 2010 (photo) Donald Woodman/Artists Rights Society (ARS), New York.

tions to world history. These run a wide gamut, from Egyptian Queen Hatshepsut to Georgia O'Keeffe. The names of 999 additional women of achievement are inscribed on ceramic tiles below the table. Each place setting includes a hand-embroidered fabric runner and a porcelain plate designed in honor of that woman. Some of the plates are painted with flat designs; others have modeled and painted relief motifs; many are explicitly sexual, embellished with flower-like female genitalia.

East Coast feminists were more pointed in their protests. Some of them formed the group Women Artists in Revolution (WAR), which picketed museums. In response to private dealers who were reluctant to show work by women, they formed their own collaborative gallery, Artists in Residence (AIR). Nancy Spero, a leader in East Coast feminist circles, participated in both groups. Her work from the late 1960s and early 1970s used uncommon media such as paper scrolls, stencils, and printing to document subjects such as the torture and abuse of women. Her later scrolls, such as *Rebirth of Venus*, attempt to present images of women different from those commonly seen in art. In the segment illustrated here, an ancient statue of the love goddess Venus is split open to reveal a woman sprinter who runs directly toward the viewer. The contrast between the two images is difficult to miss. Woman as love object gives way to woman as achiever. (Compare this work to Botticelli's Renaissance *Birth of Venus* on page 163.)

One of the most radical feminists in Europe was Orlan, who, like Judy Chicago, rejected her birth name. Her persistent theme has been the woman's body as the site of cultural debate and struggle. In 1974, she donned a nun's costume based on Bernini's *Ecstasy of St. Teresa* (see page 184) and performed a strip-tease that she documented in a series of photographs. Thus, she passed between the two poles of identity (virgin and whore) that she saw the culture allotting to women.

Her most controversial work came in 1977 when she crashed a contemporary art exhibition in Paris with *Le Baiser de l'Artiste* ("The Artist's Kiss") She was not invited to this show, but rather she set up her exhibit at the staircase leading to it. On a large black pedestal, viewers approached either

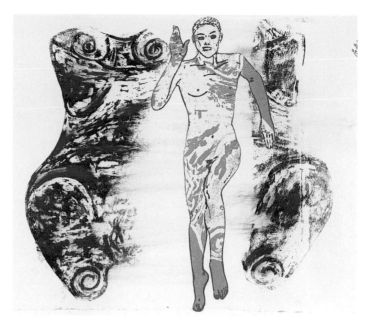

13.40   Nancy Spero.
Rebirth of Venus. Detail. 1984.
Handprinting on paper. 12″ 3 62′.
© The Estate of Nancy Spero/Licensed by VAGA,
New York, NY. Courtesy Galerie Lelong, New York.

13.41   Orlan.
Le Baiser de l'Artiste ("The Artist's Kiss"). 1976–1977.
Mixed media with paint, metal chain, photographs, wood,
blinking diode, artificial candles, artificial flowers, and CD.
86½″ 3 67″ 3 23½″.
In the collection of the Fonds Regional d'art Contemporain, Pays de la Loire, France.
© ORLAN. © 2010 Artists Rights Society (ARS), New York/ADAGP, Paris.

13.42 Joseph Beuys.
I Like America and America Likes Me. 1974.
Performance at Rene Block Gallery.
Courtesy of Ronald Feldman Fine Arts, New York. Photograph: © Caroline Tisdall. © 2010 Artists Rights Society (ARS), New York/VG Bild-Kunst, Bonn.

Orlan the Saint (a photo from the earlier strip-tease act) or Orlan the Body (the artist herself sitting behind an invented vending machine). A sound-track invited viewers to either bring a candle to the virgin, or insert a coin in the slot below the artist's chin. As the coin ran down to its receptacle, the artist dispensed kisses. This rather scandalous performance forcefully raised the issue of woman as virginal ideal or as marketable commodity; it also cost the artist her teaching position.

Researchers and art historians continue to uncover and publicize work by women throughout history, and each edition of this book has benefited from the effort by including more of them. Because feminism has influenced most contemporary art movements since the 1970s, it makes little sense to separate feminist artists in discussions of the styles of the last quarter-century.

PERFORMANCE ART

In **performance art**, artists do not create anything durable. Rather, they perform actions before an audience or in nature. Thus, this art form contains both visual art and drama, and has historical antecedents in Dada performances of the early twentieth century as well as in Expressionist painting. An Abstract Expressionist painting is the frozen record of an event (the act of making a painting). The next step was logical: Eliminate the record and concentrate on the event itself. The record was in the remembered experience of the participants and in a few photographs. The happenings movement is another important antecedent. Forms of art such as Conceptual art, which emphasize idea and process, are related to performance art.

One of the most influential performance artists of the 1960s and 1970s was German-born Joseph Beuys. He carried out actions that resonated with deep symbolic significance, as if he were a healer or shaman. For one 1965 piece, he swathed his head in honey and gold leaf, and carried a dead rabbit around an art gallery explaining to it the paintings on view, touching the rabbit's lifeless paw to each. Some people, he later said, were as insensitive in their daily lives as the rabbit was in the art gallery. Arriving in New York for the first time in 1974, he immediately plunged into a work called *I Like America and America Likes Me.* Met at the airport by an ambulance, he was wrapped in felt and taken to a gallery, where he lived for a week with a coyote. The animal symbolized the Wild West; copies of the *Wall Street Journal* were delivered daily to represent contemporary, business-oriented culture. He meant to heal the breach between the two.

Cuban émigré Ana Mendieta used her own body in several works as a symbol of the Earth and natural cycles. In the *Tree of Life Series*, she coated her body with mud and grasses and stood against ancient tree trunks. She intended in these pieces to show the essential equivalence between femaleness and natural processes such as birth and growth. For her, as for many early feminists, biology accounted for most of the differences between women and men. Through the natural cycles of their bodies, she seems to be saying, women are closer to the rhythms of the Earth.

Art viewers who wanted to "confess their intercultural fears and desires" got an opportunity to do so with the 1994 performance work *The Temple of Confessions*. The artists took on alternate identities as "living saints from an unknown border religion," as their press release put it. Here we see Guillermo Gómez-Peña sitting alternately on a wheelchair or a toilet, pretending to drink tequila as he embodies the public's fears about Mexican-Americans. About a third of the viewers actually confessed to one or the other of the "saints" on kneelers provided for the purpose. As artists have pushed out the boundaries of art, their work has at times drawn controversy, and even efforts at suppression or censorship (see page 58).

13.43 Guillermo Gómez-Peña and Roberto Sifuentes. *The Temple of Confessions*. 1994.
Site-specific performance, Detroit Institute of the Arts.
Photograph: Dirk Bakker.

Notes

1. Edward Lucie-Smith, *Sculpture Since 1945* (London: Phaidon, 1987), 77.
2. Calvin Tomkins, *The World of Marcel Duchamp* (New York: Time-Life Books, 1966), 162.
3. Richard Hamilton, *Catalogue of an Exhibition at the Tate Gallery,* March 12–April 19, 1970 (London: Tate Gallery, 1970), 31.
4. R. G. Swenson, "What Is Pop Art?" *Art News* (November 1963): 25.
5. Claes Oldenburg, "I am for an art . . ." from *Store Days,* Documents from the Store (1961) and Ray Gun Theater (1962), selected by Claes Oldenburg and Emmett Williams (New York: Something Else Press, 1967).
6. Donald Judd, "Specific Objects," *Arts Yearbook* 8 (1965): 78.
7. Patricia Failing, "James Turrell's New Light on the Universe," *Art News* (April 1985): 71.
8. Andy Goldsworthy, "Artist's Statement," http://www.thinker.org/deyoung/about/subpage.asp?subpagekey=847 (accessed July 20, 2007).
9. Lucy R. Lippard, *From the Center: Feminist Essays on Women's Art* (New York: Dutton, 1976), 48.

Chuck Close's *Stanley*

CHUCK CLOSE'S 1981 oil painting *Stanley* (**Fig. 13.45**) might best be described as "layered" pointillism (see Fig. 10.27). Like all of his paintings, the piece is based on a photograph. Close's working method is to overlay the original photograph with a grid. Then he draws a grid with the same number of squares on a canvas. Close is not so much interested in representing the person whose portrait he is painting as he is in reproducing, as accurately as possible, the completely abstract design that occurs in each square of the photo's grid. In essence, Close's large paintings—*Stanley* is nearly 8 feet high and 6 feet wide—are made up of thousands of little square paintings, as the detail (**Fig. 13.44**) makes clear. Each of these "micro-paintings" is composed as a small target, an arrangement of two, three, or four concentric circles. Viewed up close, it is hard to see anything but the design of each square of the grid. But as the viewer moves farther away, the design of the individual squares of the composition dissolves, and the sitter's features emerge with greater and greater clarity.

In an interview conducted by art critic Lisa Lyons for an essay that appears in the book *Chuck Close*, published by Rizzoli International in 1987, Close describes his working method in Stanley at some length, comparing his technique to, of all things, the game of golf:

Golf is the only sport in which you move from the general to the specific. In the beginning when you take your first shot, you can't even see the pin. And in a matter of three or four strokes, you're supposed to be in the cup, a very small, specific place a very long ways away. I thought of the gridded canvas as a golf course, and each square of the grid as

13.44 Chuck Close.
Stanley (large version), 1980–81, detail.
Oil on canvas, 108 3 84 in. The Solomon R. Guggenheim Museum, New York.
Purchased with funds contributed by Mr. and Mrs. Barrie M. Damson, 1981, 81.2839.
Photo: David Heald. © The Solomon R. Guggenheim Foundation, New York (FN 2839).

Works in Progress: Chuck Close's *Stanley* was taken from *A World of Art*, Sixth Edition by Henry M. Sayre.

a par-four hole. Then just to complicate things and make the game more interesting, I teed off in the opposite direction of the pin. For example, I knew that the color of the skin was going to be in the orange family, so I started out by putting down a thin wash of blue, green, or purple—something very different from what the final color would be. The second color then had to go miles to alter the first one. So for this big correcting stroke, I chose a hue that moved me into the generic color family I should have been aiming for. Now I had moved into orange, but it was too yellow, so in the middle of that stroke, I put down a gob of red to move into a reddish orange. Then I was at the equivalent of being "on the green" and hopefully quite close to the cup. But the color was still much too bright. So the final stroke was a little dot of blue, the complementary color, which optically mixed with the orange and lowered its intensity, dropping it down to an orangish brown. I was in the cup.

[It was possible] to have a birdie—to come in a stroke early. It was even possible to have an eagle—to come in two [strokes] under par. Of course, it was also equally possible to have a bogie or a double bogie [one or two strokes over par], and even get mired in some aesthetic sandtrap, just making strokes and getting nowhere at all.

Close's "game" with color is exacting and demanding, requiring a knowledge of the optical effects of color mixing that is virtually unparalleled in the history of art. He is able to achieve, in his work, two seemingly contradictory goals at once. On the one hand, his work is fully representational. On the other, it is fully abstract, even nonobjective in its purely formal interest in color. Close has it both ways.

13.45 Chuck Close.
Stanley (large version), 1980–81.
Oil on canvas, 104 3 84 in. The Solomon R. Guggenheim Museum, New York.
Purchased with funds contributed by Mr. and Mrs. Barrie
M. Damson, 1981, 81.2839.
Photo: David Heald. © The Solomon R. Guggenheim Foundation, New York (FN 2839).

POSTMODERNITY AND GLOBAL ART

14

In the late 1970s or early 1980s, the impulses and drives that caused modern art seemed spent. Modern art was based on rejecting tradition and breaking rules. Each new movement found some rule to break: regular perspective, recognizable subject matter, location in a gallery, and creation by hand are only a few of the rules that modern artists cast aside.

The urge to rebel against the norm lost its impact when such rebellion *became* the norm in most Western cultures. We now look intently forward: to the next medical advance, to the next presidential term, or to the next electronic innovation; not backward to the wisdom of our elders, ancient rituals, or eternal principles. Departing from the norm is widely seen as healthy. In fact, this was the slogan of a chain of fast food restaurants in the early 1990s: "Sometimes you just gotta break the rules."

Artists today are left with few rules to break. While it is still possible to create art that offends people, it is difficult to make a new style such as Cubism, Expressionism, Constructivism, or Minimalism. Most artists today are not striving for this.

In general, most artists of the present generation do not appear intent on perfecting form, creating beauty, or fine-tuning their sense of sight. They mostly want to comment on life in all of its aspects. They want to create work that illuminates the relationships between what we see and how we think. Rather than objects of timeless beauty or shocking novelty, most artists since the 1980s create objects laden with information about the period in which we live. This chapter will present some movements of the present generation; many of the artists discussed in this chapter could be placed in more than one category, but most would prefer not to be categorized at all.

POSTMODERN ARCHITECTURE

Modern architecture rejected tradition, ornament, and references to the past, and embraced modern materials and a utilitarian look. The modern movement culminated in the International Style, a glass box look that swept most Western cities in the years after World War II. However, a growing discontent with the sterile anonymity of the International Style (see the *Lever House* on page 281) led many architects to look once again at meaning, history, and context. Their departure from architectural modernism was dubbed **postmodern** in the late 1970s.

Postmodernists thought that the unadorned functional purity of the International Style made all buildings look the same, offering no identity relative to purpose, no symbolism, no sense of local meaning, no excitement. Postmodern architects celebrate the very qualities of modern life that modern architects rejected: complexity, ambiguity, contradiction, nostalgia, romance, and popular taste.

Chapter 14: Postmodernity and Global Art was taken from *Prebles' Artforms: An Introduction to the Visual Arts,* Tenth Edition by Patrick Frank.

Among the first architects to rebel against the International Style were Robert Venturi and his partner Denise Scott-Brown, and they did it by writing a book in 1976: *Learning from Las Vegas*. They urged architects to study what is local, vernacular, and even tacky. They realized that even if Las Vegas was tasteless, people loved it, and architects who refuse to recognize that fact turn the public off. The book brought the entire profession to attention.

The postmodern architecture of Michael Graves uses classical architecture in knowing and even humorous ways. His *Public Services Building* is both formal and playful. The exterior is dominated by a pair of fluted classical columns. They are brown, a color that the Greeks would never have used. They also share a single huge capital. These off-color vertical elements have no structural function, and Graves showed this by setting them in a reflecting pool of mirrored glass. The remainder of the façade consists of anonymous rows of square openings, an ironic reference to the bureaucrats inside.

If postmodernism freed architects from the rigid ideas of modernism, three-dimensional computer modeling made new shapes possible. Frank Gehry has mastered these techniques more than most architects, as his *Guggenheim Museum Bilbao* shows (see facing page).

The most creative architects today neither rebel against modernism nor quote tradition whimsically like postmodernists. Rather, they try to make visually stunning buildings that fulfill their functions with ease. Californian Thom Mayne is a leader in this new trend in combining aesthetics and utility. His *Campus Recreation Center* at the University of Cincinnati answers a list of tasks: A full gymnasium, classrooms, a food court, and student housing occupy an irregularly shaped building that responds to the surrounding topography and channels foot traffic over the shortest paths to and from surrounding buildings. "I wanted to make a village," he said of this building, and it fits seamlessly into the fabric of existing structures with an attractive, high-tech look. His firm is called Morphosis, an invented word that roughly means

14.1   Michael Graves.
Public Services Building.
Portland, Oregon. 1980–1982.
Courtesy of G. E. Kidder Smith/Corbis.

14.2   Thom Mayne and Morphosis.
Campus Recreation Center.
University of Cincinnati. 2006.
Photograph: Roland Halbe.

Frank Gehry's Guggenheim Museum Bilbao

"I start drawing sometimes," architect Frank Gehry has said, "not knowing exactly where I am going. I use familiar strokes that evolve into the building. Sometimes it seems directionless, not going anywhere for sure. It's like feeling your way along in the dark, anticipating that something will come out usually. I become voyeur of my own thoughts as they develop, and wander about them. Sometimes I say 'boy, here it is, here it is, it's coming. ' I understand it. I get all excited."

Gehry's early drawings of the north, riverfront facade for the Guggenheim Museum in Bilbao, Spain (**Fig. 14.3**), executed only three months after he had won the competition to design the building in 1991, reveal his process of searching for the form his buildings eventually take. These semiautomatic "doodles" are explorations that are surprisingly close to Gehry's finished building (**Fig. 14.5**). They capture the fluidity of its lines, the flowing movement of the building along the riverfront space.

Gehry moves quickly from such sketches to actual scale models. The models, for Gehry, are like sculpture: "You forget about it as architecture, because you're focused on this sculpting process." The models, finally, are transformed into actual buildings by means of Catia, a computer program originally developed for the French aerospace industry (**Fig. 14.4**). This program demonstrated to builders, contractors—and the client—that Gehry's plan was not only buildable, but affordably so.

14.3   Frank Gehry.
Guggenheim Museum Bilbao, north elevations, October 1991.
Sketch by Frank Gehry, 1991.
© Frank O. Gehry & Associates.

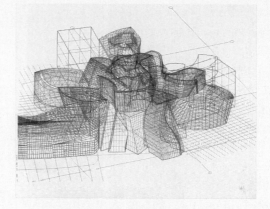

14.4   Frank Gehry.
Guggenheim Museum Bilbao.
© Gehry Partners, LLP.

14.5   Frank Gehry.
Guggenheim Museum Bilbao, 1997.
© The Solomon R. Guggenheim Foundation, New York.
Photo: David Heald.

Works in Progress: Frank Gehry's Guggenheim Museum Bilbao was taken from *A World of Art*, Sixth Edition by Patrick Frank.

14.6 Teddy Cruz.
Manufactured Sites.
Project Schematic. 2008.
ETC Estudio Teddy Cruz.

"taking shape," and his buildings take shape in highly creative ways.

Among the most influential younger architects today is Teddy Cruz, who takes inspiration not from gaudy Las Vegas but from improvisational Tijuana. Just south of the border, builders use cast-off materials, and homeowners scavenge dumpyards in search of walls, fences, structures, and roofs. Cruz's buildings, which he calls *Manufactured Sites*, pay homage to the ingenuity of people on the lower end of the economic scale. If a dominant trend today is to think green, Cruz shows us that recycling building materials is the essence of greenness.

PAINTING

As modernism came to an end, many painters in America and Europe began to revive expressive, personal styles in a movement known as Neo-Expressionism. This was partly in response to the impersonality and generally aesthetic orientation of movements such as Conceptual Art and Minimalism, and to the ironic, tongue-in-cheek quality of Pop Art and related trends.

One of the first Neo-Expressionists was Susan Rothenberg, who in the 1970s began making symbolic, heavily brushed works in which subject matter teeters on the brink of recognizability. After the cleansing blankness of Minimalism, Rothenberg could return to figurative images with original vision; what emerges is almost ethereal.

She works in a narrow range of tones, using a muted palette of white, beige, silvery or dark gray, with a bit of color. Her *Blue Head*, which outlines a

14.7 Susan Rothenberg.
Blue Head. 1980–1981.
Acrylic on canvas. 114″ 3 114″ (289.6 3 289.6 cm).
Virginia Museum of Fine Arts, Richmond. Gift of The Sydney and Frances Lewis Foundation. © Virginia Museum of Fine Arts. © 2010 Susan Rothenberg/Artists Rights Society (ARS), New York.

horse's head in front of a human hand, is a haunting image that resists explanation. It is a primal sign operating between the material world and the mystery beyond.

The German painter Anselm Kiefer combines the aggressive paint application of Abstract Expressionism with nineteenth-century feelings for history and mythology. Kiefer gives equal attention to moral and aesthetic issues. His paintings, loaded with symbolism, mythology, and religion, speak to the rest of us through powerful stories in dramatic compositions.

Osiris and Isis retells the ancient Egyptian myth of the cycle of death and rebirth. Osiris symbolized the indestructible creative forces of nature; according to legend, the god was slain and cut into pieces by his evil brother. Isis, sister (and wife) of Osiris, collected the pieces and brought Osiris back to life. In Kiefer's huge painting, a network of wires attached to fragments of the dismembered Osiris connects to the goddess Isis in the form of a TV circuit board atop a pyramid. The heavily textured surface of paint, mud, rock, tar, ceramic, and metal intensifies the image's epic treatment of the afterlife theme.

The Neo-Expressionists tend to favor painting because a seemingly infinite variety of surface textures and colors are possible. Every creative

14.8 Anselm Kiefer.
Osiris and Isis. 1985–1987.
Oil, acrylic, emulsion, clay, porcelain, lead copper wire, and circuit board on canvas. 150″ 3 229½″ 3 6½″ (381 3 560.7 3 16.5 cm).
San Francisco Museum of Modern Art. Purchased through a gift of Jean Stein, by exchange, the Mrs. Paul L. Wattis Fund, and the Doris and Donald Fisher Fund.
Photograph by Ben Blackwell. © Anselm Kiefer.

14.9 Elizabeth Murray.
More Than You Know. 1983.
Oil on nine canvases. 108″ 3 111″ 3 8″.
Photograph courtesy The Pace Gallery. © 2011 The Murray-Holman
Family Trust / Artists Rights Society (ARS), New York.

14.10 Kerry James Marshall.
Better Homes Better Gardens. 1994.
Acrylic and collage on canvas. 8′4″ 3 12′.
Collection of Denver Art Museum. Photograph courtesy Jack Shainman
Gallery, New York.

decision can leave a trace on the finished work, registering every twitch in sensibility. Other artists use the painting media because they facilitate storytelling, allowing the artist to create a two-dimensional world with the utmost freedom. This interest in narration is a dominant tendency in contemporary painting.

Elizabeth Murray combines personal meanings with explosive form in works such as *More Than You Know.* The painting dates from the time between the birth of her two children; however, beyond the general outlines of a room with two red chairs, there is little here to suggest the experience of motherhood. Her personal information is only the launching pad for a fascinatingly jagged array of canvas fragments that do not fit together but still seem to cohere. Murray's vibrant and exuberant paintings leave a great deal of the story for the viewer to make up from the suggestive shapes.

Kerry James Marshall investigates African-American life in richly textured paintings. His 1994 work *Better Homes Better Gardens* is part of a series of paintings that he made about Chicago housing projects that contain the word "garden" in their names. This one is obviously set in Wentworth Gardens, and it depicts a couple walking down a flowered pathway in a low-rise setting. At the left is a fenced area enclosing a communal flower garden. Three bluebirds fly across the upper portion of the scene, and all seems peaceful. Whatever else happens in housing projects, they are places of community and neighborhood feeling, he seems to be telling us.

Yet for all its optimism, there are ironic touches in this work. The perfectly spiraled garden hose, the white blotches over the heads of the couple, and the flowered entry with the "Welcome" sign add a note of complexity to the mood, casting a flickering shadow over its sweetness. The inscription "IL 2-8" in the upper right reminds us that this is both an illustration and a painting that is in fact rigorously composed. It is based on a solid grid of horizontals, verticals, and a few diagonals. Although the work is optimistic, Marshall is not merely painting an idealistic scene.

14.11 Gajin Fujita.
Street Fight. 2005.
24-karat gold leaf, spray paint, Mean Streak, paint marker on wood panel triptych. 24″ 3 48″.
Courtesy L.A. Louver Gallery, Venice, CA.

Los Angeles painter Gajin Fujita began his art career as a graffiti tagger in a crew known as K2S (Kill to Succeed). His recent works draw on both his past as a tagger and the high culture of Asia, in a mix that is thoroughly up-to-date in its wide cross-cultural sampling. His 2005 painting *Street Fight* begins with a layer of spray-painted graffiti, some of it by the members of his old tagging crew. A layer of gold leaf provides a sense of the sacred, alluding to ancient Buddhist and medieval Christian art; the buildings in silhouette quote both urban landscape photography and crossword puzzles in newspapers. The sky has abstract patterns based on traditional Japanese screens by Sotatsu and others. The two foreground figures come from Japanese woodblock prints, and the lettering style of the title resembles urban graffiti that decorates most cities worldwide. The theme of the work is both ancient and modern, as the title alludes to contemporary

gang life. If this painting borrows from many sources, it is also inspiring others: the L.A. Latino hip-hop group Ozomatli wrote the songs for its 2007 album *Don't Mess with the Dragon* while working in a gallery where *Street Fight* and other works by Fujita hung.

PHOTOGRAPHY

The postmodern movement has been a primary influence on recent photography. Photographers influenced by postmodernism show through their pictures that they know their medium is not an objective one and that today's cameras can easily lie. Even the most straightforward scenes can have hidden meanings. Postmodernists want to show us that the camera can influence us in ways we may not suspect, and the camera itself has a certain way of seeing.

Cindy Sherman's photographs of the late 1970s were among the first to be called postmodern.

14.12 Cindy Sherman.
Untitled Film Still #48. 1979.
Black and white photograph.
Courtesy Cindy Sherman and Metro Pictures.

14.13 Vik Muniz.
Atlas (Carlao). 2008.
Photograph from series "Pictures of Garbage."
Photograph: Vic Muniz Studio. © Vik Muniz/Licensed by VAGA, New York, NY.

She took black-and-white photos of herself, posing with props in scenes that corresponded to stereotyped female characters from popular culture. In *Untitled Film Still #48,* for example, she stands on a deserted road at dusk, her back to us, hastily packed suitcase at her side. As in many "teen movies" of the 1950s and 1960s, she is the misunderstood daughter running away from home. Other photos from the series depict the girl next door, daddy's little girl, the anxious young career woman, the oppressed housewife. Without referring to specific movies, Sherman's photos are imagined stills from popular film types that have helped to form stereotypical images of women. She knowingly quotes these stereotypes as if to satirize them; this strategy of ironic recycling is some of the purest postmodernism.

Many photographers today do not "find" their subjects; they set them up, as Sherman does. Brazilian-born Vik Muniz works hardest at this task, as we see in his work *Atlas (Carlao)* from the series *Pictures of Garbage.* The artist arranged huge amounts of trash on his studio floor, thereby "painting" a picture that he photographed. He used garbage to create a noble image of a street person, and he used the street person's materials to make it.

The photos of Lebanese artist Walid Raad are even more complicated in their relationship to reality. Raad witnessed firsthand the Lebanese civil war of the 1980s as a teenager; he often ascended to his roof and took pictures of the sky over Beirut, blackened by the smoke of aerial bombardments or artillery fire. When he developed and printed these negatives years later, he found them discolored and pockmarked, aged and damaged like the buildings of his native city. For a 2007 exhibition, he reprinted the pictures in a large format that magnified the flaws of time. *BEY82_City_IV* is a blurry and smudged photo of a bomb landing behind a hospital. The degraded quality gives the image a haunted, distant appearance that contradicts the violence that it originally recorded. His photographs thus resemble faded memories: They record not only the events, but also the tide of history since they happened.

14.14 Walid Raad.
BEY82_City_IV.
From series
"Untitled
(1982–2007)."
Archival color
inkjet print.
44″ 3 67″.
Courtesy Paula Cooper
Gallery, New York.
Photograph: © W. Raad.

SCULPTURE

The range of options available to sculptors has rarely been wider. Partly in reaction to the simplicity of Minimal and Conceptual Art, sculptors today draw on a range of techniques and materials. Many sculptors today are exploring the symbolic value of shapes. How can a shape "mean something"? What range of memories and feelings are viewers likely to attach to a given figure? At what point does a form "take shape" so that a viewer can recognize it? Are viewers likely to see what the creator had in mind? These are some of the questions that sculptors have posed in recent years.

Martin Puryear thoughtfully probes some of these issues. Combining elegant craftsmanship, organic creativity, and humor, Puryear's deceptively simple sculptures include references to shelters, canoes, trestle bridges, coffins, and basketry. Puryear's work has a distinctly American eloquence that arises from the pioneer traditions of self-reliance and craftsmanship. His *Old Mole* recalls the delicate skeleton of an animal as it combines the whimsical humor of a folktale with the austere sophistication of Minimalist sculpture.

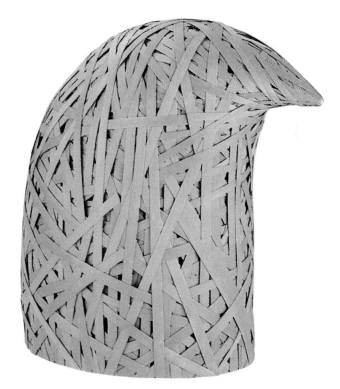

14.15 Martin Puryear.
Old Mole. 1985.
Red cedar. 61″ 3 61″ 3 32″.
Philadelphia Museum of Art. Purchased with gifts (by exchange) of Samuel S. White, III, and Vera White, Mr. and Mrs. C. G. Chaplin, and with funds contributed by Marion Boulton Stroud, Mr. and Mrs. Robert Kardon, Mr. and Mrs. Dennis Alter, and Mrs. H. Gates Lloyd. 1986-70-1. McKee Gallery NY.

Indian-born English sculptor Anish Kapoor takes such explorations in a more ritualistic direction in his work *To Reflect an Intimate Part of the Red*. He deployed across a gallery floor several shapes that allude to ancient religious structures such as Maya pyramids, Indian stupas, and onion-shaped domes. Kapoor sprinkled his sculpture with powder, an action that also seems ritualistic. The translation of these shapes into an art gallery makes us wonder how their spiritual meanings come about, and how much of that meaning persists in the new context.

Probably the most potent symbol in sculpture is the human body, and many artists today continue to find new meaning in the figure as a subject. These sculptors see it not as a vehicle for idealism or beauty, but rather for commenting on the ways in which culture shapes our bodies and how we think about them.

Like many artists today, Kiki Smith is influenced by current events. In 1995, when the frozen body of a Stone Age man was found intact in the Alps, she fashioned *Ice Man* as a commentary. The piece, showing the unclothed man in the frozen position in which he was found, is modeled life-size and cast in silicon bronze. The material gives the surface a dark color similar to that of the dead man's skin. Smith simplified the facial features, leaving the work's title the only sure clue to the source of the piece. She hung the work on the wall of the gallery, slightly above eye level, attached by its back. Thus, it became for viewers an object of curiosity, a specimen, just as the frozen Stone Age man was for the anthropologists who studied him.

14.16 Anish Kapoor.
To Reflect an Intimate Part of the Red. 1981.
Pigment and mixed media. Installation:
78" 3 314" 3 314".
Photograph: Andrew Penketh, London. Courtesy Barbara Gladstone.

14.17 Kiki Smith.
Ice Man. 1995.
Silicon bronze.
80" 3 29¼" 3 12" (203.2 3 74.3 3 30.5 cm).
Photograph by Ellen Page Wilson, courtesy The Pace Gallery.
© Kiki Smith, courtesy The Pace Gallery.

14.18 Rachel Harrison.
This Is Not an Artwork. 2006.
Polystrene, cement, Parex, wood, acrylic, X-tensions Tony G-Fire wig with label, cowboy hat, artificial potatoes and paw-paw fruit, Peter Criss action figure with drum set, Hubbcam detective surveillance camera decoy, stickers, Ikea table. Height 59″.
Jean Vong\Greene Naftali Gallery.

Just as sculptors investigate the meaning of shapes, some question the meanings of materials. They use almost any substance or object as an experiment, to see what might be said with it. One of these is Rachel Harrison, who brought together an amazing array of things and titled it *This Is Not an Artwork.* Fake vegetables, a wig model, and a cheap table only begin to list this work's components. It also includes an action figure of the famous classic rock drummer Peter Criss and a surveillance camera. The piece as a whole seems to be a meditation on what is real and what is a representation, a crucial question in today's culture.

PUBLIC ART

Public art is art that you might encounter without intending to; it exists in a pubic place, accessible to everyone. The idea of public art originated in ancient times, as government and religious leaders commissioned artists to create works for public spaces. In our time, artists still make public art that responds to the needs and hopes of broad masses of people.

The *Vietnam Veterans Memorial,* located on the Mall in Washington, D.C., is probably America's best-known public art piece. The 250-foot-long, V-shaped black granite wall bears the names of the nearly sixty thousand American servicemen and women who died or are missing in Southeast Asia. The nonprofit Vietnam Veterans Memorial Fund, Inc., was formed in 1979 by a group of Vietnam veterans who believed that a public monument to the war would help speed the process of national reconciliation and healing after the conflict.

After examining 1,421 entries, the jury selected the design of twenty-one-year-old Maya Lin of Athens, Ohio, then a student at Yale University. Lin had visited the site and created a design that would work with the land rather than dominate it. "I had an impulse to cut open the earth . . . an initial violence that in time would heal. The grass would grow back, but the cut would remain, a pure, flat surface, like a geode when you cut it open and polish the edge. . . . I chose black granite to make the surface reflective and peaceful."[1]

Lin's bold, eloquently simple design creates a memorial park within a larger park. It shows the influence of Minimalism and site works of the 1960s and 1970s. The polished black surface reflects the surrounding trees and lawn, and the tapering segments point to the Washington Monument in one direction and the Lincoln Memorial in the other. Names are inscribed in chronological order by date of death, each name given a place in history. As visitors walk toward the center, the wall becomes higher and the names pile up inexorably. The monument's thousands of visitors seem to testify to the monument's power to console and heal.

When the Museum of Modern Art in New York expanded in 2004, the neighbors in high-rise buildings complained about having to look down onto new ugly roof structures. The museum responded by turning to landscape architect Ken

14.19   Maya Ying Lin.
Vietnam Memorial, Washington, D.C., 1982.
Polished black granite, length 492 ft.
Woodfin Camp & Associates.

Smith, who said, "Let's camouflage it!" He made the humorous *MOMA Roof Garden* out of colored gravel, asphalt, and plastic bushes. The composition is a camouflage pattern, the better to "hide" the building. This piece of public art is not visible from inside the museum and, more important, requires no maintenance. When the neighbors complained yet again that the garden was completely fake, Smith responded that it was about as fake as nearby Central Park, which had been carefully planted on a stripped and leveled field. The tongue-in-cheek humor of this piece and its witty quotation of camouflage patterns make this work a rare example of postmodern landscape architecture.

A great deal of public art in the United States is created under a mandate that one-half of one percent of the cost of public buildings be spent on art to embellish them. Sometimes the results can turn out unsatisfactorily, as the case of Richard Serra's *Tilted Arc* shows (see page 55). But when a community-minded artist works with the local people, the results can be much more successful, as in the following case.

Seattle-based Buster Simpson specializes in public art, and one of his recent commissions embodies the environmental concerns of an eastern Washington agricultural community. *Instrument Implement: Walla Walla Campanile* begins with core of metal farmers' disks arranged in a repeating bell-shape pattern. Sensors track environmental conditions in nearby Mill Creek: water temperature, flow level, and amount of dissolved gases. All three of these measures are critical for the annual salmon migration, which has been diminishing in recent years. The data are processed by a computer that encodes them into musical notes. Hammers on the piece then strike the proper disks to ring a chime,

14.20 Ken Smith.
MOMA Roof Garden (Museum of Modern Art Roof Garden). 2005.
Outdoor garden at the Museum of Modern Art, New York.
Courtesy of Panoramic Images/Getty Images.

14.21 Buster Simpson.
Instrument Implement: Walla Walla Campanile. 2008.
William A. Grant Water & Environmental Center, Walla Walla Community College, Walla Walla, WA. Height 25'6".
Courtesy of the artist.

14.22   Barbara Kruger.
Untitled (I Shop Therefore I Am). 1987.
Photographic silkscreen/vinyl. 111″ 3 113″.
(282 3 287 cm).
Courtesy Mary Boone Gallery, New York. Copyright Barbara Kruger.

14.23   Fred Wilson.
Mining the Museum. 1992.
Installation. Cigar-store Indians facing photographs of Native
American Marylanders.
Museum and Library of Maryland History. Photograph: Jeff D. Goldman.

which becomes an hourly auditory update on the condition of the river. The health of the salmon is a "canary in the coal mine," an early warning of other environmental problems. Simpson included a yellow effigy of a salmon as an indicator of this. The entire piece is powered by an attached solar collector. *Instrument Implement* is located at Walla Walla Community College, within sight and earshot of hundreds of people each day.

ISSUE-ORIENTED ART

Many artists in the past twenty years have sought to link their art to current social questions. Issue-oriented artists believe that if they limit their art to aesthetic matters, then their work will be only a distraction from pressing problems. Furthermore, they recognize that what we see influences how we think, and they do not want to miss an opportunity to influence both. Some public art is issue-oriented, as we saw with Simpson's *Instrument Implement*.

Barbara Kruger was trained as a magazine designer, and this profession shows in her piece *Untitled (I Shop Therefore I Am)*. She invented the slogan, which sounds as though it came from advertising. The position of the hand, too, looks like it came from an ad for aspirin or sleeping medication. Do our products define us? Are we indeed what we shop for? Often we buy a product because of what it will say about us, and not for the thing itself. These are some of the messages present in this simple yet fascinating work. Perhaps its ultimate irony is that the artist later silkscreened it onto a shopping bag.

Artists who create works about racism and class bias show how common practices of museum display contribute to such problems. In 1992, the Maryland Historical Society invited African-American artist Fred Wilson to rearrange the exhibits on one floor to create an installation called *Mining the Museum*. He spent a year preparing for the show, rummaging through the Society's holdings and documentary records; the results were surprising. He found very little that related to Maryland's Native American population, but he did find a large collection of wooden statues of Indians that were commonly placed outside cigar stores. He dusted them off and stood them, backs to viewers, facing photographs he took of real Native Americans who lived in Maryland. In an accompanying exhibition brochure, he wrote that a museum should be a place that can make you think. When *Mining the Museum* went on display, attendance records soared.

Some artists use their work to excite debate about the ever-increasing surveillance that watches us all in this new century. In response to the threat of terrorism, governments are assuming increasing powers to watch premises, intercept communication, and detain persons. Christian Moeller

installed the public art commission *Mojo* in 2007 to raise awareness of the surveillance issue. Two cameras attached to buildings track the movements of people at night across a corner sidewalk near the port of Los Angeles. Computer software uses this input to program a spotlight (atop the striped tower) to select and follow one passerby at a time with its intense glare. The work is part lighthouse and part toy; its title seems like a pet name, but the work has caused controversy. Some resent its spying eye, but *Mojo* is only doing what passes unnoticed many times a day in most people's lives. The artist, who has installed similarly high-tech pieces in London and Tokyo, does not mind the controversy. He said, "Successful public art is indicated by how much people talk about it."

STREET ART

In the late 1990s, many galleries in various cities began to exhibit work by artists who had previously made illegal graffiti. Many of these "street artists" were based in the culture of skateboards and punk music, and they used materials bought at the hardware store rather than the art supply house. Their creations were only rarely related to gang-oriented graffiti, which usually mark out territories of influence. Nor were they mere tags with names or initials. Rather, the street artists made much broader statements about themselves and the world in a language that was widely understandable. The ancestors of the movement in the 1980s were Keith Haring (see page 91) and Jean-Michel Basquiat, both of whom worked illegally for years before exhibiting in galleries. By the turn of the twenty-first century, street art was a recognized movement, and most of its main practitioners work both indoors and out. All of our artists here create under pseudonyms. While sometimes illegal, the boldness and personal risk-taking that street artists engage in inspires many in a society with strong corporate and government power.

Faile is a collaborative of two Brooklyn-based artists. They create imagery that seems as though it were lifted from magazines and advertisements,

14.24   Christian Moeller.
Mojo. 2007.
Computer-driven sidewalk installation,
San Pedro, California. Height 40′.
Courtesy of the artist, Christian Moeller. Photograph: Anna Kwan.

14.25 Faile.
A Continuing Story. 2009.
Acrylic, spraypaint, and screenprint on canvas.
62″ square.
Perry Rubenstein Gallery, New York.

but it is their own work in silkscreen, stencil, and paint. They layer these images and then rip through them to leave a worn surface like a decaying urban wall. Some of their work at first seems self-promotional, such as *A Continuing Story*, but a better way to describe Faile is that they mock the style of billboards. The brazenness and flair of their works has attracted viewers since 1999 when the team began.

Some of today's most skillful street art is created by Swoon. She carves large linoleum blocks and makes relief prints from them, usually life-size portraits of everyday people. She prints them on large sheets of cheap (usually recycled) newsprint and pastes them on urban walls, beginning on the Lower East Side of Manhattan, but now in cities on every continent. Her *Untitled* installation at Deitch Projects was a recent indoor work. Against objections that her work is mostly illegal, she replies that her creations are far easier to look at than advertising, that they lack any persuasive agenda, and that they glorify common people. Moreover, the

14.26 Swoon.
Untitled. 2005.
Linoleum cut, newsprint, ink, and wheat paste.
Variable dimensions.
Deitch Projects, New York.

newsprint that she uses decays over time so that her work is impermanent. Although she works mostly outdoors, she sometimes shows in galleries because, she admits, "I have to make a living," but she charges far less for her work than most other artists of wide repute.

Probably the most famous street creator today is the English artist Banksy. His street art is generally witty, as we see in *Stone Age Waiter*. This piece adorns an outdoor location in a Los Angeles neighborhood with many restaurants; a cave man has apparently joined the ranks of the pleasure-seekers. Well-heeled Angelenos who walk the (always short) distance from their cars to their favorite restaurants will pass this stencil-and-spray-paint creation. Banksy is currently one of the most popular artists in his homeland, and many of his outdoor works have been preserved. When a prominent street work of his was recently defaced by another graffiti artist, protests ensued and the defacer was arrested for vandalism! Thus, street artists often blur the line between legal and illegal. Other artists who partake of a street art style are Kim McCarthy and Gajin Fujita (page 311).

THE GLOBAL PRESENT

Communication and travel technologies are making the world smaller and smaller. The Internet, air travel, mobile phones, cable television, and international migration are bringing us all into ever closer proximity. After the fall of Communism, the world is not as divided as it was for the preceding half-century, thus contributing to a more fluid world culture. Many businesses, for example, are not confined by national boundaries anymore; they may raise money in one country, buy raw materials in another, set up manufacturing facilities in a third, and sell the final product around the world.

The globalization of culture has had a profound impact on art.

Contemporary art forms such as conceptual, installation, and performance art have spread around the world. Innovative work is emerging in unexpected places, as artists in many countries use increasingly international modes of expression to interpret the contemporary world in the light of their own traditions. This union of the cosmopolitan and the local is a major source of the new creative effort that has always fertilized art. A few examples from disparate continents will have to suffice to indicate the directions that art is taking. All these works comment on issues our world faces today.

Jaune Quick-to-See Smith highlighted an important demographic shift in *The Browning of America*. Here we see a map of the continent almost covered in brown paint drips. The work seems to say that America is no longer black and white, but rather getting browner as races intermingle and immigrants arrive. Native Americans are symbolized by the shapes in the center, a strategy that gives primacy to the first Americans. (The

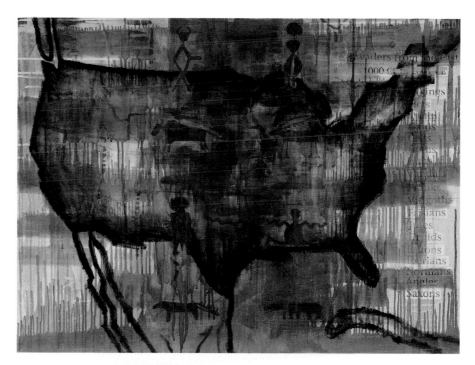

14.27 Jaune Quick-to-See Smith.
The Browning of America. 2000.
Oil, collage, and mixed media on canvas. 36" 3 48".
Courtesy of Jaune Quick-to-See Smith (An enrolled Flathead Salish, member of the Salish and Kootenai Nation Montana).

AT THE EDGE OF ART

Recent Projects

ONE MODERNIST TRADITION continued in the postmodern era: challenging the boundaries of art. Many creators today were trained as artists and call themselves artists, but create projects that do not resemble art. For the purposes of this book, we consider them artists because they use visual material in a highly creative way. Some of them comment on the art world itself; others implant their creations in the real world, like ticking time bombs.

14.28   Philippe Parreno.
Marquee, Guggenheim, NY. 2008.
Installation view. Acrylic, steel, LEDs, incandescent, fluorescent, neon lights.
During the anyspacewhatever exhibition, Solomon R. Guggenheim Museum, New York, October 24, 2008–January 7, 2009. Photograph: Kristopher McKay. © The Solomon R. Guggenheim Foundation, New York.

When Philippe Parreno was invited to exhibit at the Guggenheim Museum in New York in 2008, few knew what to expect. He has made a film about a soccer star, chalked stone words on outcroppings next to a penguin rookery, added blank books to library shelves, and once sent a truck through a Japanese city broadcasting a monologue. At the Guggenheim, he installed a huge *Marquee* over the doorway that flashed garishly all night, every night. This transformed the entrance to the museum from a contemplative passageway into a red-carpet experience, as if visitors were performers in a spectacle. The implication being, of course, that art has become a spectacle like any other in our world.

Other artists create works that cannot be illustrated, not because they are obscene but because they are invisible. Tino Sehgal in 2006 trained the guards in a museum to randomly announce aloud, for one month, each day's newspaper headlines. Thus, museum visitors who expect a quiet experience were rudely presented with the outside world within the hushed halls. He calls his pieces "structured situations," and claims that all art through history has provided these, so he is merely doing the same.

Some artists today function like visual subversives, implanting surprises in the constant flow of images that we all live with. This movement is sometimes called culture jamming. Steve Lambert bought a letter sign, of the sort that companies use to show us where to park or what is on sale that week. He set unusual or surprising, decidedly non-corporate messages on these signs and placed them in public places where thousands pass. At a cemetery in 2009, for example, he placed *You Are Still Alive* with the arrow pointing at the gravestones. The work administered a visual jolt similar to what we might feel before a surprising work of art. Lambert has also worked on other media: He developed an application, for example, that changes the advertisements in your web browser into artworks. Other artists in this book who have worked in a culture jamming mode include Jonathan Barnbrook and Heidi Cody.

14.29   Steve Lambert.
You Are Still Alive. 2009.
Archival pigment print. 30" 3 20".
Image courtesy of the artist and Charlie James Gallery, Los Angeles.

14.30 Shahzia Sikander.
Sinxay: Narrative as Dissolution #2. 2008.
Ink and gouache on paper. 82″ 3 51¼″
(208.3 3 129.9 cm).
Courtesy of the artist and Sikkema-Jenkins & Co., New York.

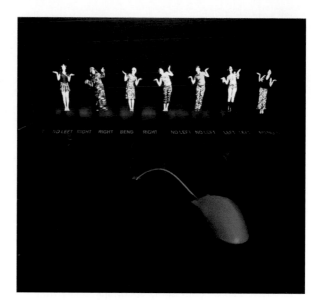

14.31 Shilpa Gupta.
Untitled. 2004–2005.
Interactive video projection; computer and
projector. Eight minutes with sound.
Courtesy of the artist and Bose Pacia Gallery, New York.

artist counts herself among these, a member of the
Flathead Indian Nation.) The first wave of immigrants, White European ethnic groups, is listed at
the right or east side from which they came. Most
of the paint drips run upward, symbolizing the
south-to-north movement of people that is helping
to transform the ethnic basis of the United States.
To make the paint run this way, she had to turn
the United States upside down, a symbolic act.

The issue of personal and ethnic identity pro-
vokes increasing soul-searching in this shrinking
world. Do artists from one part of the world need to
stick with the traditional styles still associated with
their origins? Is it appropriate for an American artist
to paint in a traditional Chinese style or vice versa?

Shahzia Sikander answers many of these questions by taking a middle ground, drawing on her

roots while giving her work a contemporary look.
Born in Pakistan, she was trained first as a traditional illustrator in the ancient gouache medium.
After moving to the West in the mid-1990s, she
studied at the Rhode Island School of Design. On
a trip to Laos in 2008, she read a translation of the
Laotian epic poem *Sang Sinxay* and created several
works in response. *Sinxay: Narrative as Dissolution
#2* uses Lao writing as a backdrop for her own cal-
ligraphic loops and swirls that are based on her earlier training. Which culture this work came from
ought not be a consideration, she says: "These days
the world is small and one should really consider
work in terms of some sort of global context of
ideas. Work I believe should stand on its own, irre-
spective of geography." In this work, an exotic text
has become a beautiful garland of careful, flower-
like paint strokes.

Contemporary artists are unlikely to specialize
in one medium or another; most prefer to work out
their ideas in whatever medium best answers the
urge to communicate. Indian artist Shilpa Gupta
has worked with sculpture, cloth, and the Internet
as she comments on how the world appears from
her perspective in Mumbai, the country's largest city. Her 2004–2005 *Untitled* work is a video
projection that shows seven figures wearing vari-

ous styles of clothing based on camouflage patterns (which she says is an increasingly important fashion statement since the American War on Terror began in 2001). Gallery viewers can use a mouse to manipulate the figures and cause them to bend, pivot, or gesture, all to the accompaniment of electronic sounds, as the command words appear on the floor. The work thus resembles a video game, but viewers soon realize that the figures do not respond perfectly to the mouse commands: Some figures imitate what others do, and sometimes a figure makes a threatening gesture to its neighbor. Thus, the artist says, the work gives us an illusion of control similar to that which we enjoy on our

daily lives. In a humorous twist, all seven figures are clones of the artist, allowing viewers to seemingly reverse the creative process by symbolically manipulating the artist.

Because human creativity is spread about equally around the globe, a good idea could emerge from almost anywhere. The African artist El Anatsui uses cast-off liquor bottle tops to weave spectacular tapestries of shimmering color. His 2007 piece *Duvor* recently entered the collection of the Indianapolis Museum of Art. *Duvor* comes from the tradition of African textiles, in which artists have used materials at hand with great resourcefulness. The bottle tops refer to the colonial

14.32   El Anatsui (b. 1944).
Duvor (Communal Cloth). 2007.
Aluminum and copper wire. 640 3 840 cm.

14.33   Renzo Piano.
Modern Wing. 2009.
Art Institute of Chicago. Photograph: Nic Lehoux, courtesy Renzo Piano Building Workshop.

Triangular Trade that sent slaves to the New World in exchange for rum. The artist has symbolically transformed that lamentable heritage into a stunning object. The title of the work means *Communal Cloth*, a reference to the many hands that helped El Anatsui to make it, and to the communal meanings that textiles have in African culture.

We will close this book with Renzo Piano's new *Modern Wing* of the Chicago Art Institute because it embodies many ideas that this book also shares. The *Modern Wing* is an addition to the earlier traditional building, which was built in 1893 from brick and stone in a classical style. The original building expressed the ideals of dignity, trust, and safeguarding the past. The new wing is almost completely glass-wrapped and open to the light. The architect said of this wing:

Today we have a different story to tell. I think the story we are telling with the new building is about accessibility . . . It's about openness. It's about a build-ing that should not be intimidating, but the opposite. It should be inviting.

This book has attempted to present a small portion of the boundless variety of art that characterizes human expression. We have seen that art comes from basic feelings that all of us share. Through their work, artists interact with life, to find purpose and meaning in it. Human life varies considerably across time and space, but the art endures. Creative expression is a response to being alive. Artists' creativity activates the artist within us.

Art offers us a way to go beyond mere physical existence. The ideas, values, and approaches that constitute the basis of the visual arts can continue to enrich our lives and surroundings. We form art. Art forms us.

Note

1. Joel L. Swerdlow, "To Heal a Nation," *National Geographic* (May 1985): 557.

Artists' Pronunciation Guide

Aalto, Alvar (<u>aal</u> tō)

Abakanowicz, Magdalena (maag daa <u>lay</u> nă / aa baa kaa <u>nō</u> vich)

Albers, Josef (<u>yō</u> sef / <u>aal</u> berz)

Anuszkiewicz, Richard (aa <u>nus</u> ke vich)

Bernini, Gianlorenzo (jaan lō <u>ren</u> zō / bair <u>nee</u> nee)

Boccioni, Umberto (oom <u>bair</u> tō / bō <u>kee</u> ō nee)

Bonnard, Pierre (peeair / bon <u>aar</u>)

Botticelli, Sandro (<u>san</u> drō / bōt ee <u>chel</u> ee)

Bouguereau, William (bu <u>grō</u>)

Brancusi, Constantin (kaan stan teen / braan <u>koo</u> sce)

Braque, Georges (zhorzh / braak)

Bronzino, Agnolo (ang <u>nō</u> lō / <u>bron</u> zee nō)

Bruegel, Pieter (<u>pee</u> tair / <u>broo</u> gĭ l)

Buonarroti, Michelangelo (mee kĕl <u>an</u> jĕ lō / booawn ă <u>rōt</u> ee)

Caravaggio, Michelangelo (mee kĕl <u>an</u> jĕ lō / kaa raa <u>vaa</u> geeō)

Cartier-Bresson, Henri (aan <u>ree</u> / kar <u>teeay</u> / bres <u>on</u>)

Cellini, Benvenuto (ben ve <u>noo</u> tō / che <u>lee</u> nee)

Cézanne, Paul (pōl / say <u>zan</u>)

Chagall, Marc (sha gal)

Christo (<u>krees</u> tō)

Cimabue (chee mă <u>boo</u> ay)

Claude Lorraine (klōd / lor <u>en</u>)

Corot, Jean-Baptiste Camille (zhaan / bap <u>teest</u> / ka <u>mee</u> / kō <u>rō</u>)

Corregio, Antonio (an <u>tō</u> nee ō / kō <u>re</u> geeō)

Courbet, Gustave (goos <u>taav</u> / koor <u>bay</u>)

Cranach, Lucas (<u>craw</u> nok)

Csuri, Charles (<u>tshoo</u> ree)

Daguerre, Louis Jacques Mande (loo ee / zhaak / man <u>day</u> / daa <u>gayr</u>)

Dalí, Salvador (sal vaa <u>dōr</u> / <u>daa</u> lee)

David, Jacques-Louis (zhaak / loo ee / dă <u>veed</u>)

Degas, Edgar (ed <u>gaar</u> / day <u>gaa</u>)

Derain, André (aan <u>dray</u> / de <u>ran</u>)

Dubuffet, Jean (zhaan / doo boo <u>fay</u>)

Duchamp, Marcel (mar <u>sel</u> / doo <u>shaan</u>)

Dürer, Albrecht (<u>aal</u> brekht / <u>door</u> ĕr)

Eames, Charles and Ray (ayms)

Eliasson, Olafur (<u>aal</u> brekht / <u>door</u> ĕr)

Escher, M. C. (<u>esh</u> ĕr)

Eyck, Jan van (yaan / van / īk)

Fathy, Hassan (<u>has</u> ăn / fat <u>hee</u>)

Fei, Cao (tow / fay)

Fortuny, Mario (<u>maar</u> ee ō / for <u>too</u> nee)

Fragonard, Jean-Honoré (zhaan / aw nō <u>ray</u> / fraw gō <u>naar</u>)

Frankenthaler, Helen (<u>fraank</u> ĕn taal ĕr)

Fukuda, Shigeo (shig <u>ee</u> o / foo <u>koo</u> da)

Gaudí, Antonio (aan <u>tō</u> neeō / gow <u>dee</u>)

Gauguin, Paul (pōl / <u>gō</u> gan)

Gehry, Frank (<u>gee</u> ri)

Gentile da Fabriano (gen <u>tee</u> lĕ / da / fab <u>ree</u> aan ō)

Géricault, Theodore (tay ō <u>dōr</u> / je ree <u>cō</u>)

Ghiberti, Lorenzo (lō <u>ren</u> zō / gee <u>bair</u> tee)

Giacometti, Alberto (aal <u>bair</u> tō / jeeaa cō <u>met</u> ee)

Giotto (<u>jeeō</u> tō)

Glaser, Milton (<u>mil</u> ton / <u>glay</u> ser)

Gogh, Vincent van (<u>vin</u> sent / van / gō)

Gorky, Arshile (ar <u>sheel</u> / <u>gōr</u> kee)

Goya, Francisco (fraan <u>sis</u> cō / <u>goy</u> aa)

Greco, El (el / <u>gre</u> kō)

Grotell, Maija (mī yă / <u>gro</u> tel)

Grünewald, Matthias (maa <u>tee</u> ăs / <u>groon</u> ĕ vaalt)

Hadid, Zaha (<u>zaa</u> hă / hă <u>deed</u>)

Heizer, Michael (<u>hītz</u> ĕr)

Hokusai (<u>hō</u> kĕ sī)

Holbein, Hans (haans / <u>hōl</u> bīn)

Ingres, Jean Auguste Dominique (zhaan / ō <u>goost</u> / dōm en <u>eek</u> / ăn grĕ)

Isozaki, Arata (ă ră tă / i sō ză kee)

Kahlo, Frieda (<u>free</u> dă / <u>kaa</u> lō)

Kandinsky, Wassily (vaa <u>see</u> lee / kan <u>din</u> skee)

Kiefer, Anselm (<u>an</u> selm / <u>keef</u> ĕr)

Klee, Paul (klay)

Kollwitz, Käthe (<u>kay</u> tĕ / <u>kōl</u> vits)

Kooning, Willem de (<u>wil</u> ĕm / dĕ / <u>koo</u> ning)

Lachaise, Gaston (gas <u>ton</u> / la <u>shes</u>)

Lalique, René (re <u>nay</u> / la <u>leek</u>)

Le Corbusier (lĕ / cōr boo <u>zeeay</u>)

Leonardo da Vinci (lay ō naar dō / daa / vin chee)

LeWitt, Sol (lĕ wit)

Lichtenstein, Roy (likh ten shtīn)

Lin, Maya Ying (mī yă / ying / lin)

Lorenzetti, Ambrogio (am brō jeeō / lor en zet ee)

Lubalin, Herb (loo ba lĭn)

Manet, Edouard (ayd waar / ma nay)

Mantegna, Andrea (aan dray ă / maan tayn yaa)

Martinez, Maria (ma ree ă / mar tee nez)

Masur (ma zoor)

Matisse, Henri (aan ree / ma tees)

Mehta, Tyeh (ti eb / may ta)

Mies van de Rohe, Ludwig (loot fik / mees / van / dair / rō ĕ)

Miró, Joan (hō awn / mee rō)

Miyake, Issey (mee yă kay)

Modigliani, Amadeo (a me dayō / mō dee glee an nee)

Mondrian, Piet (peet / mōn dree aan)

Monet, Claude (klōd / mon ay)

Morisot, Berthe (bairt / mo ree sō)

Mu-ch'i (moo chee)

Munch, Edvard (ed vart / moonkh)

Munsell, Albert (al bert / mun sl)

Nakashima, George (nă kă shee mă)

Nervi, Pier Luigi (peeair / loo ee jee / nair vee)

Nevelson, Louise (ne vĕl sn)

Newman, Barnett (bar net / noo man)

Noguchi, Isamu (i să moo / nō goo chee)

O'Keeffe, Georgia (jōr jeea / ō keef)

Oldenburg, Claes (klaas / ōl den burg)

Orozco, José (hō say / ōr ōs kō)

Otto, Frei (frī / aa tō)

Paik, Nam June (payk)

Palladio, Andrea (an dray ă / pa la deeō)

Panini, Giovanni Paolo (jeeō van ee / paō lō / pa nee nee)

Perugino (Pietro Vanucci) (pay trō / va noo kee / pe roo jee nō)

Picasso, Pablo (pab lō / pi ka sō)

Pollaiuolo, Antonio del (an tō neeō / pō la eeō lō)

Pollock, Jackson (paal uk)

Raphael (raf fī el)

Rauschenberg, Robert (row shen bairg)

Ray, Satyajit (sat ya jeet / ray)

Redon, Odilon (ō di lo / rĕ do)

Rembrandt Van Rijn (rem brant)

Renoir, Auguste (ō goost / ren waar)

Riefenstahl, Leni (len ee / reef ĕn shtal)

Rigaud, Hyacinthe (ee aa sant / ree gō)

Rivera, Diego (dee aa gō / ree ver ă)

Rodin, Auguste (ō goost / rō dan)

Rosetti, Dante Gabriel (daan tay / gab ree el / rō se tee)

Rothko, Mark (roth kō)

Rousseau, Henri (aan ree / roo sō)

Rubens, Peter Paul (roo benz)

Saarinen, Eero (saa ree nen)

Safdie, Moshe (saf dee)

Scamozzi, Vincenzo (vee chen sō / ska mō see)

Schwitters, Kurt (schvit airs)

Seurat, Georges (zhorzh / syoo raa)

Stankiewicz, Richard (stan kee ay vich)

Steichen, Edward (shtī khĕn)

Stieglitz, Alfred (shteeg litz)

Thonet, Gebrüder (ton et)

Tiffany, Louis Comfort (ti fă nee)

Tinguely, Jean (zhaan / ta glee)

Tintoretto, Jacopo (ja kō pō / tin tō re tō)

Tomazewski, Henryk (tō ma shev skee)

Toulouse-Lautrec, Henri (aan ree / too looz / lō trek)

Ugolino di Nerio (oo gō lee nō / dee / ner ō)

Van der Rohe, Mies (mees / van der rō ŭ)

Varo, Remedios (re me dee ōs / vaa rō)

Vasarely, Victor (vaa saa ray lee)

Velázquez, Diego (deeay gō / vay las kes)

Vermeer, Jan (yaan / vair meer)

Voisard (vwaa zar)

Warhol, Andy (an dee / wor haal)

Weyden, Roger van der (way dĕ)

Wyeth, Andrew (wayth)

Zapf, Hermann (her maan / zapf)

Zelanski, Paul (ze lan skee)

Glossary/Pronunciation Guide

Most words are accompanied by a guide to pronunciation. Syllables are separated by a space and those that are stressed are underlined. Letters are pronounced in the usual manner for English unless they are clarified in the following list.

a	fl*a*t
aa	f*a*ther
aw	s*aw*
ay	p*ay*
ai	th*e*re
ee	s*ee*
e	l*e*t
i	p*i*ty
ī	h*i*gh
o	n*o*t
oo	f*oo*d
oy	b*oy*
ō	n*o*
ow	n*ow*
yoo	*you*
u	b*u*t
er, ir, or, ur	f*er*n, f*ir*, f*or*, f*ur*
ă, ĕ, ĭ, ŏ, ŭ	*a*bout, ros*e*s, (to) s*u*spect: (unaccented vowels represented by "shwa" in some phonetic alphabets)
ch	*ch*urch
j	*j*et
kh	guttural aspiration (ch in Welsh and German)
ng	si*ng*
sh	*sh*ine
wh	*wh*ere
y	*y*es
zh	bei*g*e

A

Abstract Referring to the essence rather than the surface of an object, often by stripping away all nonessential characteristics.

Abstract Expressionism The post-World War II movement centered in New York in which paint was freely applied to a large canvas, expressing the energy and feelings of the artist *nonobjectively*, usually with no emphasized *focal point*.

Acoustics The science of planning the properties of sound in architecture.

Acrylic (ă krḭl ik) A water-based synthetic *medium* for painting, also called *acrylic emulsion*.

Action Painting A style of painting, most notably practiced by Jackson Pollock, in which paint is dribbled and splashed onto the *support* with broad gestural movements.

Actual Texture The true physical feeling of a form's surface.

Additive color mixing The combination of *refracted colors*.

Additive sculpture That which is created by a process of building up or combining materials.

Adze A woodcarving tool with both chiseling blade and axlike handle.

Aerial view A downward perspective on an image.

Aesthetic (es thĕt ic) Pertaining to a sense of the beautiful.

Aesthetic distance The spatial relationship between the viewer and a work of art.

Aesthetics Theories of what is beautiful.

Airbrush A tool used for blowing a fine spray of paint onto a surface, to allow smooth graduations of *values* and *hues*.

Alla prima (al ă / pree mă) See *direct painting*

Analogous colors Those lying near each other on the *color wheel*.

Anneal (ă nĕel) To heat metal to make it more malleable, to counteract the hardening typical as metal is worked.

Antique glass Sheets of glass that have been handblown as cylinders, cut, and heated to flatten them, often characterized by bubbles and warps.

Applied arts Disciplines in which functional objects are created.

Apse In church architecture, the semicircular end of the building.

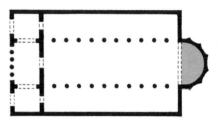

Aquatint An *intaglio* printmaking technique, producing grainy tones rather than lines, that uses acid to penetrate areas of a metal plate that are covered by porous powdered resin.

Arch A curving or pointed structural device supporting an opening, doorway, or bridge.

Archaic period In Greek arts, the 700 to 480 B.C. age during which interest in depicting the natural human body flourished.

Armature (aar mă ch ŭr) An inner skeleton that supports a sculpture made of some malleable material.

Art brut (aart / broot) "Raw art," Jean Dubuffet's term for *outsider art*.

Artisan A person who is skilled at a certain *craft*.

A secco Referring to paint applied to the surface of a fresco after the plaster has dried, in contrast to *buon fresco*.

Assemblage (ă sĕm blij) A combination of varying materials to create a three-dimensional work of art.

Asymmetrical balance The distribution of dissimilar visual weights in such a way that those on either side seem to offset each other, also called *informal balance*, in contrast to *symmetrical* or formal *balance*.

Atmospheric color The effects of lighting and environmental reflections on local colors.

Atmospheric perspective The illusion—and illusionary device—that forms seen at great distance are lower on *value* contrast and less sharply defined than objects close to the viewer.

Axis An imaginary straight line passing centrally and/or longitudinally through a figure, form, or composition.

B

Balance The distribution of apparent visual weights through a composition. See *asymmetrical balance*.

Balloon frame construction Framing for a building in which relatively small pieces of wood are nailed together rather than heavy timbers connected by joinery.

Baroque (bǎ rōk) Seventeenth-century artistic styles in Europe, characterized by swirling composition, sensuality, emotionality, and exuberant sculptural and architectural ornamentation.

Barrel vault A ceiling in the form of an unbroken tunnel.

Bas relief (bas / ri leef) See *Low relief*.

Bearing wall construction A support system in which the weight of ceiling and roof is borne by the entirety of the walls.

Binder The material used in paint and some drawing *media* to bind the particles of *pigment* together and enable them to stick to the *support*.

Bitmap A matrix of pixels (dots in the computer's memory) of which an image may be composed in computer graphics.

Blind embossing Pressing an uninked, cut plate of metal against paper to create a sculptured, uninked image.

Broken colors In contrast to areas of a single *hue*, use of fragments of different hues next to each other in a painting to approximate the dynamism of color perception.

Buon fresco (booawn / fres kō) "True fresco" in which paint is spread on wet plaster and becomes part of the wall surface itself as it dries.

Burin (byoor in) A beveled steel rod used for cutting lines in *line engravings* or *wood engravings*.

Burl A woody circular knob on the trunk of certain trees, prized for its whorled lines in woodworking.

Burnish To rub to a shiny finish.

Buttress An external supporting structure built against a wall to counteract the thrust of an arch or vault. See *flying buttress*.

Byzantine Referring to art of the Byzantine period in the eastern half of the Roman Empire, from A.D. 330 to the mid-fifteenth century. This art was primarily religious and characterized by *stylized* elongated human forms and rich ornamentation.

C

Calligraphy (kǎ li grǎ fee) The art of fine writing.

Camera obscura (kam er ǎ / ǒb skyoor ǎ) A dark chamber in which the image of an object enters through a lens or small opening and is focused on a facing wall.

Cantilever (kantī leev ĕr) A projection from a building or sculpture that is supported, anchored, or balanced at only one end.

Capital The head of a column that bears the weight of the structure above.

Cartoon A full-sized drawing for a two-dimensional work, such as a *fresco*, which is transferred to the *support* at the preparatory stage.

Casting The creation of a three-dimensional form by pouring into prepared molds a molten or liquid material that will later harden.

Ceramics The art of making objects of clay and *firing* them in a *kiln*.

Chalk Naturally deposited calcium carbonate, ground to a powder and reconstituted with a *binder* for use as a drawing *medium*.

Charcoal Charred vine or wood used in sticks as a soft drawing *medium*.

Chiaroscuro (kee aar ǎ skoor ō) The depiction in two-dimensional art of the effects of light and shadow, highly developed in *Renaissance* paintings as a means of rendering the solidity of bodies.

Chroma (krō mǎ) See *saturation*.

Cinematography The artistic and technical skills involved in creating motion pictures.

Cire perdue (seer / pair doo) See *lost-wax*.

Classical The art and culture of ancient Greece and Rome.

Classical period Greek art from c. 500 to 323 B.C., characterized by serene balance, harmony, idealized beauty, and lack of extraneous detail.

Classicism Movements, periods, and impulses in Western art that prized qualities of harmony and formal restraint and claimed direct inspiration from *Classical* models. Traditionally contrasted with *Romanticism*.

Closed form In sculpture, an unbroken volume with no projections or *voids*.

Coffer (kaw fer) A recessed panel, often repeated as a pattern, in a ceiling or vault.

Coil building A method of building a form of clay by rolling it into long ropes which are coiled in a spiraling pattern to raise the sides of the piece.

Cold color (or "cool color") A hue traditionally thought to suggest low temperature and peacefulness, chiefly blues and greens.

Collage (kǒ laazh *or* kō laaj) A two-dimensional technique in which materials are glued to a flat surface.

Color wheel Relationships among *hues* expressed in a circular two-dimensional model.

Compact disc (CD) A flat circular device on which visual and/or audio information is stored *digitally*, to be decoded by a laser beam.

Complementary hues Colors lying opposite each other on a *color wheel*.

Compositional line A line that leads the eye through a work, unifying figures or parts of figures.

Compressive strength In architecture, the amount of downward pressure a structural material can withstand without breaking.

Computer graphics Various techniques of creating two-dimensional artworks by computer.

Conceptual art Art that deals with ideas and experience rather than permanent form.

Conté crayon (kon tay / kray on) A fine-textured, non-greasy stick of powdered graphite and clay with red ocher, soot, or blackstone added for color, used as a drawing tool.

Content The subject-matter of a work of art and the emotions, ideas, symbols, stories, or spiritual connotations it suggests. Traditionally contrasted with *form*.

DRY MEDIA

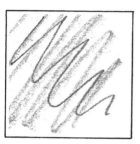
GRAPHITE

CONTÉ

COMPUTER PRINTER

LIQUID MEDIA

BRUSH AND INK

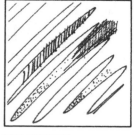
PEN AND INK

Context The surrounding circumstances.

Contour The outer edge of a three-dimensional form or the two-dimensional representation of this edge.

Contrapposto (con tra *pō* s tō) In figurative works, counterpoised *asymmetrical balance* between parts of the body, with most of the weight on one leg and an S-curve in the torso, first used by *Classical* Greek sculptors.

Contrast Abrupt change, as when opposites are juxtaposed.

Control To determine how an area will be seen or experienced.

Cool colors Those from the blue and green side of the *color wheel* thought to convey a feeling of coldness.

Corinthian (kō *rin* thee ǎn) In *Classical* Greek architecture, the lightest and most ornate order, with the appearance of outward-curling acanthus leaves on the capital.

Crafts Disciplines in which functional objects are made by hand.

Crop To delete unwanted peripheral parts of a design.

Cross-hatching Crossed parallel lines used to create the illusion of form on a two-dimensional surface, by suggesting shadows and rounding in space.

Cubism (*kyoob* iz ĭm) An art movement of the early twentieth century, dominated by Picasso and Braque and distinguished by its experiments with analyzing forms into planes seen from many sides at once and by the liberation of art from representational depictions.

Cyberspace (*sī* ber spays) The "world" of communication through international computer networks.

D

Dada (*daa* daa) An anti-rational, anti-*aesthetic* art movement begun in 1916.

Daguerreotype (dǎ ger ō tip) An early photographic process invented by Louis Daguerre.

Deconstructionist Referring to contemporary architecture which deliberately gives the impression of chaos and instability rather than order and stability.

Decorative line A line that embellishes a surface.

Defensive grid Our ability to screen out unnecessary stimuli.

Descriptive line A line that tells the physical nature of an object.

Digital versatile disc (DVD) A device for miniature storage of audio and/or visual information in *digitized* format, to be decoded by a laser beam.

Digitize In computer graphics, to convert an image into computer language so that it can be projected or manipulated by computer.

Diptych (*dip* tik) A work consisting of two panels side by side, traditionally hinged to be opened and closed.

Directional Telling the eye which way to look.

Direct painting Application of paint directly to a *support* without *underlayers*, in contrast with *indirect painting*. Also called *alla prima*.

Divisionism See *Pointillism*.

Dome A hemispherical vault over a room or building.

Doric (*daw* rik) In *Classical* Greek architecture, the simplest order, with a heavy, fluted column, a dish-shaped capital, and no base.

Download To take information from the Internet or an external storage device and save it on a computer.

Draw To make lines and marks.

Dry media A means of drawing such as graphite pencil, charcoal, pastel, *conté crayon*, or computer printer ribbon, in which the base that carries the *pigments* is not fluid. As shown in the drawing, each of these media creates a different line quality.

Drypoint An *intaglio* printmaking technique, often used in combination with *etching*, in which lines are scratched

directly into the metal plate with a sharp-pointed tool.

Ductility (duk *til* ĭ tee) The capacity for being drawn out into wires or hammered into sheets, a varying property of metals. Gold and copper are noted for their especially high ductility.

Dynamic form A mass that appears to be in motion.

Dynamic range The degree of difference between the darkest and lightest values that the sensor of a digital camera can register.

E

Earthenware *Ceramics* made from porous, coarse-textured clays such as terra cotta.

Earthwork A large-scale sculpture in which the surface of the earth is the *medium*.

Economy The use of as few means as possible to achieve a desired visual result.

Edge A boundary where two areas treated differently meet.

Elements of design The basic components of the visual arts: line, shape or form, space, texture, lighting, color, and perhaps time.

Emphasis Predominance of one area or element in a composition.

Enamel A colored glassy coating heat-fused to metal.

Encaustic (en *kaws* tik) A painting technique in which *pigment* is mixed with a *binder* of hot wax.

Engraving An *intaglio* printmaking technique in which lines are cut on a metal or wood printing surface with a sharp tool.

Enlightenment Eighteenth-century European philosophical movement promoting individual reason rather than tradition.

Entablature The horizontal member atop a column, supporting what lies above.

Entasis (en tă sis) A slightly convex curve given to the shaft of a column to correct the illusion of concavity produced by a perfectly straight shaft.

Environmental design The art of manipulating outdoor areas for practical and aesthetic purposes, from landscaping to relationships among buildings in urban settings.

Ergonomics (ur gō naam iks) The study of the mechanics and proportions of the human body, with the aim of designing products with which the body can interact efficiently and comfortably.

Etching An *intaglio* printmaking technique in which lines are produced by scratching away a protective covering of wax on a copper plate, which is then bathed in acid that bites channels where the metal has been exposed.

Expressionism An art movement particularly strong in Germany before World War I, in which the artist reports inner feelings rather than outer realities.

Expressive Giving form to emotions.

Exterior contour The outside form of a three-dimensional piece.

Eye level line In *linear perspective* drawings, the horizon line.

Eyeline The implied line along which the eyes of a human figure in a work of art seem to be looking.

F

Façade (fă saad) The front or principal elevation of a building.

Fantasy Imagery existing only in the imagination.

Fauvism (fŏ viz ĭm) An art movement of the first decade of the twentieth century, using color boldly to express the inner qualities rather than superficial appearance of things.

Fax Technology by which a facsimile of text or line art is transferred electronically from one location to another via telephone connections.

Figurative Referring to artworks based on images of identifiable objects.

Figure-ground relationship In two-dimensional art, seeing images as having been applied over a background.

Figure-ground reversal A two-dimensional work in which it is difficult to discern which is figure and which is ground, because they are visually interchangeable.

Fine arts The nonfunctional art disciplines, such as painting and sculpture.

Fire To heat *ceramics* to make them durable.

Flying buttress A *buttress* in the form of strut or segmented arch that transfers thrust to an outer support.

Focal plane shutter A common type of camera in which there is a double curtain of shutters close to the film; when a flash is used, the film must be exposed at a relatively slow speed because the double shutters take some time to open and close.

Focal point The area of a composition to which the viewer's eye is most compellingly drawn.

Folk art Works created by aesthetically untrained artists working somewhat within a community tradition.

Forced perspective The exaggerated illusion of deep space, often employed in setmaking for theatrical performances.

Foreground In two-dimensional work, the area of a composition that appears closest to the viewer.

Foreshortening Contraction of the length and adjustment of the contours of a figure perpendicular to the viewer. This is done to counteract the perceptual distortion of proportions of objects receding from the viewer into the distance.

Forge To hammer heated metal over an anvil to shape it.

Form 1. The mass or volume of a three-dimensional work or the illusion of volume in a two-dimensional work. 2. The physical aspects of a work, as opposed to its emotional and intellectual *content*.

Formal balance See *symmetrical balance*.

Formalism Art criticism concentrating on outer form rather than inner content.

Found object An object that is presented as a work of art or a part of one, but which was not originally intended as art; also called *objet trouvé*.

Fractal geometry Mathematical modeling of natural forms, often used in computer graphics.

Frame construction A building system in which spaced horizontal and vertical members are interlocked to form a solid skeleton to which an outer skin is added.

Fresco (fres kō) A wall painting technique in which *pigment* in a water base is applied directly to fresh, still-damp plaster, into which it is absorbed.

Frontal Referring to sculpture designed to be seen only from the front.

Full round Referring to sculpture that exists in fully three-dimensional space and is to be seen from all sides.

Full tonal range A term used chiefly in black and white photography to signify representation of all values in a single picture, from black through mid-grays to white.

Futurism A movement initiated in Italy in 1909 to sweep aside all artistic conventions and capture the qualities of modern industrialized life.

G

Geodesic (jee ō des ik) **dome** A structural framework of small interlocking polygons forming a *dome*.

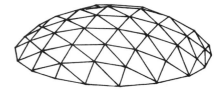

Geometric Having mathematically regular contours, such as a circle, square, or rectangle.

Geometric period A stylistic phase of ancient Greek art between c. 800 and 700 B.C. characterized by abstraction of forms to geometric elements.

Gesso (jes ō) A fluid white coating of plaster, *chalk* and *size* used to prepare a painting surface so that it will accept paint readily and allow controlled brushstrokes.

Gestural A style of painting or drawing in which the artist's arm and hand movements are apparent in the finished piece.

Glaze 1. A thinned, transparent layer of oil paint. 2. A mineral solution, applied to a *ceramic* piece, that vitrifies to a glossy and water-resistant coating when *fired*.

Golden Mean In ancient Greek *aesthetic* theory, an ideal proportional relationship between parts, whereby the smaller is to the greater as the greater is to the whole. This ratio cannot be worked out mathematically, but is approximately 5:8, or 1:1.618.

AC/AB=AB/BC

Golden Rectangle A rectangle the lengths of whose sides correspond to *golden section* proportions. Much used as a compositional and format-establishing device in *Renaissance* painting.

Gothic A style of European art from the mid-twelfth to mid-fifteenth century, especially noted for its soaring vertical cathedrals, three-dimensional sculptures, and the sense of depth and emotion in two-dimensional paintings.

Gouache (gwaash) An opaque water-soluble painting *medium* bound with gum arabic, the lighter tones being mixed with Chinese white watercolor.

Graphic design The arts involved in creating two-dimensional images for commercial purposes. Graphic designers often work with type as well as illustrations; the printed surface may range from paper to fabrics.

Graphite A soft carbon used in drawing pencils.

Groin vault In architecture, two intersecting, identical *barrel vaults*.

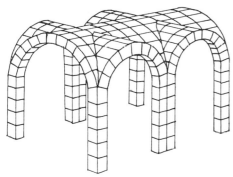

Ground 1. See *figure-ground relationship*. 2. The surface on which a two-dimensional work is developed.

H

Hard-edged A term used chiefly in referring to twentieth-century paintings in which clean, sharp edges are formed where areas of different colors meet.

Hatching Fine, short parallel lines used in two-dimensional arts to create the effect of shadow on three-dimensional forms. See also *cross-hatching*.

Hellenistic period Greek art from 323 to 100 B.C. or later, characterized by greater dynamism, emotional drama, and naturalism than that of the *Classical period*.

High contrast The polarization of the normal ranges of *values* towards the extremes of light and dark.

Highlight A spot of highest (lightest) *value* in a work—usually white.

High relief Sculpture in which figures emerge three-dimensionally from a flat surface to half or more than half of their natural depth.

High Renaissance The years between roughly 1490 and 1520 in Italy, productive of some of the world's greatest art, informed by but not bound to *Classical* traditions.

High-tech revival A late twentieth-century return to machine-like architectural structures.

Horizon line The perceived line where earth and sky seem to meet, an aspect of *linear perspective*.

Hue The property of a color that enables us to locate its position in the *spectrum* or on the *color wheel* and thus label it as "red" or "blue," etc. This is determined by its wavelength.

I

Icon A two-dimensional depiction of a sacred figure or figures, thought to work miracles, particularly characteristic of *Byzantine* sacred art.

Iconography (ī kǒ naa grǎ fee) Visual conventions and symbols used to portray ideas in a work of art.

Idealized Referring to art in which *representational* images conform more closely to ideal *aesthetic* standards than to real life.

Impasto (im pas tō) Thickly applied paint, mainly oil or acrylic.

Implied A line, shape, or form that is suggested to the eye but not actually present.

Impressionism An art movement originating in late nineteenth-century France, in which the artist attempts to capture what the eye actually sees before the brain interprets the image. This may be a surface broken by fragmented lights or an ephemeral moment in time.

Indirect painting Using a series of layers to produce a desired final effect, in contrast with *direct painting*.

Industrial design The art of creating functional products that also have *aesthetic* appeal.

Installation piece A three-dimensional designed environment set up (often temporarily) as a work of art.

Instrumentalism Art criticism focusing on how well an artwork fulfills a particular purpose.

Intaglio (in tal yō) A category of printmaking processes in which the desired image is cut into the surface of a plate, which is inked and then wiped, leaving ink only in the cut channels. Dampened paper is forced against the plate, picking up the ink.

Intensity See *saturation*.

Interior contour The form of the inside of a three-dimensional piece.

Interior design The art of decorating the insides of human environments.

International Modern Style An architectural style, originating in Europe after World War I, characterized by rectangular forms, white walls, large windows, flat roofs, and the absence of ornament.

Interpretive color Color chosen to represent an emotional atmosphere or idea rather than the visual reality of an object.

Interpretive values Lights and darks used to convey an atmosphere or idea rather than a literal description of the actual *values* of a real scene.

Intonaco (in ton ǎ kō) In *fresco* technique, the final layer of plaster, to which paint is applied during the course of the day.

Investment A heat-resistant outer mold packed around a *lost-wax casting*.

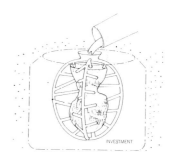

Ionic (ī aan ik) In *Classical* Greek architecture, an order characterized by fluted columns topped by scroll-like spirals.

K

Keystone The central wedge-shaped piece of masonry in an arch, added last to lock the structure in place.

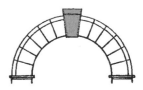

Kiln A special oven or furnace for *firing ceramics*.

Kinetic (kin e tik) **sculpture** A three-dimensional work that moves.

L

Laminate (lam i nayt) To unite flat layers of the same or different materials, such as bonded plates of wood, paper, or plastics.

Late Gothic Work produced in Europe toward the end of the *Gothic* period, characterized by increasing *naturalism* and expressiveness and by the fine details and luminosity of oil paintings.

Lead crystal High-quality, exceptionally clear and colorless glass in which a large percentage of the formula is lead oxide.

Light well 1. A shaft that allows daylight to enter the interior of a building. 2. The optical illusion of a visual pool of light created by contrast with surrounding darker areas.

Limited palette Highly selective use of only a few colors.

Line engraving A *print* made by cutting lines into a plate of metal, forcing ink into them, and printing the cut lines.

Linear perspective The illusion of deep space in a two-dimensional work through convergence of lines perpendicular to the *picture plane* toward a *vanishing point* in the distance.

Linocut (lī nō kut) A *print* made by gouging away areas of a linoleum block that are not to be inked and printed.

Liquid medium A fluid base used to carry pigments for painting or drawing, such as ink, oil, or acrylic emulsion.

Lithography (li thaa grǎ fee) A printmaking technique in which a flat stone or metal or plastic plate is drawn on with a greasy substance that retains ink when the wettened plate is inked for printing.

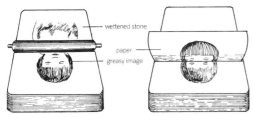

Local color The color usually associated with an object, as seen from nearby under normal daylight without shadows or reflections.

Local value The degree of light or darkness seen on an actual surface.

Logo A graphic or typographic image that identifies a business or group.

Lost-wax A *casting* process in which wax is used to coat the insides of molds and then melted away when the molds are assembled, leaving an empty space into which molten metal is poured; also called *cire perdue*.

Low relief Sculpture in which figures exist on almost the same *plane* as the background.

M

Malleability (mal ee ǎ bil ǐ tee) The capacity for being shaped by physical pressure, as in hand modeling or hammering.

Mandala A circular symbolic spiritual pattern.

Mannerism An artistic style in Italy from approximately 1525 to 1600 in which artists developed a more subjective, emotional, theatrical approach than in the preceding *High Renaissance* period.

Maquette (ma ket) A small model used for planning and guiding the creation of a sculpture.

Mass The solid content of a three-dimensional form.

Medium (plural *media*) 1. The material or means of expression with which the artist works. 2. The liquid solvent, such as water or linseed oil, in which *pigment* is suspended to make paint fluid and workable.

Mezzotint (mez ō tint) An *intaglio* printmaking technique in which an overall burr is raised on the surface of the metal plate and then smoothed in places, creating various tones and textures.

Miniature A work of art done on a much smaller scale than the object being represented.

Minimalism Use of highly simplified form devoid of representation or expressive content.

Mixed media Combined use of several different techniques—such as drawing, painting, and printmaking—in a single work of art.

Mobile See *kinetic art*.

Modeling 1. In two-dimensional art, the depiction of three-dimensional form, usually through indications of light and shadow. 2. In sculpture, creating a form by manipulating a soft *medium*, such as clay.

Modular construction A building system developed from preconstructed and perhaps preassembled parts.

Monochromatic (maan ǒ krō ma tik) Having a color scheme based on *values* of a single *hue*, perhaps with accents of another color or neutral colors.

Monotype A printmaking process in which an image is painted directly onto a sheet of metal or glass and then transferred onto paper. The process can be repeated with some repainting of the plate, but this is basically a means of creating relatively few prints of an image.

Montage (mōn taazh) 1. A composite two-dimensional image produced by assembling and pasting down cut or torn sections of photographs or drawings. 2. In cinematography, the composition of a sequence of short shots of related meaning.

Mosaic (mō zay ik) Two-dimensional art created by attaching small pieces (*tesserae*) of ceramic tile, glass, pebbles, marble, or wood to a surface.

Motif (mō teef) A recurring pattern in a work of art.

Multimedia Installation involving audio as well as visual components.

Mural (myoor ǎl) A painting, usually large, done on a wall.

N

Naive art That which is created by artists with no formal training.

Narrative Referring to art with a storytelling quality.

Naturalism A style of art that seeks to represent accurately and faithfully the actual appearance of things.

Nave (nayv) In church architecture, the central hall.

Negative space Unfilled areas in the design.

Neo-Classicism The late eighteenth- and early nineteenth-century return to *Classical aesthetics* in Europe.

Neoexpressionism A contemporary art movement in which painting is used to express the artist's feelings, projected as distorted images from the exterior world.

Nonobjective Referring to art that does not represent any known object.

Nonrepresentational See *nonobjective*.

Northern Renaissance Referring to German art from c. 1500, when the individualistic and rational aspects of the Italian *Renaissance* were adopted and adapted to north European styles.

O

Offset lithography A commercial printmaking process in which the inking of illustrations and text is offset from the plate onto a rubber-covered cylinder that transfers them to paper so that the printed image reads the same way as the original, rather than being reversed.

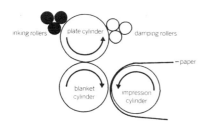

One-point perspective In *linear perspective*, the representation of parallel lines converging to a single point on the horizon, to create the illusion of deep space.

Opalescent (ō pǎl es ĕnt) **glass** Opaque glass used for art objects, with color oxides swirled through it as it is poured in a molten state into sheets.

Op Art Paintings that produce visual phenomena in the perception of the viewer that do not actually exist on the canvas.

Open form In sculpture, a volume broken by projections and/or *voids*.

Open palette Use of an unlimited range of colors in juxtaposition.

Optical color mixtures Those in which colors are mixed in the viewer's perception rather than in physically mixed *pigments*.

Outsider art Unique works created by untrained people who do not fit into any aesthetic tradition.

Overlapping Hiding of part of one figure by another, a device used to suggest depth in space.

Overpainting The final layers in an *indirect* painting, such as *glazes* or *scumbling*.

P

Pastel A chalky stick of powdered *pigment*, calcium carbonate filler, and *binder*, used as a drawing *medium*.

Pattern An all-over design created by repetition of figures.

Pediment In *Classical* architecture, the triangular area at the front of a building; also a similarly-shaped area used decoratively over a window, door, or *portico*.

Performance art Art in which the medium of expression is the artist's own body and its coverings.

Perspective See *aerial perspective*; *linear perspective*.

Photocopy A photographic reproduction of graphic material, in which a negative image is quickly taken and electronically transferred to paper as a positive.

Photogram One of the precursors of modern photography, an image made by laying objects on light-sensitive paper and exposing it to sunlight, leaving the masked areas white while the rest of the paper turns dark.

Photorealism Art that is as *representational* as a photograph, but created by other media; also called *super-realism*.

Picture plane The flat surface of a two-dimensional work, often conceived as a transparent window into three-dimensional space. See *linear perspective*.

Pigment Powdered colored material used to give *hues* to paints and inks.

Pinching A simple means of using the hands to shape a ceramic vessel from a lump of clay.

Pixel (piks ĕl) In computer graphics, one of many tiny points on the computer screen determined by intersections of *x* and *y* axis.

Placement In two-dimensional art, the positioning of images on the *picture plane*, often used with reference to the illusion of three-dimensionality.

Plane A flat surface.

Planish To hammer metal smooth.

Planographic (play naa gra fik) Referring to a printmaking technique in which images are transferred from a flat surface, as in *lithography*.

Pointed arch An arch formed by the intersection of two curves of greater radius than that of the opening; an innovation introduced in *Gothic* architecture.

Pointillism (pwan tǐ lizǐm) A technique of painting using dots of *primary* and *secondary hues* in close juxtaposition to make them mix in the viewer's perception. Also called *divisionism*.

Point of view The place from which a two-dimensional scene is reported.

Pop Art A movement beginning in the mid-twentieth century that uses objects and images from the commercial culture.

Porcelain *Ceramics* made from the finest clays, which produce an extremely smooth, glossy surface when fired.

Portico (por ti kō) A covered colonnade at the end of a building in *Classical* architecture.

Positive space Filled areas in a design, or those intended to be seen as figures.

Post and lintel An architectural construction system in which upright members support horizontal members, or lintels.

Post-Impressionism Transcendence of the perceived limitations of *Impressionism* by mid-nineteenth- and early twentieth-century artists such as Cézanne, Seurat, Gauguin, and Van Gogh.

Post-modernism An architectural movement of the 1970s and 80s, countering the glass boxes of the *International Style* with more historically eclectic forms.

Post-Painterly Abstraction Various mid-twentieth-century styles of creating *nonobjective* paintings that evoke certain responses in viewers, with the hand of the artist less obvious than in *Abstract Expressionism*.

Primary colors The set of three basic *hues* from which all other hues can be mixed; in *refracted* colors, red, green, and blue; in *reflected* colors, red, yellow, and blue.

Primary contours The outer edges of a *form*.

Principles of design The organizing factors in the visual arts, including repetition, variety, *contrast*, *rhythm*, *balance*, compositional *unity*, *emphasis*, *economy*, *proportion*, and relationship to the environment.

Print An image made by transferring ink from a worked surface onto a surface, usually paper, and usually in multiples.

Proportion Size relationships of parts to each other and to the whole.

Proscenium (prō see nee ǐm) 1. The part of a stage for theatrical production that projects in front of the curtain. 2. In ancient Greek theater, the whole of the stage.

Proscenium arch The arch that frames the stage, hiding its mechanics.

Putti (singular *putto*) (poo tee : poot tō) Chubby nude male babies often depicted in Italian art from the fifteenth century onward.

Q

Quilting Making blankets or other covers of two layers of fabric stitched together with padding in between, in which both the pieces of fabric and the pattern of stitching offer vehicles for aesthetic creativity.

R

Radial balance Symmetric arrangement of design elements around the center of a circle.

Raise In metalworking, to hammer a flat sheet over a stake to bring up the sides of a vessel and work them inward.

Read To see and assign meaning to aspects of a design.

Realism The attempt in art to capture the appearance of life as it is, as opposed to *stylized* or *Romanticized* portrayals. In mid-nineteenth-century France, the artistic movement of this name concentrated on subjects from everyday, and often working-class, life.

Reduction print A color relief print in which portions of a single block are cut away in stages, with each stage overprinted in another color, rather than creating a series of registered blocks for the various colors.

Reflected hues *Hues* seen when light is reflected from a *pigmented* surface.

Refracted colors *Hues* seen in light.

Reinforced concrete Concrete into which metal mesh or rods have been embedded so that the two interact to strengthen the structure.

Reliefs 1. A sculptured work in which an image is developed outward or inward from a two-dimensional surface. 2. A printmaking category in which areas that are not to be inked are carved away, leaving the image raised on the block.

Renaissance (ren ĭ saans) A movement beginning in fifteenth-century Italy to recapture the harmony, symmetry, and rationality of *Classical* works, with an elaboration of *linear perspective*.

Repoussé (rĕ poo say) The working of a sheet of metal from the back to create designs in relief on the front.

Representational Referring to artworks that aim to present likenesses of known objects.

Resist The waxy, acid-resistant substance used to coat the metal plate used for *etching*, into which the lines of the image are drawn.

Resolution Degree of sharpness in a *digitized* image.

Rhythm The visual equivalent of notes and pauses in music, created by repetition, variety, and spacing in a design.

Ribbed vault In architecture, a masonry ceiling in which arched diagonal ribs form a framework that is filled with lighter stone.

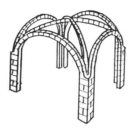

Rococo (rŏ kō kō) The late *Baroque* period, particularly in France, southern Germany, and Austria, characterized by extremely ornate, curvilinear forms in architectural decoration and delicacy and looseness in painting.

Romanesque (rō mă nesk) A style of European art from about the eleventh century to the beginning of the *Gothic* period, most notable for its architecture of rounded arches, thick walls and columns, and stone relief carvings.

Romanticism The tendency to emphasize emotion and imagination rather than logic, occurring at many times in the history of Western art, including the first half of the nineteenth century. Traditionally contrasted with *Classicism*.

Rotunda A circular building or room, especially one with a dome.

Round arch An arch formed by a semicircle; an innovation introduced by Roman architecture and much used in *Romanesque* architecture.

S

Sans serif (sanz / ser if) Referring to a *typeface* that has no fine lines finishing the major strokes.

Saturation The relative brightness or dullness of a color, also called *chroma* or *intensity*.

Scale Relative size.

Scale change Difference in size of objects, used in paintings to suggest three-dimensional depth in space, with the nearest ones being largest.

Screen print See *silkscreen*.

Scumbling In oil painting, the technique of brushing one layer of paint on top of another in a way that reveals some of the undercolor.

Secondary contours *Forms* developed across the surface of a larger form.

Secondary hues *Hues* produced by combining two *primary* hues.

Serif (ser if) In *typography*, the fine lines used to finish the heavier main strokes of letters; also used of a *typeface* that has this feature

Serigraph (ser ĭ graf) See *silkscreen*.

Sfumato (sfoo maa tō) Softly graded tones in an oil painting, giving a hazy atmospheric effect, highly developed in the work of Leonardo da Vinci.

Shading The darkening of an area in a two-dimensional work to suggest curving of a three-dimensional form away from a light source.

Shape A flat, defined area.

Silkscreen A printmaking process in which ink is pressed through a fine screen in areas that are not masked by a stencil or other material; also called *serigraph*.

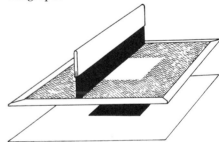

Silverpoint A drawing *medium* in which a finely pointed rod of silver encased in a holder is used to make marks on a slightly abrasive surface; the minute deposit of metal darkens by oxidation.

Simulated texture The illusion that an image would feel a certain way if touched, in contrast to the reality of its actual texture.

Site specific An installation designed for a particular location.

Size or **Sizing** A coating of glue or resin to make a surface such as canvas less porous so that paint will not sink into it.

Skene (skeen) In early Greek theaters, the building at the back of the performance area from which actors entered and exited, also used as a changing room and as a backdrop for the action.

Slab building The process of building a form of clay by attaching flat shapes to each other.

Slip A mixture of clay and water.

Soft-edged In two-dimensional work, blending of *hues* where they meet, so that no hard line forms a boundary between them.

Space The area occupied, activated, or suggested by a work of art.

Spectrum See *visible spectrum*.

Squinch A structure spanning the corner of a tower to help support a superstructure such as a dome.

Stained glass Art glass colored with chemical colorants heated in a kiln with the glass base.

State One of the stages of an *etching*, if printed separately.

Static form A mass that appears inert.

Still-life A two-dimensional representation of a group of inanimate objects such as fruit, flowers, and vessels.

Stippling Use of dots in a drawing or engraving to develop areas of a particular *value*, usually to suggest three-dimensional form.

Stoneware *Ceramics* made from clays that become very hard when *fired* at high temperatures.

Stylized Referring to distortion of *representational* images in accordance with certain artistic conventions or to emphasize certain design qualities.

Stylobate (stī lŏ bayt) In *Classical* Greek architecture, the flat base on which a series of columns rests.

Subtractive color mixing The combination of *reflected* colors.

Subtractive sculpture That which is created by the process of carving away material to reveal the desired *form*.

Super-realism See *photorealism*.

Support The solid material base on which a two-dimensional work of art is executed, such as canvas or panel in the case of a painting.

Surrealism Art based on dreamlike images from the subconscious, appearing as a recognized movement beginning in the 1920s.

Symmetrical balance Distribution of equal forces around a central point or *axis*, also called *formal balance*.

Synergistic color mixing A system of *optical color mixing* in which new *hues* are created in the spaces between colored figures.

Synthetic media Liquid media in which industrially created chemicals, such as acrylic emulsion, are used to carry the pigments.

T

Tapestry A heavy, handwoven textile with pictures woven into the surface of the fabric, usually used as a wall hanging.

Tempera A painting *medium* in which *pigments* are mixed in water with a glutinous material such as egg yolk, usually yielding a fast-drying, matt finish that cannot be blended.

Tensile strength A measure of the ability of a material to be stretched without breaking.

Tertiary hues *Hues* that are a mixture of a *primary* and a *secondary hue* lying next to each other on the *color wheel*.

Tesserae (singular *tessera*) (tes ĕr ee: tes ĕr ă) The small cubes of colored glass, *ceramic*, or stone used in *mosaics*.

Texture The surface quality of a form or the illusion that it would feel a certain way if touched.

Three-dimensional Having length, height, and width.

Three-point perspective Two-dimensional spatial illusions of forms receding toward three *vanishing points*.

Throwing See *wheel-throwing*.

Tokonoma (tō kŏ nō mă) In a traditional Japanese home, an alcove devoted to contemplation of a single scroll painting, perhaps accompanied by a flower arrangement.

Tonal range The degree to which a work (particularly a photograph) approaches the full range of *values* from black through grays to white.

Transition The abrupt or gradual change from one portion of a design to another.

Triad color scheme The use of three *hues* lying at equal distances from each other on the *color wheel*.

Trompe l'oeil (tromp / lō yee) Work that "deceives the eye" into believing it sees something other than the reality of a surface, such as architectural forms on what is actually a flat wall or ceiling.

Truss In architecture, a framework of wood or metal beams, usually based on triangles, used to support a roof or bridge.

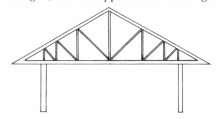

Two-dimensional Existing on a flat surface with only length and height but no depth in space.

Two-point perspective In linear perspective drawings, the representation of a three-dimensional form viewed from an angle, so that the lines formed by its horizontal edges will appear to diminish to two different *vanishing points* on the horizon.

Typeface One of many styles of letter design, in which the entire alphabet is rendered with certain repeating characteristics.

Typography The art of designing, sizing, and combining letterforms on a printed page.

U

Underpainting The initial layers of paint in *indirect painting*.

Unity Visual coherence in a work of art; also used sometimes to refer to repetition of similar motifs in a design, in contrast to *variety*.

Unsized Referring to canvas that has not been treated with a glaze or filler, leaving it porous to paint.

Upload To place *digitized* material from a computer onto the Internet or an external storage device.

V

Value Degree of dark or light.

Value scale A graded representation of differences in *value*.

Vanishing point The seen or implied spot in the distance where all lines perpendicular to the *picture plane* would appear to meet if extended. In real life, a vanishing point can only be seen where one can look across a great distance; in art, if lilies appear to converge rapidly to a vanishing point there will be an impression of great depth.

Variety Change rather than sameness in design elements.

Vellum (<u>vel</u> ŭm) A fine parchment prepared from the skin of a calf, kid, or lamb.

Veneer (vĕ <u>neer</u>) A thin surface layer, such as a fine wood placed over other woods.

Video A process of creating moving pictures by laying down images and sound as tracks on magnetic tape.

Video raster graphics Computer-generated and -manipulated *video* images.

Virtual reality Computer graphics in which the operator interacts with a scene as if existing within it.

Visible spectrum The color frequencies that humans can see; the distribution of colors produced when white light is dispersed, *e.g.* by a prism. There is a continuous change in wavelength from red, the longest wavelength, to violet, the shortest.

Visual weight The apparent heaviness of an area of design.

Void In sculpture, a hole through a work.

Volume The solid content of a form.

Voussoirs (voo <u>swaar</u>) The wedge-shaped stones in an arch.

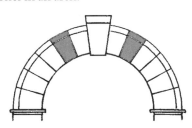

W

Walk-through Referring to large sculptures that the viewer can move through as well as around.

Warm colors Colors from the red and yellow side of the *color wheel*, associated with heat.

Watercolor A transparent water-soluble painting *medium* consisting of *pigments* bound with gum.

Website A personal domain of the Internet managed by a person or organization.

Wheel-throwing A method of creating forms of clay by centering a mass of clay on a circular slab and then pulling the sides up from it with the hands as this wheel is turned.

Woodcut A *print* made by carving away areas of a wood block and inking the remaining *relief* surfaces.

Wood engraving A *print* made by cutting the end-grain of a piece of wood, capable of rendering finer lines than the lengthwise grain used for *woodcuts*.

Wrought iron Iron that is shaped in a heated state with hand tools.

Z

Ziggurat A stepped pyramid with a temple on top.

CREDITS

page 11 © Tim Noble & Sue Webster. Courtesy of the artists
1.1 Bridgeman Art Library, London
1.3 Photo © 1998 Board of Trustees, National Gallery of Art, Washington D.C.
1.6, 1.7 Photo: Anthony d'Offay, London
1.10 © 2009 Banco de Mexico Diego Rivera & Frida Kahlo Museums Trust, Mexico D.F. / DACS
1.11, 1.12, 1.13 Photo © RMN / René-Gabriel Ojéda © Succession Picasso/DACS 2009
1.14 Kunstmuseum, Oeffentliche Kunstsammlung, Basel. Emmanuel Hoffman Foundation.
1.15 Pace Primitive Art, New York
1.16 © Georgia O'Keeffe Museum / DACS, 2009
1.17 © 2009. Digital Image, Museum of Modern Art, New York/Scala, Florencc/ © ADAGP, Paris and DACS, London 2009
1.20 Takeschi Nishikawa
1.21 © Vincenzo Pirozzi, Rome
1.22 © ARS, NY and DACS, London 2009
1.23 Victoria Miro Gallery
1.24 Archivi Alinari / Art Resource, New York
1.25 Courtesy Daniel Libeskind. Photo Jok Pottle
1.26 Chris Mellor/ Telegraph Colour Library
1.27 © DACS 2009
1.29 National Park Service, Washington D.C.
1.30 © Photo RMN / Gerard Blot
1.31 © The Isamu Noguchi Foundation and Garden Museum/ARS, New York and DACS, London 2009
1.33 © DACS 2009
1.34 © Araldo De Luca, Rome
1.35 V&A Picture Library, London
1.36 Photo South Australia Museum
1.37, 1.38, 1.41 © 2009. Digital Image, Museum of Modern Art, New York/ Scala, Florence/© DACS 2009
1.39 Photo Ju Myung Duk.
1.40 © 1998 Kate Rothko Prizel & Christopher Rothko ARS, NY and DACS, London
1.42 © 2009. Digital Image, The Museum of Modern Art, New York / Scala, Florence / © The Pollock-Krasner Foundation ARS, NY and DACS, London 2009
1.44 Photo © Christie's Images/ The Bridgeman Art Library
1.45 Photo Thibault Jeanson. Courtesy Miami Art Museum
1.47 Photo Vatican Museums
1.48 © Succession Picasso/DACS 2009
1.50 Photo Erika Barahona Ede / © FMGB Guggenheim Bilbao Museoa
2.2 Private Collection, London
2.3 Exxon Corporation, for Public Broadcasting Great Performances.
2.5 © ARS, NY and DACS, London 2009
2.7 By permission of the British Library
2.8 © ADAGP/FAAG, Paris and DACS, London 2009
2.10 Courtesy of DHM, Berlin / Sammlung Dr. Hans Sachs, Berlin
2.11 Courtesy of Wallpaper*
2.12 © RMN (Musée d'Orsay) / Hervé Lewandowski
2.13 The Mansell Collection, London
2.14, 2.17 © 2009. Digital Image, Museum of Modern Art, New York / Scala, Florence
2.19, 2.35 © V&A Images, Victoria and Albert Museum, London
2.21 Image copyright The Metropolitan Museum of Art/Art Resource/Scala, Florence
2.22 Photo courtesy of Musee Rodin
2.26 The Mansell Collection, London
2.28 Fotografica Foglia, Naples
2.30 Courtesy of Hirshhorn Museum and Sculpture

Garden, Smithsonian Institution, Gift of Joseph H. Hirshhorn, 1966
2.31 © Michael Heizer, courtesy Xavier Fourcade Inc, New York
2.33 Reproduced by permission of the Henry Moore Foundation
2.38 © Succession H Matisse/DACS 2009
2.39 © ARS, NY and DACS, London 2009
2.40 © ADAGP, Paris and DACS, London 2009
2.41 © British Musum, London
2.45 © 2009. Digital Image, The Museum of Modern Art, New York / Scala, Florence © Calder Foundation, New York / DACS London 2009
2.46 Image © 2007 Board of Trustees, National Gallery of Art, Washington, D.C.
2.47 © The Joseph and Robert Cornell Memorial Foundation/DACS, London/VAGA, New York 2009
2.48 © Witold Skrypczak / Alamy
2.49 © 2009 Olafur Eliasson. Photo Ian Reeves
2.52 Daitokuj, Kyoto, Japan
2.53 © Romare Bearden Foundation/DACS, London/VAGA, New York 2009
2.56 Photo Thijs Quispel
2.62 Courtesy of the artist
2.66, 2.69 V&A Picture Library, London
2.68 © Studio Fotografico Quattrone, Florence
2.70 M.C.Escher's "Relativity" © 1998 Cordon Art-Baarn-Holland. All rights reserved
2.71 Reproduced by permission of the Henry Moore Foundation
2.74 Werner Forman Archive, London
2.77 Reprinted by kind permission of David R Goding Inc
2.78 Bridgeman Art Library, London
2.79 © Photo Josse, Paris
2.80 Harris Works of Art, New York
2.81 Image copyright The Metropolitan Museum of Art/Art Resource/Scala, Florence
2.83, 2.93 © 2009 Digital Image, The Museum of Modern Art, New York / Scala, Florence
2.84 Courtesy of the artist
2.85 Reprinted with permission of Joanna T. Steichen
2.86 © 1990, Photo Scala, Florence / Fondo Edificio di Culto - Min. dell'Interno
2.87 Courtesy of Milton Glaser
2.89 Metropolitan Museum of Art, New York (63.210.11)
2.90 © Tim Noble & Sue Webster
2.91 Norman McGrath, New York
2.94 Sakamoto Photo Research Laboratory, New York
2.96 Sonia Halliday / © FLC/ADAGP, Paris and DACS, London 2009
2.9/ © AFP/Getty Images
2.98 Photograph Florian Holzherr © 2003 Scottsdale Cultural Council / Scottsdale Public Art Program
2.99 Arcadia University Art Gallery / Photo Aaron Igler
2.107 © 2009. Digital Image, Museum of Modern Art, New York / Scala, Florence/© Georgia O'Keeffe Museum / DACS, 2009
2.109, 2.125 Photo Scala, Florence
2.110 Courtesy of the artist
2.111 © The Isamu Noguchi Foundation and Garden Museum/ARS, New York and DACS, London 2009
2.113 Image copyright The Metropolitan Museum of Art/Art Resource/Scala, Florence (1875.1.119)
2.115 © Succession Picasso/ DACS 2009
2.116 © 2009 Digital Image, Museum of Modern Art, New York/ Scala, Florence © Succession H Matisse/DACS 2009
2.117 Photo Eduardo Calderon
2.118 © 2009 Digital Image, The Museum of Modern Art, New York / Scala, Florence/© The Josef and Anni Albers Foundation/VG Bild-Kunst, Bonn and DACS, London 2009
2.119 © Photo by Melba Levick
2.120 Photo Eduardo Calderon
2.124 Image copyright The Metropolitan Museum of Art/Art Resource/Scala, Florence (26.100.6)
2.127 © Richard Anuszkiewicz © DACS, London/VAGA, New York 2009
2.129 © 2009 Digital Image, The Museum of Modern Art, New York / Scala, Florence

2.132 © 1962 Ives Sillman, New Haven, Collection Arthur Hoener / Photo Beverley Dickinson/© Th Josef and Anni Albers Foundation/VG Bild-Kuns Bonn and DACS, London 2009
2.133 © ARS, NY and DACS, London 2009
2.134 Image copyright The Metropolitan Museum of Art/Art Resource/Scala, Florence (53.140.4) / © Succession Picasso/DACS 2009
2.135 © 2009 Digital Image, Museum of Modern Art, New York / Scala, Florence © Calder Foundation New York / DACS London 2009
2.136 Museum of Fine Arts, Houston, Texas /© ADAG Paris and DACS, London 2009
2.139 Philadelphia Museum of Art/ Bridgeman Art Library, London/© Succession Marcel Duchamp/ADAGP, Paris and DACS, London 200
2.143 © R. Todd King, www.rtoddking.com.
3.1 The National Trust, London
3.3 © Magdalena Abakowicz / © ADAGP, Paris and DACS, London 2006
3.4 © 2009 Digital Image, Museum of Modern Art, Ne York / Scala, Florence/ Licensed by DACS 2009
3.6 © Succession Picasso/DACS 2009
3.7 International Olympic Committee
3.8 © Inigo Bujedo A. Guirre, London
3.11 © John G. Walter / Alamy
3.12, 3.27 © 1990 Scala, Florence. Courtesy of Ministe Bene e Att. Culturali
3.14 Image copyright The Metropolitan Museum of Art/Art Resource/Scala, Florence (1975.1.7)
3.16 Wadsworth Atheneum Museum of Art, Hartford Conneticut/ © ARS, NY and DACS, London 200°
3.19 V&A Picture Library, London
3.22 © Nancy Graves Foundation/DACS, London/VAGA, New York 2009
3.24 Andrew W. Mellon Collection, Image © 2003 Board of Trustees, National Gallery of Art, Washington D.C.
3.29 © Araldo De Luca, Rome
3.31 © Quattrone, Florence
3.33 © imagebroker / Alamy
3.35 Image copyright The Metropolitan Museum of Art/Art Resource/Scala, Florence
3.41 Craig & Marie Mauzy, Athens mauzy@otenet.gr
3.42 Japan National Tourist Organization, London
3.43 © Marina Abramovic. Courtesy of Marina Abramovic and Sean Kelly Gallery, New York. DACS 2009
3.44 Photo Erika Barahona Ede © FMGB Guggenheim Bilbao Museoa
3.45 © 2009 Digital Image, Museum of Modern Art, New York / Scala, Florence/ © ADAGP, Paris and DACS, London 2009
3.46 © H. Mark Weidman Photography / Alamy
page 197 Courtesy of the artist and Lombard-Freid Projects, NY
4.1 National Gallery of Canada. Ottawa, Ontario/ © Succession Picasso / © Succession Picasso/DACS 2009
4.4 Froelick Gallery, Portland, Oregon
4.5 © the artist
4.7 Image © 1998, Board of Trustees, National Gallery Art, Washington D.C. / © DACS 2009
4.8 Joseph Szaszfai
4.10 A&B Courtesy of the artist
4.12 Courtesy of the artist
4.17, 4.18 © Trustees of the British Musum, London
5.1 AKG-images London
5.2 Margaret Courtney-Clarke
5.3 Image copyright The Metropolitan Museum of Art/Art Resource/Scala, Florence (29.100.16)
5.4 Carnegie Museum of Art, Pittsburgh / © ADAGP, Paris and DACS, London 2009
5.5 © Tyeb Mehta
5.6 Peter Willi/ The Bridgeman Art Library, London
5.7 Bob Shalkwijk / AMI © 2009 Banco de Mexico Die Rivera & Frida Kahlo Museums Trust, Mexico D. DACS
5.10 © 1990. Photo Scala, Florence/© 2009 Banco de Mexico Diego Rivera & Frida Kahlo Museums Trust, Mexico D.F. / DACS